CGI
Internet Programming with C++ and C

Mark Felton
Lucent Technologies Inc.

An Alan R. Apt Book

Prentice Hall
Upper Saddle River, New Jersey 07458

Library of Congress Cataloging-in-Publication Data

Felton, Mark.
 CGI : Internet programming with C++ and C / Mark Felton.
  p. cm.
 "An Alan R. Apt book."
 Includes bibliographical references and index.
 ISBN 0-13-712358-2
  1. C++ (Computer program language) 2. C (Computer program
language) 3. Internet programming. I. Title.
aspects. I. Title.
QA76.73.C153F45   1997
005.2'762–dc21   96-44083
              CIP

Publisher: Alan Apt
Editor-in-Chief: Marcia Horton
Assistant Vice President of Production and
 Manufacturing: David W. Riccardi
Managing Editor: Bayani Mendoza de Leon
Production Editor: Mona Pompili
Manufacturing Buyer: Donna Sullivan

Creative Director: Paula Maylahn
Art Director: Amy Rosen
Cover Designer: Bruce Kenselaar
Cover Illustrators: Mark Felton and Chris Cota
Copy Editor: Martha Ochs
Editorial Assistant: Toni Chavez

ABOUT THE COVER: The Star Quilt cover was created using color mapping techniques explained in Chapter 16 and other sections of the book. A single template was passed through a cgi-bin program which then remaps the colors on the fly. This technique provides a foundation for realtime image control over the Internet. With the 9 colors and 9 available positions, a single GIF template can produce 387,420,489 different GIF images. The Star Quilt can be viewed at: http://www.alphacdc.com/prentice/cgi-book.html or http://www.dash.com/netro/tribal/Quilt.html. The chess board can be viewed at http://www.alphacdc.com/chess/.

 © 1997 by Prentice-Hall, Inc.
Simon & Schuster / A Viacom Company
Upper Saddle River, New Jersey 07458

The author and publisher of this book have used their best efforts in preparing this book. These efforts include the development, research, and testing of the theories and programs to determine their effectiveness. The author and publisher shall not be liable in any event for incidental or consequential damages in connection with, or arising out of, the furnishing, performance, or use of these programs.

Printed in the United States of America

10 9 8 7 6 5 4 3 2 1

ISBN 0-13-712358-2

PRENTICE-HALL INTERNATIONAL (UK) LIMITED, *London*
PRENTICE-HALL OF AUSTRALIA PTY. LIMITED, *Sydney*
PRENTICE-HALL CANADA, INC., *Toronto*
PRENTICE-HALL HISPANOAMERICANA, S.A., *Mexico*
PRENTICE-HALL OF INDIA PRIVATE LIMITED, *New Delhi*
PRENTICE-HALL OF JAPAN, INC., *Tokyo*
SIMON & SCHUSTER ASIA PTE. LTD., *Singapore*
EDITORA PRENTICE-HALL DO BRASIL, LTDA., *Rio de Janeiro*

To my family complete.

Registered Trademarks and Copyrights

Preface

THE INTERNET IS THE FIRST network based computer that has created excitement in everyone. Many years ago, I was given the opportunity to talk to Buckminster Fuller.[1] He was fascinated by computers but thought that they would only achieve real success when a "World Computer" came into existence. He envisioned it as providing the means and information needed to allocate and distribute world resources on a global level. How much would he see his vision in the rapidly developing Internet? Certainly there is the potential for this to be accomplished.

This book is about programming the cgi-bin in C++ and C. As a programmer, you will find in this book methods to link the power of compiled languages into the Internet interfaces. I believe this is an important and powerful capability. As you will quickly discover, in many ways, it is simple. However, you will also realize quickly that what I have provided here is merely some basic connective mechanisms that will allow you to interface the wealth of GUI and other capabilities of the Internet to the massive existing and potential resources available using C++ and C languages.

The primary focus of the book is methods for using C++ and C for developing cgi-bin programs. These include important capabilities unavailable through other methods:

- Continuity across forms
- Multiple argv[]
- Get and Post methods combined
- Hidden variable files
- Server side isolation files
- Environmental variable (gets and puts)
- Image control and remapping
- stdin and stdout
- cgi HTML

---

[1] Buckminster Fuller was a philosopher-scientist. He was presented with the Presidents Award for his work which crossed over virtually every field of science and human development. One of his many noteworthy achievements was the development of the geodesic dome.

In addition, the book contains a wealth of techniques that are useful for any programming in C++ and C:

- Pointers to functions
- Pointers to images
- Class construction
- Constructor driven programs
- Parsing
- Database interfaces

Finally, there is a wealth of general material that will be of valuable to anyone working on the Internet:

- Object analysis of web pages
- Client-server control
- Devices
- Techniques of animation
- Multimedia
- PDF
- Applets and cgi

I wrote this book because I wanted to obtain real power connectivity to the Internet. I was aware of the capabilities of HTML, had worked in script languages and even had attended discussions of Hot Java. None of them seemed to be providing what I wanted. As a programmer involved in real time international network control systems, I was very aware of the embedded body of C++ and C software. It became clear to me that the alternative directions being discussed were not going to give me the interfaces I saw as necessary to provide deep level connection to the computers I work with on a daily basis. For me the answer was almost self evident. I needed a way to connect compiled objects to the Internet.

I set out with some basic objectives. The first was to "make it work." I got that one fairly quickly with a few demonstration programs written in C. The next was to push it past basic script languages. I knew that this was possible, but it was not until I was asked to do the Star Quilt program that I began to see that my instincts were correct. Later, when I developed the chess program and was able to link it to existing algorithms, I knew that this was really an unique approach.

As you progress through this text, you will find that it provides many layers. I have tried to provide various programming techniques to offer options as the reader progresses. At each new point, I have tried to combine several simple programs that let you get down to programming along with more advanced examples that can be analyzed and discussed as part of a course. Some of the more difficult examples will take some work. However, even the simple examples require you to understand several different disciplines, HTML, compiled code, and most importantly, their interactions.

Because cgi-bin programs require special skills to do debugging, I have included sections on debugging. I don't believe this is exhaustive, but do think it will allow most problems to be approached successfully.

In addition to the discussions of technical problems, I have included some discussions of technique. These include certain areas where I talk about methods I prefer. These are provided so you won't make the same mistakes I made. The cgi-bin Internet environment, unlike most other coding situations, combines multimedia with code. This can require a whole new way of examining things. Issues of performance, timing and input-output must be examined both directly and as seen across a wide variety of facilities ranging from high speed digital networks to basic modems; from high definition work stations to beginning PCs. While this can be an awesome challenge, it can also be made very manageable by preceding systematically. There is no reason that large projects can not be accomplished, provided that the ground work is put in place.

While the book is organized into progressively more difficult sections, there is nothing to stop the reader from using any section out of order. In every section, enough code is provided to make it possible to skip around once the first chapter is understood. While my own preference would be to get a grasp of FORMs before taking on image manipulation, this is certainly not necessary. Some people, having grasped the basics may find themselves skipping around different sections. Most people will head for the debugging section at some point. I think this is one of the most valuable parts of the book. Once understood, it should encourage many knowledgeable programmers to try some more difficult projects.

Acknowledgments

THERE ARE A NUMBER OF people and institutions who I would like to thank for making this book possible. Chris Cota, who came up with the idea for the Native American Star Quilt which became the initial catalyst for this project. Jeff Olson, who answered all my questions until I knew what needed to be done. Jim Smith and Stefano Mimmi who proof read the text and helped find errors in the code. Robert Klein who supplied the basic code for the section on sockets. The Colorado School of Mines, Keane Inc, Lucent Technologies, the American Indian Science and Engineering Society, Alpha Institute, The Billy Mills Foundation; all of whom assisted me with my work for the Young Scholars Math and Science Project which started me exploring the Internet. Finally, there are some special people who have protected me through out the years who are collectively known as the Lord Family. And finally there is my wife Rachel who has been a constant inspiration.

It is my fervent wish that this book will be easy enough to get basic programmers involved in cgi-bin projects for the Internet and difficult enough to advanced programmers to push the Internet envelope. Ultimately I would like to believe that I have helped to further Buckminster Fuller's vision of a world computer that will allow us to place in balance the delicate fabric of the Earth.

— *Mark Felton*

Contents

Getting Started

Introduction

IT IS PROBABLY UNNECESSARY TO tell anyone reading this book about the rapid growth of the Internet. There are countless books, articles, and even Internet Web pages available on basic Internet development. These explain in detail how to work in *HyperText Markup Language* (HTML) and how to develop hypertext links, IMaGes, and other capabilities associated with Internet Web pages. While these techniques are attractive to many non-computer-oriented people because of their

---

[1] The term cgi-bin is used throughout this book. Other texts may refer to it as "cgi" since it is possible to map areas not named cgi-bin to provide the same function. The use of cgi-bin seemed appropriate for this book since the programs are binary compiled files that provide Common Gateway Interface capability.

ease of implementation, those more versed in computer skills frequently find the lack of expected computer interfaces frustrating and wonder if there is any real programming challenge on the Internet other than working behind the scenes as a system administrator. Fortunately, the people who developed the interfaces to the Internet were not totally blind to the fact that input from programmers would be valuable. While they wanted to develop a simple, easy-to-use programming language, which became HTML, they also foresaw the need for more complex capabilities. To create these, a special area associated with the server was developed called the cgi-bin. This is an area in which programs can be placed that provide special capabilities that are more complex than those available using HTML hypertext alone.

This book is about advanced use of the cgi-bin programs. It is not a book for beginners. It provides tools to develop advanced real-time interactive control over the Internet Web pages using cgi-bin programs written in compiled C++ or C language. These techniques go far beyond the basics provided when using HTML and even beyond most of the advanced capabilities provided via cgi-bin script programs such as PERL (*Practical Extraction Report Language*) and Shell script.

The reader of this book should have some basic knowledge of both HTML and either C++ or C. Knowledge of Internet protocols is also useful, as is a UNIX background. However, to help newcomers, every attempt has been made to introduce the information in a way that will allow readers to gain understanding in areas that are lacking. Many of the programs and subroutines are shown in both C++ and C. HTML output is explained, although not as thoroughly as in a book dedicated to the subject. A number of references are included that should assist those who wish to supplement the methods provided in this text. Where areas are examined that may require advanced background, care is taken to make this clear, thus allowing less knowledgeable programmers to skip over these areas. For the most part, the material presented is straightforward and should be easily understood by anyone with reasonable programming capabilities and a moderate understanding of HTML.

Because the programs in this book are shown in both C++ and C, there was a danger of redundancy. To avoid this, subtle and often valuable modifications are made between the C++ and C versions of the same capability. Persons understanding both languages should derive valuable insights from reading both versions. When alternatives are omitted, either it is evident how to produce the other version or appendix versions have been included.

Where possible, examples have been included that use the most basic components of the language prior to the use of more advanced libraries. This should allow users with only public domain or generic compilers to provide the same capabilities as more advanced sites. Users of this book who have available more advanced functions, such as strstr(), which will search for a substring, should not hesitate to use them where appropriate. Many advanced readers will discover that there are numerous libraries available that more quickly or easily implement some of the capabilities presented in this book.

Chapter Organization

THE CHAPTERS IN THIS BOOK are structured so that the book can be read start to finish or specific sections can be read independently. A person wishing to control images could go directly to the image section (Chapter 16) and bypass all discussions of forms and other HTML capabilities. If you are planning to skip around, you may want to go through Chapter 1, which explains the basics, and Chapter 4, which explains forms.

Chapter 1. This is the most important of all the chapters. A good C++ or C programmer with an understanding of Chapter 1 and a basic grasp of HTML could easily be off and running, creating cgi-bin programs. In Chapter 1 the cgi-bin fundamentals are explained, along with the basics of how the cgi-bin programs control data and information output to the Internet client server. A simple *Hello Internet World* program is developed that can be compiled and put into the cgi-bin. An explanation is given of the various components of the program followed by methods for testing the program using an Internet browser. This is followed by several more simple examples. Finally, this book's conventions are explained.

Chapter 2. An initial example of a graphing program is used in Chapter 2 to illustrate the potential power of the cgi-bin. This simple program shows the power available from cgi-bin compiled programs over any other options available to Internet service developers. The program uses some simple conditionals and file I/O (input output). It immediately moves you outside the capabilities of other script languages. This program is then used to start the development of an object-oriented approach. The development of the initial graph class sets the foundation for the use of object design of cgi-bin programs for the Internet. This is followed by some simple do's and don'ts to get you moving down the road of object-oriented thinking.

Chapter 3. Chapter 3 provides the initial foundation for the development of C++ basic classes. In many ways this chapter should be a review chapter since much of it is focused on understanding HTML. However, the chapter provides important information because it sets up the foundation to build cgi-bin programs in a structured and organized manner. This chapter may prove especially valuable to C programmers who are transitioning to more object-based analysis. In addition, it is a good practice chapter on sending HTML from a program. This is a fundamental skill for all cgi-bin programming.

Chapter 4. The development and understanding of forms are discussed in Chapter 4. Since forms are one of the capabilities that require the use of cgi-bin programs, this is a critical chapter. The process by which information is passed from a form to a cgi-bin program is provided. The understanding of forms is required for almost any of the advanced techniques that follow. The use of Post and Get methods is explained, as well as how they are used with forms.

Chapter 5. The knowledge developed with forms is expanded in Chapter 5 to develop mail forms. Since email is so connected to the Internet and our use of computer communications, mail forms are one of the most common uses of forms. Electronic mail is the most effective way to get user input sent to someone.

Chapter 6. Heading toward more complex cgi-bin applications, methods are developed in Chapter 6 that allow a single cgi-bin program to be used for multiple applications. This is an optional approach for providing different versions of the same service or different types of services at a single site. In addition, it increases the flexibility of your programs and allows common code segments to be shared. Multiple applications are also the precursor to the more complex applications that follow. The Star Quilt shows the full extent of multiple applications.

Chapter 7. The HTML cgi-bin Thru mode, discussed in Chapter 7, provides a method for mixing HTML with cgi-bin programs interactively. The method is powerful because it is easier to maintain. By taking advantage of a great deal of the simplicity of HTML programming and mixing it with the conditional and other programming capabilities in cgi-bin programming, a powerful method is provided.

Chapter 8. Chapter 8 reviews the basics of HTML and discusses the use of tables. Methods are developed to connect the HTML table capability to the cgi-bin programs with interesting results. Tables provide an excellent method for creating formatted output with cgi-bin programs. The use of tables can produce professional results.

Chapter 9. More information on forms is provided in Chapter 9, including how to create and process different kinds of buttons and how to create a questionnaire.

Chapter 10. The use of hidden variables to pass information between cgi-bin calls, which is the focus of Chapter 10, shows how powerful cgi-bin programming is. Using this technique, a chess game that can be played over the Internet is built. The chess game is one of two larger programs developed. It will be expanded several times to illustrate new techniques.

Chapter 11. The base class is expanded in Chapter 11 to include virtually all known HTML capabilities. Examples are given that demonstrate the use of this base class. This chapter is extremely valuable for C++ and C programmers who have little knowledge of HTML. It is also an excellent reference source when developing Web page output using any of the methods discussed.

Chapter 12. Chapter 12 examines the use of the timed Meta operator with cgi-bin programs. The use of the Meta operator can provide important basic capabilities, from starting a cgi-bin program from an HTML Universal Resource Locator (URL) to very sophisticated capabilities such as a timed chess game. The Ping program shows how Meta can be expanded to access remote resources.

Chapter 13. Counters, discussed in Chapter 13, are found on many Web pages. They are used both to keep track of visits to the page and to tell others how often the page is visited. Basic counters are developed along with methods for hiding the counters from the users. The Thru mode, developed in Chapter 7, is used to provide a special *hidden counter.* Time and date control are also illustrated to show how much can be provided with good programming knowledge.

Chapter 14. In this chapter, the development of WAIS and other search engine cgi-bin programs is examined. These types of search capabilities have become a familiar part of the Internet. In this chapter methods are developed to create your own search capabilities. Fundamental database skills are discussed along with how they can be applied to Web page applications.

Chapter 15. The use of x/y coordinates from an IMaGe as the input to a cgi-bin program, which is the topic of Chapter 15, provides a totally different way of inputting to a cgi-bin program. Image maps have become a familiar part of Web pages. Programs are developed that will allow you to map out your images. Advanced techniques show how to create grided areas.

Chapter 16. Up to this point, all discussion has been about cgi-bin programs that produce HTML output to the client. In Chapter 16 cgi-bin programs are used to output GIF (*Graphic Interface Format*) images. Two methods are developed for modifying GIF files. The first is simple to use and can create remarkable color effects by changing the color maps. The second builds on this but allows even more control over the GIF images. A complete program that produces a remarkable Star Quilt is used to illustrate this and other cgi-bin capabilities.

Chapter 17. Methods for debugging cgi-bin programs are examined in detail in Chapter 17. This chapter brings together many techniques discussed throughout the book and adds to them important methods for debugging. In time, this chapter will become your most valuable resource. Any attempt to develop very complex Web pages will require you to put in place good debugging methods.

Chapter 18. Chapter 18 discusses animation techniques and other mixed mode content types.

Chapter 19. Chapter 19 discusses analysis and brings together and expands many of the principles discussed throughout this book, including both object analysis and methods for systematically approaching the development of cgi-bin programs.

Chapter 20. Advanced capabilities are developed in Chapter 20 to allow access to computer-based devices. The Complex class is developed to provide this capability. Chapter 20 is an advanced chapter that introduces ideas that will allow use of the internals of the computer as well as external devices. This chapter will probably only be valuable after you have become skilled in the other techniques.

Chapter 21. This chapter examines methods for using other code. Many cgi-bin programs are initially developed in Shell script language or in PERL script language. In this chapter techniques are examined to change these scripts into compiled C++ or C. The advantages and disadvantages of making this transition are examined, as well as how to connect up to existing C++ or C code.

Chapter 22. This chapter examines cgi-bin interfacing to Java Applets and Javascript. The differences between server-side cgi-bin programming and client-side Java programming are examined. This is followed by three important ways of providing a mixture of cgi-bin and Java programming in the same Web page.

Appendixes.

- Supplementary Listings
- Terminology
- References, URLS, and FTPS
- ASCII to HTML table (See last page of book)

What is a cgi-bin Program?

THE cgi-bin[2] IS A SPECIAL directory associated with the Internet server. Programs placed in this special bin directory are used to provide Common Gateway Interface (CGI) capabilities. The Common Gateway Interface includes a standard for interfacing applications with information servers, such as HTTP (hypertext transfer protocol) or Web Server. These capabilities extend well beyond those provided by plain HTML files.

The exact location of the cgi-bin is set up when the server is set up. As with most paths associated with servers, there will be a UNIX-specific path to the cgi-bin and a URL associated with the cgi-bin. These may or may not look similar. The cgi-bin directory and its subdirectories contain executables whose output will be sent to the client browser. Common browsers are Netscape™, Internet Explorer™, Mosaic™, or even the text browser lynx. The cgi-bin must be configured for use by the server administrator. If it is not correctly configured, the client requests will load in a text-only mode.

Each server can be set up with special requirements. For example, the server can be set up to require all files to have a .cgi extension. On many servers, any standard program name is acceptable. A server can also be set up so that subdirectories under the cgi-bin are owned by individuals. This allows programs to be segmented by whoever is creating the cgi-bin programs. Many system administrators will require that the source code be available along with the compiled code to allow inspection for security concerns.

---

[2]   While it is possible to give this a different name, the directory is normally named "cgi-bin".

The executable in a cgi-bin can be any type of executable that handles stdin and stdout. These include PERL (Practical Extraction and Report Language) scripts, UNIX Shell scripts, C++ programs, C programs, Fortran, Basic, LISP, or any other executable. While this book emphasizes C++ and C because of their execution speed, availability, and familiarity, many of the principles can be applied to other executable formats.

While the cgi-bin can provide a wide variety of capabilities, some systems provide similar features through other mechanisms such as the exec command, server capabilities or client extensions.[3]

While cgi-bin programs are the most common server-side method for providing unique capabilities that go beyond HTML, you may face situations in which you will not find cgi-bin references and will still observe unique capabilities. An example is the exec command allowed on some servers. Normally these will be server based, but they may also be client based. If they are server based, they are provided by the server-side software, which will reside on the same machine as the HTML or cgi-bin programs. If they are client based, they will be provided by Netscape, Explorer, Mosaic, or other server software at the user site. In either event, if you wish to implement similar capabilities, you should find that cgi-bin programs can be implemented that will do the same thing. This is especially valuable when server modifications would affect others or when the servers are managed by groups other than the applications developers. Even when this is not the case, few situations warrant a client or server modification as opposed to a cgi-bin application.

Developing with HTML

The developers of Internet services provided a number of methods for developing Internet Web pages. The most basic is the use of HTML (HyperText Markup Language). HTML is a user-friendly script language that is close to some of the early word processors, such as postscript, nroff and troff. However, unlike these, the HTML interpreter is run directly by the client software. The HTML is transferred through the Internet via transmission facilities such as modems, 56-kb service, 64-kb ISDN,[4] 155.54-MHz T1, or other higher-speed services to the end user's machine. There, the HTML is interpreted by the client software, and information and multimedia are presented to the user. The control language or HTML uses a simple and limited command language placed around text information, details about other documents, or multimedia output requests. The HTML's virtue and

---

3   Java™ can also provide special capabilities. However, this is a special case that is so distinct that it will require discussion in a later chapter. Persons exploring Java should be aware that it is not the same as cgi-bin and should not be seen as providing the same capabilities.

4   ISDN provides two types of service that are used for clients and servers. The *Basic Rate Interface* (BRI) has two 64-kb data channels and one 16-kb control channel. This can be used at home or office to provide combined voice and data or in place of a 5-kb server connection. The *Primary Rate Interface* (PRI) is a trunk service with 24 64-kb channels, one of which is normally for control signals. This is used as part of the backbone or large computer infastructure for the Internet.

weakness is that it has a limited command set that serves primarily to determine the format of the screen output. It contains none of the conditionals, relationals, and other control functions found in more traditional computer languages. It provides no method for accessing the internals of the computer. Since it is not a compiled language, it does not produce machine language code. Instead it requires a special interpreter that is handled through the client (such as Netscape, Mosaic, or lynx) and the server, which accesses the various Internet World Wide Web services.

HTML is very different from computer languages such as C++ and C. These languages are machine based. Once compiled, they operate at an extremely rapid speed often measured in millions of instructions per second, or MIPS. They are the reason why the latest computers promise increasingly higher processing speeds measured in megahertz, or MHz (millions of cycles per second).

Between these two extremes are script languages such as PERL and Shell script. These languages provide some of the capabilities of the compiled languages but lack the complexity and speed of execution. They do, however, provide conditionals such as If then; do while; case and relationals such as = < > !. They also allow variables, file input and output, and a host of other capabilities. None of these capabilities are available in HTML.

What is lacking in both script languages and compiled languages is a way to interface to the client-server capabilities provided on the Internet. While conditionals and variables are readily available in compiled languages, they lack a method to send out an image or to produce a hypertext anchor link. Since these are the nuts and bolts of the Internet—specifically the transfer of multimedia—this is unacceptable if compiled languages are to be used as part of Internet services. This is where the cgi-bin comes into play. This unique area provides a way to use the complexities of script languages and/or compiled languages along with the HTML, client, and server capabilities. In one special area, the cgi-bin, the best of both worlds are allowed to co-exist simultaneously.

The other alternative for Internet development is Java. With Java, an object language similar to C++ is provided. Unlike the cgi-bin programs, Java executes on the client side. The advantage of this approach is a minimization of the time spent processing on the server side. The disadvantage is the same as the advantage. While some programs may be best implemented on the client side (for example, an extended animation) others are best done on the server side (such as management of a large database). Because of this, Java is not an alternative to cgi-bin programs; it is a totally different approach. This means that projects examining both options will need to determine which approach is best for the particular goals being set.

What has become increasingly clear is that while skill in HTML can produce informative and meaningful Web pages, it represents only the most basic capabilities on the Internet. Most people who explore the Internet quickly come across Web pages that include forms, interactive control, and other exciting capabilities. Attempts to view these Web pages using the view source capability (a method for looking at source HTML documents) reveals one consistent thing: reference to the cgi-bin.

The cgi-bin is the special area designated for the host server. Unlike HTML programs that are uncompiled ASCII, the cgi-bin will include programs written in advanced languages such as PERL, C++, and C. While many discussions of cgi-bin programming have encouraged the use of PERL script language, the use of compiled languages such as C++ and C provides increased speed and expanded capability. This becomes increasingly important as more and more people access your Web pages. Compiled code will execute faster than script languages. Equally as important, it will use less computer resources when numerous users are running your cgi-bin programs simultaneously. Most programmers who have had any experience with script languages know that they can only provide limited capability. While they are useful in getting started, they soon lack the required performance. Issues such as swap space become critical as usage increases. This book focuses on the use of C++ and C to provide cgi-bin programs. While some of the basic programs could be provided in PERL or other script languages, the more advanced capabilities, such as the interactive chess game and the changes in IMaGe files, are probably only achievable in compiled languages. The goal here is to provide a method for people with programming skills to create advanced interactive capabilities for the Internet.

Locating the cgi-bin

UNLIKE HTML HYPERTEXT, the cgi-bin programs must reside in the cgi-bin or in subdirectories that are contained inside the cgi-bin. This unique area is set up as part of the installation of the Internet server. The exact location on any system must be obtained from the system administrator or the Internet provider. In much the same manner as HTML areas, cgi-bin areas can be set up on an Internet server. However, increased care is normal in allowing access to the cgi-bin. Unlike the HTML areas, which can be segmented easily to provide necessary security, the cgi-bin requires responsibility on the part of software developers because programs executed from the cgi-bin are executed by the server, not by the user. Since the cgi-bin programs do not have the highly restricted capabilities that HTML programs are given, they require an understanding of what should and what should not be done. With HTML, the only possible result of bad skills is a Web page that fails to produce the expected result. With cgi-bin programs, real problems can be created if the program is done incorrectly. This means that cgi-bin programming is a double-edged sword. On the one edge, it provides maximum control over server computer-based services. This will result in advanced interactive capability. On the other edge, it allows access to computer internals that malicious people could use to disrupt the operations of an Internet site. Because of these factors, it is unlikely that access to the cgi-bin will be given to casual parties. Instead, the cgi-bin is normally (and should be) approached with extreme caution. However, those who demonstrate the correctness of their goals can provide remarkable capabilities that go far beyond the basics of HTML hypertext.

To utilize the knowledge imparted in this book, you will need access to the cgi-bin. Whether you have this because a system administrator accepts your need or because you are the administrator for your system, you should proceed with caution. The cgi-bin programs are an exciting adventure into the Internet world, but they require professionalism and advanced skills to provide the greatest rewards.

Getting Started

EVERY ADVANCED LANGUAGE SKILL BEGINS with a simple program that will demonstrate the basic ability it will unfold. Here is a first program in both C++ and C.

Hello Internet World

Every program must have a *hello world* to get you started.

```
/*
* Type: C++ main
* Purpose: Send out Hello Message
*/
//----------------------------------
/* Name: hello.c */
#include <iostream.h>
main()
{
     cout<<"Content-type: text/html\n\n";
     cout<<"<HTML>\n";
     cout<<"<BODY>\n";
     cout<< "<H1> HELLO INTERNET WORLD </H1>\n";
     cout<< "</BODY>\n";
     cout<< "</HTML>";
     cout << endl;
}
//--------------------------------
CC -o main main.C
```

or alternatively in C the similar program becomes

```
/*
* Type: C main
* Purpose: Send out Hello Message
*/
#include <stdio.h>
#include <stdlib.h>
main()
{
     printf("Content-type: text/html\n\n");
     printf("<HTML>\n");
     printf("<BODY>\n");
     printf("<H1> HELLO INTERNET WORLD </H1>\n");
     printf("%s%s%s%s%s%ss",
          "Hola, el mundo de Internet\n",
          /* Spanish */
```

```
                    "Ciao Mondo Internet\n",
                    /* Italian */
                    " ' '\n",
                    /* Vietnamese⁵ */
                    " ` ' ^ ? \n",
                    /* Vietnamese */
                    "Chao Qui vi, the gioi Internet\n",
                    /* Vietnamese */
                    " .  \n",
                    /* Vietnamese */
                    "Hallo, Internet Wereld\n"
                    /* Netherlands */
                    "Aadab Internet Dunia\n"
                    /* India */
              );
              printf("</BODY>\n");
              printf("</HTML>\n");
        }
        cc -o main main.c
```

About this program

1. The first line is a message to the server. It says that what follows is HTML text. Since the output of the cgi-bin program will pass through the server to the client, the initial message is required to tell the server to forward the message on to the client. This line will not be sent to the client software. Only the lines that follow will go to the client. The two returns are needed to provide a single blank line after the server command.

2. The next lines are the actual HTML being sent to stdout. When a cgi program is run, stdout receives the output and routes it to the server, which then routes it to the user (client). If you are not familiar with HTML, you may want to look more closely at this output. It outputs a bare-bones HTML set of instructions along with the imbedded text *Hello Internet World*. The C++ version includes an endl[6] which can be used instead of \n and includes a flush of the buffer.

Compile this simple program. Then place it in the cgi-bin on your server. Be sure that it is totally executable. Remember that it will be executed by the server, not by the person who compiled it.

---

[5]   Vietnamese requires that all the punctuation be properly aligned to convey the meaning of the Internet World.

[6]   In most of the text, \n, which is familiar to C++ and C programmers, is used. The use of endl or fflush to clear the buffer is good practice, although it should only need to be done once at the completion of the program.

```
cp main unix_path/cgi-bin/main
chmod ugo+x unix_path/cgi-bin/main
```

This already assumes that you have access to a system and to the cgi-bin. It further assumes that your system administrator will allow you to use C++ or C scripts. Many locations will not allow access to the cgi-bin. When they do, they will require you to use PERL[7] language since it is easily inspected. The cgi-bin gives you enormous control over the computer and network. Using these techniques is only for sites where responsible people are involved in providing Internet services. Always remember the following:

> **The programs being run out of the cgi-bin are being run by the server, not by the user. This means that caution must be taken regarding who is given access to this capability.**

Viewing the cgi-bin Output

LET'S ASSUME THAT YOU have gotten past all the aforementioned obstacles, that you have your script in the cgi-bin, and that it is executable. Go into Netscape, Explorer, or another appropriate browser. Enter the URL of the cgi-bin program. This will look something like the following:

```
http://www.somename.com/cgi-bin/main
```

This is the URL associated with the cgi-bin program. This is normally http:// followed by the server name, a slash, cgi-bin, a slash, and the program name. The URL is a way of telling the Internet server where a particular HTML page or cgi-bin resource is located. Unlike UNIX paths, URLs need not exist on the local system. In fact, the purpose of the Internet is to allow access to resources that are not local. While this means that it would be possible to develop cgi-bin programs for a remote machine, for the moment assume that the cgi-bin is on the local machine. For those familiar with URLs, the cgi-bin URL will look much like other URLs. More will be said about this later. For now, simply enter the cgi-bin URL on the browser. (On Netscape, clicking on open at the top of the screen will bring up a URL entry window.) Remember that this same URL will be something that others will be able to enter to access your cgi-bin program either locally or remotely.

If you have set up the server for your system, you will know what the cgi-bin URL is. If you have not, you may need to ask the system administrator or server administrator. Since you will be using this frequently as you develop your cgi-bin

---

[7]   I have substituted PERL for any script language since it is the most common script language used. The same statements would apply to awk, Shell script, etc.

projects, you should write this down or save the URL as part of your bookmarks or favorites. Bookmarks, favorites, hotlists, or something equivalent are available on most client software. They provide an easy method to save URLS. The URL is associated with a description string and is easily accessible. (On Netscape, click on the bookmark icon at the top of the screen and then add the bookmark.) Since the real URL will take an inordinate amount of time to type, this an extremely convenient approach. In reality, the URL is even more esoteric, but that is the topic for books on client servers, not this book.

When you opened the URL from your browser, if you saw *Hello Internet World* on your browser screen, you are ready for the advanced techniques presented in this book. If you did not, you will have to find out why not. Recheck your work and recheck your permissions. If all else fails, start reading the chapter on debugging (Chapter 17).

Figure 1.1 shows step-by-step what was required to get this first program working. Once again, the steps are the following:

- Locate the cgi-bin.
- Code the initial *Hello Internet World* program.
- Compile the program.
- Place the program in the cgi-bin on the server.
- Determine the URL for the cgi-bin program.
- Enter the URL into the browser and view your output.

A More Detailed Look

BEFORE CONTINUING, TAKE A LOOK at the preceding program in more detail. First notice that the messages to the Internet server are sent as stdout using the iostream object cout or library function printf. The library function cout was used in the C++ version, but the same result was obtained by using the C printf. The C++ iostream library cout is a little easier to use since it takes most types (strings, ints, floats) without the requirement of formatting instructions. Persons familiar with either of these languages will recognize these as commands that would normally print ASCII text to the terminal screen. This is called standard output or stdout. However, much of what was being printed to the screen did not show up on the browser, because stdout is redirected to the client-server software when the cgi-bin program is run. Part of what is being sent to stdout are the hypertext (HTML) commands. In other words, the stdout for the cgi-bin program is not really the computer screen. Instead, there is an indirect routing to the screen. When the cgi program is invoked by the server, stdout goes to the server rather than directly to the screen. This is then passed through as HTML hypertext, which is interpreted, formatted, and then sent to the screen. Had the program merely printed out *Hello Internet World*, the server would not have been able to tell what kind of information it was receiving due to the missing

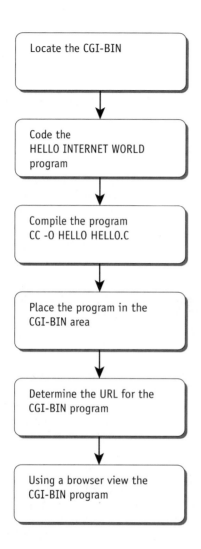

FIGURE 1.1   CGI Programming: Developing programs for the cgi-bin requires a step by step process.

Content Type:...

line. Even if this was present, the client would have no HTML instructions and the output still would be incorrect. However, in the latter case there may actually be an output since HTML interpreters tend to be forgiving.

As will become evident shortly, the fact that CGI programs go to stdout will have real advantages in developing these programs. The most important advantage is that it is possible to test the cgi-bin code by merely executing the program from the command line, as if it were a normal C program. You can then watch the screen to see if you are sending the expected information. What you will see on the screen is what would normally be sent to the server and eventually to the browser as HTML hypertext. When it is run as a cgi-bin program, it will be going through this server and then the client path to the browser and then to the user's screen. It will be received and processed in the same manner as a standard HTML page. The information is processed by the client (browser) with the same rules for hypertext as if you were writing a normal HTML Web page.

However, there is one exception: the essential first line that gives instructions to the server.

```
"Content-type: text/html"
```

This is a message to the server, and it must be exact since it tells the server how to deal with what will follow. It is the command required for the server. It tells the server what kind of information it is receiving. Without it, the message will not be sent to the browser. Later in this book, other types of server information will be discussed. For now, begin with the basic server request to send HTML command text with embedded material to the client. This messaging should be standard across servers.

The next part of the C++ and C code sends out the HTML. Again, this is sent to stdout and should be exactly what would be put in an HTML page. You may be wondering why you should go to all this trouble when you can do the same thing with standard HTML. The answer is that now you have all the tools available in compiled C++ or C at your disposal. This will allow the building of interactive displays, creation of real-time data displays, and use of sophisticated algorithms to control HTML and ultimately Web pages.

Once the *Hello Internet World* succeeds, next try viewing the source from a browser such as Netscape. Again use the view the source capability that is provided on most browsers. It is, in essence, legitimate cheating. It allows anyone to view the HTML that is used to produce an Internet Web page that is on the screen. It was developed as an easy method to get started on the Internet. If you want to give it a try, merely go to a favorite Web page and view the source. There is even a method to save the source, which can then be modified with any standard text editor. When you looked at the output of your cgi-bin program, you received your initial test of how well you understand cgi-bin program operation. Perhaps surprisingly, the source looked like a standard HTML page. The actual C++ code that sent the view to the screen was hidden from the browser. The result of viewing the source was

```
<HTML>
<BODY>
<H1> HELLO INTERNET WORLD </H1>
</BODY>
</HTML>
```

You could have saved this as an HTML page, placed it in an appropriate HTML area, and then using the URL associated with the new HTML page, created the same *Hello Internet World* on a browser. You may want to try this just to prove it to yourself. This is also a useful exercise because you will know where your available HTML area is. It will be different from the cgi-bin area. Later in this book, methods will be developed that use both areas.

The cgi-bin output will not always look exactly like standard HTML. It will quickly become evident that much of the work done by cgi-bin programs is hidden from the browser. Forms and other interactive control can only take place via a cgi-bin program.

At this point, try modifying the preceding program to put out some additional HTML. If you are knowledgeable in HTML, you could send out any acceptable HTML, including anchors, IMaGe requests, and tables. Then try the following examples. Take the time to put them into a program, compile them, and see what you get.

Example 1: C++ Creating an HTML List

```
/*
 * Type: C++ main
 * Purpose: Send out an HTML list
 */

/* Name: list.c */

#include <iostream.h>
#include <stdlib.h>

main()
{
    cout << "Content-type: text/html\n\n";
    cout << "<HTML>\n";
    cout << "<TITLE>cgi-bin list program</title>\n";
    cout << "<BODY>\n";
    cout << "<H1> cgi-bin program generating a list </H1>\n";
    cout << "<H2> Created by your name </H2>\n";
    cout << "<UL>\n";
    cout << "<LI>\n";
    cout << "List Item 1\n";
    cout << "<LI>\n";
    cout << "List Item 2\n";
    cout << "</UL>\n";
    cout << "</BODY>\n";
    cout << "</HTML>\n";
}
```

This results in the following HTML:

```
<HTML>
<TITLE>cgi-bin list program</title>
```

```
<BODY>
<H1> cgi bin program generating a list </H1>
<H2> Created by your name </H2>
<UL>
<LI>
List Item 1
<LI>
List Item 2
</UL>
</BODY>
</HTML>
```

Example 2: C Code Different Header Types

```c
/*
 * Type: C main
 * Purpose: Send out HTML Header types
 */

#include <stdio.h>
#include <stdlib.h>
main()
{
    printf("Content-type: text/html\n\n");
    printf("<HTML>\n");
    printf("<TITLE>cgi-bin header types</title>\n");
    printf("<BODY>\n");
    printf("<H1> This is a cgi-bin program </H1>\n");
    printf("<H2> Created by your name </H2>\n");
    printf("<H3> This is a header 3 </H3>\n");
    printf("<H4> This is header 4 </H4>\n");
    printf("</BODY>\n");
    printf("</HTML>\n");
}
```

One quick point of information: The carriage returns (\n) are only done for esthetics. They have no effect on the HTML output and could have been eliminated. However, if they are avoided, the view of the HTML source code may be difficult to read. Sometimes it may make sense to combine some printouts. For example, the last two lines could be combined into the single line

```c
printf("</BODY></HTML>\n");
```

This would have the same result for the HTML interpreter.

Spaces are another ignored character. Only a single space will be output by the HTML, even if there are multiple spaces in a row. This can be used to create more readable code. Here is another equivalent rewrite of the final lines in the preceding program:

```
cout << " </BODY> </HTML> \n";
```

You are encouraged to experiment in HTML or, more appropriately, use your cgi-bin program to verify some of these similarities.

Book Conventions

A WORD ABOUT THE CONVENTIONS used in this book is in order. Two types of paths reflect the distinction between C++ or C versus HTML. The first are normal UNIX paths and are shown as

```
unix_path
```

These are the paths familiar to UNIX, C++, and C developers. An example from a typical environment is as follows:

```
/home/markf/rje
```

This is the UNIX path to the rje directory under

```
/home/markf.
```

In the text of this book, the UNIX paths will normally be given as follows:

```
unix_path/myfile.txt
```

So the equivalent for the path /home/markf/rje would be

```
unix_path/rje
```

Here unix_path is substituted for /home/markf or any similar path, such as /home/joe or /usr/joe. The specific path would depend on how the system has been set up. When using real UNIX paths for your cgi-bin programs, use the command

```
pwd
```

to print the working directory, which will show the full path to a file. Always be careful about permissions. It is also a good idea to use full paths in your programs. If a file is to be read by the cgi-bin program, the permissions for reading the file will need to be at the level required by the server, not the level required by the developer (which is you), and certainly not at the user's level, since users have no permissions (they are accessing with a browser). Many UNIX systems are set up to give permissions for access only to the user who creates the files. This can make it appear that your cgi-bin program is working when you execute it directly as yourself. However, it will fail when it is executed using a URL since the server will be trying to access the file.

When examining the entire unix_path and file description, the first part tells that it is a general UNIX path. The second part, myfile.txt, is to give specific information about the file type used with the UNIX path. In this instance myfile.txt might be a text file that will be read in by the cgi-bin program. In the preceding example, the unix_path would be /home/markf/rje. This could be any UNIX path depending on how the UNIX system is set up and where files are kept. The UNIX path should be thought of as existing on the local machine or machine where the cgi-bin is located. While there are some special exceptions to this rule, such as NFS[8] mounting, which allows access to remote files through local area networks (LANs), the assumption will be more often valid than not. C++ and C programs will use UNIX paths to access files.

Any type file could be accessed by a cgi-bin program. These could be

- database files—file.db
- text files—file.txt
- HTML files—file.html
- flat files—file.txt
- GIF files—file.gif
- JPG files—file.jpg
- binary files—file.bin

or any other legitimate file type. Because C++ and C are being used, the information contained in the file can be in ASCII format, hexadecimal format, raw integer format, or any other format that can be interpreted. This means that scramblers, security algorithms, and other special capabilities could be put in place. As will be seen in the later discussions of forms and hidden variables (see Chapters 4 and 10), it is even possible to send a descrambling key to the HTML. This means that deciphering or encryption capability could be provided with a cgi-bin program.

URL Paths

Also needed are Internet or HTML paths called URLs:

internet_path

---

[8]   NFS = Network File System.

These are the paths to URLs. The cgi-bin programs will be accessed using a browser
and an Internet or URL path. Normally, an Internet path will be in the following
format:

    http://internet_path/cgi-bin/myprog

The starting http is used as a reminder that the path is a URL path—specifically a
World Wide Web address. There are other legitimate designators, such as gopher://
or ftp://. If you are interested, you should examine the numerous source books
available on these topics. The internet_path is a reminder that the cgi-bin will have an
associated path that must be determined from your system administrator. The "cgi-
bin" shows that a cgi-bin program follows. Finally, the myprog at the end is the name
of the compiled cgi-bin program. This can be any legitimate compiled name. For a
typical system, the real Internet path might look like this:

    http://www.xyz_co.com/cgi-bin/cgi_program

This would be rewritten as

    http://internet_path/cgi-bin/cgi_program

There will also be Internet paths to standard HTML Web pages. These will written to
look like this:

    http://internet_path/somename.html

The use of cgi-bin programs will still allow use of the normal hypertext capabilities,
including links to other Web pages in either HTML or cgi-bin format.

In many cases, the Internet URL path and the UNIX path will have parts in
common. For example, the cgi-bin program will have a URL that includes cgi-bin as
part of the URL, but the UNIX path that the cgi-bin program is found in will also have
cgi-bin as part of the path. If this seems confusing, remember that the UNIX path is
how the UNIX operating system locates a file on a particular computer, while the
Internet path is how the browser locates a resource (which may be an HTML file, an
IMaGe, other multimedia files, or a cgi-bin program). Even though they are in the
same location, the naming convention allows them to have different names if they
are a UNIX path versus a URL. This may have been a deliberate decision since it
hides the real location of files from the publicly accessible Internet URLs. UNIX
paths are associated with resources accessible via UNIX tools, while URL paths are
associated with resources available to the Internet client server. UNIX paths are traditionally internal to an institution, while URLs are public, like your email address.
The cgi-bin program is the unique application program that crosses both boundaries and therefore will contain both UNIX paths and Internet URL paths. UNIX files
will normally be resources used by the cgi-bin program. URLs, on the other hand,
can occur both as ways to activate the cgi-bin programs from the browser and as part
of the HTML output from a cgi-bin program.

Since this book focuses on C++ and C cgi-bin programming, many of the examples are provided in both languages. In many instances subtle differences and other capabilities are included in the alternative versions to avoid monotony. Some of the alternative programs are also available in the appendixes. The emphasis is on the use of *object analysis* for either language. *Object-oriented* languages are increasingly becoming the choice of programmers. Nonetheless, the C language, which is more function based, remains a powerful and popular language. It is also widely available and therefore may be more accessible to some readers. However, object-oriented analysis should be the preferred method for development of high-powered tools for the Internet even if the language used is C. This approach is apparent in this book. Even the C programs will frequently have an object-oriented approach, with strong emphasis on structured programming and object analysis. Because some may disagree with this approach, this book contains enough modularity in the examples in both languages to support changing to other approaches. In areas where there are fewer examples in either language, most programmers will be able to convert to the other language without much difficulty. Many of the examples are constructed in a manner that would make them easy to transport to other languages. No attempt has been made to support other languages, but the principles provided in this text would be equally applicable to Fortran, Basic, or other languages. Only in a few instances have the capabilities specific to the C++ and C languages been used.

The use of the object-oriented approach associated with C++ was chosen because it provides maximal structure. The topic of this book, cgi Internet programming, will frequently become moderately complex. The object-oriented approach provides the structure needed to help minimize the degree of complexity and make this sometimes difficult subject, which crosses several disciplines, manageable.

Most of the program modules in this book are complete. You are encouraged to use this code for building blocks for your own applications. The C++ in this book is object based and uses the user-definable class type as the major building block. While it is possible to use the programs in this book directly, real development will require studying *C++ and C coding standards* to gain an understanding of the nature of user definable classes and of *C methodology*. References in the back of the book will help interested readers enhance their skills in these areas.

To provide readability, the C++ classes in this book always begin with a capital letter followed by lowercase letters. For example, a class might be called Myclass, Abird, or Myform. The capitalized Myclass can now be used to create the instance of the class Myclass a_specific_class. This was done to make it easy to recognize classes when they are being created. This was needed in a book that crosses frequently between two compiled languages, C++ and C , and the noncompiled Internet language HTML. The HTML control statements should be moderately easy to recognize since they almost always start and end with triangular brackets ("< >"). You should find yourself quickly recognizing the different types of information.

Having done all this preliminary work, you should have the necessary tools to start your adventure in cgi-bin development. If you have worked through this introduction,

- You have access to the cgi-bin area.
- You have the ability to write C++ or C code with an editor.
- You have a compiler that will compile the C++ or C code.
- You have the ability to create the required permissions for your cgi-bin executables.
- You have access to an HTML area.
- You have an understanding of the different conventions used in this book.
- You have several working cgi-bin programs.
- You have a browser for viewing and accessing your cgi-bin and HTML projects.
- You have a basic understanding of the *control messages* required by the server before messages are sent to the client.

All that remains is for you to gain some experience and understanding of how to use these new resources. If you are like most programmers, you are already seeing options that you never thought existed and starting to experiment in new ways.

PROGRAM EXERCISES

1. Create your own version of the *Hello Internet World* program. Place it in the cgi-bin and then execute the program from the browser. Do a chmod 700 filename and execute the program as a normal program from the command line. Now reexecute the program from the browser. Explain the result.

2. Using the program from Exercise 1, execute the program from the command line and redirect the output to a filename.html. Now place the filename.html in a normal HTML area and, using the correct URL, bring up the filename.html on the browser. Correct the observed problem in the file as needed and retry. Explain what happened.

3. Using the full extent of your knowledge of HTML, create a cgi-bin program that outputs a fancy HTML Web page. Test your output using the URL from a browser. Did you do any of the following?

    a] Basic HTML output

    b] Anchors

    c] Images

    d] Tables

    e] Backgrounds

    f] Title

    g] Headings and Lists

If you did, explain what was needed to get these to work. If you did not, see if you can add any of these capabilities to your project.

4. Create a *subdirectory* under the cgi-bin with your name. Place one of your cgi-bin programs in this area. Remove it from all other areas. Determine the required URL for your program and use it to activate your program from the browser.

5. Using the program from Exercise 4, do the following. First set the cache size on your browser to a moderately large value. Next clear out all existing cached items. Execute the cgi-bin program and observe the output. Change the original source code to put out different HTML. Compile and replace the old version with the new version. Reexecute the URL from the browser. Did you get the cached version or the new version? Why? Repeat the experiment with an HTML file. Did you get the cached version or the original version? Why? Explain any differences in behavior.

PROBLEMS

1. Explain the function of "Content-type: text/html." What will happen if this line is missing? Why isn't it needed when HTML is used instead of cgi-bin programs? Is it only needed for C++ and C programs or would you also need it for script cgi-bin programs?

2. Why do cgi-bin programs have to be placed into a special area? If the directory was given the normal name of cgi-bin, what methods might you use to find it?

3. Explain why a cgi-bin program, when executed, does not result in the same output as is at the browser? What is meant by the statement "the cgi-bin program is executed by the browser"?

4. Explain the flow of information between the client, server, and cgi-bin program.

5. Explain the distinction between a URL and a UNIX path.

6. Explain the diagram shown in Figure 1.2.

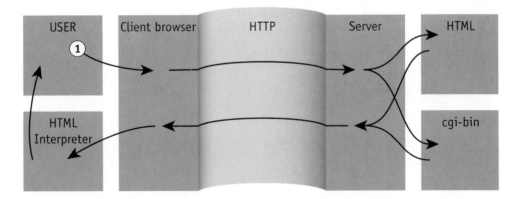

FIGURE 1.2

File I/O

Moving Forward with File I/O

NOW THAT YOU HAVE C++ or C available to create HTML output, you can do things you could not do before. The next section contains a simple program that displays data obtained at regular intervals on changes in temperature. Although it is simple in concept, with subtle changes this program will create results that are unobtainable using other script methods. The data relating to the temperature at different periods are located in a UNIX file called weatherfile. Since this is a UNIX file it can be created using any tools available from the UNIX operating system: It could be typed in by a scribe at regular intervals; it could be located in a database or obtained through a separate computer program; it could come from any source available to the computer, including satellite data, telemetry, or electronic sensors; and it could be other types of data, such as bus schedules, educational material, or stock quotes. For now, we use the weather data presented in the file in some numerical format.

Temperature Program

```
//-----------------------------------

/*
 * Type: C++ main
 * Purpose: Send weather star graph from a file
 */

/* Name: weather.c */

#include <stdlib.h>
#include <stream.h>
#include <string.h>
#include <iostream.h>
main()
{
    int i=0;
    int j;
    char c;
    filebuf fin; // buffer to read a file in

    cout<<"Content-type: text/html\n\n"; // we always send this
    cout<<"<HTML>\n";
    cout<<"<BODY>\n";
    /* open the weather data file */
    if((fin.open("unix_path/weatherfile", "input") == EOF)
    {
        cout << "<B> Sorry Could Not Get Weather Data </B>\n";
    } else
    {
        c = fin.sgetc(); // get the first character
        while(c ! = EOF)
        {
            // create the HTML
            cout << "<H1> Data " << i++ <<" "<<
                (int )((c-'0')*10) <<
                "</H1><BR>\n";
            for(j=0; j <= (c-'0') * 10; j++)
                cout << "*";        // send out the graph
            cout <<"\n";
            c = fin.snextc();        // next character
        }
        // end the HTML
        cout << "</BODY>\n" << "</HTML>\n";
        fin.close();
```

```
        }
    }
```

About this program . . . .

1. The header files include some standard C++ headers. The string.h allows string routines, and the iostream.h allows stream routines.

2. The filebuf fin is used to input the data from a unix_path file. In this case the weather data are inside the file in numerical format.

3. The output to stdout using cout is the initial HTML message. By using a high-level language, it is legitimate to send this early in the program. Remember that the compiled program will execute in millionths of a second (microseconds). However, the output to the client-server will be at the normal rate. Since the output is going through stdout, the rate will be regulated by built-in *flow control* mechanisms. This is accomplished by buffering in the UNIX operating system and need not concern the cgi-bin programmer, which means that there is no danger of going too fast and that it is highly unlikely that you will go too slow.

4. The weather file with a complete unix_path is opened using normal C++ file I/O. The decision to send out the initial HTML allows the creation of an error leg just in case the file is not there. This opens possibilities that did not exist with previous basic HTML skills. It is possible to create conditionals and error legs based on the result of the cgi-bin program's real-time processing.

5. The first character is read in, and a check is done for an End of File (EOF). If it is EOF, the error message is sent; otherwise, the normal processing occurs.

6. The data are surrounded by HTML, which is sent to stdout using cout. For these data, the preference is integer form, so it is sent through a subroutine to change ASCII called atoi.[1] The C++ stream cout knows how to determine the type going to stdout and format it correctly so there is no need for formatting directives. The value of the variable i is used to determine which data item is being shown. It acts as an *item counter.*

7. After all the data have been sent out, the final completion of the HTML is sent to the server by way of stdout.

. . . .

If the data in the weather file are 5672, this is what you see when you activate the cgi-bin weather program from a browser:

```
Data 1   50 ***************************************************
Data 2   60 **********************************************************
Data 3   70 ****************************************************************
Data 4   20 *******************
```

---

[1] atoi is ASCII to integer.

These are the four temperatures, with temperature 1 having a value of 50 degrees, temperature 2 a value of 60 degrees, temperature 3 a value of 70 degrees, and temperature 4 a value of 20 degrees. The number of asterisks corresponds to the temperature value.

Using GIF Picture Graphs

WHEN THIS WAS ACTUALLY USED in a similar project, GIF files created the slices instead of asterisks. Instead of using the number 50 for the first temperature, 50 pictures of smiley faces were output along a line. This created a line graph representation of the magnitude of the temperature. GIF and JPG are the two standard methods for picture displays used on the Internet. Both display still pictures. The GIF (pronounced jiff) format tends to be the preferred format since it often produces better pictures. The JPG (pronounced jaypeg) format has the advantage of being highly compressed. Since it uses more colors, it is also better for faces and very textured pictures. With small pictures, such as those used for this project, the GIF format will actually result in smaller, more manageable files. JPG is most valuable for large files being sent on resources with lower speed or limited access. If these pictures are small enough (in this case about 1/4 inch square), the number of pictures output can be relatively large without any degradation in performance. How large is relatively large? This depends on the number of users accessing the Web page simultaneously or using shared system resources. Recall from earlier discussions that it is possible to do some initial testing using normal HTML pages. You could even use the output of the cgi-bin program by saving it to a file.

Execute the program and send the output to a file.

```
myprogram > myhtmlfile.html
```

Then remove the first line, which is the command to the server, and use it like a normal HTML file. This is a slightly different approach from the earlier method, in which the HTML was obtained by viewing the source. Since the entire output is being redirected to a file, it will include the command that goes to the server. This command is not required for a normal HTML file since the server removes it before sending the rest of the HTML to the client. In fact, if it is left in place, it will cause problems for the client (browser) HTML interpreter, and you will get a funny display.

Using GIF Files to Create Picture Graphs

HERE IS THE PROGRAM REWORKED in C with the GIF slices added:

```
/* Temperature Program */
/*-------------------------------------------*/
```

```
/*
 * Type: C main
 * Purpose: Send weather GIF graph from a file
 */

/* Name: weather_gif.c */
#include <stdio.h>
#include <file.h>
main()
{
    int i=0;
    int j;
    char c;
    FILE *fin; /* file buffer to read a file in */

    /* send the HTML to stdout */
    printf("Content-type: text/html\n\n"); /* we always send this */
    printf("<HTML>\n");
    printf("<BODY>\n");
    if((fin = fopen("unix_path/weatherfile", "r")) == 0)
    {
        printf("<B> Sorry Could Not Get Weather Data </B>\n");
    } else
    {
        c = fgetc(fin); /* get the first character */
        while(c ! = EOF)
        {
            /* create the HTML */
            printf("%s%d%s
                    "<H1> Data ",
                    i++,
                    " ");
            for(j=0; j <= (c-'0'); j++) // number * 10
            {
                printf("%s"
                    "<IMG SRC=\"http://internet_path/smiley.gif\">"
            }
            printf("%s%s",
                    "</H1><BR>\n",
                    "*\n"
                ); /* send out the graph */

            c = fgetc(fin); /* next character */
        }
        /* end the HTML */
```

```
printf("%s%s",
    "</BODY>\n",
    "</HTML>\n");
fclose(fin);
}
```

The GIFs called smiley.gif were little smiley faces, but they could just as easily have been colored bars or other graphic images. In fact, since C++ or C is being used, it would be possible to use smiley faces if temperatures exceeded a balmy 70 degrees and frowny faces if it got too cold. Figure 2.1 shows the use of thin sliced gifs to build horizontal and vertical bar graphs. Line graphs can be constructed in a similar manner by constructing the graph from blank square sections and square sections with a dot in the middle. The smaller the files used to build the graph, the more accurate the resolution. However, the more sections, the more time it will take to build the graph. The output command in the for loop to create the IMaGes looked like this.

```
printf("%s", "<IMG SRC=\"http://internet_path/smiley.gif\">");
```

or in C++

```
cout << "<IMG SRC=\"http://internet_path/smiley.gif\">";
```

This results in the normal HTML associated with images being sent from the cgi-bin program to the client-server software. When the HTML <IMG> command arrives at the client, it is replaced by the actual GIF file with a URL=http://internet_pathsmiley.gif. What appears on the screen is the smiley face picture, not the word "smiley."

Note the backslashes inside the HTML output string. These force the quotes to stdout instead of ending the stream of characters to stdout. These are needed since quotation marks are the normal delimiter for string variables in C++ and C. Here the literal character " is part of the string so the escape character \ must precede it.

If you do not like this construction, a simple subroutine can be created to send back the escape quote sequence.

```
/*
 * Type: C++ subroutine
 * Purpose: Add backslashed quotations
 */
char* quote()
{
    return "\\\"";
}
```

Now you can write

```
cout << quote() << mytext << quote();
```

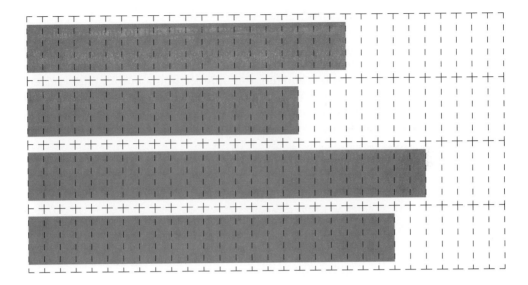

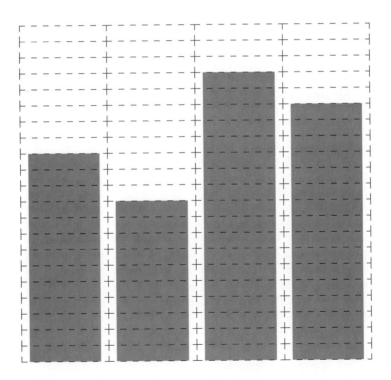

FIGURE 2.1　Each dashed rectangle is a GIF image.

The quoted text will go to stdout.

It should be self-evident that changing the data in the file will result in a totally different graph for the next person who uses the cgi-bin/main. Whatever temperatures are in the file will determine the number of GIF files output to the screen. This is accomplished by changing the number of GIF output lines created. In reality, the program would probably need to be modified to put out a GIF for every 5 or 10 degrees of temperature and to use string input. This would result in a better-looking page, and it is accomplished with a simple modification of the for loop.

```
int k=0;
char input_string[20];
    while(fgets(input_string, 20, fin) != EOF)
    {
        // HTML OUTPUT HERE
        for(j=0; j <= atoi(input_string)/10; j++)
        {
            if((k++ %10)==0)
                printf("%s"
                    "\"<IMG SRC=\"http://internet_path/smiley.gif\">"
                );
        }
        // HTML OUTPUT HERE
```

This results in images only going out every count of 10 degrees and allows real temperature values. The file might look like this

```
53
72
83
75
```

The fgets(…) reads in a line at a time. The function atoi changes the ASCII value to an integer. The K counter sends output every tenth count. You can change to every fifth count or some other modulus based on your data. For this example, fgets() may appear to be the better option unless you are seeking speed, in which case you will avoid having an ASCII file and keep your data as absolute decimal values ranging from 0 to 255 for a char data type.

This is a simple example of how real-time displays can be realized by changing files with standard computer tools. The power of such tools is that dynamic, changing information can be presented rather than static information. The Internet ceases to be a telephone yellow pages, changing only occasionally through user input, and instead becomes a dynamic information source, outputting real-time information to the public and private sectors. It may be of interest that even a simple program like this may show degradation if written in script languages. Script languages tend to produce very loose timing and could result in some of the image downloads failing.

Developing C++ Classes and Object C

HAVING MADE THE DECISION to use C++ and C to create cgi-bin programs, it makes sense to create some structure that will continue as projects become increasingly complex. An overview of the use of cgi-bin programs will provide some early direction. At the most basic level, form information will come into these programs and HTML will come out of them. This is one of the most fundamental uses of the cgi-bin programs. HTML forms provide output from the browser to the server, which is then passed to the cgi-bin program. After processing the form information, the appropriate HTML is generated, which goes back through the server to the browser and then becomes output to the user. The input will be provided from the users. The output can consist of other forms, tables, or fundamental HTML components. There will be images in GIF and JPG format. There will also be HTML anchors or hotlinks to other resources. There may also be behind-the-scenes activities such as mailers, database lookups, and image processing.

At the next level there will be project-specific details. We may want to provide a questionnaire, an interactive game, a database search tool, or a purchase request form. Each of these should provide clear definitions that allow a modular approach. There are many software tools that C++ provides that are natural for this approach. The use of *classes, polymorphism, inheritance, overloading,* and other data types familiar to object-oriented programmers will be extremely valuable. In C the modularity will not be quite as self-evident, but by working from the C++ to the C, the same result can be achieved. Ultimately the C++ will be compartmentalized into object units with their associated functionality, while the C will have systematically organized functional units that can be carried over into other projects as whole entities.

With this as a goal, let's get started by creating a data type called _Graph. Remember that *C++ classes* look like *C structs* with the addition of attached functions. While this is a simplification, it does give a basic starting point. In reality, everyone who has worked in C++ and C knows that while structs and classes look similar, they are very different approaches to programming. C++ looks at the world through user-defined data types called class objects. Each object is a self-contained module that has associated with it public interfaces and components and private functions and components. In C the commonality must be implied. However, this should not be difficult since each chapter unit should create the necessary sub-units. More will be said later about this unique approach to programming and how it relates to the Internet. For now, the best approach is to develop a simple C++ class based on the initial examples and then extend it to C.

Here is a graph class:

```
class Graph {
private:
    // Data Hiding
    int i;
    char c;
    char* mystring;
    filebuf fin;                        // the file buffer
```

```
public:
    Graph(){ i=0; };                        // constructor
    void draw();                            // class subroutine to draw the graph
    void addstring(char *string) { mystring = string; };
    };
```

About this class

1. The class is called Graph. Recall that the Caps convention is used to allow the recognition of the class name. You may prefer other conventions for naming your own classes. For example, _ (underscore) could be used for the initial class name. The method used here is merely to create some organization and should not be considered a standard for C++ class development.

2. The internal parts required to make graphs are placed in the *private*[2] area. The word *private* is used even though it is not needed. (Private is understood until public is stated.) The char* mystring is the name of the GIF file. This would make it easy to change from smiley faces to frowny faces. A simple change would allow the filename also to be an input to the program. The filename could also be passed in as a parameter to the draw routine.

3. The *constructor* merely sets the value of i to zero. It is automatically called when the class is created. Since no new or, equivalently in C, malloc() routines occur, there is no need for a *destructor* to act as a cleanup when the class ceases to exist. Since most cgi-bin programs have a very short life span, destructors will rarely be needed. Cleanup will result anyway from the program terminating. However, good programming style will be to provide cleanup destructors. The Internet protocol has often been referred to as a *memoryless protocol*. It comes into being, sends a message to the client server, and then terminates. Only the user's local information is maintained. This is done as a conscious decision to minimize the amount of time spent sending data through the network. The constructor, on the other hand, will often have a great deal of value. You may already have thought about using the constructor to open the file. In fact, constructors are prime candidates for things that always occur as part of initialization for the cgi-bin program.

4. The primary functional part is the routine draw() shown next.

```
/*
 * Type: C++ class subroutine
 * Purpose: Draw graph as part of a class
 */
#define FILENAME "weatherfile"
Graph::draw()
```

---

[2]   I have placed the private area in the same location as in most C++ texts. Some programmers prefer to reverse this order.

```
        {
            cout<<"Content-type: text/html\n\n" // we always send this
            cout<<"<HTML>\n";
            cout<<"<BODY>\n";
            if((fin.open(FILENAME, "input") == 0)
            {
                cout << "<B> Sorry Could Not Get Weather Data </B>\n";
            } else
            {
                c = fin.sgetc();
                while(c ! = EOF)
                {
                    for(i=1; i <= (c-'0'); i++)
                    {
                        // create the HTML
                        cout << "<H1> Data " << i <<
                            "</H1><BR>\n";
                        // send out the graph
                        cout << mystring;
                    }
                    cout <<"\n";
                    c = fin.snextc(); // next character
                }
                // end the HTML
                cout << "</BODY>\n" << "</HTML>\n";
        };
```

This, of course, looks very similar to the earlier program. The main difference is that the subroutine is now part of the C++ class Graph. The Graph class is also more general and can therefore be used for other graphs. This provides some initial modularity and can eventually be used to create software packages that will be usable on different Web pages as needed. This packaging of C++ classes is the basis of object design. Each class represents an object module. These neat little packages will allow a building block approach to emerge, which will eventually create complex cgi-bin capabilities quickly and easily. With good construction, class objects can also provide an easy method for creating a sophisticated development environment that can support multiple customers with multiple programmers.

Completing the picture requires a main program:

```
// now our main program looks like this:
/* Name: graph.c */
/*
 * Type: C++ main
 * Purpose: Create graph by instantiating GRAPH class
 */
#include <iostream.h>
```

```
#include <stdlib.h>
#include <string.h>
main()
{
    GRAPH myGraph;
    myGraph.addstring(
        "<IMG SRC=\"http://internet_path/smiley.gif\">\n");
    myGraph.draw();
}
```

About main   ·

1. The class type Graph is created. In this case the type is a Graph (initial capitals) and the specific graph is called myGraph.

2. The public instance mystring is set to the smiley face using the Internet path. Because mystring is a char*, the creation is straightforward. Recall that in both C++ and C, a string of characters in quotation marks represents a *pointer* to that string or a char*. This is the kind of argument that the subroutine myGraph.addstring(…) expects.

3. Finally, the draw() routine is called to complete the HTML output to the client server of the required graph.

· ·

Since the GIFs used to create the graph are very small[3]—approximately 1/4 inch square—they load very quickly even when there are a large number of them. By repeating the same GIF file over and over to build the graph, the caching capability of good browsers will only have to download the GIF file once. The graph will actually be built locally. This is a highly valuable aspect of most browsers. Once a GIF name is known to the browser, the browser will no longer download it but will instead use the locally cached version. These kinds of considerations are an essential part of cgi-bin programming. Experience with cgi-bin programming will uncover many tricks that will allow complex capabilities to be realized quickly. While C++ and C will have rapid response times, rapid responses will not be assured if other segments are not properly designed.

While the Graph class is probably not the most useful class, it does illustrate the principle of *modular object programming*. The basic steps are as follows:

1. Determine the required object.

2. Identify the components that consist of variable types: int, char, pointers, enums, and even structs.

3. Determine how much of this can be *hidden*. This is an area where many programmers fall short. While it is easier to create many public types, this is the equivalent of creating numerous global variables in C. The result will be diffi-

---

[3]   Image size is measured in points (e.g., 24×32). The size of a point is a function of the monitor used.

culty handing these modules to others since they can step on parts of the program that should have been private. The result is endless hours troubleshooting others' work. By building with minimal public access and by providing this access through public functions rather than public data, productivity will be greatly increased.

A QUICK NOTE: While our primary purpose is to create Internet cgi-bin programs, it is not unreasonable to review some basic object principles. Here is an example of something you should not do:

```
class Aclass {
public:
     int myint;
}
main()
{
     Aclass myclass;
     myclass.myint = 1;
}
```

Instead the same thing is done through function interfaces:

```
class Aclass {
private:
     int myint;
public:
     set_int(int value) { myint = value; };
}
main()
{
     Aclass myclass;
     myclass.set_int( 1 );
}
```

While this may seem a waste of a subroutine, object thinking dictates this approach. The thinking is that objects come into existence and actions change the objects. You open a door rather than repositioning the door's molecules. The movement of the molecules is the hidden part of the object. While this may seem cumbersome at first, the approach quickly grows on you, and eventually the payoffs become apparent as you continue to think in the object-based paradigm.

While it is not possible to create the same thing as a class in C, you can name your file graph.c and keep all the definitions needed for graphing local to the graph routines. You could even get closer by making a graph struct that contains all the data types used by a graph.

Summary

In this chapter you extended your skills with cgi-bin programs that allow input from files. This is a basic building block for many of the advanced techniques. The simple weather program provided an initial look at how much can be done with cgi-bin programs. This was followed by the object approach using the Graph class as an initial example.

PROGRAM EXERCISES

1. You have been given the job of sending information about a design project over the Web. Since the information will be changing at regular intervals, you have decided to keep the information in a text file and then have a cgi-bin program read the information into a Web page. Create the required cgi-bin program. Create a sample text file. Verify that everything is working properly. (**Hint:** Be sure to review Internet paths versus UNIX paths.)

2. You have been given the job of displaying the quantities of software available for a software vendor. This company sells five different software products (Product A, Product B, etc.) and wishes to make its monthly sales available over the Web to its marketing people so they will know what is selling well and what needs to be discounted. Come up with a method for showing this information using cgi-bin techniques. Change the data to get a new display.

3. Repeat Exercise 2 using any graphics tools available to you. Develop your graphics to provide the information in the best way. See if you can come up with at least three graphics methods.

CHAPTER 3

C++BaseClasses

Basic HTML C++ Classes and C Libraries

HTML Classes

C HTML Functions

Definitions of Colors

Basic HTML C++ Classes and C Modules

SINCE HTML IS A STRUCTURED LANGUAGE with organizing rules, it is straightforward to build some C++ classes or C modules that will allow basic HTML to be created easily. If these are built correctly, they should be usable for multiple cgi-bin-created Web pages. In the language of C++, these will become *base classes* or in C *standard functions* or even libraries. If you are working toward object-based C, *modules* may be a better term to use. By using C++ classes and C modules interchangeably, it will be easier to move back and forth between the two languages.

Furthermore, *derived* classes can use *inheritance* to carry these base classes forward rather than having to repeat the code ad infinitum. For C language programmers, this will be accomplished by building some functions with data types into modules. These will be accessed by other program modules to provide something equivalent to C++ inheritance.

Even if these subroutines are not used as shown here, they represent a valuable review of the HTML language. Since this is essential to the production of cgi-bin Web pages, the review will prove valuable to anyone who is serious about developing cgi-bin programs. This chapter and later chapters on base HTML classes will also provide easy reference for HTML, eliminating the need to use this book and an HTML book when developing your cgi-bin programs. This does not mean that you should not supplement this book with a reading of other HTML learning books. While HTML is a simple language, there are certain capabilities that may warrant careful examination. In this respect, this chapter is not a complete definition of all possible HTML capabilities. Instead, it is only meant to cover the more common aspects of the HTML language along with some of the special features that are available. Emphasis is on capabilities that lend themselves to cgi-bin programming. It is also important to be aware that HTML is still undergoing change. New features will be put in place; future cgi-bin programs can and should take advantage of these changes to produce new and exciting cgi-bin programs.

The routines created here are usable for C++ or C. Just change the comment line to use the familiar C

```
/* comment */
```

rather than the C++

```
// comment
```

Then change the C++ stdout library function cout to the similar C function printf. Formatting will need to be added for the printf version.

One final point before defining the base classes: The routines shown may require certain predefined inputs, such as a background color. Definitions for these are given near the end of this chapter (page 48). You may want to take a quick look at these definitions before reading the following sections.

HTML Classes

THE JOB OF DEVELOPING AND understanding the HTML base class is simplified if you understand how HTML works. HTML is a script-based control language. It consists of three basic types of commands. The simplest are unary commands that always precede the lines being controlled. A simple example would be the bold font command <B>. This precedes any text that is to be in bold font. It can be turned off by activation of a new font or by </B>.

```
<B>
This text will be printed in BOLD Font
As will this
<I>
 This text will be in italics
```

If <B> appears on a line, it sets the font type to bold until another font-affecting command occurs. The second type of commands are the binary commands, which have a beginning, imbedded information, and an end. The beginning command always appears in triangular brackets. The end command is the same command with a forward slash (/) right after the left triangular bracket. Here is an example of a title:

```
<TITLE> my title </TITLE>
```

The final commands are a mixture of all the other HTML commands. These include a wide variety of button types, form commands, IMaGe commands, anchors, tables, etc. There is no simple rule for describing these commands. The only common feature is that they begin with a left angle bracket (<) and end with a right angle bracket (>).

HTML tends to be a forgiving language. Some mistakes will be passed through without harm. Unfortunately, different client browsers will deal with these anomalies differently. Because of this and because of the increased difficulty of dealing with compiled cgi-bin programs, it is worth the time to create consistent HTML output.

Because HTML is an ASCII-based language, the subroutines provided next will use pointers to strings (char*) as their input and then format the strings with HTML and send them out to stdout. This allows the variable information fields to be the primary focus. The HTML rules handle the rest.

```
class Standard { // This will be used to standard parts
     char color[8];
public:
     Standard(); // overload constructor
     Standard(int start_color);
     void start_msg(int start_color);
     void set_color(char* color_to_set)
          {strcpy( color, color_to_set);};
     void normal_head(char* title);           // standard header
     void color_head(char* title);            // colored background header
     void end();
     void comment(char* mycomment);
     void image(char* myimage);               // overload image
     void image(char* myimage, char* alt);
     void image(char* myimage, int n, ...);
     void anchor(char* link, char* hottext);
};
```

About the Standard class   . . . .

1. The constructor Standard is overloaded. This is an unique capability in C++. It allows the same function name to call different functions. Which version is called will be determined by the function arguments. From the C viewpoint, they can be thought of as different functions with an invisible character that differentiates them. In this case the overloading is used to allow a background color to be optional. If the function receives a color as an argument, it is the background color. If there is no argument, there is no

background color selected. This is also used to make one constructor send the required server message and one that does not. This will give us the option of autosending the start message or providing it on demand.

2. The start_msg() routine is the server control start_msg sent on demand. This is the content message that is required by the server when a cgi-bin program runs. In later chapters it will be shown that there are different types of start messages (for image, animation, and other capabilities), so you will need to expand this routine.

3. The set_color() routine does just what its name implies. It sets the color, which is a private variable. The color can then be used in other class functions. This is a generic function to allow color to be used in any of your functions. The use of color plays an important part in Internet Web pages.

4. The color_head() and head() take arguments for the title and optionally the color of the background. If the color is preset, head() can be used. In HTML the <HEAD> directive is used to identify information about the Web page. It is followed by the <BODY>, which contains the components of the multimedia display.

5. The image subroutine is overloaded to support the required image (<IMG>) and the unrequired alternative (<ALT>). The third version allows additional strings, such as size. This takes advantage of the va_list and arg_ptr capability in C++. It is also available in the C language. The use of IMaGes is one of the most powerful capabilities on the Internet. In later chapters methods are developed that allow unique image control to be implemented using the cgi-bin.

6. Finally, the anchor is used to set up the hypertext links to other URLS (<HREF=...). The link and the activating text are included as the two arguments. These anchors, the name used in HTML, are familiar to anyone who has used the World Wide Web. They are what allows you to move about by clicking on text and/or pictures through various sites.

· ·

In C it will be necessary to create a more functional approach by creating a module of routines that are available for any standard HTML requests.

```
/*
 * Type: C++ constructor
 * Purpose: Send out server message and setup color
 */
/* Constructor sends the needed start of message and sets up the default color */
Standard::Standard(char* start_color)
{
    cout << "Content-type: text/html\n\n";
    strcpy( color, start_color);
}
/*
 * Type: C++ overloaded constructor
```

```
 * Purpose: Set up color to default
 */
/* Constructor does not send the start message. Used with startmsg (see below) when the
 * script can have multiple purposes.
 */
Standard::Standard()
{
     strcpy( color, DEFAULT_COLOR);
}
/*
 * Type: C++ class subroutine
 * Purpose: Force message to server and set color
 */
/* Used when the script can have multiple purposes. As an example, these classes could be
 * used to create standard HTML pages rather than cgi-bin programs. If this were the case,
 * the start message would not be needed. In other situations, it may make sense to
 * create some part of the HTML prior to sending it to the server. When this is the case,
 * there may be reasons to create the class without sending the initial message to the server
 * about the type of data being sent.
 */
Standard::startmsg(char* start_color)
{
     cout << "Content-type: text/html\n\n";
     strcpy( color, start_color );
}
/*
 * Type: C++ class subroutine
 * Purpose: Send out starting HTML for top of Web page
 */
/* This is a generic routine that sets up the beginning part of your HTML page. It creates
 * some HTML that occurs at the start of most pages. All it requires for input is the title of
 * your page.
 */
void
Standard::normal_head(char* title)
{
     cout<<"<HTML><HEAD>\n";
     cout<<"<TITLE>\n"<<title << "</TITLE>\n";
     cout<<"</HEAD>" << "<BODY>\n";
}
/*
 * Type: C++ class subroutine
 * Purpose: Just send the server message
 */
/*
 * This sends the content type message.
```

```cpp
    */
void
Standard::start_msg()
{
    cout<<"Content-type: text/html\n\n";
}
/* This is the same as the normal head, except it adds a colored background of your choice
 * to the starting HTML. The color is set either by start_msg or set_color prior to calling this
 * routine.
 */
void
Standard::color_head(char* title)
{
    normal_head(title);
    cout<<"<BODY " <<" BGCOLOR=\""<<
        color <<"\>\n" << "</BODY>\n";
}
/* This routine will provide the required HTML to end your home page that is being
 * generated from the cgi-bin. It ends the body and then ends the HTML. All other HTML can
 * be placed between this routine and the normal_head() or color_head() routines.
 */
void
Standard::end()
{
    cout<<"</BODY></HTML>\n";
}
/* This routine adds a comment to your HTML output. Comments will appear on the browser
 * screen, but can be examined by viewing the source. While their major purpose is to
 * document your HTML work, they can also represent a powerful method of passing
 * information to cgi-bin programs. This will become clearer in later chapters on Thru mode.
 */
void
Standard::comment(char* mycomment)
{
    cout<<"<!--" << mycomment << "-->\n";
}
/* The image is the method used to place a GIF or JPG image on the browser screen.
 * Images can be merely placed on the screen or they can replace text in anchors, tables, or
 * other HTML. There are a number of optional arguments that can be part of the IMaGe
 * HTML. Because of this, image capability will be overloaded to allow you to input other
 * options.
 */
void
Standard::image(char* myimage)
{
    cout<<"<IMG SRC=\"" << myimage << "\">\n";
```

```
}
void
Standard::image(char* myimage, char* alt)
{
      cout<<"<IMG SRC=\"" << myimage << "\"ALT=\"" << alt <<"\">\n";
}
/* The anchor is the other major component for HTML development. It consists of text which
 * will be highlighted on the screen and an associated URL. If the text is clicked on with the
 * mouse or in some other way activated, the associated URL is requested from the server
 * and the new page (or resource) identified by this URL is sent to the client.
 */
void
Standard::anchor(char* link, char* hottext)
{
      cout<< "<A HREF=\"" << link << "\">" << hottext << "></A>\n";
}
```

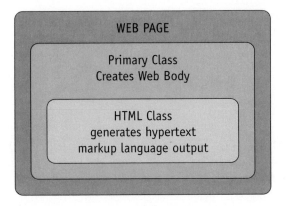

FIGURE 3.1   Base Class: Object oriented design allows systematic development of cgi-bin
procedures.

C HTML Functions

IN C, THE FUNCTIONS LOOK almost identical except that the stream operator cout is
replaced by the printf function. Since data hiding is no longer available, global definitions will be required. Good C practice will be to place these at the lowest layer
possible. In addition, the absence of overloading in C necessitates the use of different subroutine names where overloading was used in C++.

```
char color[8];
Standard(char* start_color)
{
```

```
        printf("Context-type: text/html\n\n");
        strcpy( color, start_color);
}
/* A different name is needed since overloading is not available */
Alt_Standard()
{
        strcpy( color, DEFAULT_COLOR);
}
/* used when the script can have multiple purposes */
void
startmsg(char* start_color)
{
        printf("Context-type: text/html\n\n");
        strcpy( color, start_color);
}
void
normal_head(char* title)
{
        printf("<HTML><HEAD>\n");
        printf("%s%s%s","<TITLE>\n", title, "</TITLE>\n");
        printf("%s%s", "</HEAD>\"\n");
}
void
color_head(char* title)
{
        printf("<HTML><HEAD>\n");
        printf("%s%s%s","<TITLE>\n", title, "</TITLE>\n");
        printf("%s%s%s%s", "<BODY BGCOLOR=",
                color, "></HEAD>\n", "<BODY>\n");
}
void
end()
{
        printf("</BODY></HTML>\n");
}
void
comment(char* mycomment)
{
        printf("%s%s%s", "<!--", mycomment, "-->\n");
}
void
image(char* myimage)
{
        printf("%s%s%s", "<IMG SRC=\"", myimage, "\">\n");
}
void
```

```
alt_image(char* myimage, char* alt)
{
    printf("%s%s%s%s%s%s", "<IMG SRC=\"", myimage,
        "\"ALT=\"", alt,"\">\n");
}
void
anchor(char* link, char* hottext)
{
    printf("%s%s%s%s%s",
        "<A HREF=\"",
        link,
        "\">,
        hottext,
        "></A>\n");
}
```

It is now possible to create a basic page with the following:

```
#include <stdio.h>
#include <stdlib.h>
#include <string.h>
#include <iostream.h>
main()
{
    Standard myStandard(GREY);              // create the standard class
    myStandard.color_head("Show a Blue Background");
                                            // place page stuff here using cout to stdout
    cout << "This hyperlink goes to";
    myStandard.anchor("http: //internet_path/zzz.html",
            "the zzz world");
    myStandard.comment("This is a Generic Page");
    myStandard.end();
}
The C version:
#include <stdio.h>
#include <stdlib.h>
#include <strings.h>
main()
{
    strcpy( color, GREY);
    color_head("Show a Grey Background");
    /* place page stuff here using printf to stdout*/
    printf("This hyperlink goes to");
    anchor("http://internet_path/zzz.html",
            "the zzz world");
    comment("This is a Generic Page");
```

```
        end();
    }
```

If you use #defines for your hyperlinks and hottext, it works even better.

```
#define ZZZ_LINK "http://zzz.html"
#define ZZZ_TXT "the zzz world"
        myStandard.hyperlink(ZZZ_LINK, ZZZ_TXT);
```

The HTML that will result from this page is as follows:

```
<HTML><HEAD>
<TITLE>
Show a Grey Background</TITLE>
<BODY BGCOLOR=#f0f0f0 ></HEAD>
<BODY>
<A HREF="http://internet_path/zzz.html" > the zzz world </A>
<!- This is a Generic Page -->
</BODY></HTML>
```

To complete the basic capabilities, the following section provides some definitions of colors. Colors are used in a number of places. The most basic use will be to define the color of the background for the home page.

Definitions of Background Colors

```
/* colors for backgrounds
 *   These are the hexadecimal values used to set the colors for backgrounds on an HTML
 *   page. Since you will be sending HTML code to stdout from your cgi-bin program, these
 *   can be used to set the background color appropriately. The defines are the actual strings
 *   used for background colors.
 */
#define WHITE "#ffffff"
#define BLACK "#000000"
#define GREY "#f0f0f0"
#define DARK_RED "#800000"
#define DARK_GREEN "#008000"
#define DARK_YELLOW "#808000"
#define DARK_BLUE "#000080"
#define RED "#ff0000"
#define GREEN "#00ff00"
#define BLUE "#0000ff"
#define YELLOW "#ffff00"
#define LIGHT_BLUE "#a6caf0"
```

```
#define CREAM "#fffbf0"
#define CYAN "#00ffff"
#define MAGENTA "#ff00ff"
#define GRAY GREY /* deal with alternative spellings */
#define DEFAULT_COLOR GREY /* change for your default */
```

Additional colors can be added to this color chart. Programs such as xv on UNIX and PC Paint or Photoshop on Windows can be easily used to find other colors. These can be placed in a standard .h or header file and used as needed. In color mapping, the three colors red, green, and blue are represented by three numbers. The range for each color is 0 to 255 decimal or 0 to 0xFF hexadecimal. This maps to a single byte or char. The color light blue is made up of 0xA6 hex of red, 0xCA hex of blue and 0xF0 of green. In the discussion on changing color mappings, it will be necessary to separate these three components into their individual constituents. In the case of backgrounds, the color is represented by a string in the manner shown previously. While this represents three hexadecimal numbers, the string variable is not the same as a hexadecimal variable in C++ or C. The difference is the fact that these are ASCII characters that begin with # rather than the C++ and C format 0xF0F0F0. Furthermore, the representation is placed in a string variable, not in an int or into three chars, which is how it would be done numerically. In Chapter 16, the actual numerical value will be needed to alter colors in a binary file. In the case of the background color, an HTML command is used. Since all HTML commands are ASCII strings, so is the request to change the background color.

Summary

In this chapter you developed techniques for providing HTML more quickly in your Web pages by developing standard base classes or C subroutines. Since HTML will always be needed regardless of the project being developed, this will be a good technique if you are doing a lot of Web pages on a busy schedule. (In Chapter 11, this capability will be expanded to provide a full range of HTML choices). Also in this chapter you began the process of building up object design for your Web pages using some standard HTML code and the Graph class. By doing this you have established techniques that will become more generalizable as you accumulate knowledge.

PROGRAM EXERCISES

1. Create two cgi-bin programs, one written in C++ and one written in C, that provide the same output. In the first one use the function cout<< to send the output to stdout. In the second one use the function printf() to provide stdout. Verify that you get the same results from both approaches.

2. Redesign the programs from Exercise 1 so that the first is provided from a base class and the second uses a modular subroutine. Restructure and rework until both have a minimal size main(). What can be done to minimize the size of main() even more? See how small you can make main(). Now look at the rest of your program and examine it from the object paradigm. Do the different components of the program have object names, or is the approach more functional? If it appears more functional, try reworking the project to provide more object structure.

3. Rework Program 1 as a top-down project. Begin by looking for the thing-ness that you are trying to describe first. Write down descriptive words about your project, avoiding any verbs or actions on the first analysis. Try to examine what your project is. At the highest level, it is a Web page. Perhaps it is also a graph or a store front or a chess game. It could also be an information provider, such as a weather forecaster. Perhaps it is a very specific object such as John Wilson's Computer Store. Once you have described it, explain what it does. This is where the action states become part of the process. If it is a store, it may show items with their costs and provide methods to order products. An information provider would allow searches for subjects and provide detailed data about the requested information. Finally, look at how the various components interconnect (i.e., the "software glue" that binds the elements together). Now rewrite your program and test it.

4. Create a simple base HTML class. Separate the class definitions and class functions into .h and .c files. Compile to produce .o files. Create a simple main() and compile to create an executable. Place your class in the cgi-bin and test.

PROBLEMS

1. Explain the function of a base class. What types of base classes might make sense besides an HTML class?

2. Explain different approaches that could be used to provide HTML from both C++ and C. What alternative structures are possible? If you were designing HTML capabilities, what would be the inputs and outputs? What parts do you see as using *data hiding*? Why? (Recall that data hiding is the method of placing components of a program at a layer where only their inputs and outputs are accessible.

3. Explain some of the critical factors in sending HTML from a base class. What parts of the output appear to vary? What parts are fixed? What special considerations are required to assure that the output is interpretable by the browser?

CHAPTER 4

Forms

Creating Forms

ONE OF THE MOST POPULAR uses of cgi-bin programs is to process input from forms.
A form is an HTML element that allows users to input information, which is then
used as part of postprocessing. The form is the HTML equivalent of stdin or, alternatively, argc and argv[]. But forms include many special aspects that are part of the
HTML client-server interface. Forms allow the user of a browser to provide input to
a cgi-bin program from an HTML Web page. Once the cgi-bin program has been acti-

vated, postprocessing can be used to send the user inputted information via email; to use the information to activate additional HTML output; or to provide any other computer controllable activity. This powerful capability of handling forms begins in this chapter and is expanded throughout the book. Some of the forms that most Internet users will be familiar with are search capabilities such as the Lycos™ and Yahoo™ search engines. These allow anyone to search the Internet for Web pages that relate to a particular topic.

But these are only the most popular forms. There are many other custom forms that may be of particular value for the applications you are developing. Groups or individuals that wish to allow input from those accessing their Web pages will want to use forms as part of their systems. Very sophisticated forms can be created by using C++ and C. In reality, the tools that will be developed to create and respond to forms can open up new ways of using the Internet. Later in Chapter 10, a program is presented that uses form input to make chess moves on a GIF chess board. This demonstrates just how far this capability can be extended.

Fundamentals of How Forms Work

To CREATE OUR BASIC FORMS interface, it is necessary to understand how forms work. There are two methods used to input data from an HTML form into a cgi-bin program: Get and Post. For C++ and C programmers, these can be compared to input via command line arguments (argc and argv[]) versus direct input using stdin, such as getchar() and gets(). The argc and argv[] map to the Get method, while the getchar() and gets() map to the Post method. For a number of reasons that will become clear shortly, the Post method is easier to use. For this reason, it is used in the initial examples. Later you will examine the use of Get method.

The normal way to complete a form from an HTML Web page is to submit the form. This is a button option that is placed on the user's browser screen. Here is an example HTML form including the submit button.

```
<HTML><HEAD><TITLE>MYFORM</TITLE></HEAD><BODY>
<H1>Project Schedule Updates </H1>
```

Fill out the form below and submit.

```
<FORM ACTION="http://internet_path/cgi-bin/form" METHOD=POST>
<P>
<B>Task Name </B>: <INPUT TYPE=text VALUE="" SIZE=30 NAME="taskname"><BR>
<B>Owners Initials </B>: <INPUT TYPE=text VALUE="" SIZE=3
        NAME="initials"><BR>
<B>Start Date </B>: <INPUT TYPE=text VALUE="" SIZE=8 NAME="startdate"><BR>
<B>End Date </B>: <INPUT TYPE=text VALUE="" SIZE=8 NAME="enddate"><BR>
<B>% Complete </B>: <INPUT TYPE=text VALUE="" SIZE=3 NAME="percent"><BR>
```

```
<P>
<B> Notes or Dependencies </B><BR>
<INPUT TYPE=text NAME=mytext VALUE=""></P>
<P><INPUT TYPE="submit" VALUE="submit ">
<INPUT TYPE="reset" VALUE=" start over"></P>
</FORM>
<P>
</BODY></HTML>
```

If you have never worked with HTML forms, you may want to take some time to study this section. Briefly, the form is broken up into several areas.

1. The beginning section is normal HTML; something similar would be found at the start of any HTML Web page.

2. The next section starting with the line that reads

```
<FORM ACTION="http://internet_path/cgi-bin/form" METHOD=POST>
```

is the actual form. The <FORM ACTION... line tells the URL of the cgi-bin program that is to be used when the form is submitted and the manner in which the information is to be carried. In this case the Post method will be used. Recall that this is like gets() in C++ and C. If the method is not included on this line, the default is used, which is the Get method. Do not get confused here: The HTML Get method does not map to the C++ and C gets() routine; it is the Post method that maps to the gets() routine. The output of a Post is passed to your cgi-bin program as stdin, while the output of a Get is sent as command line arguments to argc argv[].

3. The Action is followed by the various input types. There are a number of ways to input data to a form. All the various input types will be explained shortly. In the preceding form there are text input sections that look like this:

```
<INPUT TYPE=text VALUE="" SIZE=30 NAME="taskname">
<INPUT TYPE=text VALUE="" SIZE=3 NAME="initials">
<INPUT TYPE=text VALUE="" SIZE=8 NAME="startdate">
<INPUT TYPE=text VALUE="" SIZE=8 NAME="enddate">
<INPUT TYPE=text VALUE="" SIZE=3 NAME="percent">
```

4. Then there is the line that reads like this:

```
<INPUT TYPE="submit" VALUE="submit ">
```

This will create the submit button. This button allows the form to be sent to the cgi-bin program. The cgi-bin program to execute was specified in the

Action section. The method to use, Get or Post, was also specified. These were in the earlier Form part of the HTML. This is often followed by

```
<INPUT TYPE=reset>
```

which provides an additional button that will allow the user to clear all input fields back to their default values at any time.

5. Finally there is the form end directive

```
</FORM>
```

The rest of the HTML can be any standard HTML, including the termination of the HTML Web page. You can also surround the form sections with additional text, using standard HTML. The form HTML is an enclosed unit. It has a *binary* logic structure, meaning that it has a beginning and an end. It also contains content fields between the start and end. Most important, it includes the action directive, which tells what cgi-bin program to execute, and the submit line, which creates the button that will send the information to the server and request that it be processed by the cgi-bin program.

Because the HTML for a form has a beginning and an end, there is nothing to stop you from putting more than one form section onto the same HTML Web page. These could even be associated with different cgi-bin programs. While such complexities may have value, this is only occasionally done.[1] Therefore, it makes more sense to think in terms of a single entry form.

When a form is submitted using the Post method, the information is sent in a standard format to the server. The server uses the action field to start up the correct cgi-bin program and then sends the user's input to the cgi-bin programs. Forms cannot work without cgi-bin programs.

The only actions that are allowed for forms are the executions of programs in the cgi-bin area using the associated URL. Initial cgi-bin programs can be written in PERL or other script languages. The problem with this approach is the response time and flexibility of the script. In addition, script programs will tend to use more processor swap space. Most programmers work in script languages for early development, but quickly transfer the programs to compiled code. The forms process consists of the following:

1. An HTML input part that allows data to be entered into it
2. The cgi-bin program, which processes the form request
3. The programmed responses, which can consist of sending email and performing data lookup and interactive functions
4. The HTML responses, such as sending requested information back to the screen

---

[1] Forms should not be nested.

The input part of the form can be built as a standard HTML program or by using another cgi-bin program or another part in the same cgi-bin program. (See the discussion of multiple use of cgi-bin programs in Chapter 5.)

Before continuing, let's review the steps that take place when a form is used:

1. The user brings up the form. This is done by requesting a URL associated with the form. It will normally be a standard HTML Web page, but it could be a cgi-bin program that outputs the HTML form.

2. The user enters his or her information into the form using buttons and text fields.

3. The user submits the form using the submit button.

4. The information from the user along with the form action and the form method are sent to the server. There is also some extra environmental information, which will be discussed later.

5. The server uses the action to start up the appropriate cgi-bin program. It also sends the user information to the program using the method requested (Get or Post).

6. The cgi-bin program must now retrieve the user information. It then processes it using the cgi-bin program. Having processed the information, it can send the information as email to a user, put the information into a file, or use it in other programmable manners.

7. The cgi-bin program should also send HTML back to the client. This could be some acknowledgment that the message has been processed or a response based on the user's input or any other desirable HTML. This output will become a new Web page for the user.

Get and Post

WHEN THE FORM IS SENT to the cgi-bin program, it contains the user entered information. Several methods are supported for sending data. The two primary methods are Get and Post. The Get option is the default if none is stated in the HTML document. The Get data arrive as argc and argv[] information, while the Post data are sent as stdin. For some browsers, Get will not work since there is no method for passing command line arguments. For example, early versions of lynx and Mosaic would not handle the Get method but did handle Post. Because of this, and since argc and argv[] are always more difficult to deal with, the initial forms shown here are developed with the Post method. This does not mean that Get should never be used. As will become evident, Get can provide some important capabilities. If all this seems overwhelming, it will become clearer as the cgi-bin form program is developed.

While we began with the more familiar HTML-generated form, it is important to remember that the form itself can also be provided by a cgi-bin program. In fact anything that can be done in HTML can also be done from a cgi-bin program, as was shown with our initial *Hello Internet World* program. Many examples in this book may use this fact even though it is frequently easier to do the same functionality directly in HTML. When both options are available, standard HTML should usually be preferred since it is easier to make minor modifications and will result in comparable response times. However, when both sides of the form are under cgi-bin program control, the number of alternatives open to the Web page developer increase. For this reason, there are many instances in which both the initial form and the response should both be done as cgi-bin programs. (Later, in Chapter 7, a Thru mode technique will be provided that takes advantage of both the HTML flexibility and the cgi-bin robustness.) Figure 4.1 shows the basic steps for forms.

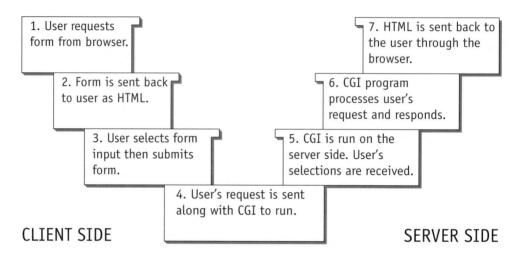

FIGURE 4.1   Interactive forms provide the foundation the critical building block for complex programs.

Another Example Form

```
<!-- An example input FORM in HTML -->
<HTML> <HEAD> <TITLE> Input Form </TITLE></HEAD>
<!-- end of the normal starting stuff -->
<FORM METHOD=POST ACTION="http://internet_path/cgi-bin/cgi_main" >
<!-- now create the form -->
<P> <STRONG> SEND MAIL TO: </STRONG>
<SELECT NAME="mailto_name" >
<OPTION SELECTED> Technical Support
<OPTION> Field Support
<OPTION> Product Support
<OPTION> Engineering
</SELECT>
<P> <STRONG> ENTER YOUR EMAIL ADRESS: </STRONG>
```

```
<!-- This is needed since mail will have the cgi program address -->
<P> INPUT TYPE="text" NAME="your_email" VALUE="" SIZE=60>
<P> <STRONG> ENTER MESSAGE: </STRONG> <P>
<TEXTAREA COLS=50 ROWS=6 NAME="message" VALUE="">
</TEXTAREA>
<P> <INPUT TYPE="submit" VALUE="Mail Message"> <INPUT TYPE="reset"> </FORM>
</BODY>
</HTML>
```

Decomposition of the Basic Form

1. The initial lines are standard HTML.
2. The form begins with the line

   ```
   <FORM METHOD=POST ACTION="http://internet_path/cgi-bin/cgi_main" >
   ```

   This line specifies the start of a form. It states that the user data will be sent to the cgi-bin program using the Post method. It states that the cgi-bin program or action to take when the form is submitted can be found at

   ```
   URL="http://internet_path/cgi-bin/cgi_main"
   ```

3. Next is the form itself. The form is made up of input areas and text that requests the input from the user. HTML supports a number of different ways to provide input. The input line also contains the name of the variable that can be used by the cgi-bin program to identify the input information.

   ```
   ==== An HTML comment ====
   <!-- now create the form -->
   ==== Text to tell the user what the input will do ====
   <P> <STRONG> SEND MAIL TO: </STRONG>
   ==== The first variable is called "mailto_name"
   This uses the option input mode, which allows the user to select from a finite number of
   choices available through a pull down menu ====
   <SELECT NAME="mailto_name" >
   <OPTION SELECTED> Technical Support
   <OPTION> Field Support
   <OPTION> Product Support
   <OPTION> Engineering
   </SELECT>
   ==== More text about what the input will do ====
   <P> <STRONG> ENTER YOUR EMAIL ADDRESS: </STRONG>
   <!-- This is needed since mail will have the cgi program address -->
   ```

==== Another variable is called "your_email". It has an initial value of "" (null character) and could be preset to some default value, but this would be inappropriate for this example. The size of the input string is limited to *60 alphanumeric characters.* ====
<P> INPUT TYPE=text NAME="your_email" VALUE="" SIZE=60>
==== More text about what the input will do ====
<P> <STRONG> ENTER MESSAGE: </STRONG> <P>
==== A text area of 6 rows and 50 columns. This variable is called "message". It begins with a null value. The user can type into the area until any part or the entire area is filled with alphanumeric characters. ====
<TEXTAREA COLS=50 ROWS=6 NAME="message" VALUE="">
</TEXTAREA>
==== The required submit field. Activating this field will send the variables, with their content, to the server and then to the cgi-bin program. Two types are provided. The *submit* sends the data to the cgi-bin program listed in the initiation of the form. The *reset* clears all values inside the form and allows the user to start over. ====
<P> <INPUT TYPE="submit" VALUE="Mail Message"> <INPUT TYPE="reset">

The user of this form enters the data into the various user locations. When the form is submitted, the cgi-bin/cgi_main will execute. The cgi-bin program is determined in the HTML line that reads

<FORM METHOD=POST ACTION="http://internet_path/cgi-bin/cgi_main" >

A QUICK NOTE: The HTML control language is normally not case sensitive. Only URLs (normally in quotations) and variable values (also in quotations) will be case sensitive. All other HTML may include any mixture of upper and lowercase letters and still have the same meaning. The commands <BODY>, <Body>, and <body>, and even <bODy> all have the same meaning in HTML. Actual content text will be displayed with the case specified.

The variables for this particular form are as follows:

mailto_name This is selected with option type choices. The options are field support, product support, and engineering.

your_email This is a variable string of up to 60 characters with no default value.

message This is a text message of up to 6 rows with 50 characters per row.

After submit is activated, the data will be sent to the cgi-bin program.

User Data, Stdin, and Stdout

NOW IT IS THE JOB of the cgi-bin program to retrieve the user data. Since the method is Post, the C++ function cin>> and C function gets() can be used to retrieve

the user's input. The input will consist of a single continuous ASCII string containing *all* the user's data.

Here is a cgi-bin program to retrieve the data:

```
/*
* Type: C++ main
* Purpose: Retrieve FORM data development
*/
#include <iostream.h>
#include <stdlib.h>
#include <string.h>
main()
{
     char indata[10000]; // allow for up to 10,000 characters
     cin >> indata;
      // The data come in as a continuous stream to stdin

}
```

What would happen if you added the line

```
cout<<indata;
```

to produce this program?

```
/*
 * Type: C++ main
 * Purpose: Retrieve FORM data development
 */
#include <iostream.h>
#include <stdlib.h>
#include <string.h>
main()
{
     char indata[1000]; // allow for up to 1000 characters
     cin >> indata;
     cout << indata;
}
```

Where would the data go? If you guessed right back to the server and then back to
the browser, you are correct. Since the data are not in HTML format, you would get
a time-out on your screen. It would improve the program by changing it to

```
/*
 * Type: C++ main
 * Purpose: Retrieve FORM data and echo
 */
```

```
#include <iostream.h>
#include <stdlib.h>
#include <string.h>
main()
{
    char indata[MAXLINE];
    cin>>indata;
    cout << "Content-type: text/html\n\n" <<
        "<HTML><HEAD>data test</HEAD>\n" <<
        "<BODY><H1>Got Your Data</H1><BR>\n" <<
        indata <<
        "\n</BODY></HTML>\n"
}
```

This version includes the required Content-type... and the necessary HTML.
The output of the indata will echo the user request back to the browser.

The C version using the HTML subroutines will look like this:

```
#include <stdio.h>
/*
 * Type: C main
 * Purpose: Retrieve FORM data and echo
 */
main()
{
    char indata[1000];
    STANDARD Standard(WHITE);
                                        /* be sure to send the content-type */
    gets(indata);                       /* read in user FORM input */
    normal_start("Got Your Data");      /* base call for start HTML */
    printf("%s\n", indata);             /* echo the data back to browser */
    end();                              /* base call for end HTML */
}
```

The C++ version using the base class Standard with HTML subroutines looks like this:

```
/*
 * Type: C++ main
 * Purpose: Retrieve FORM data echo using base class
 */
// Includes Here
main()
{
    char indata[1000];
    STANDARD Standard(WHITE);
    cin >> indata;
```

```
        // use the base class routines to send the HTML
        Standard.normal_start("Got Your Data");
        cout << indata;
        Standard.end();
    }
```

About the program . . . .

1. This is a simple program with which to read a line of input from standard in or stdin. It is the reverse of stdout: It is the information coming into a program. If the program was executed from the command line rather than by the server, the program would have paused and waited for the user to type something in and press return before continuing. However, when it is run by the server, the input is sent by the server from the form and the program continues immediately.
2. In the final C version, the data are then sent back to the client screen.
3. The rest of the program involves just sending additional HTML back to the client software using stdout routines.

. . . .

Now you have sent something appropriate back to the server. But what about the data? Unfortunately, it will be necessary to do some work on the data before they can be used. The HTML server will send the data in the following format:

mailtoname=MAIL_STRING&emailad=EMAIL_STRING&message=MESSAGE_STRING

The parts in capitals are the variable information coming from the user. The lower-case are the names of the variables followed by the equal sign and separated by the ampersands. Although this is OK if it is going to you, it would be inappropriate if it is going to others. Since the objective here is to prepare polished cgi-bin programs, the latter should be assumed. If this is the case, the input string will need to be separated into its constituent parts.

To put this in terms more familiar to programmers, the string needs to be parsed into a usable format. There are actually two types of parsing that will be of value. In the first type, the user's input is *cleaned up* so it can be sent by mail or placed into a file. In the second case, the string values of individual variables are separated out for use in *decision making*. The use of variable isolation is needed when specific contents have a critical meaning. The former (cleanup) will be needed if the message is going to be forwarded (for example, as email). The latter (isolation) is needed if a subpart of the message, such as the value of a single variable, is needed. An example of this would be pulling out the person's email address and separating it from the message to be sent.

Parsing the Form Data

HERE ARE THE RULES for parsing:

1. Each variable except the last one will end with an *ampersand* (&) sign to identify it. The final variable ends with a *carriage return* (\n). There will be an *equal sign* before the actual user value. All variables are sent as a single string. Each variable includes a *name field,* an *equal sign,* and the *string value* of the variable. The variables are separated by an *ampersand.* The final variable, and *only* the final variable, is terminated by a *carriage return.*[2]

2. Spaces appear as %20. Carriage returns appear as %0A and/or %0D inside the form data. Users familiar with ascii will recognize these as carriage return and line feed in hexadecimal format, with the % sign used to designate the start of a hexadecimal character. You may get one or both depending on the implementation on the terminal being used. A normal carriage return (^M, 13 decimal, or 0D hex) will be at the end of the entire string. The fact that all of the form carriage returns are remapped means that the input will be a continuous string.

   In general, all punctuation or control characters appear with a % sign followed by two ASCII characters, which represent the hexadecimal value of the character. These will be any control characters, such as space, return, tab, as well as punctuation (".':;-/, etc.). Only the letters and numbers are sent in their normal ASCII manner.

3. String concatenation can be sent as a plus (+). The plus will be replaced by a space in the cleanup routines. The plus will later be shown to have special uses.

   Form output arrives at the cgi-bin program in the unusual format (using %xx for hexadecimal) shown previously. The following are the critical factors:

1. Variables are separated by ampersands (&) at the end and equal signs (=) between the value and the variable name. The last variable has no ampersand at the end, but includes the carriage return termination. Here is a typical string of variables.

   variable1=hello&variable2=internet&variable3=world

   Here is a repeat of the same input with the variable names in bold, the user input or values of the variables in italics, and the parts added by the client server in normal font.

   variable1=*hello*&**variable2**=*internet*&**variable3**=*world*

2. Checkbox variables (an HTML type that allows you to check a box) will only be in the string if they have been checked. For other types, if no value is entered

---

[2]   In the parsing routines, provisions are made for the final character to be either \n (carriage return) or 0 (null). This is done to allow debugging since an echoed string will terminate with a null.

for a variable, the default value will be sent. This can be a null string ("") or an actual value.

3. Text boxes will provide control characters as a percent sign % followed by an ASCII representation of the hexadecimal value. For example, a space is represented by %20 (20 hexadecimal or 32 decimal).

4. Extra spaces can occur in text input. This often results from arrow keys or other ways of moving through the text area.

5. Spaces can also appear as a plus key (+).

Because the data at stdin or the argv[1] data will be in this *unusual format* of variable name, variables, punctuation and control characters, and ampersands, parsing routines are needed to change the data back to normal format. Some applications may choose not to do this; however, these routines are recommended since they will make the final output much more readable.

To handle this unusual input to the cgi-bin program from the form, new classes and modules that include parsing routines are developed for handling forms. If they are developed correctly, it becomes possible to use them in any future development of forms. Since the submit capability of the form is extremely critical in many advanced capabilities, this is an important part of the class arsenal.

```
/**********************************************************************
 * _Form
 *   Usage: handle forms, including the parsing of form input into readable format
 */
class _Form
{
private:
    /*
     * These are the general subroutines required for parsing.
     * clear_space - removes double spaces that can result from using arrow keys to
     *    navigate a text area.
     * clear_amp - will change the ampersands in user input into carriage returns. This is
     *    especially useful when the information will be sent by mail or saved in a file for
     *    later processing.
     * clear_plus - will change '+' to a space.
     * clear_control - changes the control characters in the %XX format to their real
     *    hexadecimal value.
     * ahextoi - is used to change an ASCII representation of a hex value into its decimal
     *    equivalent. It is used in conjunction with clear_control.
     */
    /* Cleanup Routines */
    char* clear_space(char* msg);
    char* clear_amp(char* msg);
    char* clear_plus(char* msg);
    char* clear_control(char* msg);
    int ahextoi(char* msg);
```

```
        char input_msg[2000];        // message sent to parsing
        char out_msg[2000];          // message returned from parsing
public:
    /*
     * These are the public interfaces for the FORM class.
     * clear_all - takes an input message and does all the required private clear functions
     *    to provide normal output for mailers or files.
     * get_variable - is used to retrieve a value for a single variable that has been input to
     *    a FORM. It is used to provide information about the user's input that can then be
     *    used for further processing in the program. The return value is the actual value
     *    user variable string.
     * check_msg - is used along with get_variable(). It takes as arguments the string
     *    value of the variable and an expected value. It returns TRUE if they are the same
     *    and FALSE if they are different.
     */

    _Form() {;};
    char* clear_all(char* msg );
    /* Decision-making Routines */
    char* get_variable(char* msg, char* start);
    int check_msg(char* variable_value, char* expect_value);
    /* inline routine to move the output string to the input string */
    inline char* out_to_in(char* output_message)
    {
        strcpy( input_msg, output_message);
        return( input_msg );
    };
};
```

About the Form class

1. The first private subroutines are the critical components for clearing the message and separating messages.
2. The clear_all() creates a user-friendly message.
3. The get_variable() locates a specific message that is a subsection of the whole message. This is used to pull out the value of a single variable.
4. The check_msg() compares a variable message value with an expected message value to see if they are the same.

Cleanup Routines, C++ Version

```
#define EOM 0 /* End of Message (EOM) is always a null character */
#define NULL 0 /* NULL termination for strings */
```

```
/*
 * Type: C++ class subroutine
 * Purpose: Clear double spaces from a user string from a FORM
 * Note: These can occur due to use of arrow keys
 * Input:     char* msg - pointer to user's message
 * Output:    char* - pointer to msg with double spaces removed
 */
/*
 * subroutine to clear double spaces from a string that can result from arrow keys or other
 * factors
 */
char*                   /* return pointer to cleared message */
_Form::clear_space(
    char* msg     /* pointer to message to clear */
    )
{
    int i = 0;  // temp message counter
    char tmp_msg[MAXLINE];
    while(*msg != EOM)
    {
        if((*msg ==' ') && (*(msg+1) == ' '))
        {
            ++msg; // skip this space
        } else
        {
            tmp_msg[i++] = *msg;
        }
        ++msg; // go to the next character
    }
    tmp_msg[i] = NULL; // terminate the string
    strcpy( out_msg, tmp_msg );
    return ( out_msg );
}
/*
 * Type: C++ class subroutine
 * Purpose: Change ampersand (&) separating variables to a
 *   return ("\n") for readability
 * Input:     char* msg - pointer to user's message
 * Output:    char* - pointer to msg with ampersands replaced by return
 */
char* _Form::clear_amp(char* msg)
{
    int i = 0;      // temp message counter
    char tmp_msg[MAXLINE];
    while(*msg != EOM)
    {
```

```cpp
            if(*msg =='&')
            {
                tmp_msg[i++] = '\n' ;
                // replace ampersand with cr
            } else
            {
                tmp_msg[i++] = *msg;
            }
            ++msg;   // go to next character
        }
        tmp_msg[i] = NULL;
        strcpy( out_msg, tmp_msg );
        return ( out_msg );
}
/*
 * Type: C++ class subroutine
 * Purpose: Change plus (+) to a space for readability
 * Input:      char* msg - pointer to user's message
 * Output:    char* - pointer to msg with plus replaced by space
 */
char* _Form::clear_plus(char* msg)
{
    int i = 0; // temp message counter
    char tmp_msg[MAXLINE];
    while(*msg != EOM)
    {
        if( *msg == '+' )
        {
            tmp_msg[i++] = ' ' ;
            // replace plus with space
        } else
        {
            tmp_msg[i++] = *msg;
        }
        ++msg;// go to next character
    }
    tmp_msg[i] = NULL;
    strcpy( out_msg, tmp_msg );
    return ( out_msg );
}
/*
 * Type: C++ class subroutine
 * Purpose: Change %0x0x to decimal value (0-255)
 * Input:      char* msg - pointer to user's message
 * Output:    char* - pointer to msg with %0x0x replaced by decimal value
 */
```

```cpp
char*      /* return pointer to cleared message */
_Form::clear_control(
    char* msg                /* pointer to message to clear control character from */
)
{
    char val_msg[3];          // holder for the hex part of the message
    int i = 0;
    char tmp_msg[MAXLINE];    // character counter
    while(*msg != EOM)        // check for end of message string
    {
        if(*msg == '%')       // locate the initial %
        {
        /* Change the next two values into a string, then send them to an ASCII to integer
         * conversion routine. Continue after incrementing the pointer past the three
         * characters.
         */

            val_msg[0]=*(msg+1);
            val_msg[1]=*(msg+2);
            val_msg[2]=0;
        /* Versions of atoi will not handle hexadecimal input; if yours won't, use the
         * routine ahextoi() given below.
         */
            tmp_msg[i++]=ahextoi(val_msg);
            msg +=3;
        }else
        {
            msg++;
        }
    }
    tmp_msg[i] = NULL; // add a null termination to the string
    strcpy( out_msg, tmp_msg );
    return(out_msg); // send the message pointer back
}
/*
 * Type: C++ or C subroutine
 * Purpose: Convert a hex string to its equivalent decimal ASCII value
 * Input:    char* value - pointer to hex string
 * Output:   int - decimal ASCII value
 */
int              /* return converted value */
ahextoi(
    char* value /* ASCII string to convert */
)
{
    int dec_value =0;
```

```
        int i =0;
        /* turn hex ASCII to decimal equivalent */
        while(*(value+i) != EOM)
        {
            if((*(value+i) >= '0') &&
               (*(value+i) <= '9'))
            {
                        /* calculate the decimal value mod 16 */
                dec_value = (*(value+i) - '0') +
                (dec_value * 16));
            } else
                        /* check for upper case */
                if((*(value+i) >= 'A') &&
                   (*(value+i) <= 'F'))
                {
                dec_value = (((*(value+i) - 'A') + 10)
                + (dec_value * 16));
            } else
                /* check for lower case */
                if((*(value+i) >= 'a') &&
                   (*(value+i) <= 'f'))
                {
                dec_value = (((*(value+i) - 'a') + 10)
                + (dec_value * 16));
            }
            ++i;
        }
        return(dec_value);
}
/*
 * Type: C++ class subroutine
 * Purpose: Clear all parts of a message
 * Input:      char* msg - pointer to user's message
 * Output:     char* - pointer to msg with everything cleared
 */
/*
 * This is the public interface for clearing out the message part of a form of all extraneous
 * characters.
 */
char* _Form::clear_all(char* msg)
{
    char local_msg[MAXLINE];            /* set to expected message size */
    strcpy( local_msg, clear_space(msg));
    strcpy( local_msg, clear_amp(local_msg));
    return( clear_control(local_msg));
}
```

Alternatively, you can use the routine out_to_in()

```
char* _Form::clear_all(char* msg)
{
    char local_msg[MAXLINE];         /* set to expected message size */
    return(
    clear_control(
    out_to_in(clear_amp(
    out_to_in( clear_space(msg))))));
}
```

Decision Routines, C++ Version

```
/*
 * Type: C++ class subroutine
 * Purpose: To get the user inputted value of a variable
 * Input:      char* msg - pointer to user's message
 *             char* start_msg - pointer to string with variable name=
 * Output:     char* - pointer to user input string requested
 */
char* _Form::get_variable(char* msg, char* start_msg)
{
    int start_flag=0;
    int length;
    int start_length;
    int j;
    int i = 0;
    char tmp_msg[MAXLINE];
    length = strlen(msg);
    start_length = strlen(start_msg);
    tmp_msg[0]=0;
    while(i <= length)
    {
        if(strncmp(msg+i, start_msg, start_length-1) !=0)
        {
            i++;
        } else
        {
            start_flag=1;
            break;
        }
    }
    if(start_flag==0)
    {
```

```
                // error condition
                return "";
        }
        i+=start_length;
        j=0;
        while(i <= length)
        {
            if((*(char *)(msg+i) == '&') || /* 38 */
                (*(char *)(msg+i) == ' ') ||
                (*(char *)(msg+i) == 13) ||
                (*(char *)(msg+i) == 0))
            {
                break;
            }
            tmp_msg[j++]=*(msg+i);
            i++;
        }
        tmp_msg[j]=0; // null terminate the string
        strcpy( out_msg, tmp_msg );
        return(out_msg);
}
#define TRUE 1
#define FALSE 0
/*
 * Type: C++ class subroutine
 * Purpose: Check if a user value is equal to an expected value
 * Input:    char* value - pointer to string with user's value
 *
 *           char* expect_value - pointer to string with expected value
 * Output:   BOOLEAN state - TRUE or FALSE
 */
int
check_msg(char* variable_value, char* expect_value)
{
        /* compare the two strings to see if they are the same */
        if(strcmp(variable_value, expect_value) == 0)
        {
            return TRUE;
        } else
        {
            return FALSE;
        }
}
```

Cleanup Routines, C Version

IN THE C VERSION, THE output message is passed into the routines as the first argument rather than being hidden inside the class.

```
/*
 * Type: C subroutine
 * Purpose: Clear extra spaces
 * Input:      char* retmsg - pointer to return message string
 *             char* msg - pointer to user's message string
 * Output:     char* - pointer to msg without extra spaces
 */
char* clear_space(char* retmsg, char* msg)
{
    char tmp_msg[200];
    int i = 0;  /* temp message counter */
    while(*msg != EOM)
    {
        if((*msg ==' ') && (*(msg+1) == ' '))
        {
            ++msg; /* skip this space */
        } else
        {
            tmp_msg[i++] = *msg;
        }
        ++msg; /* go to the next character */
    }
    strcpy(retmsg, tmp_msg);
    return ( retmsg );
}
/*
 * Type: C subroutine
 * Purpose: Change ampersand to return
 * Input:
 *    char* retmsg - pointer to return message string
 *    char* msg - pointer to user's message string
 * Output:
 *    char* - pointer to msg with ampersand changed to returns
 */
char* clear_amp(char* retmsg, char* msg)
{
    char tmp_msg[MAXLINE];
    int i = 0;       /* temp message counter */
    while(*msg != EOM)
    {
        if(*msg =='&')
```

```
        {
            tmp_msg[i++] = '\n' ;
            /* replace ampersand with cr */
        } else
        {
            tmp_msg[i++] = *msg;
        }
        ++msg; /* go to next character */
    }
    strcpy(retmsg, tmp_msg);
    return ( retmsg );
}
/*
 * Type: C subroutine
 * Purpose: Change plus to spaces
 * Input:      char* retmsg - pointer to return message string
 *             char* msg - pointer to user's message string
 * Output:     char* - pointer to msg with plus changed to space
 */
char* clear_plus(char* retmsg, char* msg)
{
    char tmp_msg[MAXLINE];
    int i = 0;       /* temp message counter */
    while(*msg != EOM)
    {
        if(*msg =='+')
        {
            tmp_msg[i++] = ' ' ;
            /* replace plus with space */
        } else
        {
            tmp_msg[i++] = *msg;
        }
        ++msg; /* go to next character */
    }
    strcpy(retmsg, tmp_msg)
    return (retmsg);
}
/*
 * Type: C subroutine
 * Purpose: Clear %0x%x to decimal ASCII equivalent
 * Input:      char* retmsg - pointer to return message string
 *             char* msg - pointer to user's message string
 * Output:     char* - pointer to msg %0x0x replaced by ASCII equivalent
 */
char* clear_control(char* retmsg, char* msg)
```

```
{
    char tmp_msg[MAXLINE];
    char val_msg[3];        /* holder for the hex part of the message */
    int i = 0;              /* character counter */
    while(*msg != EOM)      /* check for end of message string */
    {
        if(*msg == '%') /* locate the initial % */
        {
            /* Change the next two values into a string then send them to an ASCII
             * to integer conversion routine. Continue after incrementing the pointer
             * past the three characters.
             */
            val_msg[0]=*(msg+1);
            val_msg[1]=*(msg+2);
            val_msg[2]=0;
            /* Versions of atoi will not handle hexadecimal input, if yours won't, use the
             * routine ahextoi() given below
             */
            tmp_msg[i++]=ahextoi(val_msg);
            msg +=3;
        } else
        {
        tmp_msg[i++] = *msg;
        }
        }
    tmp_msg[i]=0;       /* add a null termination to the string */
    strcpy(retmsg, tmp_msg);
    return(retmsg);     /* send the message pointer back */
}
```

The typical message parsing routine will look like this:

```
/*
 * Type: C subroutine
 * Purpose: Clear all characters
 * Input:      char* retmsg - pointer to return message string
 *             char* msg - pointer to user's message string
 * Output:     char* - pointer to retmsg totally cleared
 */
char* clear_all(char* retmsg, char* msg)
{
    return( clear_space (retmsg,
        clear_amp (retmsg,
        clear_plus (retmsg,
        clear_control (retmsg, msg))))));
}
```

Decision Routines, C Version

```c
/*
 * Type: C subroutine
 * Purpose: Get the user's value of a specific variable
 * Input:      char* retmsg - pointer to return message string
 *             char* msg - pointer to user's message string
 *             char* start_msg - pointer to name of variable and =
 * Output:     char* - pointer to user's input to the variable
 */
/*
 * This is the public interface for getting the string value of a variable input via the client
 * software. Example usage: get_variable(output_msg, input_msg, "myvariable=")
 */
char* get_variable(char* retmsg, char* msg, char* start_msg)
{
    char tmp_msg[MAXLINE];
    int start_flag=0;
    int length;
    int start_length;
    int j;
    int i = 0;
    length = strlen(msg);
    start_length = strlen(start_msg);
    tmp_msg[0]=0;
    while(i <= length)
    {
        if(strncmp(msg+i, start_msg, start_length-1) !=0)
        {
            i++;
        } else
        {
            start_flag=1;
            break;
        }
    }
    if(start_flag==0)
    {
        /* error condition */
        return "";
    }
    i+=start_length;
    j=0;
    while(i <= length)
    {
        if((*(char *)(msg+i) == '&') || /* 38 */
```

```
                    (*(char *)(msg+i) == ' ') ||
                    (*(char *)(msg+i) == 13) ||
                    (*(char *)(msg+i) == 0))
            {
                break;
            }
            tmp_msg[j++]=*(msg+i);
            i++;
        }
        tmp_msg[j]=0; /* null terminate the string */
        strcpy(retmsg, tmp_msg);
        return( retmsg );
}
```

The routine to get a variable will look like this:

```
/*
 * Type: C main
 * Purpose: Get and test a user variable
 */
/* Includes Here */
void main()
{
    char retmsg[MAXLINE];
    char input[MAXLINE];
    gets(input);
    if(strcmp("some_value",
            get_variable(retmsg, input, "myvariable=") == 0)
    {
        /* variables value is a match to some_value */
    } else
    {
        /* not a match */
    }
}
```

It is worth your time to get these routines working the way that you prefer. Forms are so critical in the use of cgi-bin programs that you will find yourself using these *cleanup* and *decision* capabilities over and over again. Because these routines are so critical, they are repeated in other formats throughout this book.

Response to the Form

```
/* Handling the message coming to the cgi script */
#include <string.h>
```

```
#include <stdio.h>
#include <stdlib.h>
#include <iostream.h>
main()
{
     char indata[MAXLINE];
     STANDARD Standard(GRAY);
     char mailtoname[MAXLINE];
     char emailad[MAXLINE];
     char msg[MAXLINE];
     cin >> indata;
     /* process the data */
     strcpy(mailtoname, get_msg(indata,
          "mailtoname="));
     strcpy(emailad, get_msg(indata,
          "&emailad="));
     strcpy(msg, clear_all(get_msg(indata, "&message")));
     /*
      * do something with the data and then
      *    send a message back to the server
      */

     Standard.normal_start("Got Your Data");
     /* place message to the server here */
     cout << "Got Your Input\n";
     Standard.end();
}
```

C version using the same routines:

```
#include <stdio.h>
#include <stdlib.h>
#include <string.h>
main()
{
     char indata[MAXLINE];
     char mailtoname[MAXLINE];
     char emailad[MAXLINE];
     char msg[MAXLINE];
     gets(indata);
     /* process the data */
     strcpy(mailtoname, get_variable(indata, "mailtoname="));
     strcpy(emailad, get_msg(indata, "&emailad="));
     strcpy(msg, clear_all(get_msg(indata, "&message")));
     /* do something with the data and then send a message back to the server */
```

```
        normal_start("Got Your Data");
        /* place message to the server here */
        printf("This is your data\n %s\n", indata);
        end();
    }
```

Get Method

IF THE Get METHOD IS used instead of the Post method, the user information from the form will be sent as a command line argument to argv[1] rather than into stdin.

Here is an example form using the Get method:

```
<HTML><BODY>
<H1> This is an example of a Get method form </H1>
<FORM ACTION="http://internet_path/cgi-bin/cgi_program" METHOD=GET >
<INPUT TYPE="checkbox" NAME="understand" VALUE="yes" >
Do you understand the use of Get method?
<INPUT TYPE="checkbox" NAME="location" VALUE="yes" >
Will the user data be in stdin?
<INPUT TYPE="submit" VALUE="Enter Your Choice" >
</FORM></BODY></HTML>
```

When you submit this form, the user data (in this case the input to the checkbox) will be sent as a command line argument to argv[1].

The cgi-bin program looks like this:

```
void main( int argc, char* argv[])
{
    char out_msg[MAXLINE];
    if(argc <= 1) /* the first argument argv[0] is the program name */
    {
        /* send back an error message */
        exit;
    } else
    {
        /*
         * use the normal parsing routines, but instead of getting input from stdin, the
         * argv[1] contains the user information
         */
        clear_all ( out_msg, argv[1] );
    }
    /*
     * Send back HTML with the user's message echoed back to the screen
     */
```

```
printf("Content-type: text/html\n\n");
printf( "%s\n%s\n%s\n%s\n%s\n",
    "<HTML><BODY><H1>YOUR DATA WAS<H1>",
    "<H4>",
    out_msg, /* cleaned up message */
    "</H4></BODY></HTML>" );
}
```

Because the Get method is the default method for forms, the line that read

```
<FORM ACTION="http://internet_path/cgi-bin/cgi_program" METHOD=GET >
```

could have been replaced by

```
<FORM ACTION="http://internet_path/cgi-bin/cgi_program">
```

When the method is unspecified, it defaults to Get method. When the method is Get, there is no need to specify it.

Another distinction between the Get method and the Post method is how the user data from the form are sent. With Post, the information was sent through stdin and was hidden from the user. With the Get method, the argv[1] user information will appear along with the URL associated with the form action. This is what you will see on the browser:

```
http://internet_path/cgi-bin/cgi_program?understand=yes&location=no
```

The variables (*understand* and *location*) and their values ("yes" and "no") are seen appended to the requested action. A "?" separates the URL from the user information. Later, we will see that there are ways to force argv[] by using a "?" to force the arguments.

Here is one more example that responds to the same form but uses *decision* routines for the *parsing*.

```
void main (int argc, char* argv[])
{
    char out_msg[MAXLINE];
    if(argc <= 1) /* the first argument argv[0] is the program name */
    {
        /* send back an error message */
        exit;
    } else
    {
        cout << "Content-type: text/html\n\n";
        if( ( chk_msg(
            get_msg(out_msg, argv[1], "understand=" ),
```

```
            "yes" ) == TRUE ) &&
            ( chk_msg(
            get_msg( out_msg, argv[1], "location=" ),
            "no" ) == TRUE )
        ) {
            /* both answers are right */
            cout << "<HTML><HEAD>"
                    << "<TITLE>mytitle</TITLE>"
                    << "</HEAD><BODY>"
                    << "<H1>"
                    << "Your answer was correct"
                    << "</H1></BODY></HTML>";
        } else
        {
            /* something was wrong */
            cout << "<HTML><HEAD>"
                    << "<TITLE>mytitle</TITLE>"
                    << "</HEAD><BODY>"
                    << "<H1>"
                    << "Your answer was wrong"
                    << "</H1></BODY></HTML>";
        }
    }
}
```

Because the Get method provides a number of capabilites that cannot be obtained with the Post method, you are cautioned about the use of this method. In the next section, you will discover just how powerful the use of argc and argv[] can be.

Getting Started with Debugging

BEFORE CONTINUING WITH OUR understanding of forms, let's make a slight divergence. At this point, your cgi-bin programs are getting slightly more complex. In Chapter 17, extensive methods are developed to debug cgi-bin programs. Here are some simple beginning methods to allow impatient readers to get started. If you are feeling like you want to move full speed ahead, you may want to turn to the debugging chapter (Chapter 17) and take a look at it. On the other hand, if you are working through these chapters systematically, this initial discussion of debugging should suffice.

There are a number of things that are essential to do when testing a cgi-bin program. First test with Netscape or any other appropriate browser. When submitting a form or calling a cgi-bin program, watch how the browser sends it to your program. Use examples like the one shown in the preceding section to send requests

right back to the screen and to determine exactly what the cgi-bin program is receiving. Where necessary, create logging facilities to accomplish the same goal. Providing debugging capability early in the design cycle will guarantee more sophisticated
cgi-bin programs as development progresses.

The first fundamental of debugging is to determine what goes to argv[] and
what goes to stdin. Here is a simple debugging program that does both. If you are
making sure that you are only using Post, you can use the earlier program that
sends back the stdin.

```cpp
// C++ Form Debugging Program
#include <iostream.h>
#include <stdlib.h>
#include <string.h>
main()
{
    char indata[MAXLINE];
    STANDARD Standard(WHITE);
    if(strcmp(getenv(REQUEST_METHOD), "POST") == 0) // optional check
        cin>>indata;
    Standard.normal_start("Got Your Data");
    if(strlen(argv[1]) > 0)
    {
        cout << "The argv data is " << &argv[1];
    }
    if(strlen(indata) > 0)
    {
        cout << "The stdin data is " << indata;
    }

    Standard.end();
}
```

The next thing to remember is that you can test a form cgi-bin by executing it
and entering a string from the terminal. Since this is stdin when the program is normally run, the cgi-bin program will process it and send back whatever you programmed.

With the ability to obtain information from Internet users via form input, you
now have the capability to create many of the common cgi-bin programs seen on
the Internet. As we have seen, Post forms are relatively simple. All that is required is
a cgi-bin program capable of retrieving information from stdin and some postprocessing to decode the input information. Get forms are only slightly more complicated and use argc and argv[]. The Get form does have the advantage that you will
see the user's data appended to the requested action URL when it is sent from the
browser.

PROGRAM EXERCISES

1. Create the clearing parsing routines. Create an HTML form that sends at least three variables. Using your parsing clearing routines, create a cgi-bin program to respond to your form. Using any method you wish, show that your clearing routines are removing %hex values, extra spaces, plus to space, etc.

2. Create a form with three user defined variables. Develop a cgi-bin program that uses the decision-making routines. Have your program send back different HTML to the user based on the user's input to the variables from a form. Verify that the program works. (**Hint:** Stay away from text input if you want to make things simple.)

3. Create a form with at least one hidden variable. Using decision routines and clearing routines, verify that you can isolate the predefined value of the hidden variable. Send the value back to the user inside HTML. Change the value of the hidden variable and repeat.

4. Use the beginning debugging tools to test your cgi-bin programs. Verify that you can debug using stdin and stdout. If the output to stdout is in HTML, remove the Content Type line and then display the output on your browser. (**Hint:** You can use a URL that starts with "file://" or one that starts with "http://".)

5. Create a Post cgi-bin program and a Post method form. Test to verify that it is operational. Now change each to use the Get method and retest.

PROBLEMS

1. Explain the rules of parsing. Explain the difference between clearing routines and decision routines. State which clearing routines will not be needed when decision routines are used, and explain why.

2. Explain the difference between the Post and Get methods. Explain the distinction between stdin and argc, argv[] for the two methods. What do you see as the advantages or disadvantages of the two methods?

3. Explain in detail the steps that take place when a form is submitted. Include details, starting from the structure of the initial HTML form and ending with the output to the user. Explain some of the different ways this can be accomplished. Add any additional options that you think might work. Explain how you might go about testing your added capabilities.

4. Explain some of the differences and similarities between debugging forms with cgi-bin programs and debugging normal C++ and C programs. Set up a step-by-step methodology that you might use to debug a problem. Explain some of the special things that must be checked. Explain things like these:
   - The server runs the program.
   - There is one continuous string.
   - The stdout does not go directly to the user.

- The stdin is not the keyboard.
- The distinction between the unix_path and the internet_path.

5. Using Figure 4.2, explain the sequence of events for using forms. Add any missing parts needed to help the explanation.

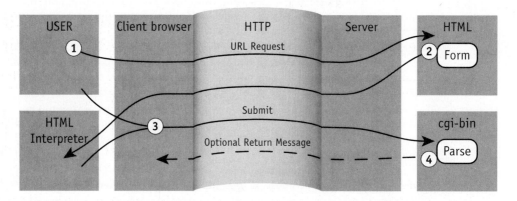

FIGURE 4.2

5

Emailers

Emailing Form Data

Using the Process ID (PID) in a Simple Mailer

Emailing Form Data

ONE THING THAT CAN BE done with the form data is to mail them to someone. This is one of the most common uses of the form. For businesses, educational facilities, and other institutions, forms represent a way to get input from users of their Internet services. Anything that is input to a form, such as a questionnaire, a purchase request, customer feedback, or service request, can be mailed to an appropriate person. The steps that are required are straightforward:

1. Provide the form for inputting the information you require. This can be done with standard HTML.
2. Create a cgi-bin program that will read in the data and then clean up any extraneous information and retrieve any needed variables.
3. The cgi-bin program then emails the information out to the correct person and sends back an HTML confirmation.

Using the Process ID (PID) in a Simple Mailer

IN THE SIMPLEST VERSION of an emailer, the person to send the email to is fixed, so all that is needed is the user information.

Here is a simple mailing routine that is easy to create. To accomplish the emailing, the text to be emailed is output to a file in a temporary directory. The C

language call system(argument) is used to allow a standard UNIX mailer to mail the
program out.

```cpp
/*
 * Type: C++ subroutine
 * Purpose: Send a user message out using email
 * Note: Uses UNIX system call
 * Input:      char* msg - pointer to user's message
 */
void
send_mail(char* msg)
{
    filebuf f;
    char filestring[MAXLINE];
    char mailstring[MAXLINE];
    /* Open the temporary output file that will be sent to the UNIX mailer */
    /*
     * Use the process identification (pid) to create a unique filename just in case two or
     * more people try to send email at the same time.
     */
    strcpy(filestring, "/unix_path/tmp/tmpfile."
    strcat(filestring, itoa( (int )getpid()) );
    if(f.open(filestring, output) == EOF)
    {
        return; // file unavailable so abort
    }
    /*  Ostreams are a powerful part of the C++ language. They make it easy to send
     *  different types of information to a file. The similarity of the ostream and cout is
     *  evident.
     */
    ostream dest(&f);
    dest << msg; // put the message in the file
    f.close();
    /*  To use the system() call requires a string, which is the UNIX command to execute.
     *  Since part of the string is based on the input variable, string functions are
     *  used to build up the entire string prior to the system call.
     */
    strcpy(mailstring,
        "mail myname@mycompany <");
    strcat(mailstring, filestring);
    system(mailstring);
    /*
     * Now repeat the string building process to remove the temp file.
     */
    strcpy(mailstring, "rm ");
    strcat(mailstring, filestring);
```

```
            system(mailstring);
      }
```

In the next program you will need a simple lookup table to translate the mailtoname into an email address. This could be as simple as case statement, or if the mailtoname changes frequently, use file I/O to read in the email address from a flat file.

```
#include <sys/types.h>
#include <unistd.h>
#define TEMPSPACE "/home/tmp/tmp.space" /* define a tmp file */
/*
 * A word of caution: When the cgi-bin program runs, it will be the server that is running
 * the program, not the user. Permission for any files must be set up so the server can access
 * the file. Many mailers let the user enter the email address. This has two disadvantages.
 * First, mail to multiple people can clutter your machine by sending mail to people not on
 * your system. Second, users may not know the email addresses for critical people you want
 * them to mail to. You will have to take charge of forwarding mail if this is the case. When
 * you create a mailer, always remember that the mail will come from the server, not from
 * the user. If you want the person's email address, include a text entry field for the required
 * information.
 */
/*
 * Type: C++ subroutine
 * Purpose: Send a user message out in email
 * Caution: Multiple users could collide
 * Input:      char* to - who the email is sent to
                char* msg - pointer to user's message
 */
void
send_mail(char* to, char* msg)
{
      filebuf f;
      char mailstring[MAXLINE];
      /* Open the temporary output file that will be sent to the Unix mailer. */
      if(f.open(TEMPSPACE, output) == 0)
      {
            return; // file unavailable so abort
      }
      /*  Ostreams are a powerful part of the C++ language. They make it easy to send
       *  different types of information to a file. The similarity of the ostream and cout is
       *  evident.
       */
      ostream dest(&f);
      dest << msg; // put the message in the file
      f.close();
```

```
/*   To use the system() call requires a string, which is the UNIX command to execute.
 *   Since part of the string is based on the input variable, string functions are
 *   used to build up the entire string prior to the system call
 */

sprintf(mailstring, "%s%s%s%s",
     "mail",
     to,
     " < ",
     TEMPSPACE);


system(mailstring);
/* Now repeat the string building process to remove the temp file. Some sophisticated
 * readers will see a possible problem here if more than one user is trying to send mail
 * at the same time. These types of problems can be handled with slightly more
 * sophisticated routines (e.g., lock files) or by appending the process number to the
 * file to assure that it has a unique name. The time.h routines can also be used
 * to create file extensions that provide the same uniqueness. Since cgi-bin programs
 * can be called by multiple users, this is a legitimate concern.
 */
strcpy(mailstring, "rm ");
strcat(mailstring, TEMPSPACE);
strcat(mailstring, itoa( (int )getpid()) );
system(mailstring);
}
```

Finally, we present a similar program in C with two important additions: (1) the email address is an input to the routine, and (2) UNIX pipes are used to avoid the temp file. The use of popen() is the better option, but it may not be available on all systems. The system() command used earlier is standard C++ and C and should be readily available. See Figure 5.1 for an overview of the creation of email routines.

```
#define NULL 0
/*
 * Type: C subroutine
 * Purpose: Send user message out as email
 * Note: Uses popen to set up a pipe
 * Input:     char* to - who the email is sent to
 *            char* msg - pointer to user's message
 */
void send_mail(char* to, char* msg)
{
     FILE* stream;
     char tempstring[MAXLINE];
```

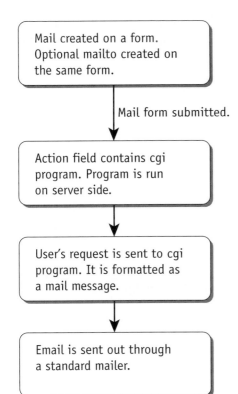

FIGURE 5.1   Mailers: The email interface creates important flexibility for information gathering.

```
strcpy(tempstring,"mail ");
strcat(tempstring, to);
if((stream = popen(tempstring, "w")) == NULL)
{
      return; /* abort */
}
fprintf(stream, "%s\n", msg); /* mail message */
pclose(stream);
}
```

Here is an HTML form that provides a variable email address.

```
<HTML> <HEAD> <TITLE> Mail Form </TITLE></HEAD>
<!-- end of the normal starting stuff -->
<FORM METHOD=POST ACTION="http://internet_path/cgi-bin/cgi_main" >
<!-- now create the form -->
<P> <STRONG> SEND MAIL TO: </STRONG>
<INPUT TYPE="text" NAME="email" VALUE="markf@xxx.com" SIZE=20>
<STRONG> ENTER YOUR EMAIL ADDRESS: </STRONG>
```

```
<!-- This is needed since mail will have the cgi program address -->
<P><INPUT TYPE="text" NAME="your_email" VALUE="" SIZE=60>
<P> <STRONG> ENTER MESSAGE: </STRONG> <P>
<TEXTAREA COLS=50 ROWS=6 NAME="message" VALUE="">
</TEXTAREA>
<P> <INPUT TYPE="submit" VALUE="Mail Message"> <INPUT TYPE="reset"> </FORM>
</BODY>
</HTML>
```

The critical input line is as follows:

```
<INPUT TYPE="mailto" NAME="email" VALUE="markf@xxx.com" SIZE=20>
```

This line sets the variable email to a particular email address. Unless it is changed, the mail will be sent to the required party.

The send mail routine can also be part of a class that allows the use of inheritance to connect the form class to it. The whole thing looks like this:

```
class _Send_mail : public _Form
{
private:
    void send_mail(char* to, char* msg); // see routines above
    char tmp_msg[1000];
public:
    _Send_mail() {;};
    void out()     // send the mail out
};
#define TEMPSPACE "/home/tmp/tmp.space" /* define a tmp file */
/*
 * Type: C++ class subroutine
 * Purpose: Send message via email using C++ class structure
 */
void
_Send_mail::out()
{
    char indata[1000];
    char mailtoname[50];
    char msg[1000];
    cin>>indata;
    /* process the data */
    strcpy(mailtoname, clear_msg(indata,
        "mailtoname=", "&emailad="));
    strcpy(msg(clear_msg(get_variable(indata,
        "&emailad=")));
    strcat(msg, clear_msg(get_variable(indata, "&message=")));
```

```
        send_mail(mailtoname, msg);
}
/*
 * Type: C++ main
 * Purpose: Send message via email using C++ class structure
 */
#include <iostream.h>
#include <stdlib.h>
#include <string.h>
main()
{
     Send_mail mySend_mail;
     mySend_mail.out();
}
```

Here is one more version in C:

```
/*
 * Type: C subroutine
 * Purpose: Send message via email
 * Special Note: Uses malloc and popen
 */
#include <malloc.h>
void
_Send_mail_out()
{
     FILE* stream;
     char indata[MAXLINE];
     char mailtoname[MAXLINE];
     char* msg;
     msg = malloc (sizeof(char) * 1000); /* malloc the space */
     gets(indata);
     /* process the data */
     strcpy(mailtoname, variable(indata,
          "email="));
     strcpy( msg, clear_sp(clear_amp(clear_plus(indata))));
     /* mail to is known so hard code it into the pipe */
     if( stream = popen("mail joe@testmachine", "w") == 0)
     {
          return; /* pipe unavailable so abort */
     }
     fprintf(stream, "%s\n%s\n", mailtoname, msg);
     pclose(stream);
}
```

The addition of *mailers* makes it possible to take input from users via forms and send it using the system's email to a particular user. This is helpful since the other option of sending it to a file would require that periodic checks be made of the file. With email, most mailers will tell you when new mail arrives. If this is important information that requires a fast turnaround, the email option will be the obvious choice. On the other hand, if it was a questionnaire or some information-gathering function, it might make sense to use file output with an occasional check for status.

PROGRAM EXERCISES

1. Create a cgi-bin program that sends a fixed mail message to you when activated. After it sends the mail out, have it send back a message in HTML that says "Message Sent."
2. Create a form with a text area. Have a cgi-bin program parse the text and then send it to you as email. Have it send a carbon copy to someone else. Test your ability to parse correctly by entering the following into the text area:

   There are 30% more apples than   oranges;!:)

3. Create a form that contains three text areas. In the first enter the person's email name; in the second their email location; in the third the email text.

PROBLEMS

1. Explain the difference between the system() call and the popen() call. Why would you tend to prefer one over the other? Where might you be forced to use one over the other? Using the command man on a UNIX to get the manual pages, explain in detail the way popen() is used.
2. Explain situations in which built-in capabilities might be preferred over a cgi-bin mailer. (**Hint:** This problem requires knowledge of HTML and client-server capabilities. These may not be present on all systems.)
3. The popen() routine is a method of providing a pipe. In the examples in this chapter, the pipe was used to provide a conduit to mail capabilities. How else might pipes be used as part of the cgi-bin development process?
4. The object-oriented paradigm might lead us to think in terms of a mail station, a mailbox, or even a post office. Continue with this line of analysis and see how the mail routines might be restructured.
5. Explain how a mailer operates using Figure 5.2.

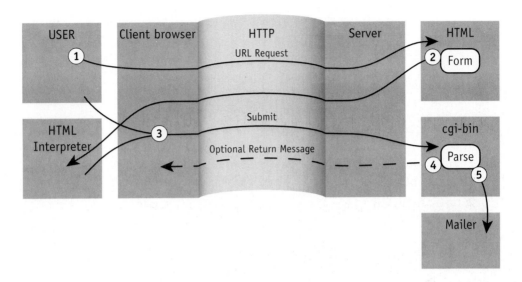

FIGURE 5.2

6

Multiple
Applications

Developing Multiple Applications in a Single Program

IF YOU HAVE FOLLOWED THIS BOOK to this point, you may be getting good at creating cgi-bin programs and may be finding that you are handling a multitude of requests. If this is the case, you are probably looking for ways to cut down on your work load or methods to provide more complex capabilities.

This section provides methods that will enable you to use all or parts of the same program over again. Methods are also developed to pass options into a program. In many ways, this is the critical reason for selecting compiled languages over other methods. The ability to create complex programs is more quickly and easily achieved in these programming environments.

There are several possible strategies to consider when examining these issues. One approach is to develop some standard code that can be placed in libraries.

This is certainly a good approach for the form parsing routines and for the HTML BASE class. These can be classes and associated functions for C++ or function libraries for C. The additional approach that can be used is to provide multiple Web pages from the same cgi-bin program.

By combining into a single cgi-bin program multiple applications, it is possible to produce common routines only once. This will make the most sense if a unique group of Web pages is being developed for a single site. Libraries might not make sense if the commonality across the Web pages was a customer logo or a customer address. In many instances the differences will be part of a single picture, as in the Star Quilt (see Chapter 16) where colors are changed but the star remains constant.

The idea of having the same cgi-bin program send the initial screen and the response screen has already been mentioned. But it may also make sense to use the same cgi-bin program for multiple forms with a common thread. The specifics of groupings will need to be determined on a case-by-case basis.

There are a number of ways to differentiate calls to the same cgi-bin program. The first identification that can be made is contained in the the HTTP[1] server message.

Accessing the Server Environment

RECALL THAT EVERY cgi-bin program is run by the server. When the cgi-bin program runs, it is provided environmental variables known to the server. These special environmental variables have the same format as any UNIX environmental variable, such as your PATH or TERM type. The server has a unique environment that can be accessed by the user program. Certain environmental variables used by the server can provide valuable information to your cgi-bin program.

The command getenv(ENVIRONMENT_NAME) can be used to get any of the server environmental information. Here is a simple program that retrieves all known information about the *server environment*.

```
/*
 * Type: C++ main
 * Purpose: Get the server environment
 */
#include <iostream.h>
#include <stdlib.h>
main()
{
    cout << "Content-type: text/html\n\n" <<
        "<HTML><BODY>"
        << "Your Remote Address (IP Address) is " <<
```

---

[1]   The HTTP is the protocol used by client and servers on the Internet to transfer messages.

```
            getenv("REMOTE_ADDR") << "\n"
      << "Your Server Software is " <<
            getenv("SERVER_SOFTWARE") << "\n"
      << "Your Server Name is " <<
            getenv("SERVER_NAME") << "\n"
      << "Your Gateway Interface is " <<
            getenv("GATEWAY_INTERFACE") << "\n";
      << "Your Server Protocol is " <<
            getenv("SERVER_PROTOCOL") << "\n"
      << "Your HTTP Accept is " <<
            getenv("HTTP_ACCEPT") << "\n"
      << "Your REQUEST METHOD is " <<
            getenv("REQUEST_METHOD") << "\n"
      << "</BODY></HTML>\n";
}
```

However, more often than not, you will not want all the environmental variables. Depending on your application, you may want the REMOTE_ADDR (remote address) for security reasons. Or you may want the Request method, which can separate out a Post from a Get. To determine what will be of value, examine the following Environment class. Each of the server environmental variables is explained along with code for retrieving any or all of them.

```
/*
 * _Environment
 *
 *   Usage: Retrieve server environmental variables
 */
class _Environment
{
     int environment_type;
public:
     _Environment(){ environment_type = -1; } ;
     char* retrieve(char* env_str);
};
/*
 * Type: C++ class subroutine
 * Purpose: Get a specific server environment variable
 * Input:     char* env_str - pointer to the environment string requested
 * Output:    char* - pointer to value of environmental variable
 */
char*
_Environment::retrieve(char* env_str)
{
     switch(environment_type)
     {
```

```
        default:
        case NO_TYPE:
            env_str="";
            break;
        /*
         * The name and version of the information server software answering the request and
         * running the gateway. The format is Name/Version
         */
        case SERVER_SOFTWARE:
            env_str=getenv("SERVER_SOFTWARE");
            break;
        /*
         * The server's hostname. DNS alias or IP address as it would appear in self-referencing
         * URLs
         */
        case SERVER_NAME:
            env_str=getenv("SERVER_NAME");
            break;
        /*
         * The revision of the CGI specification to which this server complies.
         * Format: CGI/Revision
         */
        case GATEWAY_INTERFACE:
            env_str=getenv("GATEWAY_INTERFACE");
            break;
        /*
         * The name and revision of the information protocol this request came in with.
         * Format: Protocol/Revision
         */
        case SERVER_PROTOCOL:
            env_str=getenv("SERVER_PROTOCOL");
            break;
        /*
         * The port number to which the request was sent
         */
        case SERVER_PORT:
            env_str=getenv("SERVER_PORT");
            break;
        /*
         * The method with which the request was made. For HTTP the methods are Get, Head,
         * and Post. This can be useful for using the same script to start a form screen and to
         * handle the POST request from the form screen.
         */
        case REQUEST_METHOD:
            env_str=getenv("REQUEST_METHOD");
            break;
```

```
                    /* Extra path information provided by the client. This is useful if the same script will
                     * function differently based on a virtual pathname. This information is valuable for
                     * server decoding if a cgi-bin program comes from a URL before it is passed on to the
                     * program.
                     */
                    case PATH_INFO:
                        env_str=getenv("PATH_INFO");
                        break;
                    /*
                     * A virtual path to the script being executed, used for self referencing URLs.
                     */
                    case SCRIPT_NAME:
                        env_str=getenv("SCRIPT_NAME");
                        break;
                    /*
                     * If the Get method is used or with ISINDEX (detailed later) this information will
                     * follow the ? in the URL that referenced the script. This is the query information. It
                     * will normally not be decoded in any way. This variable is always set when there is
                     * query information, regardless of command line decoding.
                     */
                    case QUERY_STRING:
                        env_str=getenv("QUERY_STRING");
                        break;
                    /*
                     * The IP address of the remote host making the request
                     */
                    case REMOTE_ADDR:
                        env_str=getenv("REMOTE_ADDR");
                        break;
                    /*
                     * When the input type is POST, this is the content type of the data. Presently there is
                     * only one content type: x-www-form-urlencoded.
                     */
                    case CONTENT_TYPE:
                        env_str=getenv("CONTENT_TYPE");
                        break;
                    /*
                     * The number of bytes of input data to read from the stdio (standard in) stream when
                     * the post method is used.
                     */
                    case CONTENT_LENGTH:
                        env_str=getenv("CONTENT_LENGTH");
                        break;
                    /*
                     * The MIME types that the client will accept, as given by the HTTP headers. Other
                     * protocols may need to get this information from elsewhere. Each item will be
```

```
        * separated by commas. The format is: Type/Subtype, Type/Subtype...
        */
       case HTTP_ACCEPT:
            env_str=getenv("HTTP_ACCEPT");
            break;
       }
       return( env_str );
}
/* Here is a partial version in C */
/*
 * Type: C subroutine
 * Purpose: Get a specific server environment variable
 * Input:      char* env_str - pointer to the environment string requested
 * Output:     char* - pointer to value of environmental variable
 */
char* retrieve(char* env_str)
{
       switch(environment_type){
       default:
       case NO_TYPE:
            env_str="";
            break;
       /*
        * The name and version of the information server software answering the request and
        * running the gateway. The format is Name/Version
        */
       case SERVER_SOFTWARE:
            env_str=getenv("SERVER_SOFTWARE");
            break;
       etc.
       /* continue rest of C program here
        *
        *    return env_str and end C program
        */
```

These are #defines that can be used to map numerals into each of the environmental capabilities. They are arbitrary values for use in your programs.

```
#define NO_TYPE -1
#define SERVER_SOFTWARE 0
#define SERVER_NAME 1
#define GATEWAY_INTERFACE 2
#define SERVER_PROTOCOL 3
#define SERVER_PORT 4
#define REQUEST_METHOD 5
#define PATH_INFO 6
```

```
#define SCRIPT_NAME 7
#define QUERY_STRING 8
#define REMOTE_ADDR 9
#define CONTENT_TYPE 10
#define CONTENT_LENGTH 11
#define HTTP_ACCEPT 12
```

By reading specific environmental variables, it is possible to create more control over the cgi-bin program. For example, here is a program that uses REQUEST_METHOD to determine how the same script is being invoked. This will allow the Get and Post to be separated out. In many cases, the Get will occur if someone uses the cgi-bin program directly as a URL, while the Post will occur if the cgi-bin program is invoked from a form. When the Get method occurs, it will make sense to send back something in HTML that is appropriate.

```
/*
 * Type: C++ main
 * Purpose: Demonstrate use of environment to select Get or Post method
 */
#include <iostream.h>
#include <stdlib.h>
#include <strings.h>
void main(int argc, char* argv[])
{
    char input[MAXLINE];
    cout << "Content-type: text/html\n\n";
    if( strcmp( getenv("REQUEST_METHOD"), "GET") == 0)
     {
        /*
         * Do Get method stuff. For Get there may not be any arguments since Get method
         * will be the method if the program is invoked directly as a URL. To find out check
         * argc.
         */
        if ( argc > 1)
        {
            /* Process using argv[1] */
        } else
        {
            /* Send default HTML */
        }
     } else
     if( strcmp( getenv("REQUEST_METHOD"), "POST") == 0)
     {
        /* Do Post method stuff */
        gets( input );
        /* Do processing on input data */
```

```
        } else
        {
            /* error routine */
        }
    }
```

Hidden Variables

HIDDEN VARIABLES WERE INITIALLY INTRODUCED in the discussion of forms. A hidden variable is a preset piece of information that is sent along with other information when a form is submitted. It is a form variable that does not leave an input field and is not seen on the client screen. Since the user cannot change the hidden variable,[2] the value sent to the program is whatever value the variable is set to in the HTML. This can be used for a number of different purposes. One of these is the separation of two forms that request the same cgi-bin program. If the program determines the value of the variable immediately after retrieving the stdin information, the value of the hidden variable can be used to follow separate paths in the program. This is an especially valuable approach if the different paths are relatively close. For example, suppose a group of HTML pages is presenting the local news of the day. It might be that the user is given the option of selecting different stories of the day. If all stories are shown with a standard identification logo and always end with a standard ending banner, a hidden variable can be used to determine the selected story.

Here is a typical hidden variable input line:

```
<!-- COMMENT html VERSION OF A HIDDEN VARIABLE -->
<P><INPUT TYPE="HIDDEN" NAME="myhidden" VALUE="hide1"></P>
```

In C++ it is this:

```
cout<< "<!-- HTML VERSION OF A HIDDEN VARIABLE -->\n";
cout<< "<P><INPUT TYPE=\"HIDDEN\" NAME=\"myhidden\" VALUE=\"hide1\"></P>\n";
```

In C it is this:

```
printf( "<!-- HTML VERSION OF A HIDDEN VARIABLE -->\n");
printf( "<P><INPUT TYPE=\"HIDDEN\" NAME=\"myhidden\" VALUE=\"hide1\"></P>\n");
```

Since the variable myhidden= will always be set to hide1 for this form, you can use this variable to differentiate two forms that use the same cgi-bin program with only

---

[2]   In reality, a user could change a hidden variable by saving your HTML page and then modifying it. Because of this, protective measures may be needed against maliciousness.

subtle differences. Here is an example program that shows how this would work. First we have the HTML for the first hidden variable form

```
<FORM METHOD=POST ACTION="http://internet_path/cgi-bin/cgi_main" >
<P> <STRONG> ENTER MESSAGE: </STRONG> <P>
<TEXTAREA COLS=50 ROWS=6 NAME="message" VALUE="">
 </TEXTAREA>
<INPUT TYPE="HIDDEN" NAME="myhidden" VALUE="hide1"></P>
<P> <INPUT TYPE="submit" VALUE="Mail Message"> <INPUT TYPE="reset"> </FORM>
</BODY>
</HTML>
```

Then we have the HTML for the second hidden variable:

```
<FORM METHOD=POST ACTION="http://internet_path/cgi-bin/cgi_main" >
<P> <STRONG> ENTER MESSAGE: </STRONG> <P>
<TEXTAREA COLS=50 ROWS=6 NAME="message" VALUE="">
 </TEXTAREA>
<INPUT TYPE="HIDDEN" NAME="myhidden" VALUE="hide2"></P>
<P> <INPUT TYPE="submit" VALUE="Mail Message"> <INPUT TYPE="reset"> </FORM>
</BODY>
</HTML>
```

The only distinction between these two HTML forms is that the first contains the hidden variable named hide1 and the second contains the hidden variable named hide2. Here is the cgi-bin program:

```
/*
 * Type: C++ main
 * Purpose: Get and respond to a hidden variable
 */
main()
{
     FORM myform;        // create a form type
     char indata[MAXLINE];
     cin > indata;
     // send out the Content-type ...
     ...
     if(check_msg (get_variable(indata,"myhidden="), "hide1")) == TRUE)
     {
          // do hide 1 stuff
     } else
     if(check_msg (get_variable(indata,"myhidden="), "hide2")) == TRUE)
     {
```

```
            // do hide 2 stuff
        } else
        {
            // error condition
        }
        // send the final HTML
    }
```

About the program . . . .

The initial check_msg() determines whether the variable myhidden is equal to hide1 or hide2. In the former case it does the functions and outputs the HTML associated with hide1. In the other case it does the same type of thing for hide2. If neither are the case, an error output results. You may be thinking that this error could not possibly occur. This is not true. Anyone can write HTML to call your URL-based cgi-bin program. They could save your HTML page to their local site and then put the code in an editor and change hide1 to hide3. Always remember that the Internet is a public resource. Of course, in this case all that would occur if you did not put the error leg in is that nothing would go back to the client server and eventually the malicious person would receive a time-out. Nevertheless, the error leg is still a good idea.

. . . .

argc and argv[]

ANOTHER METHOD FOR PROVIDING different output paths is to use the argc (the count of the number of arguments) and argv[] (the actual arguments) capability in C++ and C. Command line arguments, familiar to most programmers, can be sent to a cgi-bin program. There are several methods available to accomplish this. One is to use the Get method rather than the Post method. The second is to invoke the cgi-bin program followed by a "?" and the command line arguments. This can be done from an HTML anchor (<A>) or as a direct input URL (http://...cgi_prog?args).

Case 1: argv[] with forms (Get method)

In the first case the form would look like this:

```
<FORM ACTION="http://internet_path/cgi-bin/myprog" METHOD=GET >
```

or

```
<FORM ACTION="http://internet_path/cgi-bin/myprog" >
```

The second one works because the default method is Get.

Case 2: cgi-bin Activation from an Anchor

The second option looks like this:

```
<A HREF="http://internet_path/cgi-bin/myprog?myargs" > text </A>
```

In case 2 an anchor is used instead of a form. This will only be useful if the value of myargs is all that is needed by the cgi-bin program. In the anchor case, no user entered values are sent. Instead the arguments placed on the command line are directly put into the URL line.

More on "?"

WHEN THE EXAMPLES IN case 1 are used, the same "?" followed by arguments will be sent, but it will be the string from the form that will follow the question mark. It may already be apparent why in the earlier forms it was suggested that you begin by using Post. Using argc and argv[] will clearly provide more complexity since they can be used in places other than forms. There is one other compelling argument— namely, that some browsers will not send a Get but will send a Post. While this will probably not be true for long, it was a strong reason for beginning with Post. The other motive is esthetics. The Post moves invisibly between the client-server software while the Get will appear on the URL line. In other words, the unparsed string will appear along with the rest of the URL. Despite this fact, there are some cases in which Get will be the preferred method. For example, there is no way to have the same program use input from anchors to do different things when using the Post method. The only way to obtain the same result with the Post method would be to have two different versions of the cgi-bin program with different names.

Here is a simple example of a program using Get instead of Post in a form. Start with a simple form that sends out user information:

```
<FORM METHOD=GET ACTION="http://internet_path/cgi-bin/cgi_main" >
<!-- now create the form -->
<P> <STRONG> ENTER YOUR EMAIL ADDRESS: </STRONG>
<P> INPUT TYPE="text" NAME="your_email" VALUE="" SIZE=60>
<P> <STRONG> ENTER MESSAGE: </STRONG> <P>
<TEXTAREA COLS=50 ROWS=6 NAME="message" VALUE="">
 </TEXTAREA>
<P> <INPUT TYPE="submit" VALUE="Mail Message"> <INPUT TYPE="reset"> </FORM>
</BODY>
</HTML>
```

Here is the routine to retrieve the user information:

```
/*
 * Type: C++ main
 * Purpose: echo back argv[]
 * Input:
 *    argc and argv[]
 */
#include <iostream.h>
#include <stdlib.h>
#include <string.h>
main(int argc, char* argv[])
{
    normal_head("Show a GET");
    cout << "Your input data is " <<
            argv[1];
    normal_end();
}
```

The data appear in argv[1], the normal command line argument. When the data appear back on the client screen, they will have everything except the "?". This was used by the server to determine that what followed was command line arguments. When it arrived at the program, it had been replaced by a space. Now you could continue the same way as you would have if a Post method had been used. The parsing routines would take argv[1] for the input instead of stdin, which was used with the Post method. Since argv[1] is a char*, the same routines will work just fine.

So far, what has been passed has been the form information. In the following example, the argv[] information comes from the anchor and is processed by option-handling library function.

Here is typical code for determining options that can be used with Get:

```
/*
 * Type: C++ or C main
 * Purpose: Evaluate argv[1]
 * Input:      argc and argv[] - based on user input to a FORM
 */
#include <iostream.h>
#include <stdlib.h>
#include <string.h>
#include "cgi-defines.h"
extern int opterr;
extern int getopt();
void
main(int argc, char* argv[])
{
    int optchar; /* arg for getopt */
    int option_o = 0;
    opterr = 1; /* used for logging errors */
```

```
while((optchar = getopt(argc, argv, "o:")) != EOF)
{
    switch(optchar)
    {
    case 'o':
        /*
         * optarg contains the string following the selected option
         */
        option_o = atoi(optarg);
        break;
    default:
        /* error routine */
        break;
    }
    switch(option_o)
    {
    case 1:
        /* do send_mail */
        break;
    case 2:
        /* do send form */
        break;
    case 0:
        /* do the default operation */
        break;
    default:
        /* send an HTML error message */
        break;
    }
    /* send another HTML error message */
} // end main
```

More on Command Line Arguments

THIS TYPE OF CODE IS familiar to most C++ and C programmers. The getopt() library routine is a way to identify options entered from the command line. Here the options are being sent between the client-server software. Many, however, may not know that this capability is available in cgi-bin programs. This capability is activated with the "?" option. For example,

```
http://www/mypath/cgi-bin/main?-o1
```

will invoke the cgi-bin program main as if you had executed

```
main -o1
```

from the command line.

Now it becomes possible to use a single cgi-bin program to activate multiple Web pages from an anchor. The advantage of this approach is obvious. Library routines and common routines need not be reproduced every time a new form or capability is to be developed. Modules can be built, tested, and then enabled. Traditional .o files with standard routines, classes, and functions can be developed, compiled, and then reused. Standard source control can be used. In short, a development environment can be put in place.

It is important to notice the final comment:

```
/* send another HTML error message */
```

If there were no command line arguments, the code would reach this point. This would happen if someone happened to view your source and tried invoking the program as a URL without any arguments. These types of fundamental protections make for good programming. The default option is also important since someone could use a URL with an unknown argv[]. It cannot be stressed too often that the Internet is open to the public. If you put cgi-bin programs out there, someone is going to try something incorrectly, perhaps due to lack of understanding or deliberately. In either event, protecting against these contingencies is good practice.

argv[] and Post Combined

THIS SECTION PRESENTS ANOTHER argv[] cgi-bin program. It combines both command line arguments and the Post method; this is done by setting up the form action with command line arguments. The Post method forces stdin to be passed by the server, while the argv[] is appended to the cgi program as part of the action.

The HTML will look like this:

```
<FORM ACTION="http://mycgi_directory/cgi-bin/main?-d2" METHOD=POST>
```

Since the actual user information is sent as a Post to stdin, there are no additional arguments added to the line. This is similar to the anchor discussed earlier, except in this case argc and argv[] are being forced onto the form action request. Error paths are included throughout the program, which uses a password file that contains multiple entries for each user. The first is the user's name, followed by the first user password, the user key, and then a second user password. The user enters his or her name and the first password on a form screen. If a match is found, the key is sent back in the second password request. The user enters his or her name and the second password. Using command line arguments to the cgi-bin program allows the same program to call different sections at each juncture. If a match occurs, secure information is sent back to the user. If the user tries to call the second section of the password code directly, he or she is rejected since the REQUEST_METHOD will be Get rather than Post and the needed Post information will not be present. While this may seem like a lot of work just to get a couple of passwords, it illustrates just how much is possible to do with the basic HTML capabilities once cgi-bin programs are added. Another thing that has been added to this program is sending the first HTML page directly from the program. This is a good idea since it will allow you to add more complex encryption if security is a real concern.

Steps in the program are as follows:

1. The program is first called either directly or from an HTML anchor. When this is done, there are no Post data, but there is an attached argv[1].

2. In this case the argv[1] will be

```
<A HREF="internet_path/cgi-bin/main?-d1>
```

which will arrive at the program as

```
main -d1
```

This will cause the first password form to be sent back to the user. The action field for this first form will be a request for the same cgi-bin program, but with the argv[1] set to -d2. The action line will look like this:

```
<FORM ACTION="http://internet_path/cgi-bin/main?-d2 METHOD=post">
```

The user then enters his or her first name and first password. This is sent back to the same cgi-bin program, but in this case it contains both argv[1] as -d2 and the user's Posted data, which include the user's first user ID and first password.

3. The argv[1] is processed first, which results in the next form routine being called. Since the option -d2 has resulted in the routine that processes the first password request, this routine can check in the password file for a user ID with the first password field a match to the user's password. If a match is found, a second password form is sent back. This contains a new action line, which will request the same cgi-bin program again, but this time the value of argv[1] will be -d3. The action line will look like this:

```
<FORM ACTION="http://internet_path/cgi-bin/main?-d3 METHOD=post">
```

The process repeats, but now the check is against the user ID and the second password field.

```
/*
 * Type: C++ main
```

```
     * Purpose: Check one of three passwords using argv input to getopt
     *    Combines command line arguments (argv[]) and stdin (Post method) in a single program.
     * Note: argv[1] contains the password, but stdin is the password string
     * Input:      argc and argv - tells which password to read
     */
// externs here
#include <iostream.h>
#include <stdlib.h>
#include <string.h>
extern int opterr;
extern int getopt();
main(int argc, char* argv[])
     Password myPassword;
     int optchar; // arg for getopt
     int option_o = 0;
     opterr = 1; // used for logging errors
     while((optchar = getopt(argc, argv, "o:")) != EOF)
     {
          switch(optchar)
          {
          case 'o':
               option_o = atoi(optarg);
               break;
          default:
               // send an error
               return;
          }
          switch(option_o)
          {
          case 1:
               /* 1st Password Request */
               myPassword.form_1();
               break;
          case 2:
               /* 2nd Password Request */
               myPassword.check_1();
               break
          case 3:
               myPassword.check_2();
               break;
          case 0:
               /* do the default operation */
               break;
          default:
               /* send an error message */
          }
```

```
                        /* send an error message */
            } // end main
```

About the main program . . . .

1. The options in argv[1] are turned into an integer by the command

   ```
   option_o = atoi(optarg);
   ```

   This causes the same program to go to the different subroutines. A default operation is also provided so the program can be requested with the 0 option. If an illegal option is used or if no option is used, error messages are sent to the client software and then to the user.

2. The command line arguments or Get method are used so the password request will only be sent if a command line argument is present.

3. When the forms are sent out, they include a cgi-bin with command line arguments along with the Posted information. The options route the request to the appropriate subroutine. The Posted data are then retrieved and processed.

. . . .

```cpp
class _Password: public _Form : public _Standard {
    void form_2(char* key); // 2nd password form
    void form_3(); // form after password clearance
public:
    _Password(){ ; };
    void form_1(); // 1st password form
    void check_1(); // check for the 1st password
    void check_2(); // check for the 2nd password
};
void
_Password::form_1()
{
    start_msg();
    color_head("PASSWORD SECURITY PASSWORD 1");
    cout<< "<BR>\n";
    cout<<
        "<FORM ACTION=\"http://internet_path/cgi-bin/main?-d2\" METHOD=POST >\n"
        << "<BR>\n"
        << "<!-- now create the form -->\n"
        << "<P> <STRONG> ENTER YOUR 1st Password: </STRONG>\n"
        <<
        "<P> INPUT TYPE=\"password\" NAME=\"password1\" VALUE=\"\" SIZE=60>\n"
        <<
        "<P> INPUT TYPE=\"text\" NAME=\"name\" VALUE=\"\" SIZE=60>\n"
        <<
```

```
          "<P> <INPUT TYPE=\"submit\" VALUE=\"\"><INPUT TYPE=\"reset\"> </FORM>\n";
     end_msg();
}
```

About subroutine form_1 . . . .

1. The subroutine is the startup subroutine. It will occur the first time the cgi-bin program is invoked. Its job is to send back an HTML form to the user. It could be expanded to include an encryption key or other security.

2. Be sure to notice that the form action includes a call to

   main?-d2

   Remember, this is the same as running the program with

   main -d2

. . . .

The HTML output will look like this:

```
<HTML><TITLE>PASSWORD SECURITY PASSWORD 1</TITLE>
<BODY>
<BR>
<FORM ACTION="http://internet_path/cgi-bin/main?-d2" METHOD=POST>
<BR>
<!-- now create the form -->
<P> <STRONG> ENTER YOUR 1st Password: </STRONG>
<P> INPUT TYPE="password" NAME="password1"
     VALUE="" SIZE=60>
<P> INPUT TYPE="text" NAME="name"
     VALUE="" SIZE=60>
<P> <INPUT TYPE=\"submit" VALUE="submit"> <INPUT TYPE="reset"> </FORM>
</BODY></HTML>
```

The next subroutine is used to check the input from the first submit by the user. The user will have entered his or her first password. The subroutine will check for a match of this to the predefined common password. The NAME field is for the user's identification name. This will be used to determine the requirements for the second password.

```
#define PASSWD_FILE "/mypath/passwd.file"
/*
 * Type: C++ class subroutine
 * Purpose: Check a password sent by a user from a FORM
```

```
                */
           void
           _Password::check_1()
           {
                /*
                 *   It is possible to add scrambling algorithms to the password program
                 */
                char indata[MAXLINE];
                char passwdname[MAXLINE];
                char username[MAXLINE];
                filebuf fin;
                char c;
                char tmp_data[MAXLINE];
                char key[20];
                int i = 0;
                int field_cnt;
                int match = NOMATCH;
                cin >> indata;
                /* process the data */
                strcpy(passwdname, clear_msg(get_variable(
                     indata, "password1=")));
                strcpy(username, clear_msg(get_variable(
                     indata, "name=")));
                /*
                 * Now check to see if the password is valid for the user name. This is a character-by-
                 * character search.
                 */
                fin.open(PASSWD_FILE, input);
                /*
                 * The format for field in the password file is username key1 password_1 key2
                 * password_2
                 */
                c = fin.sgetc();                           // get the first character from the file
                while((c != EOF) && (c != ' '))            // looking for a space
                {
                     tmp_data[i++] = c;
                     c = fin.sgetc();
                                                           // get the first character from the file
                }
                if( (strncmp(username,
                     tmp_data, strlen(username)) == 0)     // match
                {
                     match = MATCH;
                     break;                // break out of the while loop
                }
                /*
```

```
      * If no match occurred send back an error message
      */
     if(match != MATCH)
     {
         send_error();
         // subroutine to send back an HTML error
     }
     /*
      * continue into the string to validate the user password. If this does not
      * match, send back an error message again
      */
     /* continue into the string to get the key */

     if(match == MATCH)       // everything matches
     {
         start_msg();          // send the start message
         form_2(key1);         // add second form to message
         end();                // end the HTML page
     } else
     {
         /* send back bad password */
         start_msg();
         color_head("BAD PASSWORD REQUEST");
         end();

     }
 }
```

About the subroutine check_1 . . . .

1. The subroutine retrieves the user data that have been Posted.
2. The two variable inputs password1 and username are pulled from the data.
3. A check is made for the username. If it is not found, an error message is sent out.
4. A check is then made for the user's first password. If it does not match, an error message is sent out.
5. If both match, the key is retrieved from the password file. This is a critical part of the program. The key will be passed into the next request; if it was not, there would be no way to create continuity between the first stage and the second stage in the password request. By creating this continuity, it is possible to stop a person from saving the first stage page and then just using it to request the second stage. A number of methods could be used for this purpose. For example, the day of the month could be added to the key and then removed from it on the second request. This is a fairly simple security. More complex ones could clearly be put in place.

. . . .

The HTML sent back to the user looks almost identical to the first password request except that it tells them that they are to enter their second password and, more important, it contains the hidden variable with the "key" in its encrypted state.

```cpp
/*
 * Type: C++ class subroutine
 * Purpose: Get the second password sent from a user's FORM
 */
void
_Password::form_2()
{
    start_msg();
    color_head("PASSWORD SECURITY PASSWORD 2");
    cout<< "<BR>\n";
    cout<<
        "<FORM ACTION=\"http://mycgi_directory/cgi-bin/main?-d3\" METHOD=POST >\n"
        << "<BR>\n"
        << "<!-- now create the form -->\n"
        << "<P> <STRONG> ENTER YOUR 2nd Password: </STRONG>\n"
        << "<P> INPUT TYPE=\"password\" NAME=\"password2\"" <<
            "VALUE=\"\" SIZE=60>\n"
        << "<P> INPUT TYPE=\"HIDDEN\" NAME=\"your_key\""
            << "VALUE=\"" << key << "\" SIZE=60>\n"
        << "<P> <INPUT TYPE=\"submit\" VALUE=\"NULL\"> " <<
            "<INPUT TYPE=\"reset\"> </FORM>\n";
}
```

About this subroutine . . . .

Be sure to notice that the form action includes a call to

    main?-d3

Remember, this is the same as running the program with

    main -d3

. . . .

```cpp
/*
 * Type: C++ class subroutine
 * Purpose: Get the third password sent from a user's FORM
 */
void
_Password::form_3()
{
```

```
        /* see above */
    }
```

The second check is similar to the first except that the encrypted key is also retrieved. Matches are required for the name, second password, and key.

```
    /*
     * Type: C++ class subroutine
     * Purpose: Validate the user's password
     */
    void
    _Password::check_2()
    {
        ...
        /*
         *   variable for the key information
         */
        char your_key[20];
        /* same as check_1 */
        strcpy(your_key, clear_msg(get_variable(
            indata, "your_key=")));
        /*
         * check for the user's name
         */
        /*
         * check for the second password
         */
        /*
         * encrypt the key
         */
        /*
         * check for the key
         */
    }
```

Multiple Arguments, argv[1], argv[2]...

ONE QUESTION ABOUT argc and argv[] still remains unanswered: Can multiple argv[] be sent to the server? Could there be an argv[1] and an argv[2]? This would be the same as multiple command line arguments to a C++ or C program.

```
    myprogram -iI_option -j -kK_option...
```

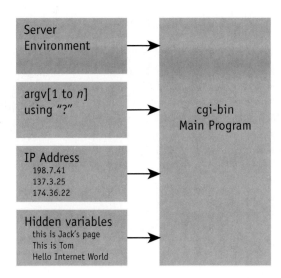

FIGURE 6.1   Multiple Applications: A cgi-bin program can respond differently based on input information from the user, command line or server.

The answer appears to be *no*. If you try something like

```
URL="http://internet_path/cgi-bin/myprogram?-iI_option?-j?-kK_option …
```

a single argv[1] is sent to the script that looks like this:

```
-iI_option\?-j\?-kK_option…
```

The second ? is replaced with a \?, not a second space with two arguments.

You could develop your own parsing routine to separate these into different arguments, but there is an easier way. Replace the second ? and any subsequent ones with a +. This will create the desired multiple arguments. So the URL is

```
URL="http://internet_path/cgi-bin/my_program?arg1+arg2
```

or, in the example,

```
URL="http://internet_path/cgi-bin/myprogram?-iI_option+-j+-kK_option…
```

This is the same as

```
myprogram arg1 arg2
```

or, in the example,

```
myprogram -iI_option -j -kK_option ...
```

This program takes three arguments in the argv[1-3] sent along with the request for
the cgi program. The first is a start message, the second an end message, and the
third a UNIX path to the file that contains the message. The program can be used to
search through folders or archives of mail items and select out a single message to
be included on a Web page. All that is required is a unique start and end word to
show where the message starts and ends. The three arguments are given, with the
first separated by a ? and the subsequent arguments by a +. The clear_hex routine is
also shown for completion.

```c
/*
 *    multi_prog.c
 *    usage: <A href=
 *      "http://internet_path/multi_prog?startmsg+endmsg+unixpath" >
 */
/*
 * Type: C++ main
 * Purpose: Demonstrate the use of argv[1], argv[2] ...
 * Input:      argc and argv{1-n}
 */
#include <stdio.h>
void main(int argc, char* argv[])
{
    FILE* stream;
    char start_string[MAXLINE];
    char end_string[MAXLINE];
    char u_path[MAXLINE];
    char buffer[MAXLINE];
    char out_msg[MAXLINE];
    int start_flag=0;
    // cleanup and copy the three strings to local variables
    strcpy(start_string, clear_hex(out_msg, argv[1]));
    strcpy(end_string, clear_hex(out_msg, argv[2]));
    strcpy(u_path, clear_hex(out_msg, argv[3]));
    // send the starting HTML
    cout <<
        "Content-type: text/html\n\n" <<
        "<HTML><BODY><PRE>\n";
    stream= fopen(u_path, "r");
    while(fgets(buffer,80,stream) != 0)
    {
        if(strncmp(start_string,
             buffer, strlen(start_string)) ==0)
        {
            start_flag =1;
```

```
                    }
                    if(start_flag==1)
                    {
                            cout << buffer;
                    }
                    if((start_flag==1) &&
                     (strncmp(end_string,
                            buffer, strlen(end_string)) ==0))
                    {
                            break;
                    }
            }
            fclose(stream);
            // final HTML - it is a good idea to always flush stdout
            cout << "</PRE></BODY></HTML>\n" << fflush;
}
/*
 * Type: C++ or C subroutine
 * Purpose: Change %0x0x strings to ASCII equivalent
 * Note: Also changes plus to a space
 * Input:
 *   char* out_msg - pointer to cleared message
 *   char* message - pointer to message to be cleared
 * Output:
 *   char* - pointer to cleared output message
 */
char* clear_hex(char* out_msg, char* message)
{
        char tmp_hex[3];
        int i = 0;
        char* xmessage;
        char in_msg[MAXLINE];
         strcpy(in_msg, message);
         xmessage = in_msg;
        while(*xmessage != 0)
          {
                if(*xmessage == '+') *(out_msg+i) = ' ';
                else if(*xmessage != '%') *(out_msg+i) = *xmessage;
                else
                {
                        xmessage++; tmp_hex[0] = *xmessage;
                        xmessage++; tmp_hex[1] = *xmessage;
                        tmp_hex[2] = 0;
                        *(out_msg+i) = ahextoi( &tmp_hex[0] );
                }
                        xmessage++; i++;
```

```
                    }
                    *(out_msg+i) = 0;/* null termination */
                    return(out_msg);

            }
```

Case Study 1: Using Interface Protocol Addresses

In the next program a check is done of a table of legitimate Interface Protocol (IP) addresses. The cgi-bin program will only allow mail to be sent by those that are in the list. The IP address is a unique address associated with the user's machine. Unfortunately, this is not totally true. For example, some proxy servers (a system method of security) will select an IP address from an available list. This means that the user's address will change every time he or she uses the system. However, if security is a real issue, proxy servers with dynamic IP addressing can be avoided and unique IP addresses will be associated with each user.

Client-Server Isolation

WHILE IT IS NOT SHOWN in any of these examples, it would be possible to set-up a server with special environmental variables not included in the standard server environment. This would require customization of the server environment and is beyond the scope of this book. In dealing with environmental variables, it is most important to remember that the environmental variables are coming from the server, not the client. Only client information available to the server, such as IP addresses, will be user specific. What will never be available are the actual environmental variables of the user. In fact, since more often than not the user is located on a remote machine, the passing of this information would be a violation of the most basic concepts of the Internet—namely, the isolation of the user's environment from the Web page environment. A little reflection will make it apparent that such a state would be extremely dangerous in a system that allows so much public access. The vision of the Internet was to provide a highly usable protocol that still maintained sharp divisions between the user and the client software (specifically the browser) and the HTML pages and cgi-bin programs, with their associated server software.

Before proceeding, let's look at the subsections of the IP program.

1. A primary class IP_address is used to verify the user's IP address against a list of legitimate addresses in a file. The IP_address class inherits the previously developed Environment class, which allows it to read the server environment. In this case it is the user's IP address that is read. The verification will return a MATCH or NOMATCH to the main program.

2. The second class is a new class that is our first introduction to counters. It reads in a counter from a file, increments the counter, and then puts the new value back into the file.

3. The third class is a mailer. It inherits the counter since the only time the counter will be increased is if a valid IP address is confirmed and the mailer is sent to the user.

4. The main has only a couple of decisions to make. First it is determined if there is a valid or invalid IP address. If the address is valid, the mailer is sent to the user, which also increments the counter. If the IP address is invalid, an error message in HTML is sent to the user.

With that information, let's proceed with the program. First set up a class to handle IP address verification:

```
class _IP_address :: public _Environment
{
public:
    _IP_address() { ; };
    int verify();
};
```

About the IP_address class . . . .

This is a very simple class. It does only one thing: It checks to see if the user's IP address is part of a list of valid IP addresses. In addition, it inherits the capabilities of the Environment class, so it can read the environmental variables. This is needed because the IP address is a server environmental variable.

. . . .

```
/*
 * Place these in the cgi_defines.h file
 *    These are the two possible return states. Either there is a match or there is not a match.
 */
#define NOMATCH 0
#define MATCH 1
/*
 * Type: C++ class subroutine
 * Purpose: Verify that a person's IP address is in the validation file
 * Output:    int - valid or invalid
 */
/*
 * Member Function to verify IP addresses
 */
int
_IP_address::verify()
{
    char* ip_ptr;         // pointer to the IP Address
    filebuf fin;          // a file buffer
    char inbuf[MAXLINE];  // A string of characters
    char c;               // Used to read a character at a time
```

```
        int i;                        // Used as a counter in loops
        /*
         * Using the environmental capability, retrieve the remote address or IP address of the
         * user
         */
        ip_ptr = retrieve(REMOTE_ADDR);
        /*
         * Since it may be preferable to change the acceptable valid IP addresses, let's use a
         * flat file to create the valid addresses. Therefore, the next step is to read in the valid
         * addresses and see if any match the remote address obtained from the environment.
         */
        fin.open("/path/ip_flatfile", input);
        c = fin.sgetc(); // get the first character from the file
        while(c != EOF)
        {
            i=0;
            while(c != '\n') // each IP address will end in a cr
            {
                inbuf[i++] = c;
            }
            inbuf[i]=0; // null terminate
            if(strcmp(ip_ptr, &(inbuf[0])) == 0)
            {
                /*
                 * got a match
                 */
                fin.close(); // remember to clean up
                return MATCH;
            }
            fin.getc();// get next character
        }
        /*
         * Nothing ever matched so tell the next part of the program
         */
        fin.close();
        return(NOMATCH);

    }
```

C version of the same function

```
    /*
     * Type: C subroutine
     * Purpose: Verify that a person's IP address is in the validation file
     * Output:
     *    int - valid or invalid
```

```
     */
int
verify()
{
     char* ip_ptr;
     FILE* fin;
     char inbuf[MAXLINE];
     char c;
     int i;
     ip_ptr = retrieve(REMOTE_ADDR);
     fin = fopen("/path/ip_flatfile", "r");
     while(fgets(fin, 50, inbuf) != 0)
     {
          if(strncmp(ip_ptr, &(inbuf[0]), strlen(ip_ptr)) == 0)
          {
               /* got a match */
               fclose(fin);
               return(MATCH);

          }
     }
     fclose(fin);
     return(NOMATCH);

}
```

A typical IP address flat file of valid addresses

```
//--------------------------------
135.11.124.22
135.11.124.27
135.11.125.67
//--------------------------------
```

Other routines for the IP program

The next step is to define a new function type for the Send_mail class. This will be the function that sends the form from the cgi script. It will be activated if a Post method comes to the script. Recall from previous discussions that a form can select the Get or Post method. However, since it is illustrating cgi-bin differentiation using Get and Post, this program will deal with both methods. We can also add a simple counter to the Post to keep a record of how many times this page is accessed from the form using Post. We will discuss counters in greater detail in Chapter 13.

```
#define CNT_FILE "/path/countfile.out"
#define TMPCNT_FILE "/path/tmpcnt.out"
/* count how many times this page has been accessed */
```

```
class _Count
{
public:
    _Count(){ ; };
    void up(char* count_file);
};
/*
 * Type: C++ class subroutine
 * Purpose: Initial counter
 * Input:
 *   char* - pointer to the count file
 */
void
_Count::up(char* count_file)
{
    FILE* stream;
    char buffer[MAXLINE];
    int i;
    stream = fopen(count_file, "i");
    fgets(buffer, 20, stream);
    fclose(stream);
    i= atoi(buffer); // turn the counter into an int
    i++;             // increment the counter
    stream = fopen(TMPCNT_FILE, "o");
    /*
     * Turn the integer to a string of chars then put the new counter into the file
     */
    fprintf(stream, "%s\n", itoa(buffer));

    fclose(stream);
    /* Use a move to minimize the time of the file change; if there is a lot of traffic we will
     * need to use file locking. This is necessary since it is possible for more than one
     * person to be trying to increment the counter at the same time. A locking file would
     * prevent this, but if you are not that worried about a couple of missed counts
     * occasionally, this method will work just fine.
     */
    strcpy(system_buf, "mv ");
    strcpy(system_buf, TMPCNT_FILE);
    strcpy(system_buf," ");
    strcpy(system_buf, count_file);
    system(system_buf);
}
```

Other examples of counters are included in Chapter 13.

About the class Counter and subroutine up() . . . .

1. The count file is opened and the value is read into the program.
2. The file is closed and then the counter is turned into an integer using atoi().
3. The integer is increased by 1, which moves the count up one unit.
4. The temporary file is opened and the new count value is sent to the temporary file.
5. The temporary file is then closed and a system call is set up to move ("mv") the file over into the original count file, which causes it to be replaced with the new count.
6. Finally, the temporary file is removed. Lost counts could occur if two or more people tried to up the count at the same time. For example, if the count was 5 and both of them retrieved the value 5 before either put in their increment of the counter, then the new count would be 6, not 7, when they were done. If absolute accuracy were needed, a method would be required to stop the second person from retrieving the count until the first user was done incrementing the count. While this is possible, it is rarely needed and so is only mentioned for the sake of thoroughness.

. . . .

The next section is the actual mailer. It is just one of many choices of things to do based on the IP address. For example, we could just as easily have refused access to some information in HTML or some other format. The only thing unique about this mailer is that it includes the *counter* at the beginning. The counter will only be increased for legitimate access to the system with a valid IP address in the IP address file. To do this, the mailer will have to inherit or include the Counter class. This required inheritance is shown next. Because only the mailer will increment the counter, this provides the kind of data hiding that is an indication of good C++ programming.

```cpp
// See earlier class declarations of mailers
class _Send_mail : public _Form, public _counter
{
    // rest of class
};
/*
 * Type: C++ class subroutine
 * Purpose: Send FORM from a cgi-bin program for mailing
 */
void
_Send_mail::memoform()
{
    /* increment the counter */
    up(CNT_FILE); // increment the count file
```

```
        /*
         * Send out the mailer HTML
         */
        cout<< "<HTML> <HEAD> <TITLE> Input Form </TITLE></HEAD>\n"
            << "<BODY BGCOLOR=#f0f0f0 >\n"
            << "<!-- end of the normal starting stuff -->\n"
            << "<BR>\n"
            << "<FORM ACTION=\"http://mycgi_directory/cgi-bin/main\" >\n"
            << "<BR>\n"
            << "<!-- now create the form -->\n"
            << "<P> <STRONG> SEND MAIL TO: </STRONG>\n"
            << "<SELECT NAME=\"mailto_name\" >\n"
            << "<OPTION SELECTED> Technical Support\n"
            << "<OPTION> Field Support\n"
            << "<OPTION> Product Support\n"
            << "<OPTION> Engineering\n"
            << "</SELECT>\n"
            << "<P> <STRONG> ENTER YOUR EMAIL ADRESS: </STRONG>\n"
            <<
            "<!-- Needed since mail has the cgi program address -->\n"
            << "<P> INPUT TYPE=\"emailad\" NAME=\"your_email\"" <<
                "VALUE=\"\" SIZE=60>\n"
            << "<P> <STRONG> ENTER MESSAGE: </STRONG> <P>\n"
            << "<TEXTAREA COLS=50 ROWS=6 NAME=\"message\" VALUE=\"\">\n"
            << "</TEXTAREA>\n"
            << "<P> <INPUT TYPE=\"submit\" VALUE=\"Mail Message\">" <<
                "<INPUT TYPE=\"reset\"> </FORM>\n"
            << "<P><H3>This Page Has Been Accessed " << counter <<
                "Times</H3><BR>\n"
            << "</BODY>\n"
            << "</HTML>\n";
    }
```

Finally, the main() program is created.

```
    /*
     * Type: C++ mail
     * Purpose: Combined use of IP addressing and mailer
     */
    #include <iosteam.h>
    #include <stdlib.h>
    #include <string.h>
    #include "cgi_defines.h"        // pick up all the defines from a file
    main()
    {
        IP_ADDRESS myIP;       // IP address class
```

```
    SEND_MAIL myMail;        // set up a _Send_mail class
    STANDARD Standard;       // create _Standard without start msg
    /*
     * Send out the initial HTML to the client
     */
    Standard.start_msg(GREY);
    Standard.color_head("Environment Program Match");


    /*
     * Check for a valid IP address
     */
    if(myIP.valid() == MATCH)
    {
         myMail.out();
    } else
    {
         // send the error HTML
         cout<<"<H2> Bad IP Address Message Not Sent</H2>\n";
    }

    Standard.end();
}
```

You should have noticed that there is still a need for a cgi-bin program to handle the output of the mailer. This could be a separate cgi-bin program or could use argc and argv[] to take the same program down a different pathway.

Having completed this section, you should be able to use the Get method by passing argc and argv into your program. You have also obtained the ability to use hidden variables to have the same cgi-bin program do different things. Finally, the server environmental variables can be used to send your program down different paths based on specific information known by the server. With all these options, it is apparent that the same cgi-bin program can provide multiple capabilities in a number of ways. Any or all of these may be used simultaneously in developing your cgi-bin program; this provides flexibility. Most important, the methods established in this chapter provide means to send status information from the HTML to your program. This is a very different capability from the conditional capabilities that exist within the C++ and C programs, and it establishes a method of communicating states between the HTML Internet programming language and the cgi-bin programming language. This method differs from the user defined states, since it is under complete control of the person developing the Web page. Later, in the Chess program (see Chapter 10), it will become evident that this can be a two-way path, with the cgi-bin program receiving information from the hidden variables in the submitted form and sending back status in the HTML message back to the client server. In this way continuity can be established between successive pages, allowing each user to have a uniquely defined state with each successive page. With these tools you are establishing the ground work for continuity between pages, which will be affected by the user's input and by previous states. This capability will enable you to create the two large programs, the Chess program and the Star Quilt program. In addition, it creates methods that should have far-reaching implications for the use of the Internet.

PROGRAM EXERCISES

1. Using the server environment, develop a cgi-bin program that sends Hello Internet World in one language if the method is Post and in another language if the method is Get. Using this methodology as a starting point, expand or rework the program to use the server environment. When you have finished, test your program in the following ways:
   - Start from a form (Post or Get method).
   - Start from an anchor (with or without arguments).
   - Start as a URL (with or without arguments).
2. Create a cgi-bin program that uses a hidden variable to branch in several different directions. Make the program work whether the method is Post or Get. (**Hint:** Use the environment to determine the method.)
3. Create a program that uses IP addresses to provide security. First create the program with hard coded IP addresses. Next alter the program so the IP addresses are read in from a file. Be sure that the IP address file is not in the cgi-bin area. (**Hint:** Watch the file permissions.)
4. Create a program that gets two arguments from argv[1] and argv[2]. The first argument is a string of letters A to Z. The second argument is whether to alphabetize them from A to Z or backward from Z to A. Verify that the program sends back to the browser and then to the user the correct response based on the arguments provided.

PROBLEMS

1. Explain as many methods as you can think of for providing alternative branches in a cgi-bin program. Include any that you think were missed in the text.
2. Create a test to determine the maximum length of a form variable for your system. Run the test and report your results.
3. Create a program that uses both stdin and argc, argv[] at the same time. Have the program produce different results depending on the values of both stdin and argv[]. Before testing, try to determine what will happen to your program if either value is missing. Come up with a way to make the values not be present. Test to validate your assumptions. If the result was not as expected, why not? Do anything needed to assure that there are error legs for these contingencies if they were not present.

Thru mode

The cgi-bin Thru Mode

The cgi-bin Thru mode[1] is a special capability that can only be provided through a cgi-bin program. You can think of it as a cgi-bin program that passes an HTML file out to the client server. As simple as this may sound at first, it will shortly become apparent that this is a powerful technique that will provide important flexibility in your development process.

We begin the development of this technique with a simple program. Interestingly, this program will look almost identical to one of the first programs we developed, in which a text file was read into a cgi-bin program. The major distinction is that the text file is in HTML format instead of normal ASCII text. This will mean that only the Content message will need to be added inside the program.

---

[1] Object-oriented purists may find the use of the name *Thru mode* offensive, but it seemed the best way to describe this capability.

Here is a simple program. First we have the HTML file:

```
<!- Comment: save as file.html -->
<HTML><HEAD><TITLE>THRU MODE</TITLE></HEAD>
<BODY>
<H1> This is a test of the THRU MODE </H1>
</BODY></HTML>
```

Now we have the cgi-bin program:

```
/*
 * Type C main
 * Purpose: demonstrate Thru mode
 */
#include <iostream.h>
#include <stdlib.h>
#define MY_HTML "unix_path/file.html"
void main()
{
    FILE* stream;
    char buffer[MAXLINE];
    printf("Content-type: text/html\n\n");
    stream = fopen ( MY_HTML, "r" );
    while(fgets ( buffer, MAXLINE, stream ) != EOF)
    {
        printf("%s", buffer) ;
    }
    fclose ( stream );
}
```

About this program. . . . .

1. The Content-type message is sent out to the client.
2. The HTML is then read into the cgi-bin program and sent back out to the client server.
3. The file is then closed.

. . . .

Name this file "my_program.c" and then compile the program:

```
cc -o my_program my_program.c
```

Now place the program in the cgi-bin and call it using the cgi-bin URL. The output will be the same as if you had used the original HTML directly as a URL—not very exciting. You may be thinking, why go to all this trouble when the same thing can be done with the HTML directly?

To understand just how powerful this program is, let's look at some things we have discovered so far. First let's review the process used for cgi-bin programs.

CGI Steps

1. Activate the cgi-bin program either directly with a URL or more frequently with a form.
2. Do the conditional and other software processing.
3. Do any mailing or other activities associated with the cgi-bin program.
4. Send the HTML back to the user.

An obvious first use of the Thru mode is in the fourth step. Instead of creating the HTML in the cgi-bin program using cout or printf, you can now create the final output as HTML and then put a Thru mode class or subroutine into your program. The advantage of this method is that you will not have to recompile every time you want to make a subtle change in the HTML output. All you will need to do is modify the HTML text. The second advantage is that you will also have the HTML page available in case you want to use it directly. For example, it may be the main entry to your Web pages that you wish to return your users to after the form is completed.

With all these initial gains in mind, let's develop the required Thru mode class.

```cpp
class _Thru_mode
{
private:
    FILE* stream;
    char buffer[90];
public:
    _Thru_mode(char* html); // use the constructor
};
#define THRU_MODE class _Thru_mode /* done for emphasis in text */
/*
 * Type C++ constructor
 * Purpose: demonstrate Thru mode
 * Input:
 *    char* htmlfile - pointer to file containing html
 */
_Thru_mode :: _Thru_mode(char* htmlfile)
{
    cout << "Content-type: text/html\n\n";
    stream = fopen ( htmlfile, "r" )
    while(fgets ( buffer, 80, stream ) != EOF)
    {
        cout << buffer ;
    }
```

```
        fclose ( stream );
    }
```

About the subroutine. . . . .

The only difference is that the subroutine is built into the constructor for the class
and the subroutine takes a string argument that points to any HTML file. Remember, the string must be a unix_path to the file since the server will be running the
program. The path must be complete (not relative) and is *not* a URL.

   With this subroutine you can now replace any sending of HTML with the Thru
mode class. All you have to do is instantiate the class, and the constructor does
the rest.

. . . .

Here is a simplified main() that uses the Thru mode class to send out HTML.

```
    /*
     * Type C++ main
     * Purpose: demonstrate Thru mode
     * Input:
     *    argc and argv[]
     */
    void main(int argc, char* argv[])
    {
        _Thru_mode* myThruMode;
        myThruMode = new (sizeof(class _Thru_mode))(argv[1]);
    }
```

To get a C version, change the initial program to a subroutine called
thru_mode and then create a main.

```
    /*
     * Type C subroutine
     * Purpose: create Thru mode
     * Input:      char* htmlfile - html file
     */
    void thru_mode(char* htmlfile)
    {
        FILE* stream;
        char buffer[80];
        printf("Content-type: text/html\n\n");
        if((stream = fopen ( htmlfile, "r" )) == 0)
        {
            /* do error recovery HTML */
            return;
        }
```

```
        while(fgets ( buffer, 80, stream ) != EOF)
        {
            printf("%s", buffer) ;
        }
        fclose ( stream );
    }
    /*
     * Type C main
     * Purpose: demonstrate Thru mode subroutine use
     * Input:
     *   argc and argv[]
     */
    void main(int argc, char* argv[])
    {
        thru_mode(argv[1]);
    }
```

About the main . . . .

Just call the Thru mode subroutine with argv[1] the path to your HTML file. For example, if the file is in /unix_path/file.html, then the URL to use the Thru mode would look like this:

```
URL="http://internet_path/cgibin/thru_mode_prog?/unix_path/file.html"
```

The thru_mode_prog is any of the Thru mode cgi programs. The argv[1] following the ? is the unix_path to the HTML file that will be sent out by the cgi-bin program.

You can send other files through the same subroutine by merely changing the part after the question mark (?). The Thru mode can be used in a wide variety of places. The most basic use is to call it directly. The second most basic is to use the cgi-bin program that uses the Thru mode as an HTML anchor.

Send the

```
<A HREF="http://internet_path/cgi-bin/thru_mode_program?/unix_path/file.html">
```

Thru mode </A> to the client server. Include this line on your favorite HTML page to make a hotlink to the cgi-bin program. In either of these cases, the Thru mode could send other data types out to the screen (see Figure 7.1). For example, the output could be PDF, PostScript, Framemaker or other document types. All that is required is that the type be an acceptable MIME type. (A MIME type is a file type that is acceptable to the client software. MIME types specified in the HyperText Transfer Protocol (HTTP) translate to content types in the cgi-bin programs). The other requirement is that the first line that sends the Content type to the server specify the correct type, as shown in the MIME types file.

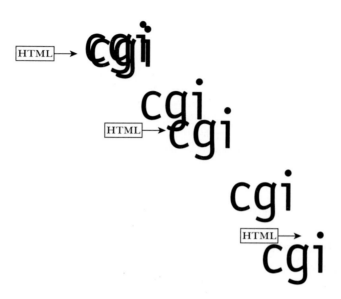

FIGURE 7.1   Thru mode: Combining HTML and compiled code provides quick turn around of changes with minimal effort.

Examples of PDF Files

HERE ARE SOME EXAMPLES THAT show a MIME type; the browser mailcap entry and the resulting content type message. MIME types are the designations for the messages sent through the HyperText Transfer Protocol (HTTP). If a helper application is required for the browser, an entry is placed in the mailcap file (UNIX only). The cgi-bin program send the required MIME type as a content type to stdout.

```
example .mime.types
application/x-acrobat pdf

example .mailcap
application/x-pdf;acroread %s

example C++ or C type line
printf("%s\n\n", "Content-type: text/pdf");
```

The PDF[a] file format supports document anchors and has become a standard for providing complex documentation across the Internet.

---

[a] The primary source for PDF tools and readers is Adobe, URL= http://www.adobe.com.

Comment Capability

IF THIS WERE ALL THAT the Thru mode could do, it would be enough. By providing this capability, it is now possible to segment work into HTML development and cgi-bin development. This will allow artists and layout people to go merrily on their way while the C++ and C programmers do their work. But this is not all that the Thru mode gives you. Having created this capability, it is now possible to place retrieval instruction inside the HTML. These can be done by putting coded comments inside the HTML text. A coded comment is a line in the HTML file that can be identified by a string search. The recommendation is to use HTML comment strings since this will allow the HTML file to be used independently of the cgi-bin program for certain parts of your application.

Recall that a comment in HTML has the format

```
<!- text of my comment -->
```

A simple C++ or C routine can easily be developed to read in the contents of the comment. It can then use this to put additional HTML information into the output to the client server. In this manner a second bridge is developed between the easily created HTML and the highly flexible cgi-bin program.

What can the cgi-bin program do when it deciphers the comment? There are limitless possibilities. It could provide a page counter. It could output some variable information from a file. It could provide a variable IMaGe (see Chapter 16). It could read a database and create a database table, and so on.

First develop the required classes and functions to decipher the comment. To make this generic, the routines will be built to have two arguments. The first will be a pointer to the line read in from the HTML. The second will be a pointer to the matching comment string being searched for in the HTML. The routine will return either a MATCH or NOMATCH. In the actual program body, if a MATCH occurs, the program will do something else, such as read some information from a file and then send it to the screen or send out an incremented counter.

```
class _Comment
{
private:
public:
    _Comment(){ ; };
    int check (char* html, char* comment);
};
/*
 * Type C++ class subroutine
 * Purpose: Check for a comment during a Thru mode
 *    char* html - html line
 *    char* comment - comment line being watched for
 */
int
```

```
_Comment :: check(
    char* html, // A line of HTML read in from the file
    char* comment // The comment being matched
)
{

    if(strcmp(html, comment) == 0) // do string & comment match
    {
        return MATCH;
    }
    return NOMATCH;

}
```

About the check subroutine. . . . .

The subroutine compares the line from the file with the expected comment. If they match, it returns MATCH; otherwise, it returns NOMATCH. The C subroutine looks almost identical. However, the class does have some real advantages. For example, by encapsulating in an object, it is possible to develop different comment types. Look at this modified class.

. . . .

```
#define COUNTER "<!-- counter -->
#define FILE "<!-- file -->
class _Comment
{
private:
    int check (char* html, char* comment);
public:
    _Comment(){ ; };
    int check_count(char* html)
        { return check(html, COUNTER); };
    int check_file(char* html, CNT)
        { return check(html, FILE); };

};
#define COMMENT class comment /* for readability in the text */
;
```

About the new _Comment class . . . .

Now the class provides a number of different subroutines that are specific to the kinds of comments expected. Additional subroutines could be built into the class regarding what to do for each of the comment types. The object approach continues to produce the preferred modularity.

Now you can re-create the THRU_MODE to inherit the Comment class and overload the constructor to use or not use the comment mode.

```
class _Thru_mode : public _Comment
{
private:
    FILE* stream;
    char buffer[90];
public:
    _Thru_mode(char* html);  // use the constructor
    _Thru_mode(char* html, char* comment); // use the constructor
};
/*
 * Type C++ constructor
 * Purpose: Combine Thru mode and check
 * Input:
 *   char* html - pointer to html file
 *   char* comment - pointer to comment to look for.
 */
_Thru_mode :: _Thru_mode(char* html, char* comment)
{
    cout << "Content-type: text/html\n\n";
    stream = fopen ( html, "r" )
    while(fgets ( buffer, 80, stream ) != EOF)
    {
        if(check(html, comment) == MATCH)
        {
            // Do comment stuff here
        } else
        {
            cout << buffer ;
        }
    }
    fclose ( stream );
}
```

Here is a typical main() to use the _Comment capability with the _Thru_mode.

```
/*
 * Type C++ main
 * Purpose: demonstrate Thru mode and Comment using constructor
 * Input:     argc and argv[]
 */
void main( int argc, char* argv[])
{
_Thru_mode myThruMode(argv[1], COUNTER);
            // let the constructor do it all
            ; // nothing left to do
}
```

The C version requires a modification of the Thru_mode subroutines to include the call to the comment subroutine.

```c
/*
 * Type C subroutine
 * Purpose: demonstrate Thru mode and Comment capability
 * Input:
 *    char* html - pointer to html line
 */
void thru_mode(char* html)
{
    /* read in the html */
    if(comment(html, COUNTER) == MATCH)
    {
        /* do comment stuff */
    } else
    {
        /* send out the html */
    }
}
/*
 * Type C main
 * Purpose: demonstrate Thru mode and Comment using argv[]
 */
void main( int argc, char* argv[])
{
    thru_mode(argv[1]);
}
```

The C++ again produces more modular code, even when object coding is forced onto the C code.

Sending Comment Messages

HAVING DEVELOPED THE COMMENT CAPABILITY, it is now possible to move one more step using the Thru mode. Since many of the more complex examples require sending back HTML, why not replace the comment section with a comment that includes instructions for the next input from the user? This would allow us to use comments in much the same way as hidden variables. The string check would have to be a little more intelligent since the comment string would be made up of a fixed part and a variable part. The comment would look something like this:

```
<!-- FIXED STRING -- VARIABLE STRING -->
```

Now the comment routine would have to look for a string match of

```
"<!-- FIXED STRING -- "
```

Then, instead of returning MATCH or NOMATCH, it would return a pointer to the variable string. If NOMATCH is found, a null pointer of zero (0) will be returned. Here is a routine that provides this capability:

```c
/*
 * Type C subroutine
 * Purpose: comment with pointer to variable string
 * Input:      char* html - pointer to html line
 *             char* fixed_string - pointer to string to match on
 * Output:     char* - pointer to variable part of the comment line
 */
char* comment( char* html, char* fixed_string)
{
    char* return_ptr;
    int i=0;
    if( strncmp( html, fixed_string, strlen(fixed_string)) != 0)
    {
        return NOMATCH; /* no match return the null pointer */
    } else
    {
        /*
         * Set the return pointer to the start of the variable string
         */
        return_ptr = html + strlen(fixed_string) + 1;
        /* now null terminate the end of the variable string */
        while (strncmp((return_ptr + i), "-->", 3) != 0)
        /*
         * You could add a safety check here in case someone forgets the end of comment
         * string
         */
        {
            i++;
        } else
        {
            *(return_ptr + i)=NULL; /* terminate */
        }
        return return_ptr;
    }
}
```

If the comment string looks like

```
<!-- chess location -- a1b1a1c1a1c3 -->
```

then the call

```
comment(html, "<!-- chess location -- ");
```

will return a pointer to the variable string

```
"a1b1a1c1a1c3"
```

In C++ you could overload this function and have two versions of the same subroutine. In either case, you can now use comments for message passing between HTML Thru mode pages.

Back Button

HERE IS ANOTHER UNIQUE use of Thru mode. The objective is to create a button that will take you back to either of three previous Web pages depending on which one you started from when you accessed the present Web page.

```
/*
 * Type C main
 * Purpose: back button using Thru mode
 */
void
main(int argc, char* argv[])
{
    FILE* stream;
    char buffer[MAXLINE];
    char out_msg[MAXLINE];
    if(argc < 3) /* program name and two arguments */
    {
        /* error path */
    }
    printf("Content-type: html/text\n\n");
    /*
     * argv[1] is the unix path to the HTML output file
     */
    stream = fopen(clear_hex(out_msg,argv[1]), "r");
    while(fgets(buffer, MAXLINE, stream) !=0)
    {
    /*
```

```
 * If the HTML comment is found on a line, the value of argv[2] replaces it in an HTML
 * anchor. The string in argv[2] is an internet (URL) for the go back anchor
 */
    if((strncmp(buffer, "<!- Anchor -->", 10) ==0))
    {
        printf("%s%s%s\n",
                "<A HREF=\"",
                clear_hex(out_msg, argv[2]),
                "\"> Previous Page ></A>\n");
    } else
    {
        puts(buffer);
    }
  }
}
```

On each of the HTML pages, the anchor to go to this new Web page will look like this:

```
<A HREF=
"internet_path/cgi-bin/return_cgi?to_unix_path_to_nextpage+go_back_to_url" > your text</
A> to go forward to the next page.
```

The go_back_to_url is the URL for the Web page where the anchor is located. The to_unix_path_to_nextpage is the path to the HTML file that will be sent back to the user. It must contain a line with the comment:

```
<!- Anchor -->
```

When that line is read in, the line will be replaced with an anchor back to the originating page, which was sent as a URL in argv[2]. The Web page that this is placed onto is located by the cgi-bin program using the UNIX path to the HTML file. The path is sent to the cgi-bin program in argv[1]. The cgi-bin program is invoked when the initial anchor is clicked using the mouse. The value of argv[1] follows the ? which acts as a space when the cgi-bin program is invoked. The argv[2] follows the +, which acts as the second space when the cgi-bin program is invoked.

The Thru mode can be used for a wide variety of applications. Decorative fonts created with GIF files can be sent out in response to Comment messages; file types can be sent in the comments. By using the Thru mode, it becomes possible to increase the degree of customizing done for users.[2]

In Chapter 16, on IMaGes, other examples of the use of Thru mode will become apparent. One of the most useful is providing different HTML Web pages from IMaGe forms that send back cursor x and y coordinate information. The Thru mode and its companion comment messaging add another powerful enhancement to the cgi-bin library of tools.

In this chapter, you have learned how to use one of the most powerful capabilities available with compiled program, the Thru mode. You have learned how to pass HTML files out of a cgi-bin program, and you have learned how to send messages to the cgi-bin program to do additional actions while passing the file through to the client-server software. You have also learned that the file read in and sent out during the Thru mode can reside anywhere accessible to the server. This means that it can be a visible HTML file (one that is viewable directly as HTML) or a hidden file (one that is located in a UNIX directory not available via a URL but accessible by the server software).

PROGRAM EXERCISES

1. The HTML I/O station or Thru mode provides the following services:
   - Reads in HTML (or other MIME types)
   - Checks for critical information in the input stream
   - Alters the data stream per requirements
   - Sends the data back out to the browser

   With these guidelines, create a class that provides these services. Develop it in a way that will allow usage in a wide variety of applications. Place the class definitions in an .h file. Place the function definitions in a .c file. Compile to obtain an .o file. Now create a main to use the newly created class. Compile the main along with the .o file to produce a cgi-bin executable. Verify the expected functionality.

2. Using the comment capability that is part of the Thru mode, create a program that replaces a comment line with an IMaGe. Do it in such a way that the image can be changed easily. Show that you can change the image output by changing the comment line. Add fields to the comment to include the height and width of the image.

3. Create a program that uses case statements or their equivalent to read in a comment and output different types of information based on the comment. Some alternatives are as follows:
   - Include the name of a text file that will be used as part of the HTML. (See Chapter 2 on file I/O.)
   - Include multimedia, such as audio or film based on the comment.
   - Use the comment to perform an action, such as setting the header size.

4. Develop a program that provides a count of the number of times your Web page has been accessed using the Thru mode.

---

[2]   Today when a person searches for "rockets" on the Internet, he or she can get anything back from information about model rockets to advanced physics. But why shouldn't the next generation of the Internet have the capability to take input about the level of a person's background and then decide which information should be sent back? With the intelligent use of cgi-bin programming, including the Thru mode capability, this is a realistic objective for the future.

PROBLEMS

1. Explain some of the stated reasons for providing the Thru mode. What other possible uses can you think of for this capability? When would it be better to use the Thru mode as opposed to the direct output of HTML from the cgi-bin program?

2. What are the path level concerns for the Thru mode? Explain how you might use the Thru mode for other MIME types, such as PDF files. Explain the difference between the Thru mode and the earlier file I/O. Are there instances when both can be used in the same program?

3. Create a list of the different kinds of information that could be used with the comment mode. For each item in the list, give an example (at a descriptive level) of a program that could use this capability.

4. Explain how a comment is placed onto an HTML page. Explain the steps in reading in the HTML page using the Thru mode. Explain how a comment is parsed out of an HTML page during the Thru mode and then replaced with alternative HTML. What must be added by the cgi-bin besides the changes to the comment string?

5. If the Thru mode is used for information other than HTML, for example PDF, what other changes are required to the cgi-bin program? Why? What will need to be present for the browser if these alternative types are used?

6. Make a list of some of the various enhancements the comment mode could provide when used in conjunction with the Thru mode. Include two types of lists—one that is general, such as "name of the image," and one that is specific to your field, such as "The software percentage completed on the xyz project."

8

Tables

Basics of Tables
An HTML Table
Generating a Table from an Equation
Unformatted Output

Basics of Tables

ONE OF THE EXCITING CAPABILITIES available in HTML is the ability to define tables.[1] A *table* is a row-and-column-formatted HTML Web page. It includes a number of ways to add titles and to manipulate the row and column structure. Furthermore, the table can contain active links to other documents and images. Because of these factors, cgi-bin programs can add important capabilities to table generation. Since the generation of an HTML document can be based on data or instructions in flat files or other input data obtained from the computer, it is possible to have the table continuously updated with respect to the data they contain. Furthermore, they can grow in size as new data become available. The use of dynamic links or anchors can make it possible to link the items in a table to actual related documents or to link the table headings to other related tables or other associated information. Tables, like other HTML, can also be generated using the Thru mode and comment capability explained in Chapter 7.

We begin by reviewing the basics of HTML table generation. Then we show how to create the same basic table using C++ and C. Next dynamic input is added to our table cgi-bin program, and then dynamic linking. Finally, some advanced table capabilities are demonstrated.

---

[1]   Tables are not available for all browsers.

An HTML Table

IN HTML A TABLE CONSISTS of the standard beginning and ending information, with some table elements in the body of the document. Here is an example of a simple HTML table:

```
<HTML> <HEAD> <TITLE> TABLE 1 </TITLE></HEAD>
<BODY> <H1> TABLE 1 </H1>
<TABLE BORDER=5 CELLPADDING=8>
<CAPTION>PROJECT RESULTS IN Millions of Units</CAPTION>
<TR><TD></TD><TD>CHINA</TD><TD>JAPAN</TD><TD>CANADA</TD>
<TR><TD>1995</TD><TD>15.2</TD><TD>12.2</TD>
<TD>1.6</TD>
<TR><TD>1994</TD><TD>14.2</TD><TD>27.4</TD>
<TD>1.7</TD>
<TR><TD>1993</TD><TD>11.1</TD><TD>20.7</TD>
<TD>2.5</TD>
<TR><TD>1992</TD><TD>15.8</TD><TD>16.4</TD>
<TD>2.7</TD>
<TR><TD>1991</TD><TD>12.6</TD><TD>19.0</TD>
<TD>2.1</TD>
<TR><TD>1990</TD><TD>10.5</TD><TD>12.7</TD>
<TD>2.3</TD>
</TABLE>
</BODY>
</HTML>
```

The table begins with the directions for laying out the table:

```
<TABLE BORDER=5 CELLPADDING=8>
```

The border and cellpadding directives tell how to space the items in the table. This is followed by table cells:

```
<TR><TD>1990</TD><TD>10.5</TD><TD>12.7</TD>
```

    <TR><TD> starts a new row.
    <TD> starts a new column cell on the present row.
    Finally, the table is ended:

```
</TABLE>
```

The rest is standard starting and ending HTML.

While the preceding example will result in a nice-looking table, it will probably be looked at once and then forgotten. But what if it could read the data in on the fly and have some program running from a shell program or a *crontab* that would update the data at regular intervals? Now the topic or content reported could change daily or even hourly. The table could generate a stock report page that would have current prices on stocks or a weather page with present weather conditions. It could put up the locations of marketing people or provide updated schedules.

Generating a Table from an Equation

THE NEXT PROGRAM USES an equation to generate the table from the cgi-bin program. It outputs the payments for an investment. Figure 8.1 shows a matrix equation being used to generate a table.

<Table>

<TR><TD>

$$\Psi \int_I^N 3x = 1$$

<TD>

$$\begin{bmatrix} I & -1 & 9 \\ 0 & J & 1 \\ 1 & -1 & K \end{bmatrix}$$

</TABLE>

FIGURE 8.1   Tables: Equations, tables, and cgi-bin programs combine to produce formatted data.

```
/*
 * Type C main
 * Purpose: demonstrate equation from to a table
 */
void main()
{
    FILE *fp;
    char buffer[40];
    int i = 0;
    float rate;
```

```
float balance;
float payments;
float interest;
rate = .08;
balance = 80;
payments = 9;
printf("Content-type: text/html\n\n");
printf("%s%s",
    "<HTML><HEAD><TITLE>Equation</TITLE>\n",
    "</HEAD><BODY>\n");
printf("%s\n%s\n%s\n%s\n",
    "<H1>COMPOUND INVESTMENT PROBLEM </H1>",
    "<H2>Balance = $80</H2>",
    "<H2>Interest = 8%</H2>",
    "<H2>Payments = 9</H2>");
fp=popen("date", "r");
fgets(buffer, 80, fp);
printf("%s<BR>\n", buffer);
fclose(fp);
/* Equation */
printf("%s%s%s",
    "<TABLE BORDER>\n",
    "<TH> Balance </TH>\n",
    "<TH> Interest </TH>\n"
);
for(i=1 ; i<= payments; i++)
{
    printf("<TR><TD> ");
    interest = balance * rate;
    printf("%3.2f</TD>\n", balance);
    printf("<TD> ");
    printf("%3.2f</TD>\n", interest);
    balance = balance + interest;
}
printf("</TABLE>\n");
printf("</BODY></HTML>\n");
}
```

About the Program

The program calculates the interest on an investment over a given period. The balance and interest are put onto a table along with the other needed HTML.

The HTML output looks like this:

```
Content-type: text/html
<HTML><HEAD><TITLE>Equation</TITLE>
</HEAD><BODY>
<H1>COMPOUND INVESTMENT PROBLEM </H1>
<H2>Balance = $80</H2>
<H2>Interest = 8%</H2>
<H2>Payments = 9</H2>
Wed Feb 28 15:48:03 MST 1996
<BR>
<TABLE BORDER>
<TH> Balance </TH>
<TH> Interest </TH>
<TR><TD> 80.00</TD>
<TD> 6.40</TD>
<TR><TD> 86.40</TD>
<TD> 6.91</TD>
<TR><TD> 93.31</TD>
<TD> 7.46</TD>
<TR><TD> 100.78</TD>
<TD> 8.06</TD>
<TR><TD> 108.84</TD>
<TD> 8.71</TD>
<TR><TD> 117.55</TD>
<TD> 9.40</TD>
<TR><TD> 126.95</TD>
<TD> 10.16</TD>
<TR><TD> 137.11</TD>
<TD> 10.97</TD>
<TR><TD> 148.07</TD>
<TD> 11.85</TD>
</TABLE>
</BODY></HTML>
```

By adding form input, it would be possible to allow the user to input the amount, interest, payments, etc.

Unformatted Output

THE NEXT PROGRAM IS a calendar keeper. It uses the HTML PRE to output unformatted calendar information. The HTML <PRE> operator allows raw text to be output on a Web page. Since it may be of use to a number of people, the example is a basic calendar program. This is a great program for people who need to let others know when they will and will not be available. If it is built correctly, it should be possible to put it in a central place and use a hidden variable to tell where the flat file is located. This will mean that the same program will be usable by multiple people.

```
class Calendar : Public _Standard
{
char* calendar_file;
File* stream;
public:
    Calendar(){ ; };
    void select();
    void show(char* calendar_file);
};
/*
 * Type C++ class subroutine
 * Purpose: Initial calendar HTML
 */
void
Calendar.select()
{
    start_msg();
    color_head("MARK FELTON'S CALENDAR");
    cout<< "<FORM ACTION= <<
        "\"http://mycgi_directory/cgi-bin/main?/markf/calendar\" >\n"
        <<"<P> SELECT NAME=\"dayofweek\">\n"
        << "<OPTION> MONDAY</OPTION>\n"
        << "<OPTION> TUESDAY</OPTION>\n"
        << "<OPTION> WEDNESDAY</OPTION>\n"
        << "<OPTION> THURSDAY</OPTION>\n"
        << "<OPTION> FRIDAY</OPTION>\n"
        << "</SELECT>\n"
        << "<P> <INPUT TYPE=\"submit\" VALUE=\"NULL\"> </FORM>\n";
    end();
}
```

Since you want multiple people to be able to use the program, you will also need a standard HTML version. All they will have to do is modify the VALUE field and keep the flat file up to date. With a little luck, someone may find that there is a standard calendar program that creates the needed flat file. Then all that will be necessary is modification of the cgi-bin program to work with the format of the canned flat file.

```
<FORM ACTION=
"http://mycgi_directory/cgi-bin/main?/markf/calendar" >
```

```
<P> <SELECT NAME="dayofweek">
<OPTION> MONDAY</OPTION>
<OPTION> TUESDAY</OPTION>
<OPTION> WEDNESDAY</OPTION>
<OPTION> THURSDAY</OPTION>
<OPTION> FRIDAY</OPTION>
</SELECT>
<P> <INPUT TYPE="submit" VALUE="NULL"> </FORM>
</BODY> </HTML>
```

Now create the flat file in the form

```
DATE DAY TIME "EVENT"
DATE DAY TIME "EVENT"
```

Here is a typical calendar flat file:

```
10/16 MON 08:00 "Meeting with Joe"
10/16 MON 08:20 "Programming project"
10/16 MON 09:30 "Analyzer Meeting"
10/16 MON 11:00 "Lunch Meeting with Raghu"
10/16 MON 12:00 "Off for an hour"
10/16 MON 13:00 "2 HOURS OF LAB"
10/16 MON 15:00 "Work on Design"
```

Finally, create the response cgi-bin program:

```cpp
/*
 * Type C++ class subroutine
 * Purpose: show the calendar
 * Input:      char* calendar_file - pointer to calendar information file
 */
// First the subroutine
void Calendar::show(char* calendar_file)
{
    char msg[MAXLINE];
    /* get the hidden variables */
    cout<< "<H1> Schedule For The Week </H1>\n";
    cout << "\n<PRE>";
    stream = fopen(calendar_file, "r");
    while(fgets(msg,90,stream) !=0)
    {
        /* check against the hiddens */
        if (date and day from hiddens)
```

```
            cout<<msg;
        }
        cout << "</PRE>\n";
        fclose(stream);
    }
```

The C version

```
/*
 * Type C subroutine
 * Purpose: show the calendar
 * Input:     char* calendar_file - pointer to calendar information file
 */
void show(calendar_file)
char* calendar_file
{
    FILE* fp;
    char msg[MAXLINE];
    /* Retrieve hidden variables */
    ...
    printf("<H1> Schedule For The Week </H1>\n");
    printf("\n<PRE>");
    fp = fopen(calendar_file, "r");
    while(fgets(msg, 90, fp) !=0)
    {
        /* check against the hiddens */
        if (date and day from hiddens)
            printf("%s", msg);
    }
    printf("</PRE>\n");
    fclose(fp);
}
```

The C++ main program

```
/*
 * Type C++ main
 * Purpose: show the calendar
 * Input:     argc and argv[]
 */
main(int argc, char* argv[])
{
    Calendar myCalendar;
    myCalendar.show(argv[1]);
}
```

The same program in C

```
/*
 * Type C main
 * Purpose: show the calendar
 * Input:
 *    argc and argv[]
 */
main(int argc, char* argv[])
{
    show(argv[1]);
}
```

Once compiled, rename the program mycalendar_file and place it in the cgi-bin. It can now be called with

```
URL="http://path/cgi-bin/main?mycalendar_file"
```

In this chapter you learned how to provide table output from your cgi-bin program. Tables are an excellent way to organize data being provided on Web pages. By adding cgi-bin capability, you can provide increased flexibility, which allows presented information to change on a regular basis. Finally, you learned how to create unformatted output with <PRE>.

PROGRAM EXERCISES

1. Create a cgi-bin program that outputs a table based on information in a flat file. The flat file should be field based, with each field representing an item in the table. For example, a list of products would include

   ```
   product_name quantity_available cost markup
   ```

   Demonstrate the program and verify that it is operational from a browser.
2. Create an equation table that takes at least three inputs based from a form. Using these data, generate a table. (**Hint:** One approach is to use two of the inputs as start and end points to provide a range. The additional value[s] can be an actual part of the equation used to generate the table.)
3. Use the Thru mode (see Chapter 7) to generate a table based on the comment field in the HTML. Include at least one equation as part of the algorithm. Use the comment as input to the equation.

PROBLEMS

1. A table is a way to format output. Describe in as much detail as possible some of the kinds of information that will most benefit from this kind of formatted output. Include examples that contain anchors, graphics, or other media as part of the table.

2. Considering your own field of expertise, how might the ability to provide equation-based output benefit your needs to present data effectively? Demming, the famed statistician, equated quality with the ability to make measurements and improvements based on the data. How might your processes be enhanced by presenting measurements in tabular format across the Internet? What kind of organizational feedback could you provide through this methodology?

3. Many actuarial practices, such as accounting and engineering, use tables of data for their work. Give some examples of approaches to these kinds of data that might benefit from Internet-based tables. How could ranging be included as part of the output? How could tables and forms be combined effectively? Give examples of some projects that would benefit from combining the two.

4. Explain the purpose of each of the following:

        <TR>
        <TD>

9

Buttons and Questionnaires

More on Forms

Types of Buttons

Creating a Questionnaire

More on Forms

WHEN CREATING YOUR FORMS, you will want to provide variety. There are many ways to accomplish this, including the use of good art work, the combining of different techniques, and the use of the different kinds of form formatting elements provided from HTML.

Types of Buttons

IN CREATING FORMS, it is important to understand how buttons and other inputs will be displayed. Buttons and inputs provide the interface to the users. Proper use of the different input types can be critical in the layout and development of your Web page. The following types of buttons and other input fields are presently supported by HTML:

- **Option or Drop Down List** This provides a choice to the user of a pull-down list of options. Only the presently selected choice is shown until the down arrow is pressed or the mouse pulled over the drop-down area. The user may select only one of the optional choices provided. When the form is submitted, the user choice is sent to the cgi-bin program along with the name of the

153

variable that identifies the choice. The input information will be included in the string sent to the server in the format

    variable_name=option_choice

- **Checkboxes**   A checkbox consists of a square box that can be clicked on or off. Normally a checkbox will be preceded by text or other identifying information to tell the user what checking the box indicates. The user clicks on the particular checkbox to select it. Once selected, the user can deselect by clicking again. While checkboxes default to off (or unchecked), it is possible to have them originally show up as selected or checked. The user can select multiple checkboxes since each checkbox is unique. A variable name is used to identify each of the checkboxes. While there is nothing to stop you from using the same variable name for multiple checkboxes, doing so will rarely serve any purpose. If this were done, the cgi-bin program would have to separate the different answers by sequentially moving through the input string and finding each occurrence of the variable. Since it is much easier to write subroutines to separate out different variables, this is the suggested technique. Unlike other input types, only the checkboxes selected are sent after the user submit. Any unchecked boxes will not appear in the input string. While each checkbox can have a value that is sent, this may be redundant information for many applications since the only concern is if the box is checked or not. The format for the information sent from a checkbox is as follows:

    variable_name=check_box_value

- **Radio Buttons**   These buttons are usually done in groups. A radio button can be used in a manner similar to the option list mentioned earlier. The main difference is that all options are simultaneously visible to the user. A group of radio buttons will all have the same variable name, so when the user selects one, any previously selected ones with the same name are deselected. The choices grouped under the same name are mutually exclusive. Only the one checked is sent after the submit. However, unlike the checkbox, there will normally be one and only one radio button sent. While it is normal to provide one of the choices as the default selection, it is possible to begin with none of the choices selected. If the user leaves none of the choices selected, then none are sent.

- **Default Text**   There are also two types of text areas. If a form input type is specified with a type that is not part of the standard HTML choices, it defaults to a text field. When this is done, a SIZE=number should be included to define the number of characters allowed in the field.

- **Text Area**   The second type of text area is specified as text. This text field also includes the number of rows and columns. The user sees a large text box, which includes the specified rows and columns. The text box has a variable name. A user can move around inside the text box using arrow keys, the mouse, or standard character input. The text box is sent along with the rest of the input in the format

```
variable_name=text_string
```

The text string will consist of a string of ASCII characters separated by control characters. These include spaces, returns, tabs, etc. The punctuation and control characters are represented by a % followed by the hexadecimal value of the control character. Here is a partial list of the more common punctuation and control characters (see also back page).

- %20 -> space
- %0D -> carriage return (usually implies line feed also)
- %0A -> line feed

■ **Text Type**   A text type is a single row of text. The user can navigate with arrows, tabs, etc. The entire text type is sent out as a single continuous string variable.

■ **Password Type**   This is similar to the default text type except that the user's input will not appear on the screen when it is typed in; instead the screen will show an asterisk (*) each time a character is entered. Because much of the Internet was not established with high levels of security, care should be taken in the use of the Password Type.

There are two other buttons that will appear for all forms that use buttons:

■ **Submit Type**   This allows the user to submit the form to the cgi-bin program.

■ **Reset Type**   This allows the user to reset all the input fields back to their original values.

Buttons can be created with standard HTML, or they can be sent as HTML output from a cgi-bin program. The following is a simple button class with subroutines to provide the different button and input types. This class can be used to create any requested button. A comment is included in each subroutine to show the equivalent HTML.

```
class _Button
{
Public:
    _Button(){ ; };
    virtual void option(
     char* first_option, char* second_option, ...);
    virtual void check_box(char* text, char* variable_name);
    virtual void radio(
     char* variable_name, char* first_text, char* first_value,
         char* second_text, char* second_value, ...);
    virtual void default_text(
         char* text, char* type, char* variable_name);
```

```
            virtual void text_area(char* text, char* rows, char* columns);
            virtual void password(char* text, char* variable_name);
        };
        /*
         * Type C++ class subroutine
         * Purpose: create an option button
         * Input:      char* name - pointer to the name of the button
         *             char* selected - pointer to the item to make selected
         *             char* ... - varargs of the options
         */
        #include <iostream.h>
        #include <stdarg.h>
        void _Button::option
            (char* name, int selected, int n, char* option1, ...)
        {
            va_list arg_ptr;
            char *entry;
            int i;
            cout << "<SELECTED NAME=" << name << ">\n";

            /*
             * va_... allows a variable number of arguments to be sent to the subroutine
             */
            va_start(arg_ptr, n);
            for( i=1; i <= n; i++)
            {
                entry = va_arg(arg_ptr, char *); // get an entry
                cout << "<OPTION " <<
                    (i==selected) ? "SELECTED>" : ">" <<
                    entry;
            }
            va_end(arg_ptr);
            cout << "</SELECTED>\n";
        }
```

About Option ·

1. This subroutine uses the vararg capability. The routine is sent a name, which is the name of the variable. The next argument is an int that tells which of the items is to be selected. The next integer tells how many option fields there are. Finally, there is the actual text for the option fields.

2. The start of the options is sent out first and includes the name field. This is followed by a variable argument routine, which reads in the option text one at a time. HTML is created around the text to provide the option button. If the argument count is equal to the select counter, an additional string is sent showing that this item is to be selected initially. In HTML, this will cause the

selected button to be the one that shows on the screen initially. Others are obtained through a pull-down menu. When all the options texts are exhausted, the end of the options button is sent out to stdout. Option buttons are excellent when there are lots of choices since the pull-down menu will show the selected item. The option button can include an extra field called size. When size is included along with a count, the value of the count will determine how many of the option choices are shown in the default state prior to using the pull-down menu. The mouse-activated pull-down will show the other available options. One other field that can be added is multiple. If this is present, more than one option can be selected.

```
/*
 * Type C++ class subroutine
 * Purpose: create an checkbox
 * Input:      char* name - pointer to the name of the button
 *             char* value - pointer to the default value
 *             int checked - initially checked or not
 */
void _Button::checkbox(
     char* name, /* variable name */
     char* value, /* value of the variable */
     char* text, /* associated text */
     int checked /* checked or not initially */
     )
{
     cout << "<INPUT TYPE=\"checkbox\" NAME=" <<
          name <<
          "VALUE=\"" <<
          value <<
          "\"" <<
          (checked == YES) ? "CHECKED >": " >" <<
          text << "\n";
}
```

With checkboxes, each one is standalone, so you can select as many as you want.

```
/*
 * Type C++ class subroutine
 * Purpose: create a radio button
 * Input:
 *    char* name - pointer to the name of the button
 *    char* value - pointer to the default value
 *    int checked - initially yes or no
 *    char* text - text to show user
 */
void _Button::radio(
```

```
    char* name, /* name of the variable */
    char* value, /* value of the variable if checked */
    int checked, /* initially checked YES or NO */
    char* text /* visible text for the user */
    )
{
    cout << "<INPUT TYPE=\"radio\" NAME=" <<
        name <<
        "VALUE=\"" <<
        value <<
        "\"" <<
        (checked == YES) ? "CHECKED >": " >" <<
        text << "\n";

}
```

With radio buttons, any that have the same name are considered the same button, and only one can be checked with the specific name. If another is checked with the same name, the original will automatically be reset.

```
/*
 * Type C++ class subroutine
 */
void
_Button::text(
    char* text, /* text associated with the button */
    char* name,/* name of the button */
    char* value,/* initial default string for button */
    int size   /* number of text characters allowed */
)
{
    cout << text <<
        "<INPUT TYPE=\"text\" NAME=" <<
        name <<
        "VALUE=\"" <<
        value <<
        "\" SIZE=\"" <<
        size << "\">\n"

}
```

The text button is a single-line text entry field:

```
/*
 * Type C++ class subroutine
 */
```

```
void
_Button::textarea(
    char* text,          /* text associated with the button */
    char* name,          /* name of the button */
    int rows,            /* number of text character rows */
    int columns          /* number of text character columns */
)
{
    cout << text <<
        "<INPUT TYPE=\"textarea\" NAME=" <<
        name <<
        "\" ROWS=\"" <<
        rows << "\""
        " COLUMNS=\"" <<
        columns << "\">\n";
}
/*
 * Type C++ class subroutine
 */
void
_Button::submit_reset(
    char* name
)
{
    cout << "<INPUT TYPE=\"submit\" VALUE=\"" <<
        name << "\">" <<
        "<INPUT TYPE=\"reset\">";
}
```

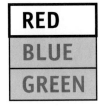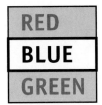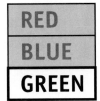

FIGURE 9.1   Buttons: the cgi-bin program provides direct control over the form control GUI devices.

Creating a Questionnaire

ONE OF THE MAJOR ADVANTAGES of the Internet is its ease of access. Many companies use questionnaires to do both internal and external analysis. One of the most frequent problems with questionnaires is lack of response. By providing an on-line questionnaire, the users receive an easier access than is normally available. Furthermore, the questionnaire will not be lost in the avalanche of papers that frequently arrive daily in many offices. As will be seen, the use of Internet questionnaires also provides some unique capabilities.

An immediate concern may be how to provide anonymity. Many questionnaires are done with the assurance that the person will not be identified. Fortunately, the Internet can do the same thing. Since any material obtained will come from the server, not from the individual's login or ID, the person will only be identified if he or she chooses to fill in a name field or other identification fields. Even if the form is mailed to a particular user, it will come from the server, not from the individual who filled out the questionnaire.

With this foundation, let's begin with a simple questionnaire in HTML that sends output to a cgi-bin program.

```
<HTML><HEAD>
<TITLE>Questionnaire Page</TITLE>
<link rev=made href="mailto:markf@xyz.com">
</HEAD>
<BODY bgcolor=#f0cfc0 </BODY>
<BODY>
<H1> INTERNET QUESTIONNAIRE </H1>
<BR>
<FORM ACTION="http://internet_path/cgi-bin/questionaire?-p1"METHOD=post >
<H4> CHECK ONE </H4>
<BR>I Find the Internet Home Pages Useful <BR>
<INPUT TYPE="radio" NAME="Q1" VALUE="SA"> Strongly Agree
<INPUT TYPE="radio" NAME="Q1" VALUE="A"> Agree
<INPUT TYPE="radio" NAME="Q1" VALUE="D"> Disagree
<INPUT TYPE="radio" NAME="Q1" VALUE="SD"> Strongly Disagree
<INPUT TYPE="radio" NAME="Q1" VALUE="U"> Undecided
<BR>The Internet Home Pages Are Easy To Use <BR>
<INPUT TYPE="radio" NAME="Q2" VALUE="SA"> Strongly Agree
<INPUT TYPE="radio" NAME="Q2" VALUE="A"> Agree
<INPUT TYPE="radio" NAME="Q2" VALUE="D"> Disagree
<INPUT TYPE="radio" NAME="Q2" VALUE="SD"> Strongly Disagree
<INPUT TYPE="radio" NAME="Q2" VALUE="U"> Undecided
<BR>The Internet Home Pages Contain Information That Helps Me Get My Job Done <BR>
<INPUT TYPE="radio" NAME="Q3" VALUE="SA"> Strongly Agree
<INPUT TYPE="radio" NAME="Q3" VALUE="A"> Agree
<INPUT TYPE="radio" NAME="Q3" VALUE="D"> Disagree
<INPUT TYPE="radio" NAME="Q3" VALUE="SD"> Strongly Disagree
<INPUT TYPE="radio" NAME="Q3" VALUE="U"> Undecided
```

```
<BR>The Internet Home Pages Are Well Organized <BR>
<INPUT TYPE="radio" NAME="Q4" VALUE="SA"> Strongly Agree
<INPUT TYPE="radio" NAME="Q4" VALUE="A"> Agree
<INPUT TYPE="radio" NAME="Q4" VALUE="D"> Disagree
<INPUT TYPE="radio" NAME="Q4" VALUE="SD"> Strongly Disagree
<INPUT TYPE="radio" NAME="Q4" VALUE="U"> Undecided
<BR>The Internet Home Page Search Tools Are Useful<BR>
<INPUT TYPE="radio" NAME="Q5" VALUE="SA"> Strongly Agree
<INPUT TYPE="radio" NAME="Q5" VALUE="A"> Agree
<INPUT TYPE="radio" NAME="Q5" VALUE="D"> Disagree
<INPUT TYPE="radio" NAME="Q5" VALUE="SD"> Strongly Disagree
<INPUT TYPE="radio" NAME="Q5" VALUE="U"> Undecided
<H4> CHECK ANY THAT APPLY </H4>
<BR>I Use the Internet Home Page <BR>
<INPUT TYPE="checkbox" NAME="ch1_1">AT WORK
<INPUT TYPE="checkbox" NAME="ch1_2">AT HOME
<INPUT TYPE="checkbox" NAME="ch1_3">OTHER
<BR>I Use the Following Pages <BR>
<INPUT TYPE="checkbox" NAME="ch2_1">Project & Management
<INPUT TYPE="checkbox" NAME="ch2_2">Lab Resources
<INPUT TYPE="checkbox" NAME="ch2_3">OS
<INPUT TYPE="checkbox" NAME="ch2_4">Tools<BR>
<INPUT TYPE="checkbox" NAME="ch2_5">Training
<INPUT TYPE="checkbox" NAME="ch2_6">Affirmative Action
<INPUT TYPE="checkbox" NAME="ch2_7">Other
<INPUT TYPE="submit" VALUE="submit">
<INPUT TYPE="reset" VALUE="reset">
</FORM>
</BODY>
</HTML>
```

The cgi-bin program can be a simple mailing program that sends the responses to someone for collating. It could also place the responses into a file.

Here is the output from this file when it is sent out from a mailer after being passed through the cleanup routines.

```
From: wwwexe@drmail.dr.com <wwwexe@drmail.dr.com
Q1=A
Q2=A
Q3=A
Q4=A
Q5=A
ch1_1=on
```

```
ch1_2=on
ch2_1=on
ch2_2=on
SEND=SEND
```

> **Note: The sender is wwwexe which is the World Wide Web Server, not the user's ID. The final variable "SEND" is added to show a submit occurred.**

In a more advanced questionnaire, additional cgi-bin capabilities could be added to the initial questionnaire part that is presented to the user.

1. The first page could be sent out followed by a second page of questions. This would be done by using argv[] to keep track of which section of the questionnaire has been answered. This technique is good if you will lose some of your people with too many questions, but want to see if you can get detailed answers. To do this, you begin with your basic questions, let the user submit these, and then send the next set of questions. The chapter on hidden variables (Chapter 10) provides methods for linking successive inputs to each other.

2. The first Web page could be added to a file and the second page sent out with a hidden variable containing the name of the second page. The second page would then be concatenated to the first page.

3. Different second pages could be made available depending on how the questions were answered. For example, persons who find Internet pages useful would be asked a different set of questions than those who find them less useful. Another option is to email each successive questionnaire page that has been submitted and include a hidden variable with the initial date and PID for identification. (These types of techniques are developed in Chapter 10.)

4. The second page of the questionnaire is then followed by a third or final page, which is common to both either positive or negative responses.

Here is how example 3 might be implemented. In this case, one of the earliest programs will be expanded. First create Web pages that provide the questions for the two possible types—specifically, those who tend to like the Internet resources and those who do not.

```
<!- filename question.good.html -->
<HTML>
<HEAD>
<TITLE>Questionnaire</TITLE>
<link rev=made href="mailto:markf@xyz.com">
</HEAD>
<BODY bgcolor=#c0c0c0 </BODY>
<BODY>
```

```
<H1> QUESTIONNAIRE LIKE THE INTERNET</H1>
<BR>
<FORM ACTION="http://internet_path/cgi-bin/questionaire?-p2 "METHOD=post >
<H4> THE THINGS I LIKE ARE <BR> CHECK ANY THAT APPLY </H4>
<INPUT TYPE="checkbox" NAME="lk1_1">GUI INTERFACE
<INPUT TYPE="checkbox" NAME="lk1_2">EASY TO USE
<INPUT TYPE="checkbox" NAME="lk1_3">CONVENTIENT
<INPUT TYPE="checkbox" NAME="lk2_1">PRINTER OPTION
<INPUT TYPE="checkbox" NAME="lk2_2">TEXT SIZE
<INPUT TYPE="checkbox" NAME="lk2_3">FORMAT
<INPUT TYPE="checkbox" NAME="lk2_4">FAMILIAR<BR>
<INPUT TYPE="checkbox" NAME="lk2_5">GOOD SUPPORT
<INPUT TYPE="submit" VALUE="submit">
<INPUT TYPE="refresh" VALUE="refresh">
</FORM>
</BODY>
</HTML>
```

The negative response page looks like this:

```
<!- filename question.bad.html -->
<HTML>
<HEAD>
<TITLE>Questionnaire Dislike</TITLE>
<link rev=made href="mailto:markf@xyz.com">
</HEAD>
<BODY bgcolor=#c0c0c0 </BODY>
<BODY>
<H1> QUESTIONAIRE DISLIKE THE INTERNET </H1>
<BR>
<!- The cgi request is the same for both forms since all questionaires end with the final page -->
<FORM ACTION="http://internet_path/cgi-bin/questionaire?-p2 "METHOD=post >
<H4> THE THINGS I DISLIKE ARE <BR> CHECK ANY THAT APPLY </H4>
<INPUT TYPE="checkbox" NAME="lk1_1">INTERFACE
<INPUT TYPE="checkbox" NAME="lk1_2">DIFFICULT TO USE
<INPUT TYPE="checkbox" NAME="lk1_3">TOO SLOW
<INPUT TYPE="checkbox" NAME="lk2_1">CAN'T LOCATE OPTIONS
<INPUT TYPE="checkbox" NAME="lk2_2">TEXT SIZE
<INPUT TYPE="checkbox" NAME="lk2_3">FORMAT
<INPUT TYPE="checkbox" NAME="lk2_4">UNFAMILIAR<BR>
<INPUT TYPE="checkbox" NAME="lk2_5">BAD SUPPORT
<INPUT TYPE="checkbox" NAME="lk2_6">HAVEN'T REALLY CHECKED IT OUT
```

```
</FORM>
</BODY>
</HTML>
```

Here is the final page:

```
<!- filename final.html -->
<HTML><HEAD>
<TITLE>Final Page of Questionnaire</TITLE>
<link rev=made href="mailto:markf@xyz.com">
</HEAD>
<BODY bgcolor=#c0c0c0 </BODY>
<BODY>
<H1> QUESTIONAIRE FINAL PAGE </H1>
<A HREF="http://internet_path/mainpage.html">
<IMGSRC="http://internet_path/logo.gif"></A>
<BR>
Thank You for Your Participation
</BODY> </HTML>
```

Save the first as question.good.html, the second as question.bad.html, and the third as final.html. Now add the cgi-bin program.

```
/*
 * Type C main
 * Purpose: questionnaire
 */
/* to compile use cc -o questionnaire questionnaire.c */
void main(int argc, char* argv[])
{
    /* instantiate required FORM Classes */
    int option_p = 0;
    char* opinion;
    FILE* file;
    char indata[1000]
    char* page_to_show;
    /* getoption code here */
    switch()
    {
    case p:
        option_p = atoi(optarg);
        break;
    }
```

```
cin >> indata;
switch(option_p)
{
case 1: // coming from page 1
        opinion = variable(indata, "Q1=");
        if((strcmp(opinion, "SD")==0) ||
            (strcmp(opinion, "D")==0))
        { /* disagree or strongly disagree */
                page_to_show=
                "unix_path/question.bad.html";
        } else
        {
                page_to_show=
                "unix_path/question.good.html";
        }
        break;
default:
case 2:
        page_to_show="unix_path/final.html";
        break;
}

/* send out the server request */

file=fopen(page_to_show, "r");
while(file != EOF)
{
        fgets(buffer,80, file);
        puts(buffer);
}
/* If it is page 1 -
 * create a file for the data
 * then add a hidden to the bottom
 */
/* If it is page 2 - read the hidden
 * concatenate the data to the file
 * mail the data or mail directly with ID
 */
}
```

In this chapter you learned how to create HTML input buttons and fields. This is a critical capability if you are going to create interactive Web pages. You also learned how to develop a questionnaire using these inputs. In the extended questionnaire, the first input was provided by standard HTML, but the secondary inputs were output from your cgi-bin program.

PROGRAM EXERCISES

1. Create a group of cgi-bin programs that provide each of the different button types. Using one of the multiple usage methods (see Chapter 6), combine the programs into a single program. Add to this a response to the different forms based on the button used.

2. Create a questionnaire that will be sent to the server after receiving user responses. (**Advanced:** Develop a background process that can read in the results of your questionnaire and display it on a separate HTML page.)

3. Create a cgi-bin program that reconfigures the button display based on the user's input. An example would be using the option buttons, and then returning the same form with the same options but having the select connected to the user's choice.

PROBLEMS

1. Explain each of the different kinds of buttons. Explain how each operates when it is sent as part of the form data going to the cgi-bin program. Show examples of what the variable information would look like for each button type.

2. Explain the submit and reset buttons in detail. Show examples of what they look like. Is it possible to make the submit button a graphic image? If yes, how?

3. Give examples from your field where questionnaires might provide valuable feedback on status. A common practice in some fields is a report card, which allows people to evaluate the performance of teachers and trainers. How might you benefit from this approach? Do you think Internet-based questionnaires would get better or worse response than desk-to-desk or mailed questionnaires? How could you improve your response rate? Frequently questionnaires use incentives to get responses. What kinds of incentives might be provided through the Internet? Through mailers? Through other methods?

CHAPTER 10

Hidden Variables

Using Hidden Variables

Hidden Variable Counter on Request

State Transition Machines

IMaGe *Pointers*

Encryption

Creating a Hidden Variable File

Using Hidden Variables

HIDDEN VARIABLES PROVIDE A UNIQUE way to pass information through a cgi-bin program. A hidden variable is sent just like any other variable when the form is sent to the cgi-bin program. However, it does not appear on the user screen, and the user has no way to change its value. Hidden variables provide a mechanism for passing information between successive user screens.

Here are a few of the many examples of information that could be passed through hidden variables:

1. The name of a file that stores relevant information
2. The state of a game
3. An encryption code
4. The user's identified IP address
5. The user's entered ID
6. The type of browser the person is using
7. Whether a person is using a modem or a high-speed link
8. The number of cards that have been dealt in a card game

9. The person's age range

10. The difficulty level a person has selected to play a game at

11. Personal access privileges

Before examining the use of hidden variables with cgi-bin programs, it is essential to understand what a hidden variable is and what it is not. Hidden variables are parts of a form and are carried along with the form as part of the data sent to argc and argv[] (Get method) or to stdin (Post method). When it is said that the variables are hidden, all that this implies is that the HTML interpreter in the browser will not display them on the user's screen. This is a very low level of hiding since all you need to do is view the source from the browser to see the hidden variables. In this regard, hidden variables are anything but secret; they are merely below the surface. However, this does not mean that they are not useful. In fact, there are many instances in which you are unconcerned about a person seeing the hidden information. You just find it inappropriate to show that information on the screen. In addition, The use of hidden variables can provide continuity between successive Web pages.

All of the examples in the previous list are parameters that the person has provided in some manner, so the users know the value in the hidden variable. The users do not want to see this information on the screen. It is information that you as a Web page developer wish to pass into the different steps of a cgi-bin program as the user selects various choices.

By using cgi-bin programs and passing hidden variables along, it becomes possible to maintain continuity between consecutive accesses of the same cgi-bin program or of different cgi-bin programs. The basic idea is that the user enters some information onto an initial form. For example, there might be checkboxes for the person's background level. The form is submitted and the value is sent to the cgi-bin program. The cgi-bin program then sends back a new form that includes, as a hidden variable, the previously entered value. The person makes some choices or decisions on the new form and then submits it. Since the hidden variable is also sent with the information, this can be used to decide what form to send back next. If the cgi-bin program was generating some type of step-by-step learning, the hidden variables could also contain information about which problem the person is working to solve.

Later in this chapter we discuss encryption of hidden variables. While encryption is interesting, a great deal can be done with hidden variables without the use of encryption. This is fortunate since it is not easy to implement real encryption on the Web. In the next example, a hidden variable interpreter is used to send the next hidden variable to the newly generated form. To illustrate this principle, we will have the interpreter increment the value of the hidden variable by one on each new access. This technique will have very little use, since all it is doing is keeping track of how many times in succession the person uses the same form. However, it is a simple illustration of the use of hidden variables and at the same times demonstrates the ability to have continuity from one form to the next form to the next form. As this technique is developed, the word *form* becomes less and less meaningful, and the continuity has more resemblance to a game or an interactive environment. As will be seen shortly, this is exactly where we are heading.

Hidden Variable Counter on Request

SINCE IT WILL BE NECESSARY to start from somewhere, begin by developing an initial HTML Web page as a starting point.

```
<HTML><HEAD><TITLE>
Hidden Variable FORM
</TITLE></HEAD>
<BODY>
<H1> This FORM includes a Hidden Variable with the number 1</H1>
To increase the number to 2, submit the FORM
<FORM METHOD="post"
 ACTION="http://internet_path/cgi-bin/cgi_hidden" >
<INPUT TYPE="hidden" NAME="myhidden" VALUE="1" >
<INPUT TYPE="submit" NAME="Enter">
</FORM>
</BODY></HTML>
```

Here is a simple C program to deal with the submitted form:

```
/*
 * Type C main
 * Purpose: demonstrate html hidden variables
 */
main()
{
    char input[MAXLINE]; /* holder for the input data  */
    char value_string[10];
    int value;
    gets(input);
    /* get the value of the hidden variable  */
    strcpy(value_string, get_variable(input, "myhidden="));
    /*
     * The value of the variable is now in the input buffer. Turn it into an integer and
     * increment it by +1
     */
    value = atoi(value_string) + 1;
    /*
     * Now send out the HTML. It will look exactly like the original except that the number
     * will be increased by 1
     */
    /* Don't forget to tell the server */
    printf("Content-type: text/html\n\n");
    /* Now the HTML */
    printf("%s%s%s%s%s%s%d%s%s%s%s%d%s%s%s%s%d%s%s%s%s%s%s",
```

```
            "<HTML><HEAD><TITLE>\n",
            "Hidden Variable FORM\n",
            "</TITLE></HEAD>\n",
            "<BODY>",
            "<H1> FORM with a Hidden Variable number ",
            value,
            "</H1>\n",
            "To increase the number to ",
            value+1
            " submit the FORM\n",
            "<FORM METHOD=\"post\"",
            "ACTION=\"http://internet_path/cgi-bin/cgi_prog\">",
            "\n",
            "<INPUT TYPE=\"hidden\" NAME=\"myhidden\" VALUE=\"",
            value,
            ">\n",
            "<INPUT TYPE=\"submit\" NAME=\"Enter\">\n",
            "</FORM>\n",
            "</BODY></HTML>\n");
    }
```

The new form looks just like the original one except that the count, including the hidden value count, is increased by 1. Submit again and you will get a new form with the numbers increased again. You can keep going until you reach the limits of your ability to submit new forms or until you reach the maximum value for integers.

State Transition Machines

THIS NEXT EXAMPLE ILLUSTRATES THE manner in which a state transition machine can be developed using hidden variable cgi-bin programs. The principle behind a state transition machine is to provide a way to move from one state to a new state. The decision about which new state to move to is based on the responses that occur in the previous state. More complex state transition machines use more than one input and/or more than one previous state. While the example shown is for an incremental learning environment with which to teach cgi-bin programming, state transition machines can be developed for many applications. Figure 10.1 shows hidden variable transitions.

The idea behind this example is that any question can be answered correctly or incorrectly. For each question there is a single state transition if the answer is correct and another transition if the answer is wrong. In other words, there is a backward directive and a forward directive based on whether a question is answered correctly. More complex transition machines can be built that include *fuzzy logic* or that take into account multiple factors. State transition machines can be used for on-line price configurators, such as allowing a person to select a com-

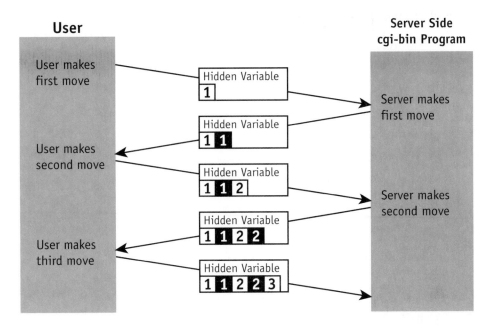

FIGURE 10.1   Hidden Variables: Passing hidden information back and forth creates continuity across Internet requests.

puter for purchase by first entering the hard disk size, the screen type, etc. At each transition the previous information about selections is passed along in the hidden variables. State transition machines could also be used to provide on-line parts information, allowing a person to locate a needed part through successive steps. For this type of application, GIF displays would provide visual information about the parts. For example, automobile parts could provide different levels of blowup of the subsections as the person stepped through the forms. This type of capability would be advantageous to both the person looking for the part and the person selling the part. Both would save valuable time by allowing the user to do the initial determination of the part needed using the Internet.

A state transition machine builds on the previous counting example with the addition of a flat file or text file, which represents the information for each of the states. The method developed here is relatively simple to implement. Each state is represented by a number and each type of information by a type string. Each line begins with a #. This allows comments to be added using lines that start with anything but a #. The next characters are an ASCII representation of a state number. This is followed by a | separator, which is then followed by the ASCII representation of the type of information. This is followed by another | and finally the actual information. For example, the question for state 1 might look like this:

    #1|Question|A program run by the server is called a _____ .

Here is a different example of a partial file for a cgi-bin learning environment:

```
#1|Correct|2
#1|Back|1
#1|Forward|2
#1|New1|The cgi-bin is the area used to hold special
#1|New2|programs. These can be written in compiled languages
#1|New3|or script languages. Since the cgi-bin is a special
#1|New4|area, you may need permission to use the area.
#1|Question|The special area used for internet programs is _____ .
#1|Answer1|compiled
#1|Answer2|cgi-bin
#1|Answer3|script languages
#1|Answer4|none of above
#2|Correct|3
#2|Back|2
#2|Forward|4
#2|New1|Compiled programs provide capabilities not
#2|New2|available in script languages. This is because
#2|New3|compiled languages provide increased response
#2|New4| speed.
#2|Question|The people allowed to use the cgi-bin are _____ .
#2|Answer1|anyone
#2|Answer2|only programmers
#2|Answer3|people given permission
#2|Answer4|none of above
```

Additional state information

Each line is made up of fields. The fields are defined as shown in Table 10.1.

TABLE 10.1 *Transition Machine Fields*

Field 1 State	Field 2 Information Type	Field 3 Information
State Number $1-n$	Back	What to send if answer is wrong
	Forward	What to send if answer is correct
	New{$1-n$}	New information to be presented to the user
	Question	The question being asked of the user
	Answer{$1-n$}	The multiple choice answers
	Correct	The correct answer

Here is how the state transition machine operates:

1. The cgi-bin program receives a hidden variable that corresponds to the state number and a standard variable with the person's choice for an answer.

2. It searches the file for the answer to that state number. When it finds it, a check is done to see if it is correct or not.

3. If the answer is correct, the program checks for the forward state; otherwise, it finds the back state.

4. This state is used by the HTML routine to send out the new information and the question and possible answers associated with this state. The information retrieved from the file is surrounded with the required HTML to create a new form, which will allow the next answer to be entered by the user. A hidden variable is created that includes the new state so the process can be repeated.

5. A number of routines are left to the readers. (For example, the file can be read into a buffer to avoid multiple file I/O.)

Other things can be added to this program. For example, the program can include what section of text to read before proceeding. This should show the flow of states in a diagrammatic manner. The program can also maintain a hidden variable with a count of correct and wrong answers with which to generate a score at the end. It can contain the URLs for anchors or GIFs that will be shown on the screen with each new question.

A state transition provides a means to transition from one condition to another based on user input. When developing this kind of capability, it is often valuable to draw a state transition diagram before starting. Doing so can give valuable clues about how the program will work. To provide a generic state transition machine, begin by analyzing the required components. A transition_file class will be needed. This class will include functions that have the ability to read the transition_file and to return the critical information fields in the file. Three passes through the file's information will be required.

■ In the first pass, the correct answer is read for the present state.

■ In the second pass, the forward or back value is read to determine the next state.

■ In the final pass, the new state's information is retrieved and sent out as HTML.

The strategy that emerges is a single object that calls private member functions when it is first instantiated. These functions determine what question is being answered and what answer is given. The program takes this information and sends it to a subroutine, which will locate the item answered and determine if the given answer is a match. If it is a match, it will return the next item to try. If it is not a match, it will return the previous item to retry. A new search is made of the file for the new item. The fields required for the next HTML page are obtained and packaged into a form, which is then sent out to the client server. The problem being worked is included as a hidden variable. The process continues until the user exhausts all possibilities or until the user leaves the Home pages.

```
#define FIELD_SEPARATOR '|'
class _Transition_machine : public html
{
private:
    /* strings for critical information fields */
    char state[MAXSTATE];
    char type[MAXTYPE];
    char answer[MAXANSWER];
    char input[MAXLINE];          // input from the FORM submitted

    FILE* stream;                 // file stream pointer
    char buffer[MAXBUFFER];       // the state file is read into the buffer
    /*
     * retrieve the FORM input, get the user's answer from the FORM input then determine
     * if it is correct or not
     */
    void get_user_input();        // call routines below to set new state
    void get_user_state();
    void get_user_answer()
    void decide();                // set the new state
    void read_state_file();       // read the state file into the buffer
    /*
     * based on the state, send out the fixed and variable HTML to the user
     */
    void send_html();
    void send_state_info;
public:
    _Transition_machine();        // constructor
    ~_Transition_machine();       // destructor
};
```

About the _Transition_machine class . . . .

1. There are only two public interfaces, the constructor and the destructor. This is all that is needed, since the program will run everything anytime it is called. The constructor can do the entire job. The destructor does any required cleanup.

2. Three strings are used to hold the critical values. The state is the ASCII value of the state being examined. It can be used to hold the incoming state from the submitted form and then later the outgoing state based on the correctness of the person's response. The type string is a similar variable used to hold the particular kind of information being accessed (for example, the question or one of the possible answers). The third variable is used to hold the answer that the person has selected.

3. These are the class functions:

get_user_input()   Retrieves the information in stdin (Post method) and places it in the appropriate variables.

get_user_state()   Gets the user's present state from the hidden variable

get_user_answer()   Gets the user's answer

retrieve_state_info()   Retrieves state info from the buffer (third field)

decide()   Determines if the answer is the correct one for the problem and sets the forward or backward state

send_html()   Creates the new page that is sent to the user from the cgi-bin program

send_state_info()   Used with send_html to send the variable information to the user based on the decided state.

. . . .

The flat file where the state information is kept is set up as a definition. It could be passed in as an argv[].

```
#define STATE_FILE "unix_path/state_file"
/*
 * Type C++ class subroutine
 * Purpose: get the present state of the user from the FORM input
 */
#include <iostream.h>
#include <stdlib.h>
#include <string.h>
void _Transition_machine::get_user_state()
{
    strcpy(state, get_variable(input, "state="));
}
/*
 * Type C++ subroutine
 * Purpose: determine the answer given by the user from the FORM input
 */
void _Transition_machine :: get_user_answer()
{
    strcpy(answer, get_variable(input, "answer="));
}
/*
 * Type C++ class subroutine
 * Purpose: get the users state and answer from the FORM input
 */
void _Transition_machine::get_user_input()
{
    /*
     * This is a normal FORM reading routine. It reads in the hidden variable and the answer
```

```
                * and puts them in the appropriate variables
                */

                // see other FORM input for details
                get_user_state()
                get_user_answer();
        }
        /*
         * Type C++ class subroutine
         * Purpose: get information from the state file
         *    state is preset prior to this call
         */
        void _Transition_machine::read_state_file()
        {
                char tmp_buffer[MAXLINE];
        stream = fopen(STATE_FILE, "r");
        while(fgets(tmp_buffer,MAXLINE,stream) != EOF)
        {
                /*
                 * The present state, forward state, and back state all need to be read into the buffer.
                 * This could be made more intelligent, but for simplicity the whole file is read into the
                 * buffer
                 */
                strcat(buffer, tmp_buffer);
        }

                fclose(stream);
        }
        /*
         * Type C++ class subroutine
         * Purpose: decide what state to move to next
         */
        char* _Transition_machine::decide() /* return the new state */
        {
                if(strcmp(answer, get_state_info("Answer|")
                {
                        return get_state_info("Forward|");
                } else
                {
                        return get_state_info("Back|");
                }
        }
        /*
         * This routine uses two arguments, the state (a private class variable) and the
         * information type. It then sends all information that meet these two criteria out to
         * stdout. The required HTML must be sent before and after the call to this routine.
         */
```

```
/*
 * Type C++ class subroutine
 * Purpose: using state and information type send html
 */
void _Transition_machine::send_state_info()
{
    sprintf(tmp, "#%s|%s|", state, type);
    stream=fopen(STATE_FILE, "r");
    while(fgets(buffer,80,stream) != 0)
    {
        if(strncmp(buffer,tmp,strlen(tmp)) == 0)
        {
            cout << buffer + strlen(tmp);
        }
    }
    fclose(stream);
}
/*
 * This routine uses two arguments, the state (a private class variable) and the
 * information type. It then returns a pointer to the information in field 3 that
 * meets this criteria.
 */
/*
 * Type C++ class subroutine
 * Purpose: using state and information type return information field
 */
char* _Transition_machine::retrieve_state_info(char* tmp_ptr, char* which_type)
{
    char tmp[MAXLINE];
    char tmp_buffer[MAXLINE];
    sprintf(tmp, "#%s|%s|", state, which_type);
    // retrieve a line from the buffer (class variable)
    while(fgets(tmp_buffer, MAXLINE, buffer) != NULL)
    {
        /*
         * The function strstr returns a pointer to the string in tmp that is the state and
         * the type string that consists of the first two fields. The length of the fields is
         * added to this pointer to get to the third field, which is the content field. A
         * pointer to this field is returned.
         */
        if((tmp_ptr = strstr(tmp_buffer, tmp) != NULL)
        {
            return(tmp_ptr + strlen(tmp));
        }
    }
    return(NULLPTR); // error leg
```

```
}
/*
 * This routine is used to create the new FORM that is sent to the client and then to the
 * user's screen
 */
/*
 * Type C++ class subroutine
 * Purpose: send next FORM to user includes
 *          new information or repeated information if back state
 *          hidden variable containing present state
 *          question to answer
 *          answer choices
 *          a FORM for sending back the answer
 */
void _Transition_machine::send_html()
{
    /*
     * See earlier discussions about the base class and how to inherit this class.
     */
    start_msg();
    normal_head();
    cout "<B>" << get("new:") << "</B>\n";
    cout << "<FORM ACTION=" <<
        "\"http://internet_path/cgi-bin/this_program\"" <<
        "METHOD=\"post\">\n" <<
        "<INPUT TYPE=\"hidden\" NAME=\"state\" VALUE=\"" <<
            state <<"\">\n" <<
        send_state_info("Question:") <<
        send_state_info("Answer1:") <<
        "<INPUT TYPE=\"radio\"" <<
            NAME=\"Answer\" VALUE=\"1\" >\n" <<
        send_state_info("Answer2:") <<
            "<INPUT TYPE=\"radio\"" <<
            NAME=\"Answer\" VALUE=\"2\" >\n" <<
        // continue for other answers
        "<INPUT TYPE=\"submit\"> </FORM>\n" ;

    end();
}
```

Finally, a constructor and a destructor are needed.

```
/*
 * Type C++ class constructor
 * Purpose: activate the state transition machine
 */
```

```
// constructor does it all
_Transition_machine::_Transition_machine()
{
        read_state_file();       // read state file information into buffer
        cin >> input;            // retrieve input from the FORM
        get_user_input();        // get the state and selected answer
        state = decide();        // set the new state
        send_html();             // send out the fixed and variable HTML


}
/*
 * Type C++ class destructor
 * Purpose: cleanup
 */
~_Transition_machine::_Transition_machine()
{
        cout << fflush;          // clean up


}
/*
 * Type C++ main
 * Purpose: cgi transition machine activation
 */
void main()
{
        TRANSITION_MACHINE* my_transitions;
        my_transitions = new(TRANSITION_MACHINE);
}
```

You may want to add some intelligence, such as ways to search and exit the file more quickly. You can exit if the state is greater than the state being searched.

Case Study 2: An Internet Game of Chess

IN THIS CASE STUDY, a chess game uses hidden variables to provide continuity between successive moves. The chess game combines a number of interesting techniques. First it uses GIF images to produce the chess board with the pieces. Then it uses pointers to rearrange the board after a move. Next it uses hidden variables to create continuity. (Chess is the type of game that is very playable over the Internet, since it need not have a short response time. See Figure 10.2.)

The Internet protocol is said to be a *memoryless* protocol. In other words, on each retrieval the total information present is sent and then the server forgets everything about what it has sent. This creates a difficult problem for persons wishing to develop continuity between screens, especially if continuity is based on the

You are white Computer's move was c6

Example Input: a2a4 [send] [Reset]

FIGURE 10.2

state of a previous screen. In the chess game that follows, the hidden variable techniques developed previously are extended to allow continuity to be preserved. This is accomplished by

1. Using the cgi-bin program to generate the hidden variables.
2. Creating the hidden variables based on the previous hidden variables passed into the cgi-bin from the form input and the new states entered by the user into the form. In the chess example, the new state is the piece being moved and its new position. The old state, in the hidden variables, is the present configuration of the board. The new hidden variables are a representation of the board after the move(s) has occurred. The program rebuilds the state of the board from these hidden variables.

The chess game developed in this case study provides a number of capabilities explained up to this section. The program is given in abbreviated format for readability. The complete listing is given Appendix 3.

The initial game does not include algorithms for playing chess against the computer. In Appendix 3, methods are shown to connect to real playing algorithms to allow competition against the computer. Algorithms are easily located with the various netsearch tools available.

We begin with an object analysis of the game of chess and its various components. Part of our analysis will require us to focus on how Internet chess differs from normal chess and part of our analysis must examine how programmed cgi-bin chess will differ from normal chess. In other words, we will have to understand the limitations and capabilities of our programming tools and of the Internet protocol to accomplish this task.

The Board and Pieces

A chess board is made up of an 8×8 array of squares that alternate between two colors, traditionally red and black. This provides an interesting challenge. The chess pieces come in two colors, usually black and white. There are a number of possible approaches to this problem. The one chosen here is to think of a single square on the chess board, with a piece on the square as a single entity. (There are also special entities, consisting of an empty gray or an empty black square. If you think of an empty square as just another piece, this is easily handled.)

This is a very workable approach. By focusing on the visual aspect of the chess game, an effective method becomes available. This approach will allow us to deal with a manageable number of Internet objects when creating our HTML.

Board Memory

Since we are dealing with the Internet, we will need to provide a memory to the Internet's memoryless protocol. This will be accomplished using hidden variables. What needs to be passed from event to event? The present state of the board prior to the move and which piece will be moved from where to where are the information that must be passed. Since the present state of the board is always visible to a person playing chess, there is no problem if the user looks at the source to see the hidden variables.

Why are the hidden variables needed at all? You must remember that *each time the new move is submitted, the cgi-bin program will run as if it had never run before.* If you do not let your program know the present state of the board, there will be no way to determine where the pieces are. Some users may be thinking, Why not put the board state into a file? Remember that the chess game will frequently be played by multiple people at the same time over the Internet. This means that files would need to be kept for each person playing. You would still need to pass the filename through as a hidden variable. The advantage of storing the board state in the hidden variables is that it can be different for each person playing. When the cgi-bin program is invoked by the user submit, a process identification will connect that version to the user's request. The information about the board state will be uniquely carried for the user's game and only his or her game. Furthermore, since the latest version of the game will reside on the user's machine (remember, all Web pages exist locally), the user can save the page and start up where he or she left off on another day. This is the real advantage of using hidden variables: The information resides on the user's machine, not in files on the remote site. If a person decides to quit playing in the middle of a game, there is no file left behind to clear up. This creates a manageable approach if handled correctly.

Next, the program uses a number of the capabilities discussed previously. Form capabilities are used to enter the *x* and *y* position of the piece to be moved and the *x* and *y* coordinates of the end position.

Special Capabilities

There are also a number of special capabilities that can be passed over by readers in a hurry to get to the heart of the program.

The server environment is obtained to determine whether the program is being started up or if a move is occurring. When Get is the method (the default), the program assumes there are no data being input and instead checks for either a file or the default configuration. If Post is the method, the program Gets the data from stdin and then interprets the meaning using arrays and parsing routines. The file mode is a special mode that is provided to select a starting position, such as those found in newspaper chess problems. This allows practice of end games or other best-move strategies.

There are numerous capabilities that could be added to this basic program. One simple one has been added: the ability to tell whose move it is. Other challenges for interested programmers include the following:[1]

- Tests for legitimate moves with error responses
- The ability to put a piece on the board when a pawn reaches the end row
- Actual chess playing algorithms for one of the players
- The ability to show which pieces have been taken. (These could be put into other hidden variables.)
- The ability to show best moves in puzzle problems (another hidden variable challenge)
- The use of standard letter and number notation. This would require a little more work in the C++ or C code to translate the coordinate information.

The cgi-bin Algorithms

The actual algorithms found in the cgi-bin program are the critical part of the project. They take the input from the user and regenerate the board as it exists in the hidden variables. The new move is then made. The new move plus the history of moves are used to generate a new hidden variable of the board's new state and to

---

[1]   Appendix 3 includes an example that connects up to actual chess algorithms and that uses most of the listed expansion features.

generate the HTML to create the new board. It is sent along with the form, which allows the user to make his or her next move out to the client and then to the user screen.

The Hidden Variable and Redundant Information

Because the chess board is a finite space (eight rows by eight columns) a decision was made to use eight hidden variables representing each of the eight rows. The pieces on each square are represented by two characters. The first gives the color of the piece, and the second is a number that maps to the individual piece. Blanks are represented as white pieces. (This was arbitrary.) The actual virtual space that describes a chess board is 6 (pieces + blank) × 2 (colors of pieces) × 2 (colors of background squares).

When designing hidden variables, a simple notation should be used. This will make the job of decoding the variables easy to program. It is also advisable to use a brief notation scheme. The compiled program can work a lot faster than the Internet client server protocol. Contention for resources should be a consideration when designing your variable notation. A good idea is to design your hidden variables to use numbers or letters. This eliminates the need to change control characters from the % format to their normal state. It also avoids two extra characters.

The Program

Different critical sections of the C++ Chess program are partially reproduced here. These sections should provide important insights into how to develop interactive games on the Internet. Details of the Chess program are included in Appendices 2 and 3.

```
/* C++ Version of the Chess Program */
#include <iostream.h>
#include <stdlib.h>
#include <string.h>
/*
 * Developed in the Forms section, this subroutine will read back the string value of a
 * submitted variable. This will be used to read in the start and end x and y coordinates
 * and to read in the hidden variable representing the present state of the chess board.
 */
extern char* variable(char* msg, char* start_msg);
```

The next section contains the actual strings that will be sent out as HTML to represent all the combinations of pieces on the two background squares. These defines can create any of the nearly infinite possible chess board layouts. The defines consist of the unique part of the IMaGe string. The rest of the string is provided each time an image is sent out as HTML. An ALT is included to allow the Chess game to be played without a graphics browser.[2] A word about the notation: The first letter B or W is the color of the piece, either black or white. The middle part is the piece, and the last part is the color of the background square, either gray or white.

```
/*
 * defines for the HTML IMaGes used to create the chess board on the screen
 */
#define B_ROOK_G "http://mypath/rk.gif\" ALT=\"B_RK\""
#define B_KNIGHT_G "http://mypath/kt.gif\" ALT=\"B_KT\""
#define B_BISHOP_G "http://mypath/bi.gif\" ALT=\"B_BI\""
#define B_QUEEN_G "http://mypath/qu.gif1\" ALT=\"B_QU\""
#define B_KING_G "http://mypath/ki.gif\" ALT=\"B_KG\""
#define B_ROOK_W ...
#define B_KNIGHT_W ...
#define B_BISHOP_W ...
#define B_QUEEN_W ...
#define B_KING_W ...
#define W_ROOK_W ...
#define W_KNIGHT_W ...
#define W_BISHOP_W ...
#define W_QUEEN_W ...
#define W_KING_W ...
#define W_ROOK_G ...
#define W_KNIGHT_G ...
#define W_BISHOP_G ...
#define W_QUEEN_G ...
#define W_KING_G ...
#define W_PAWN_G ...
#define W_PAWN_W ...
#define B_PAWN_G ...
#define B_PAWN_W ...
#define BLANK_W ...
#define BLANK_G ...
```

The next section shows what typical hidden variables would look like. These are the actual hidden variables used for the default board or the start of a chess game. Each piece is represented by a number from 1 to 5, and a blank is represented by 6. The color of the piece precedes the piece. Blanks are sent as white pieces. This is an arbitrary choice. Each of the eight rows of the chess board are represented, so there are eight hidden variables. There is one extra variable called WHO; this is used to tell whose move it is. If the other side is played by the computer, WHO is not needed.

---

[2]   The HTML ALT replaces a graphics file with words when graphics are not available for the browser.

```
/*
 * Continuity is provided by passing the chess board as eight strings, each one representing
 * a row of the chess board. The nomenclature used is
 *    b | w => black or white
 *    1-6 represent pieces and blank (see defines for pieces)
 * default board strings
 */
#define ROW1 "\"b0b1b2b3b4b2b1b0\""
#define ROW2 "\"b5b5b5b5b5b5b5b5\""
#define ROW3 "\"w6w6w6w6w6w6w6w6\""
#define ROW4 "\"w6w6w6w6w6w6w6w6\""
#define ROW5 "\"w6w6w6w6w6w6w6w6\""
#define ROW6 "\"w6w6w6w6w6w6w6w6\""
#define ROW7 "\"w5w5w5w5w5w5w5w5\""
#define ROW8 "\"w0w1w2w3w4w2w1w0\""
#define WHO "\"B\""
/*
 * Each piece on the chess board is represented by a define. The black and white pieces are
 * offset by +7. This allows the black or white pieces to be sent in the strings along with the
 * background color. The blank is always sent as a white piece (arbitrary choice).
 */
/*
 * This number plus the piece color will be used along with the background color to read in
 * the hidden variables and then to find the correct IMaGe pointer (arbitrary choices).
 */
#define ROOK 0
#define KNIGHT 1
#define BISHOP 2
#define QUEEN 3
#define KING 4
#define PAWN 5
#define BLANK 6
// Definitions for the offset between black and white pieces
#define BLACK_PIECE 0
#define WHITE_PIECE 7
/*
 * The defines for the background square colors and piece colors
 * and an offset to separate black and white pieces from each other
 */
#define WHITE 0 /* piece and background */
#define GRAY 1 /* background */
#define BLACK 1 /* piece */
```

To provide methods for the program to run efficiently, a macro definition is developed that will determine the background color based on the *x* and *y* coordinates of the piece. The algorithm is fairly simple—if both x and y are even or both x and y are odd, the square is gray; otherwise, the square is white.

```
/*
 * This macro is used to determine the background color
 * based on the x and y coordinates
 */
#define background(x, y) ( ((x) % 2) == ((y) % 2) ? GRAY : WHITE )
```

The game of chess is provided using manipulation of three arrays:

Images array: Fixed pointers to the IMaGe strings

Position array: Pointers to the images for each x/y position on the board

Hidden array: The hidden variables that contain the board status

This is followed by four integers for the x and y start and end positions for the piece being moved. This will come in as part of the variable input from the submit.

```
class Chess {
private:
/*
 * To make the board easy to change, arrays are manipulated. The arrays are
 *          xpos = pointers to the IMG strings
 *          pos = pointers to the 8 x 8 squares on the chess board
 *          hidden = pointer to the hidden variables
 */
static char* xpos[13][2];
char* pos[8][8];
char hidden[8] [8 * 2]; /* strings sent in HTML hidden variables */
int xstart, ystart, xend, yend; /* Move X Y start & end position */
char color; /* The color of the square the piece is on */
void send_html();
public:
    Chess();                  // constructor
    void move();              // move the piece
    void set_default();       // set up the default board
};
#define CHESS Chess/* for readability */
```

IMaGe Pointers

THE CONSTRUCTOR IS USED TO set up an array of constant IMaGe pointers to all the possible IMaGe strings that are required to create any chess board. These fixed pointers can later be loaded into the variable position pointers that represent the 8×8 chess squares, allowing the program to move and remove pieces. A piece is moved by replacing its position pointer with a pointer address of a new square with the appropriate background color. A piece is removed by replacing its location with another piece that made the capture. Remember that the Internet has no memory so the program will be rerun from the start each time a move is made. The constructor will have to run every time a move occurs. Since this is done in the compiled program, it is not a concern.

The use of IMaGe pointers is a powerful technique. In this case, it allows the billions of possible chess board layouts to be created from a finite number of GIF images. (**Note:** The chess game runs very fast since all the possible images, except four, are cached when the initial board appears. The four that are not cached immediately are the kings and queens on their opposite colors.)

The image control is done by

1. Determining the fundamental subsections of the total image. In this case, a square on the board with a piece on it is the basic unit.
2. Providing an array of static pointers to these basic IMaGes.
3. Providing an *x* and *y* array of variable pointers for placing fundamental images onto the screen.
4. Moving the address of the statics pointers into the variable pointers to produce different square IMaGes that build up the playing board.

```
Chess::Chess()
{
/*
 * Set up the static multidimensional array to point at all the possible IMaGes. The piece
 * color uses a define to separate the black and white piece pointers. The second dimension
 * in the array is the background color.
 */
    piece_color = BLACK_PIECE;
    background_color = GRAY;
    image[ROOK+piece_color][background_color] = B_ROOK_G;
    image[KNIGHT+piece_color][background_color] = B_KNIGHT_G;
    image[BISHOP+piece_color][background_color] = B_BISHOP_G;
    // continue to set other static image pointers
    image[QUEEN+piece_color][background_color]= ...
    image[KING...][]=B_KI_G = ...;
    image[PAWN...][]=B_PN_G = ...;
    background_color = WHITE;
    image[ROOK+piece_color][background_color] = B_ROOK_W;
    // other black pieces static image pointers

    piece_color = WHITE_PIECE;
    background_color = GRAY;
    image[ROOK+piece_color][background_color] = W_ROOK_G;
    image[KNGT+piece_color][background_color] = W_KNIGHT_G;
    // other white pieces here
```

```
    // don't forget the blanks
    image[BLANK][GRAY] = BLANK_G;
    image[BLANK][WHITE] = BLANK_W;
}
```

The move routine uses the hidden variable notation. The use of a good notation is well worth time spent. Anything that can be done to add efficiency in moving information between the client and server, which may be on different continents, will add response time to your Web page.

```
void Chess::move()
{
    /*
     * Retrieve the user's request. The eight chess rows are placed in the hidden variables r1
     * to r8. These are given in the format
     * Piece Color ->    b= black w=white
     * Piece ->          0 = Rook
     *                   1 = Knight
     *                   2 = Bishop
     *                   3 = Queen
     *                   4 = King
     *                   5 = Pawn
     * The variable who tells whose turn it is
     */
    gets(input);
    get_variable(hidden[0], "row1=");
    get_variable(hidden[1], "row2=");
    // do the other rows of hidden variables
    get_variable(hidden[7], "row8=");

    // retrieve the start and end x and y coordinates
    get_start_X();
    get_start_Y();
    get_end_X();
    get_end_Y();

    // get who made the last move and switch it
    get_variable(who, "who");
    who = (who=='W') ? 'B' : 'W');

    // move piece in the hidden variables
    move_hidden();
    // move the piece with the pointers to the images
    move_image();
    // send out HTML with the images, the hidden variables
    // and the FORM to input the next move
```

```
        send_html();
}
/*
  * This subroutine creates the user's move in the strings that are sent
  * out as hidden variables in the HTML message.
  */
void Chess::move_hidden(...)
{
      /* 1st the hidden  */
      hidden[yend][xend*2]=hidden[ystart][xstart*2];
      hidden[yend][xend*2+1]=hidden[ystart][xstart*2+1];
      hidden[ystart][xstart*2]='w';
      hidden[ystart][xstart*2+1]='6';
}
/*
  * This subroutine moves the piece as part of the image pointers that
  * will be used to create the chess board on the browser screen.
  */
void Chess::move_piece()
{
      // Set up the board like it was in hidden variables
      for(Y=0; Y <= 7; Y++){
      for ( X=0; X <= 7; X++) {
          piece_color = (hidden[Y][X*2]=='w')
              ? WHITE_PIECE : BLACK_PIECE;
          // use the macro to set the background color
          background_color= background(Y, X);
          /* Use hidden variable to set the position pointer to
            * point at the image */
          position[X][Y] =
              set_position(X, Y, background_color);
      }
      }
      // now move the piece by moving its position pointer and
      // putting a pointer to a blank where it used to be
          position[yend][xend]=image[hidden[yend][xend*2+1]-'0'+
          (hidden[yend][xend*2]=='w' ? WHITE_PIECE
          :BLACK_PIECE)][background(xstart, ystart)] ;
          position[ystart][xstart] =
              image[BLANK][background(xstart, ystart)];
}
```

Here is the subroutine to send out the HTML to the client sofware and then to the user's screen:

```cpp
/*
 * This subroutine sends out the HTML including the
       Content-type ...
       HTML to show the board images
       FORM HTML for the next move
       All surrounding HTML
 */
void Chess::send_html()
{
    /*
     * The board is now reconfigured to the new state. This is sent out as HTML code
     * to the client.
     */
    // Tell the server HTML is coming
    cout << "Content-type: text/html\n\n";

    // send some basic HTML stuff
    cout << "<HTML> <HEAD> <Title>CHESS GAME</Title>\n" <<
            "<BODY bgcolor=#f0f0f0 </BODY>" <<
            "</HEAD> <BODY>\n";
    // send out whose move it is
    cout << (who=='W' ? "WHITES" : "BLACKS") << " MOVE<BR>\n";
    /*
     * The pointers to the IMaGes are in the position array.
     * Use them to create the HTML
     * version of the chess board.
     */
    for (Y=ROW_START; Y <= ROW_END; Y++)
    {
        // send out a row of chess squares
        for (X=COLUMN_START; X <= COLUMN_END; X++)
        {
            show_chess_square (position[Y][X]);
        }
        // move to next row on the chess board
        cout<<"<BR>\n " << flush;
    }
    /*
     * Send HTML FORM to allow the user to make the next move
     */
    cout << "<FORM ACTION =" <<
            "\"http://internet_path/cgi-bin/chess \"METHOD=POST>\n";
    cout << "<BR><I>START</I>\n" <<
            "<B> X POS</B>\n" <<
            "<SELECT NAME= \"x_start\">\n" <<
            "<OPTION SELECTED> 1\n" <<
```

```
        "<OPTION> 2\n" <<
        "<OPTION> 3\n" <<
        "<OPTION> 4\n" <<
        "<OPTION> 5\n" <<
        "<OPTION> 6\n" <<
        "<OPTION> 7\n" <<
        "<OPTION> 8\n" <<
        "</SELECT>\n";

cout << "<B> Y POS</B>\n" <<
        "<SELECT NAME= \"y_start\">\n" <<
        "<OPTION SELECTED> A\n" <<
        "<OPTION> B\n" <<
        "<OPTION> C\n" <<
        "<OPTION> D\n" <<
        "<OPTION> E\n" <<
        "<OPTION> F\n" <<
        "<OPTION> G\n" <<
        "<OPTION> H\n" <<
        "</SELECT>\n";
cout << "<BR><I>FINAL</I>\n" <<
        "<B> X POS</B>\n" <<
        "<SELECT NAME= \"x_end\">\n" <<
            // continue as above

cout << "<B> Y POS</B>\n" <<
        "<SELECT NAME= \"y_end\">\n" <<
        "<OPTION SELECTED> A\n" <<
            // continue as above
/*
 * The HIDDEN values are sent to pass along the present state
 * of the board.
 */
cout << "<BR>\n"
        << "<INPUT TYPE=\"HIDDEN\" NAME=\"row1\" VALUE="<<hidden[0]
            << ">\n"
        << "<INPUT TYPE=\"HIDDEN\" NAME=\"row2\" VALUE=" << hidden[1]
            << ">\n";
        // other hidden rows
cout << "<INPUT TYPE=\"HIDDEN\" NAME=\"row8\" VALUE=" << hidden[7]
        << ">\n"
        << "<INPUT TYPE=\"HIDDEN\" NAME=\"who\" VALUE=" <<who
        << ">\n";
cout << "<INPUT TYPE=\"submit\"> <INPUT TYPE=reset>\n"
        << "</FORM>\n" <<
```

```
                    "</BODY></HTML>\n";
            }
```

As is traditional in object programming, main() has very little to do.

```
    /*
     * The C++ main for the chess program
     */
    void main(int argc, char* argv[])
    {
        CHESS Chess;
        char* env;
        // If there is an argument, it is the path/filename
        if(argc > 1)
        {
            Chess.filemode(argv[1]); /* file mode */
            return;
        }
        // Check to be sure this is a user input POST
        if(strcmp(env=getenv("REQUEST_METHOD"), "POST") == 0)
        {
            // Make the requested move and send it back
            Chess.move();
            return;// all done
        }
        // Someone directly invoked the cgi-bin program as a URL
        Chess.set_default(); /* Start Page using Thru mode */
    }
    /* END OF MAIN() */
```

About main . . . .

1. First check for argv count greater than one. (One is the program name. If it is greater than one, the argument is a filename that contains a way to set up the screen.)

2. If it is not filemode, check the environment to be sure there is Posted information. If there is not, someone has directly invoked the cgi-bin program without Posted information.

3. If there is no Post, send back the HTML page that is normally used to start the program using the Thru mode.

. . . .

This routine is needed in case a call is made to the cgi-bin program without any Post. This would occur if someone invoked the cgi-bin program directly. To handle this, use the Thru mode to send out the HTML page to start up the program.

```
void Chess::set_default()
{
    // use Thru mode to pass the start HTML page out
}
```

About this program. . . . .

A large number of comments have been included in this program to help the reader understand its operation.

1. The program is called with argc greater than 1 only if a filename is present.
2. The program can pass through three possible paths:

   Default = no filename and server mode is Get

   Move = no filename and server mode is Post

   Filemode = a filename is present (shown on page 194)

3. In the default mode, the internal string pointers are set up to point toward a standard chess board. This is done in the subroutine setdefault(). The hidden variables are set to this default setup, and then the HTML is sent out to the server. (The HTML is explained in item 8 of this list.)
4. In the move mode, the board's present configuration is retrieved from the hidden variables. The person's move is obtained from the entered variables, which consist of x and y starting coordinates and x and y ending coordinates. The coordinates represent the start and end position of the piece on the 8×8 positions of the chess board.
5. The move must also be made in the hidden variables before they are sent out to the client. This preserves the new status for the next move.
6. The move is made by replacing the end position pointer with the piece that is in the start position. Because the piece may land on the opposite color background, an algorithm is needed to determine the background color. This is done by taking advantage of the fact that if both coordinates are even values, or both coordinates are odd values, the color is white. If, on the other hand, one coordinate is even and the other is odd, the squares are not white. The *modulo* (%) operator in C++ and C can be used to decide which is the case. The start position of the piece is easier, since it always becomes an empty or blank space. Only the color background needs to be determined.
7. The file mode is similar to the default mode except that the initial state comes from a file. The file contains the eight strings that represent the rows for each of the eight rows of the chess board. The rest is the same as the original default coding.
8. The HTML consists of four parts. The first part is the normal HTML initiation. It includes the message to the server that HTML text is coming. It also includes some startup HTML, including the BODY BACKGROUND COLOR TITLE, etc. The next part is the actual chess board. It is generated using the pointers to the IMaGe strings. These strings include ALT values to allow the game to be played by persons without graphic viewers. The next section is the form information. It

includes the OPTION input variables for the *x* and *y* start and end coordinates. It also includes the hidden variables that represent the present state of the board prior to the next move. It ends with the submit or reset HTML, which allows the form to be input by the user. The final section completes the HTML using </BODY></HTML>. This completes the HTML output. As is traditional in object-based programming, the main is very small, merely calling the chess routine with either a filename or a null filename.

. . . .

Miscellaneous Additional Routines

Filemode

This routine sets up the hidden variables based on a file that contains the strings saved in the hidden variable format. Since it uses the same strings as in the hidden variables, you can merely save the chess page and edit out the hidden variable into a file. A C utility to do this automatically is provided in Appendix 2.

```
void Chess::filemode(char* filename)
{
    /*
     * The filemode provides a method for the user to read in a partially played chess game
     * and start from that point. This allows chess setups, such as those found in the
     * newspaper, to be played and could also allow games to be continued by saving their
     * state at an FTP site.
     */
    fp= fopen(filename, "r");i=0;
    // read lines from the file into the C++ hidden variables
    for(i=0; i <= 7; i++)
    {
        fgets(buffer, 16, fp);
        strncpy(hidden[i++], buffer, 16);
    }
    // whose move is a single character
    who = *buffer;
    fclose(fp);
    // reverse whose move it is since this was a Home Page Save
    //You have to remember this if you build files from scratch
    who = (hidden[8][0]=='W') ? 'B' : 'W');
    for (Y = 0; Y <= 7; Y++)
    {
        for (X = 0; X <= 7; X++)
        {
            // Determine which color the piece is
            piece_color =
```

```
                              (hidden[Y][X*2] == 'w') ? WHITE_PIECE :
                                  BLACK_PIECE;
                      // determine the background color
                      background_color= background(Y, X);
                      // Set the position pointer to IMaGe for this location
                      // The '0' is subtracted to change ASCII to INT
                      pos[Y][X] = xpos[hidden[Y][(2*X)+1] - '0'
                              + piece_color][background_color];
              }
      }
      // Send everything out to the client
      send_html();
}
```

These are some of the low-level routines required to complete the chess program. This is only one possible implementation. As is traditional in C++, these routines are private routines that are normally hidden at the lowest layers of the program. The x axis is number, while the y axis is letters. This is the reason for the special function alpha_atoi for the y axis.

```
void Chess::get_start_X()
{
      xstart = atoi(variable(input, "x_start="));
}
void Chess::get_start_Y()
{
      ystart = alpha_atoi(variable(input, "y_start="));
}
void Chess::get_end_X()
{
      xend = atoi(variable(input, "x_end="));
}
void Chess::get_end_Y()
{
      yend = alpha_atoi(variable(input, "y_end="));
}
void Chess::show_chess_square(char* position)
{
      cout << "<IMG HEIGHT=20 WIDTH=20 SRC=" <<
          position <<
          ">\n";
}
char* Chess::set_position(
      int X,          /* X coordinate */
      int Y,          /* Y coordinate */
      int background_color
```

```
)
{
    return ( image[hidden[Y][(2*X)+1] -
        '0'+piece_color][background_color] );
}
void Chess::get_variable(char* name, char* hidden_name)
{
    strcpy(name, variable(input, hidden_name));
}
```


Encryption

IT IS DIFFICULT but possible to use encryption algorithms built into the cgi-bin program to provide some real security[3] and still use hidden variables. This will allow
real hidden data to be created. Again, extreme caution should be maintained if any
type of real security is the issue. The required encryption[4] is provided by generation of a key along with the encrypted data. Without knowledge of how to use the
encryption key, there will be no easy way to decipher the other encrypted information located in other hidden variables. This technique would certainly make sense
for games, where the result of someone figuring out the encryption would not be
catastrophic.

The encryption key is done by providing a message and a key. In the example
that follows, the message is made up of the letters A to Z, which are mapped into
the numbers 1 to 26. The key is made up of the letters a to z, which are also
mapped into the numbers 1 to 26. For simplicity, spaces are ignored. Suppose you
have the message

HELLO INTERNET WORLD

with the key

adwlq

To encrypt the message, take the value of H (in HELLO), which is 8, and add it to the
value of a (in the key), which is 1. This gives 9, or the letter I. Now take the value of
E, which is 5, and add the value of d, or 4, to get 9, or another I. Continue the process. When the key is exhausted, return to the beginning and repeat. If the value of

---

[3]   RSA Public Key Cryptography is the most often used. It is used by secure HTTP servers such as SSL
      (Secure Sockets Layer Protocol). The examples shown here are for lower-level encryption over pub-
      lic access facilities.

[4]   RSA is a public-key cryptosystem that uses relatively prime numbers to provide encryption and
      authentication. Users wishing to provide real encrypted data should examine the literature on RSA.

the addition exceeds 26, subtract 26 to get the new value. You will now have two hidden variables. The first is the encrypted message. The second is the key.

For HELLO INTERNET WORLD the encrypted message will be

IIIXF JRQQIMIQ IFJPA

The key is, of course, adwlq. You decode the message by reversing the procedure—that is, subtracting instead of adding.

The code to accomplish the encoding and decoding is straightforward.

```
/*
 * Type: C++ or C
 * Usage: decode an encrypted message
 */
char*            /* return decoded message */
decode (
    char* return_msg;/* message returned */
    char* message,/* message to decode */
    char* key /* key to use to decode */
) {
    int key_length = strlen(key);
    int key_location = 0;
    int msg_location = 0;
    while((message + msg_location) != NULL)
    {
        return_msg[msg_location] =
            *(message + msg_location) - 'A' +
            *(key + key_location) - 'a' + 2;
        if ( return_msg[msg_location] > 26 )
        {
            return_msg[msg_location] -= 26;
        }
        return_msg += ('A' - 1);
        ++msg_location;
        ++key_location ;
        if ( key_location > key_length )
            key_location = 0;
    }
    return ( & return_msg[0] );
}
/*
 * Type: C++ or C
 * Usage: encode an encrypted message
 */
char*            /* return encoded message */
encode (
```

```
        char* return_msg;  /* message returned */
        char* message,     /* message to decode */
        char* key          /* key to use to decode */
    ) {
        int key_length = strlen(key);
        int key_location = 0;
        int msg_location = 0;
        while((message + msg_location) != NULL)
        {
            return_msg[msg_location] =
                *(message + msg_location) - 'A' -
                *(key + key_location) - 'a' + 2;
            if ( return_msg[msg_location] < 0 )
            {
                return_msg[msg_location] += 26;
            }
            return_msg[msg_location += ('A' - 1);
            ++msg_location;
            ++key_location ;
            if ( key_location > key_length )
                key_location = 0;
        }
        return ( & return_msg[0] );
    }
```

More complex keys systems can be easily developed to provide increased security.

Hidden variables are not the same as comments, even though both are not visible when viewed by the browser. While comments are hidden from the normal HTML view, they are not passed along when a form is submitted. The one partial exception is the Thru mode described in Chapter 7. In the combined THRU_MODE and Comment mode, a certain part of the comment is passed to the next step. But this is not a passing along in the normal sense of the word since it is not sent using client-server HTTP protocol. In the case of the hidden variables, real information can be passed along from one form to the next. Hidden variables are passed along with the user input when the submit occurs.

Here is an HTML form with a hidden variable and an encryption key.

```
<HTML><HEAD><TITLE>
Hidden Variable FORM
</TITLE></HEAD>
<BODY>
<H1> This FORM includes a Hidden Variable </H1>
<FORM METHOD="post"
 ACTION="http://internet_path/cgi-bin/cgi_hidden" >
```

```
<INPUT TYPE="hidden" NAME="myhidden" VALUE="somevalue" >
<INPUT TYPE="hidden" NAME="encryption" VALUE="a1v34579" >
<INPUT TYPE="submit" NAME="Enter">
</FORM>
</BODY></HTML>
```

When this form is submitted, both the variable myhidden and the variable encryption will be sent to the cgi-bin program. The variable myhidden will have a fixed value (myhidden = somevalue), as will the variable encryption. The encryption variable is used as a key in the cgi-bin program.

To use the encryption hidden variable(s), a cgi-bin program with a special hidden class is created. The hidden variable could be dealt with like any other variable, but our intention is to use it in a special manner.

Here is a C++ class to provide hidden encryption capabilities:

```
class _Encryption :: public _Form
{
Private:
    char key[MAX_SIZE];
    char return_msg[MAX_SIZE]
Public:
    _Encryption() { ; };
    /*
     * create a hidden variable to become part of the HTML output
     */
    virtual char* create_hidden (char* name, char* input_string);
    /*
     * The key routine can be enchanced to create more complex keys.
     */
    virtual void create_key(char* seed){ strcpy(key, seed);
    /*
     * See earlier routines
     * Returns decoded or encode message
     */
    virtual char* encode(char* message);
    virtual char* decode(char* message);
};
```

About the hidden class . . . .

First we provide the hidden class with the form capability discussed earlier. This will allow us to read in the value in the hidden variable(s). Next we provide the actual class with two capabilities. The first is to produce a new hidden variable in HTML. This can be the regeneration of the hidden variable that was sent, or generation of a new hidden variable, which can be based on the old hidden variable and what the user input to the form. The second function is the capability to create an encryption key. Finally, there are the decode and encode routines, which share the private variable return_msg.

The steps in encryption are as follows:

1. Create an encryption key.
2. Encode any message using the key.
3. Create the hidden variable, which includes the key and encoded message.
4. Send the hidden variable included as part of a form or other HTML output.

The steps in decoding of an encrypted message are as follows:

1. Receive the hidden variable containing the key.
2. Receive the message as either part of the hidden variable or separately.
3. Using the key, decode the message.
4. Send the message out as either a hidden variable or visibly along with other HTML content.

· ·

This subroutine returns an HTML string that contains the input string as a hidden variable.

```
/*
 * Type C++ class subroutine
 * Purpose: create the encryption hidden variable
 */
char*
_Encryption::create_hidden( char* name, char* input_string)
{
    char buffer[MAXLINE];
    sprintf(buffer, "%s%s%s%s%s",
        "<INPUT TYPE=\"hidden\" NAME=\"",
        name,
        "\" VALUE=\"",
        input_string,
        "\" >" );
    return( buffer );
}
/*
 * Type C++ class subroutine
 * Purpose: encryption
 */
/*
 * This subroutine encrypts an input string and then creates a hidden variable with the
 * encrypted data
 */
char* _Encryption::encode(char* input_string )
```

```
{
    char buffer[MAXLINE];
    /*
     * encrypt using the key - persons interested in encryption will need to study texts
     * on ways to encrypt information
     */
    // Do encryption
    return( buffer );
}
```

When doing encryption, you will also need to send out the key. It will be sent as an unencrypted hidden variable. Since the decoding algorithms will be built into the cgi-bin program, it will use them along with the key to determine the value of the encrypted hidden variable. The key can then be passed to the next stage.

Creating a Hidden Variable File

IN MANY SITUATIONS, CONTINUITY between events for a standard program will normally be provided by a file that is updated with each new change. If this is done over the Internet using cgi-bin programming, the files will end up on the server side. This could create numerous problems that are best avoided (e.g., disk usage and files that are never removed). To provide a similar capability, a hidden variable file can be created.

In the next partial version of the chess program, the user's history of moves is used to re-create the board after each new move. This differs from the earlier version, in which the board state was maintained. Here, the actual move history is used to rebuild the board. This move history is sent as a hidden variable file.

Unlike the previous example, there is no finite length to the hidden variables. The number of moves can vary depending on the state of the game. This will require a history file. To accomplish this, a virtual file is created in the hidden variables. By using the C++ operator new or the C operator malloc, it is possible to manage this situation without allocating over large areas in memory. This is done by providing a hidden variable with a count of how many strings of variable information will follow. The user's move and the counter are retrieved from the stdin using character-by-character reads. When both variables have been read from stdin, the next characters in stdin will be the move history. The counter is then used to determine the required space needed to retrieve the rest of the message from stdin. The space allocation is done by sectioning the moves into strings of 80 characters maximum kept in hidden variables. The counter is used to determine the size of the move history. The move history is the virtual file. The counter is multiplied by 80 plus the length of the variable names. This is used to determine the maximum space that is needed to retrieve the virtual file. The new or malloc are then used to allocate the required space. If there is only one hidden variable representing the file, the count will be one (1). This will result in 80 plus the length of the variable name characters of space being allocated, for 1 to 80 characters of data. When the count is two (2), there are two hidden variables for the file and the space allocated is 160 characters plus 2 times the length of the variable names, for 81 to 160 characters. The process continues as the hidden file grows in size with more and more user moves. Surplus space will never be more than 79 characters.

Table 10.2 shows the variables being sent to the program from the form.

TABLE 10.2 new *or* malloc *Hidden Variables*

Variable Name	Content
move=XXXXX	The user's new move in chess notation.
counter=XX	A count of the number of hidden variables there are that contain moves.[a]
board00=XXXX…X	The variables used to re-create the board. The value of xx is a number from 00 to 99. The data are the virtual file. Only the needed hidden variables will be present.
board01=XXXX…X	Next section of virtual file.
boardNN=XXXX…X	*N*th section of virtual file.

[a] This is not the number of moves, since the length of a move string may vary. It is the number of hidden variables, each of which contains a number of moves.

The steps to create a new chess move are as follows:

1. The user enters a move into the chess board form and submits it to the cgi-bin program.
2. The program retrieves the new move using character-by-character retrieval. This is required since the length of the entire input string is not yet known.
3. The program retreives the counter value character by character.
4. The counter is changed to an integer and used to malloc or new the space required to retrieve the rest of the message (i.e., the previous moves).
5. The moves are retrieved and then used to re-create the board state.
6. The new move is added to the board state.
7. The new move is added to the previous moves, and a new hidden variable is created.
8. The chess board form is sent back to the user along with the hidden file containing the move history.

```
/*
 * Type C++ or C subroutine
 * Purpose: character read of stdin to get the count before the "free"
 */
```

```
char* get_next_variable(char* variable)
{
    char c;
    char* tmp_ptr = variable;
    while((c = getc(stdin)) != '=') ;
    while(c != '&') { *tmp_ptr++ = c; }
    *tmp_ptr = 0; /* null terminate */
    return(variable);
}
/*
 * Type C++ class subroutine
 * Purpose: use free to read in variable length hidden variables
 */
void main()
{
    char move[20];
    char tmp_bcnt[20];
    char board_string[20];
    char* move_ptr;
    char* line;
    char* mymoves;
    int bcnt;
    /*
     * Read the new move from the user.
     */
    move_ptr = get_next_variable(move);
    /*
     * Read the counter that tells how many additional hidden variables there are.
     */
    bcnt = atoi(get_next_variable(tmp_bcnt));
    /* Do any out-of-range checking */
    /*
     * NEW or MALLOC the required space for the state of the chess board.
     */
    gets(line = new char[90 * bcnt]);
    /*
     * This is smaller because it doesn't include the variable name, equal signs, and
     * ampersands.
     */
    mymoves = new char[80 * bcnt];
    /*
     * Get the state of the chess board based on previous moves that have been made and
     * are in hidden variables starting from board0 and continuing through board1,...
     */
    *mymoves=NULL; /* start with a null string */
    int i=0;
    /*
```

```
          * Append any other board variables
          */
         while(i< bcnt )
         {
              sprintf(board_string, "board%d=", i);
              strcat(mymoves, variable(line, board_string)); i++;
         }
         /*
          * Regenerate the board from the string mymoves
          */
         /*
          * Using the user's input, make the user's move and then let the computer make its
          * move.
          */
         /*
          * Generate the HTML to output the new board to the user.
          */
     }
```

About this program. . . . .

This program uses new or malloc to determine the size of the variable required for
the user's chess moves. This is equivalent to using hidden variables to replace a file
that changes size each time a new move is made. The size of the hidden variable
strings is determined by reading in a hidden variable that contains a multiplier.
The multiplier is then used to set the size at

> multiplier times the maximum size of the hidden variables

which in this example is set to 90 characters. The first variables, which include the
user's move and the number of hidden variables that follow, are pulled off a character at a time since they are relatively small strings. The longer strings, which are the
representation of a file in hidden variables, are retrieved after the new or malloc of
the required space. This is a very powerful technique since it allows the equivalent
of a file to be kept in hidden variables. In this case the hidden variable file represents the history of moves made by the user in the chess game, which will be used to
regenerate the chess board for each new move made by the user and then by the
computer. The power of this technique is that hidden variable files can be kept for
any number of users without having any effect on disk or memory space on the host
computer. The files exist at the user's site, not at the server site.

1. The first two hidden variables are the user's new move on the chess board
   and a count of how many hidden variables containing previous moves
   (board configuration) information have been created.

2. Space is then newed or malloced to retrieve the previous moves based on how
   many hidden variables have been set up. The hidden variables contain 80
   move characters plus the variable name, the equal sign, and the ampersand.

3. The board moves are retrieved and then the extraneous information is removed so that only the moves are in the string mymoves.

4. The previous moves will then be sent to a routine that reads the moves and reconfigures the board. Remember, the Internet is memoryless. This may seem like a lot of overhead for each move, but it actually occurs very quickly.

5. Once the board is reconfigured, the new user move will be sent to the program.

6. The rest of the code is similar to the chess routines shown earlier. Two changes are required. First, the board needs to be generated from a sequence of moves rather than a static picture of the board. This is consistent with many chess playing programs that save moves to a file. Second, the HTML has to generate the new hidden variables, which consist of the number of hidden variables and the boardN= hidden variables. Partial code for these is shown next.

```
/*
 * Subroutine to output the number of hidden variables based on the length of the string
 * containing all the previous moves plus the new user move and the new computer move.
 */
/*
 * Type C class subroutine
 * Purpose: determine number of hidden varialbles
 */
int get_total_cnt(char* all_moves)
{
    int tmp_cnt;
    tmp_cnt = strlen(all_moves);
    tmp_cnt = tmp_cnt/80 + (tmp_cnt % 80 == 0 ? 0 : 1);
    return(tmp_cnt);
}
/*
 * Subroutine to put out the move history into hidden variables.
 */
/*
 * Type C subroutine
 * Purpose: create the new html hidden variables
 */
char* hidden_board(char* next_moves, int hidden_cnt)
{
    int k = 0;
    printf(
        "<INPUT TYPE=\"hidden\" NAME=\"board%d\" SIZE=\"80\" VALUE=\"",
            hidden_cnt );
    while(k<80)
    {
        printf("%c", *next_moves);
        next_moves++; k++;
```

```
            if(*next_moves == 0) break;
        }
        printf("\">\n");
        return(next_moves);
    }
```

· ·

In C, add the include

```
#include <malloc.h>
```

and change the new line to use malloc

```
line = malloc (sizeof(char) * 90 * bcnt);
```

Summary

In this chapter you have learned how to pass information between Internet pages using hidden variables. By changing the content of the hidden variables in the C++ program, you are now able to create a continuous flow of events. The transition state machine provides a method to move forward or backward and could even support fuzzy logic. The chess game adds to this the manipulations of IMaGe pointers to create a constantly reconfigured screen based on the user's input and the previously established state found in the hidden variables. Other variables, such as the WHO variable, can provide toggles or other state changes. Two methods are provided in the chess game to start from a predefined state. In the first, the present state is saved from the browser. When the user calls up this page locally, the hidden variables are already set to the previous value. A move is made and the process continues. Two people could actually play a game of chess by sending the saved HTML page through email. The person receiving the email would invoke the sent page through his or her browser and the person's move would appear on his or her browser screen. The person would then make a move and repeat the process. In the second method, a filemode is provided. This allows users to use conventional FTP (the file must be at the server site) to start a game from a given state. This mode is especially good for setting up chess problem like those found in the newspaper columns.

The methods provided here can be extended to any situation in which an Internet page will provide systematically changing output.

In this chapter additional techniques for using hidden variables were developed. While the example was a chess game, the techniques developed are expandable to many continuity problems on the Internet. The chess cgi-bin program also developed a new technique for building up graphic images with GIFs. The hidden variable file provides a means to obtain extended continuity between accesses.

PROGRAM EXERCISES

1. Develop a game of tick tack toe using hidden variables to maintain status. Verify that the game can be played. (**Note:** You can make the game a two-person game or you can play against the computer.)

2. Develop a cgi-bin program that receives input initially from the user about his or her age group. Based on this input, provide at least three more outputs that use the age group. (**Hint:** You can use the Thru mode to make it easier to create the different outputs.)

3. Develop a multiple cgi-bin program. On the first request get the user's IP address from the environment. Use this in hidden variables to block access to certain requests on subsequent forms. (**Advanced:** See if you can come up with a way to send only part of the HTML back to the user if his or her IP address is restricted rather than sending back a blocked message.)

4. Using the hidden variable file technique, provide an output table that is based on the hidden variable file and that grows with each new input from the user. (**Hint:** Parse out the hidden variables and use them along with the user's input to generate the table followed by a new form that includes the previous hidden variables plus a new one generated from the user's input.)

PROBLEMS

1. Explain in detail how hidden variables can provide continuity between form accesses to Web pages. Explain the difference between static continuity, in which the user provides a specific piece of information that is maintained between each access, and dynamic continuity, in which the hidden variable is changed on the fly depending on each input from the user. Provide a specific project in which each type could be used. Are there situations that might require both?

2. Explain how hidden variables can be seen by the users. What does this mean in terms of using hidden variables for security?

3. In the chess game, hidden variables are used to maintain the status of the board. Why is this needed? Examine a different project and explain how you would structure the hidden variables to provide continuity. See if you can come up with at least one example in which the hidden variables will be restricted to a finite number of items. If this is not the case, how can you provide some limits on the size of your hidden variables?

CHAPTER 11

Base Class Expanded

Organizing Base Classes and Derived Classes

Rules

Developing the Base HTML Class

Derived Classes

Organizing Base Classes and Derived Classes

To USE THE POWER OF object-oriented programming, it is necessary to set up a structure from which to grow future cgi-bin programs. Doing so requires that you first think about what the Internet objects should look like and then examine the interfaces between these objects.

The most obvious object is the HTML Web page. For the Internet, the Web page is the basic object that interfaces to the user. The main page is, of course, the Home page, while other pages are related pages or subpages or just Web pages. In defining objects that relate to pages, one readily usable structure emerges. At the base level will be the actual HTML modules. These will provide an easy way to create any HTML output from your cgi-bin programs. To create these, begin by analyzing the HTML language. While there are probably numerous ways to categorize this language, the one presented here is provided to fit into the way programmers tend to think about languages. HTML modules divide into several broad categories:

1. Modules that are contained in between begin and end HTML delineators and contain a body of material, such as the headings (<H1>...</H1>).
2. Modules that are contained in between begin and end HTML delineators and also have additional arguments, such as the IMaGe (<IMG SRC=... >).

<span></span>

<span></span>

209

3. Delineators that are placed either at the beginning or the end of an item (break <BR> and paragraph <P>).

4. Modules that contain multiple strings, such as the anchor (<A HREF=... > anchor text</A>).

5. Modules that are always imbedded inside another HTML argument, such as list items (<LI>).

6. Multiply-defined modules that fall into more than one of the preceding categories. For example, IMaGe can take optional arguments, so it could be included in category 3 or 4. For this reason, you should consider modules with variable arguments as a special case. In many instances, a default number of arguments will be used for the more frequent way a multiple-argument capability is used and alternatives will be provided for the other situations.

Rules

A SET OF RULES DETERMINES what can and what cannot be placed inside different HTML elements. The rule structure will need to be built into the classes to prevent bad requests. Rules will map into class functions.

To realize these capabilities, a base HTML class needs to be developed. The foundation for this was begun previously. This class will either return pointers to strings, which can then be placed in a buffer and sent to stdout, or directly send output to stdout. In either case, the final output will go to stdout, which is sent to the Internet server and then to the client software. By returning a pointer to a string, a subroutine can pass the string to another subroutine for further imbedding, send the string to the buffer, or pass the string to stdout. The other alternative—direct output to stdout—is provided for quick creation of HTML output from your cgi-bin programs. Depending on your preference for creating HTML, you can select either approach. This modular approach will allow easy implementation of HTML output to produce Web pages.

Above the base class, you can build classes that will send out common sequences. Above these you can build classes to send out entire Web pages. These Web pages, which will be specific to your applications, can then be connected with standard interfaces to other C++ or C modules.

In this way, the base HTML class provides a building block for any future development. When connected to other classes, such as the Form class and the Mailer class, it can provide simple building blocks for future cgi-bin projects.

Developing the Base HTML Class

THE BASE HTML CLASS WILL be developed with several goals in mind:

1. It will provide the various alternatives allowed for the same HTML element. For any HTML that allows optional arguments, a routine will be provided to

create the most frequent occurrence and one or more to handle the optional alternative arguments. This will provide a quick method to produce HTML output and slightly more complex routines for handling additional options. For example, the routine for sending out images will have a basic routine, which takes a single argument of the image to be sent to the screen, and secondary routines, which include the optional arguments for sizing the image and presenting alternative text to nongraphic browsers. For most applications the basic routine will allow you to get started. Later, you can change over to the more complex versions to optimize your projects.

2. For any HTML type of output that can be imbedded in another HTML type, options will be provided that either directly send the output to stdout or that return a pointer to a string, which can then be imbedded into another HTML layer. The ability to imbed is widespread in HTML. (For example, an image and/or an anchor can be placed inside a table.) In C++ this can be accomplished easily with overloading, while in C alternative names will be required for the different subroutines. By allowing ways to create the same HTML, you provide yourself with a means to create buffers or directly send HTML, depending on your specific situation.

3. For C++, overloading will be used extensively to accomplish these goals, while for C, alternative but similar program names will be used. The C++ overloading capability allows two functions with the same name to exist as long as there is a way for the compiler to distinguish them. In the case of the base class, the distinction will be additional arguments when optional arguments are included or different returns. An example of this second case would be one routine that sends its output to stdout and returns a void versus a second routine, with the same name, that returns a pointer to the HTML string.

For the HTML class, the structure looks like this:

```
class _Html_page // base class for HTML
{
private:
    int type;
    char msg_buffer[MAXLINE];
public:
    _Html(){ type=0;};
                        // no args
    char* cgi();        // string version
    void cgi();         // stdout version
                        // subroutines to return a string pointer
                        // single argument
    char* li(char* msg);
    void li(char* msg);
    char* hx(char x, char* msg);
    void hx(char x, char* msg);
    char* html(char* msg, int type);
```

```
void html(char* msg, int type);
char* title(char* msg);
void title(char* msg);
char* body(char* msg, int type);
// the rest of the routines are shown below
char* blockquote(char* msg);
char* form(char* msg);
char* select(char* msg);
char* option(char* msg);
char* textarea(char* msg);
char* hn(char* msg); // HTML+
char* dl(char* msg);
char* dt(char* msg);
char* dd(char* msg);
char* ol(char* msg);
char* ul(char* msg);
char* dir(char* msg);
char* menu(char* msg);
char* li(char* msg);
char* pre(char* msg);
char* b(char* msg);
char* i(char* msg);
char* tt(char* msg);
char** u(char* msg);

char* table(char* msg);
char* th(char* msg, char* align, char* colspan, char*rowspan);
char* td(char* msg, char* align, char* colspan, char*rowspan);
char* tr(char* msg);
char* caption(char* msg);

char* cite(char* msg);
char* code(char* msg);
char* dfn(char* msg); // HTML 2.0
char* em(char* msg);
char* kbd(char* msg);
char* samp(char* msg);
char* strike(char* msg);
char* strong(char* msg);
char* var(char* msg);
/* HTML + */
char* arg(char* msg);
char* text(char* msg);
char* abbrev(char* msg);
char* cmd(char* msg);
char* person(char* msg);
char* q(char* msg);
```

```
char* abstract(char* msg);
char* fig(char* msg);
char* footnote(char* msg);
char* lit(char* msg);
char* margin(char* msg);
char* math(char* msg);
char* note(char* msg);
char* online(char* msg);

// multi arguments
// overload anchors
char* a(char* anchor, char* msg);
char* a(char* anchor,
     char* msg, char* rel,
     char* name, char* rev,
     char* urn, char* title,
     char* method, char* effect,
     char* print, char* type);
char* img(char* src, char* align, char* alt);
char* meta(char* http_equiv, char* name, char* content)
char* input(char* type, char* name, char* value, char* size);
// empty
char* head(char* msg);
char* base(char* msg);
char* isindex(char* msg);
char* link(char* msg, char* title);
char* nextid(char* msg);

// no args
char* hr();
char* arg(char *); // Use for br, p
// overloading to send directly to stdout
void body(char* msg, int type);
void blockquote(char* msg);
void form(char* msg);
void select(char* msg);
void option(char* msg);
void textarea(char* msg);
void hn(char* msg); // HTML+
void dl(char* msg);
void dt(char* msg);
void dd(char* msg);
void ol(char* msg);
void ul(char* msg);
void dir(char* msg);
void menu(char* msg);
void li(char* msg);
```

```
void pre(char* msg);
void b(char* msg);
void i(char* msg);
void tt(char* msg);
void u(char* msg);

void table(char* msg);
void th(char* msg, char* align, char* colspan, char*rowspan);
void td(char* msg, char* align, char* colspan, char*rowspan);
void tr(char* msg);
void caption(char* msg);
void cite(char* msg);
void code(char* msg);
void dfn(char* msg); // HTML 2.0
void em(char* msg);
void kbd(char* msg);
void samp(char* msg);
void strike(char* msg);
void strong(char* msg);
void var(char* msg);
/* HTML + */
void arg(char* msg);
void text(char* msg);
void abbrev(char* msg);
void cmd(char* msg);
void person(char* msg);
void q(char* msg);
void abstract(char* msg);
void fig(char* msg);
void footnote(char* msg);
void lit(char* msg);
void margin(char* msg);
void math(char* msg);
void note(char* msg);
void online(char* msg);
// multi arguments
// overload anchors
void a(char* anchor, char* msg);
void a(char* anchor,
     char* msg, char* rel,
     char* name, char* rev,
     char* urn, char* title,
     char* method, char* effect,
     char* print, char* type);
void img(char* src, char* align, char* alt);
void meta(char* http_equiv, char* name, char* content);
void input(char* type,char* name,
```

```
            char* value, char* size);
        // empty
        void head(char* msg);
        void base(char* msg);
        void isindex(char* msg);
        void link(char* msg, char* title);
        void nextid(char* msg);

        // no args
        void hr();
        void arg(char *); // Use for br, p
};
```

For the C language, the same approach will be a group of functions that look very similar to the C++ class functions shown in the following computer program. The advantages of overloading functions will not be available, which means C programs will need to use slightly different names for alternative versions of the same basic functionality. Since many of the C routines require only a change from cout to printf and the omission of the class name, only a few examples have been included at the end of this chapter to illustrate the subtle differences.

The routines shown here include extensive comments to assist users who have minimal knowledge of HTML and to provide an HTML reference source for those with more knowledge. The code segments can also serve as examples when providing HTML from your cgi-bin programs. Figure 11.1 shows some of the many expansions provided by the base class.

```
char* _Html_page::li(
    char* msg     // message string
    )
{
/*
  * Rules:     Can be contained in DIR, MENU, UL, or OL.
  *            String can contain anchors, images, text, and any of the following: BR,
  *            DL, MENU, OL, UL, BLOCKQUOTE, FORM, P, PRE, ISINDEX
  * Use:  Formats a list item
  */
    ostream dest(MAXLINE, msg_buffer);
    dest<<"<LI> " << msg <<" </LI>\n";
    return(&msg_buffer[0]);
}
char* _Html_page::hx (
    char x,
    char* msg     // string characters or reference
    )
{
/*
  * Rules: String can contain
```

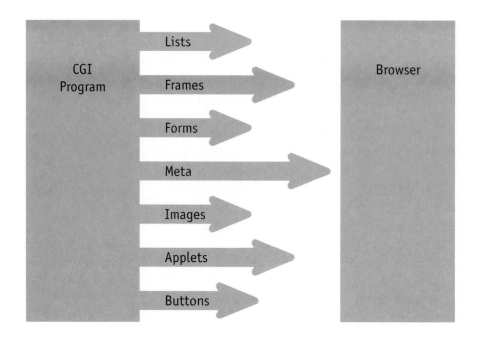

FIGURE 11.1   Base Class Expanded: Increased combining of HTML and cgi-bin programs pro-vides extensive control.

```
  *         anchors, images, text, and any of the following: CITE, CODE, DFN, EM, KBD,
  *             SAMP, STRIKE, STRONG, VAR, B, I, TT and U
  * Use:   Creates a header at level x (1-6). The exact display is determined by the browser.
  */
    ostream dest(MAXLINE, msg_buffer);
    dest<<"<H" << x << "> " << msg <<" </H" << x << ">\n";
    return(&msg_buffer[0]);
}
```

C Version

```
hx (char x, char* msg)
{
    fprintf(msg_buffer, "%s%c%s%s%s%c%s",
        "<H", x, "> ", msg, " </H", x, ">\n");
    return(&msg_buffer[0]);
}
/* Places these defines in an appropriate header file */
#define START 0
#define END 1
#define START_END 2
or alternatively
```

```
enum
{
    START,
    END,
    START_END
}
char* _Html_page::html(
    char* msg,      // string
    int type        // allow start & end due to document size
    )
{
/*
 * Rules: Contain all HTML and HTML messages
 * Use:   Tells where HTML starts in the page
 */
    ostream dest(MAXLINE, msg_buffer);
    if(type==START)
    {
        dest<<"<HTML>";
    }
    else
    if(type==END)
    {
        dest<<"</HTML>";
    else
    if(type==START_END)
    {
        dest<<"<HTML> " << msg <<" </HTML>\n";
    }
    return(&msg_buffer[0]);
}
```

C Version

```
char* html(char* msg, int type)
{
    if(type==START)
    {
        fprintf(msg_buffer, "<HTML>");
    }
    else
    if(type==END)
    {
        fprintf(msg_buffer, "</HTML>");
    else
    if(type==START_END)
    {
```

```
        fprintf(msg_buffer, "%s%s%s",
            "<HTML> ",msg, " </HTML>\n");
    }
    /* add an error leg here */
    return(&msg_buffer[0]);
}
char* _Html_page::head(
    char* msg      // string
    )
{
/*
 * Rules: Contained in HTML. The head contains general information about the document. It
 *        is not displayed in the document, but can determine attributes of the document
 *        such as background color, title, etc. Can contain TITLE, ISINDEX, BASE, NEXTID,
 *        LINK, META, BKGRND
 * Use:   Create the structure and title of the document.
 */
    ostream dest(MAXLINE, msg_buffer);
    dest<<"<HEAD> " << msg <<" </HEAD>\n";
    return(&msg_buffer[0]);
}
char* _Html_page::base(
    char* msg      // string
    )
{
/*
 * Rules: Inside the HEAD. Contains an HREF that is the base for other HREFs, anchors,
 *        images, text, and any of the other linkable resources.
 * Use:   This is an offset HREF. It allows subsequent HREFs in the document to be relative,
 *        (i.e., only include the final part of the HREF). Some systems automatically provide
 *        relative addressing from the existing URL.
 */
    ostream dest(MAXLINE, msg_buffer);
    dest<<"<BASE> " << msg <<" </BASE>\n";
    return(&msg_buffer[0]);
}
char* _Html_page::title(
    char* msg      // text string only
    )
{
/*
 * Rules: Contained in the head. The title appears in a special area on most browsers. Titles
 *        should be picked carefully since some search tools use the title to search.
 * Use:   Puts up a text only title, differs from the head normally found at the top of a
 *        document.
 */
    ostream dest(MAXLINE, msg_buffer);
```

```
            dest<<"<TITLE> " << msg <<" </TITLE>\n";
            return(&msg_buffer[0]);
    }
    char* _Html_page::body(
        char* msg,      // string
        int type        // allow start & end due to document size
        )
    {
    /*
      * Rules: Contained inside HTML. The BODY contains the HTML document, including all the
      *         HTML formatting elements. The BODY can contain most HTML elements: Hx, P, HR,
      *         DIR, DL, MENU, OL, UL, ADDRESS, BLOCKQUOTE, FORM, PRE, ISINDEX, TABLE,
      *         ANCHOR, IMG, ACTION...
      * Use:    Tells where the body of the document begins and ends
      */
        ostream dest(MAXLINE, msg_buffer);
        if(type==START)
        {
            dest<<"<BODY>";
        }
        else
        if(type==END)
        {
            dest<<"</BODY>";
        else
        if(type==START_END)
        {
            dest<<"<BODY> " << msg <<" </BODY>\n";
        }
        return(&msg_buffer[0]);
    }
    char* _Html_page::blockquote(
        char* msg       // string
        )
    {
    /*
      * Rules: The BLOCKQUOTE can contain most HTML, including Hx, P, HR, DIR, DL, MENU, OL,
      *         UL, ADDRESS, BLOCKQUOTE, FORM, PRE, ISINDEX
      * Use:    Marks a block of text as a quotation
      */
        ostream dest(MAXLINE, msg_buffer);
        dest<<"<BLOCKQUOTE> " << msg <<" </BLOCKQUOTE>\n";
        return(&msg_buffer[0]);
    }
    char* _Html_page::form(
        char* msg       // form string
        )
```

```
{
/*
 * Rules: Examples of forms have been given in earlier sections. The FORM needs to be
 *        developed as modules and then placed inside the FORM HTML
 * Use:   Surrounds a FORM
 */
    ostream dest(MAXLINE, msg_buffer);
    dest<<"<FORM> " << msg <<" </FORM>\n";
    return(&msg_buffer[0]);
}
char* _Html_page::select(
    char* msg      // string
    )
{
/*
 * Rules: Contains OPTIONS. Will be inside of a FORM.
 * Use:   Creates the HTML element around options that are pull-down choices used in forms
 */
    ostream dest(MAXLINE, msg_buffer);
    dest<<"<SELECT> " << msg <<" </SELECT>\n";
    return(&msg_buffer[0]);
}
char* _Html_page::option(
    char* msg      // string
    )
{
/*
 * Rules: Contains text. Can be inside of a SELECT
 * Use:   Provides OPTIONs that will normally show as a pull-down screen as part of the
 *        choices in a FORM
 */
    ostream dest(MAXLINE, msg_buffer);
    dest<<"<OPTION> " << msg <<" </OPTION>\n";
    return(&msg_buffer[0]);
}
char* _Html_page::textarea(
    char* msg      // string
    )
{
/*
 * Rules: Contains text. Can be inside of a FORM
 * Use:   Allows entry of a block of text inside of a FORM. The text is then sent to the cgi
 *        script as part of the message.
 */
    ostream dest(MAXLINE, msg_buffer);
    dest<<"<TEXTAREA> " << msg <<" </TEXTAREA>\n";
    return(&msg_buffer[0]);
```

```
}
char* _Html_page::dt(
     char* msg      // string
     )
{
/*
 * Rules: Contains characters, anchors <A> and images <IMG>. Can be inside of DL.
 * Use:   Contains the glossary or description list. Typically a few words or a short anchor.
 */
     ostream dest(MAXLINE, msg_buffer);
     dest<<"<DT> " << msg <<" </DT>\n";
     return(&msg_buffer[0]);
}
char* _Html_page::ol(
     char* msg      // string
     )
{
/*
 * Rules: Contains LI. Can be inside of BLOCKQUOTE, BODY, DD, FORM, LI.
 * Use:   Creates an ordered list. The list items are delineated by LI.
 */
     ostream dest(MAXLINE, msg_buffer);
     dest<<"<OL> " << msg <<" </OL>\n";
     return(&msg_buffer[0]);
}
char* _Html_page::ul(
     char* msg      // string
     )
{
/*
 * Rules: Contains LI. Can be inside of BLOCKQUOTE, BODY, DD, FORM, LI.
 * Use:   Creates an unordered list. The list items are delineated by LI.
 */
     ostream dest(MAXLINE, msg_buffer);
     dest<<"<UL> " << msg <<" </UL>\n";
     return(&msg_buffer[0]);
}
char* _Html_page::dir(
     char* msg      // string
     )
{
/*
 * Rules: Contains LI. Can be inside of BLOCKQUOTE, BODY, DD, FORM, LI.
 * Use:   Creates an directory list. The list items are delineated by LI.
 */
     ostream dest(MAXLINE, msg_buffer);
     dest<<"<DIR> " << msg <<" </DIR>\n";
```

```
        return(&msg_buffer[0]);
}
char* _Html_page::menu(
        char* msg      // string
        )
{
/*
  * Rules: Contains LI. Can be inside of BLOCKQUOTE, BODY, DD, FORM, LI.
  * Use:   Creates a menu list. The list items are delineated by LI.
  */
        ostream dest(MAXLINE, msg_buffer);
        dest<<"<MENU> " << msg <<" </MENU>\n";
        return(&msg_buffer[0]);
}
char* _Html_page::li(
        char* msg      // string
        )
{
/*
  * Rules: Contains list items, including anchors <A>, images <IMG>, other lists, emphasis
  *          <B> <I> etc. Can be inside of UL, OL, DIR, MENU
  * Use:   Delineates a list element in a list of items. The items of the list can be text,
  *          anchors, or images or combinations of these items.
  */
        ostream dest(MAXLINE, msg_buffer);
        dest<<"<LI> " << msg <<" </LI>\n";
        return(&msg_buffer[0]);
}
char* _Html_page::pre(
        char* msg      // string
        )
{
/*
  * Rules: Contains raw text. Can be inside of BLOCKQUOTE, BODY, DD, FORM, LI.
  * Use:   Marks text to be displayed with a fixed width type font. Typically used for raw text.
  *          For example, email can be displayed as HTML formatted text.
  */
        ostream dest(MAXLINE, msg_buffer);
        dest<<"<PRE> " << msg <<" </PRE>\n";
        return(&msg_buffer[0]);
}
char* _Html_page::b(
        char* msg      // string
        )
{
/*
  * Rules: Contains text. Can be inside of most HTML.
```

```
 * Use:   Tells the browser to boldface the text.
 */
    ostream dest(MAXLINE, msg_buffer);
    dest<<"<B> " << msg <<" </B>\n";
    return(&msg_buffer[0]);
}
char* _Html_page::i(
    char* msg      // string
    )
{
/*
 * Rules: Contains text. Can be inside of most HTML.
 * Use:   Tells the browser to italics the text.
 */
    ostream dest(MAXLINE, msg_buffer);
    dest<<"<I> " << msg <<" </I>\n";
    return(&msg_buffer[0]);
}
char* _Html_page::u(
    char* msg      // string
    )
{
/*
 * Rules: Contains text. Can be inside of most HTML.
 * Use:   Tells the browser to underline the text.
 */
    ostream dest(MAXLINE, msg_buffer);
    dest<<"<U> " << msg <<" </U>\n";
    return(&msg_buffer[0]);
}
char* _Html_page::tt(
    char* msg      // string
    )
{
/*
 * Rules: Contains text. Can be inside of most HTML.
 * Use:   Tells the browser to set the font to fixed width typewriter.
 */
    ostream dest(MAXLINE, msg_buffer);
    dest<<"<TT> " << msg <<" </TT>\n";
    return(&msg_buffer[0]);
}
    // empty
char* _Html_page::head(
    char* msg
    )
{
```

```cpp
    ostream dest(MAXLINE, msg_buffer);
    dest<<"<HEAD> " << msg <<" </HEAD>\n";
    return(&msg_buffer[0]);

}
char* _Html_page::base(
    char* msg
    )
{
/*
 * Rules:
 * Use:
 */
    ostream dest(MAXLINE, msg_buffer);
    dest << "<BASE HREF=\" << msg << "\">\n";
    return(&msg_buffer[0]);
}
char* _Html_page::isindex(
    char* msg
    )
{
/*
 * Rules:
 * Use:
 */
    ostream dest(MAXLINE, msg_buffer);
    dest << "<ISINDEX>\n";
    return(&msg_buffer[0]);
}
char* _Html_page::link(
    char* msg,
    char* title
    )
{
/*
 * Rules:
 * Use:
 */
    ostream dest(MAXLINE, msg_buffer);
    dest << "<LINK HREF=\"" << msg << "\"";
    if(strlen(title) > 1)
    {
        dest << " TITLE=\"" << title <<"\"";
    }
    dest << ">\n";
    return(&msg_buffer[0]);
}
```

```
char* _Html_page::meta(
    char* http_equiv,          // either this or name but not both
    char* name,
    char* content             // mandatory
    )
{
/* Rules: Can be inside HEAD
 * Use:   Allows a place for meta information such as push and pull. The browser must know
 *        how to interpret the meta information.
 */
    ostream dest(MAXLINE, msg_buffer);
    dest << "<META ";
    if(strlen(http_equiv) > 1)
    {
        dest << "HTTP-EQUIV=\"" << http_equiv << "\"" ;
    } else
    if(strlen(name) > 1)
    {
        dest << "NAME=\"" << name << "\"";
    }
    dest << "CONTENT=\"" << content << "\">\n";
    return(&msg_buffer[0]);
}
char* _Html_page::nextid(
    char* msg
    )
{
/*
 * Rules:
 * Use:
 */
    ostream dest(MAXLINE, msg_buffer);
    dest << "<NEXTID N=" << msg <<">\n";
    return(&msg_buffer[0]);
}
char* _Html_page::input(
    char* type,
    char* name,
    char* value,
    char* size
    )
{
/*
 * Rules:
 * Use:
 */
    ostream dest(MAXLINE, msg_buffer);
```

```
        dest << "<INPUT TYPE=\"" << type << "\"" <<
            "NAME=\" << name << "\"" <<
            "VALUE="\" << value << "\"" <<
            "SIZE=" << size << ">\n";
        return(&msg_buffer[0]);
}
char* _Html_page::hr()
{
/*
 * Rules:
 * Use:
 */
        ostream dest(MAXLINE, msg_buffer);
        dest << "<HR>"\n;
        return(&msg_buffer[0]);
}
char* _Html_page::arg(
        char* msg       // html string
        )
{
/*
 * Rules: Any string
 * Use:   For single-string HTML (e.g., BR and P)
 */
        ostream dest(MAXLINE, msg_buffer);
        dest << "<" << msg << ">\n";
        return(&msg_buffer[0]);
}
char* _Html_page::text(
        char* msg       // text string
        )
{
/*
 * Rules: Any string
 * Use:   For single string of text (e.g., after an anchor).
 */
        ostream dest(MAXLINE, msg_buffer);
        dest << msg << "\n";
        return(&msg_buffer[0]);
}
char* _Html_page::a(
        char* anchor,
        char* msg
        )
{
/*
 * Rules: Can be inside of ADDRESS, headers <Hx>, P, DT, DD, LI. Can contain Images or Text
```

```
 *          (which can include highlights; plus a URL).
 * Use:    An anchor is used to create an active part of the HTML page. Clicking the mouse on
 *          the anchor will cause the browser to go to a new HTML page referenced in the
 *          anchor. The msg is the section that is seen and that is clicked on to move to the
 *          new page. The anchor is a URL that is where the anchor will go when activated.
 *          The msg can be an image.
 */
    ostream dest(MAXLINE, msg_buffer);
    dest << "<A HREF=\"" << anchor <<"\">" << msg <<"</A>\n";
    return(&msg_buffer[0]);


}
char* _Html_page::a(
        char* anchor,       // URL
        char* msg,          // active msg can be an image
        char* rel,          // release
        char* name,         // name
        char* rev,          // revision
        char* urn,          // ??
        char* title,        // title
        char* method,       // method
        char* effect,       // effect
        char* print,        // print
        char* type          // type
        )
{
/*
 * Rules: Can be inside of ADDRESS, headers <Hx>, P, DT, DD, LI. Can contain Images or Text
 *          (which can include highlights; plus a URL).
 * Use:    An anchor is used to create an active part of the HTML page. Clicking the mouse on
 *          the anchor will cause the browser to go to a new HTML page referenced in the
 *          anchor. The msg is the section that is seen and that is clicked on to move to the
 *          new page. The anchor is a URL that is where the anchor will go when activated.
 *          The msg can be an image.
 */
    ostream dest(MAXLINE, msg_buffer);
    dest << "<A " <<
    if(strlen(anchor) > 1)
        {
            dest << "HREF=\"" << anchor <<"\">" << msg <<"</A>\n";
        } else
    if(strlen(name) > 1)
        {
            dest << "NAME=\"" << name <<"\";
        }
    if(strlen(rel)>1)
        {
```

```
            dest << "REL=\"" << rel << "\" ";
      }
      if(strlen(rev)>1)
      {
            dest << "REV=\"" << rev << "\" ";
      }
      if(strlen(urn)>1)
      {
            dest << "URN=\"" << urn << "\" ";
      }
      if(strlen(title)>1)
      {
            dest << "TITLE=\"" << title << "\" ";
      }
      if(strlen(method)>1)
      {
            dest << "METHOD=\"" << method << "\" ";
      }
      if(strlen(effect)>1)
      {
            dest << "EFFECT=\"" << effect << "\" ";
      }
      if(strlen(print)>1)
      {
            dest << "PRINT=\"" << print << "\" ";
      }
      if(strlen(type)>1)
      {
            dest << "TYPE=\"" << type << "\" ";
      }
      dest << ">" << msg << "</A>=n";
      return(&msg_buffer[0]);
}

char* _Html_page::img(
      char* src,
      char* align,
      char* alt
      )
{
/*
  * Rules: Can be inside Highlighting, Anchors <A>, Headers, P, ADDRESS, DD, DT, and LI.
  * Use:   Places an image on the screen. Images are normally in GIF or JPG format, although
  *           some implementations may accept other formats, such as TIF or BMP. The ALT is
  *           text that will be displayed in place of the picture on browsers without the ability
  *           to show pictures (e.g., lynx). The ALIGN tells how the picture will be placed on the
  *           page with respect to the neighboring text. ALIGN options are bottom, middle, or
```

```
 *          top.
 */
     ostream dest(MAXLINE, msg_buffer);
     dest << "<IMG SRC=\"" << src <<"\" ALT=\"[" << alt
            << "]\" ALIGN= " << align << ">\n";
     return(&msg_buffer[0]);
}
char* _Html_page::frameset (
     char* rows,
     char* columns,
     char* marginwidth,
     char* marginheight
     )
/*
 * Rules: String can contain frameset, frame, noframe. Allowed inside of HTML.
 * Use:   The frameset element is used instead of the BODY element. It is used in an HTML
 *        documents whose sole purpose is to provide a layout of the Web page into column-
 *        and row-seperated segments. The rows and columns are a comma separated list
 *        describing the row heights and column widths. These can be given as percentage
 *        values or an asterisk for equal spacing.
 */
{
     ostream dest(MAXLINE, msg_buffer);
     dest << "<FRAMESET " <<
          (rows=="") ? "" : ("ROWS = " << rows);
     dest << (cols=="") ? "" : ("COLS = " << cols);
     dest << (marginwidth=="") ? "" : ("MARGINWIDTH = " << marginwidth);
     dest << (marginheight=="") ? "" : ("MARGINHEIGHT = " << marginheight);
     dest << ">\n";
     /* Note: The frameset end element is created separately since a variable number of
      * frame elements can be inside a frameset element
      */
     return(&msg_buffer[0]);
}
char* _Html_page::frameset_end ()
{
     return("</FRAMESET>\n");
}
char* _Html_page::frame (
     char* src,          /* SRC URL */
     char* name,         /* hyperlink name */
     char* scrolling,
     char* resize
     )
/*
 * Rules: String can contain nothing.
 * Use:   Defines a single FRAME inside of a FRAMESET. The SRC is the URL to place in the
```

```
*           FRAME. It can be an HTML URL or a CGI-BIN URL. The NAME assigns a name to the
*           FRAME for hyperlinks. The SCROLLING attribute determines whether scrolling is
*           allowed in the FRAME. Scrolling can be on, off, or auto. The NORESIZE attribute
*           can be used to prevent the user from resizing the FRAME area.
*/
{
    ostream dest(MAXLINE, msg_buffer);
    dest << "<FRAME " <<
        (src=="") ? "" : ("SRC = " << src);
    dest << (name=="") ? "" : (" NAME = " << name);
    dest << (scrolling=="") ? "" : (" SCROLLING= " << scrolling);
    dest << (resize=="") ? "" : ( " RESIZE = " << resize);
    dest << "></FRAME>\n";
    return(&msg_buffer[0]);
}
char* _Html_page::noframe (
    char* text
    )
/*
 * Use:   Send the noframe alternative text for browsers that do not support FRAMEs.
 */
{
    ostream dest(MAXLINE, msg_buffer);
    dest << "<NOFRAME>\n" << text << "\n</NOFRAME>\n";
    return(&msg_buffer[0]);
}
char* _Html_page::applet(
    char* codebase,    /* Optional field specifying the base URL of the APPLET. If not
                        * specified, current document's URL is used.
                        */
    char* code,        /* Required applet class name, it must be relative to the codebase.
                        */
    char* width,       // Required width of applet frame on screen.
    char* height,      // Required height of applet frame on screen.
    char* alt,         // Optional alternative text if APPLETS are not supported.
    char* name,        /* Name fields allows APPLET to communicate to another APPLET.
    char* align,       // Alignment on the page - same as IMG align
    char* vspace,      // Margin above - same as IMG vspace
    char* hspace,      // Margin to side - same as IMG hspace
    int count,         // Number of parameters
    char* param,       /* Multiple parameters and
    char* value,        * Multiple value fields for the parameter
                        * These can be used to allow APPLETS to communicate to each
                        * other or to provide input information to the APPLET
                        */

    ...
```

```
                    )
           {
           /*
            * Rules: Inside of HTML. Standalone HTML element
            * Use:   Request for a Java applet
            */
           {
               ostream dest(MAXLINE, msg_buffer);
               dest << "<APPLET " << "CODEBASE=\"" << codebase <<"\" " <<
                   "CODE=\"" << code <<"\"" <<
                   (width==NULL ? " : "WIDTH=\"") << width << "\"" <<
                   (height=NULL ? " : "HEIGHT=\"") << height << "\"" <<
                   " [ALT=" << alt << "] " <<
                   " [NAME=" << name << "] " <<
                   " [ALIGN=" << align <<"] " <<
                   " [VSPACE=" << vspace <<"] " <<
                   " [HSPACE=" << hspace <<"] " <<
                   ">";
               while(count-- > 0)
               {
                   dest "<PARAM name=\" <<
                   // varargs routine here
                   dest << "value=\"" <<
                   // varargs routine here
               }
               dest << "</APPLET>\n";
               cout << dest;
           }
```

Example Applet in HTML

```
<APPLET code="myApplet.class" width=30 height=40
[ALT="applet image"]
[NAME="myApplet"]
[ALIGN="center"]
[VSPACE=10]
[HSPACE=10] >
<PARAM name="coordinates" value="04.01">
<PARAM name="image" value="mypicture.gif">
</APPLET>
```

Proposed Embed tag

```
       char* _html_page:embed(
           char* src,
```

```
        int count,
        char* param,
        char* value,
        ...
    )
    {
    /*
     * Rules: Inside of HTML. Standalone HTML element.
     * Use:   Request for an executable content.
     */
        ostream dest(MAXLINE, msg_buffer);
        dest << "<EMBED src="\" << src << "\ ";
        while(count-- > 0)
        {
            dest "<PARAM name=\" <<
            // varargs routine here
            dest << "value=\"" <<
            // varargs routine here
        }
        dest << "</EMBED>\n";
        cout << dest;
    )
```

Derived Classes

HAVING DEVELOPED THE BASE CLASS, it is now possible to develop derived classes.
Here is the "Hello Internet World" page.

```
class Hello : public _Html_page
{
public:
    Hello();
};
Hello::Hello ()
{
    cout << start_msg()
        << html("", START)
        << head(title("Hello Internet"))
        << body("1", hx("Hello Internet World"), START_END)
        << html("", END);
}
```

Here is a slightly more compact version:

```
Hello::Hello ()
{
```

```
        cout << start_msg()<< html("", START) <<
            head(title("Hello Internet")) <<
            body(hx("1","Hello Internet World"), START_END) <<
            html("", END);
}
```

C Version

```
void Hello ()
{
    printf("%s", start_msg());
    printf("%s", html("", START));
    printf("%s", head(title("Hello Internet")));
    printf("%s", body(hx("1", "Hello Internet World"), START_END));
    printf("%s", html("", END));
}
```

Now our program looks like this:

C++ Version

```
main()
{
HELLO Hello;
    ;
}
```
        The constructor does the whole thing :)

C Version

```
main()
{
    Hello();
}
```

While the base class approach is very useful as one starts developing more and more Web pages, for smaller Web sites there are alternative approaches:

1. Create stdout using cout or printf. After developing numerous Web pages, it became apparent that for many projects it is useful to develop a standard HTML page and then modify it to C++ or C. This is done by taking the HTML file and adding the needed printf or cout to turn it into C++ or C. For example, the HTML

```
<TITLE> My Title </TITLE>
```

is modified to

```
cout << "<TITLE> My Title </TITLE>\n"
```

This approach lets the programmer see what the page will look like at a basic level before starting to do the cgi-bin modifications. Editors, such as the UNIX-based vi and emacs, make it very easy to read in an HTML file and then modify it to C++ or C using the appropriate method to send the output to stdout.[1] The C++ is especially easy. You merely add cout << in front of the HTML and then place the HTML in quotes. Finally, terminate with a ;. Adding an \n at appropriate places will make it easier when you view the source, but this is not necessary. The only other thing is to be certain that any HTML quotation marks (") are preceded by a backslash (\"). Some readers may prefer one approach while others prefer another.

2. Thru mode, discussed elsewhere, provides another way to use HTML files as part of your cgi-bin program. This method is also useful since you can modify the HTML file without having to change the cgi-bin program and then recompile.

In many situations any of the various approaches may be better. This is especially true where one section of the cgi-bin program puts out a fixed HTML, such as a mailer, while another section is varying under program control.

In this chapter you learned the primary rules for creating HTML for your cgi-bin programs. The methods and rules for creating HTML in C++ or C are essential knowledge for creating cgi-bin Web pages.

PROGRAM EXERCISES

1. Take any two programs developed in earlier chapters and rework them using the base class. Demonstrate as many object principles as possible in your program, such as inheritance, overloading, and derived class.

2. Develop two new cgi-bin programs that use the base class to derive a new class.

3. Place the base class in an .h file and the associated subroutines into a .c file. Compile to provide .o files. Create a class that derives the base class in a new .h and .c file. Create all required externs and demonstrate the use of this file structure.

---

[1]   A backslash will be required before any quotation marks in the HTML.

12

Meta Control

Unleashing the Power of Timed HTML Control

IN THIS CHAPTER WE ARE going to examine use of the Meta operator and how it can benefit your cgi-bin program control. While this operator is not available for all browsers, it offers an important capability that will be explored here. The Meta operator is an original HTML control code, and it has several modes. One particular value will allow an HTML Web page to change after a settable time period. When this is done, the initial Web page will appear and then, after the time interval, automatically activate a secondary URL. This second URL can be a new URL or a reactivation of the same URL. As will be seen, when used with cgi-bin programs, both have value.

Here is an example of a Meta operator:

```
<META HTTP-EQUIV="Refresh" CONTENT="1"
URL="http://internet_path/anyname.html">
```

Here is an alternative using a cgi-bin URL:

```
<META HTTP-EQUIV="Refresh" CONTENT="1" url="http://internet_path/cgi-bin/program">
```

The Meta operator will always be placed in the <HEAD> section of the HTML document.

About the Meta Operator . . . .

1. The HTTP-EQUIV is a directive to the client software. It tells the client what kind of Meta operation to expect.
2. In this case, the HTTP-EQUIV is a request for a refresh. This tells the client to change or refresh to the associated URL.
3. The Content is the time in seconds that the initial URL is allowed to stay on the screen before refreshing. If the Content is set to zero (0), the refresh will occur immediately.

. . . .

When the time interval completes, the Meta operator will access the URL included as part of the Meta request. The reader should understand by now that the new URL could be a cgi-bin script and the Meta operator can be sent in a cgi-bin script.

Meta Activation from an Index File

LET'S BEGIN BY CONSIDERING an initial case, in which the Meta operator appears on an HTML page but the secondary URL is for a cgi-bin program. One of the most basic uses of the Meta operator is to have the original connection page be an HTML page. The Meta operator is used with a zero-second delay to go directly to a cgi-bin program. This has a number of advantages. First, the outside world will see a traditional URL when entering your system. Users will not be asked to type in the URL to your cgi-bin program, which may be a relatively meaningless string. Instead they will enter the name of your organization or an equally relevant identifying URL. This is especially useful when index.html pages are used. These allow HTML addresses to look very professional (for example, by only providing the company name).

```
URL="http://www.mycompany.com
```

While there are other methods that produce this same effect, the use of the Meta operator is simple and straightforward.

There is another advantage that can also prove beneficial. If you are designing public Web pages, you should have set maximum accessibility as one of your goals. This means that there will be people who access your page with different capabilities. Some users may have an advanced browser, while others are using simple text browsers. Some are turning on their graphics, while others are zipping around in a text-only mode. If you are designing for these people, the Meta operator provides additional opportunities. For example, if the Meta operator fails (as it will on some browsers, such as lynx or older versions of Mosaic), you can have an alternative Web page appear. An anchor to your cgi-bin program will be included. In this way, you provide immediate access to your advanced capabilities for those with advanced browsers, secondary access for those with less advanced browsers, and perhaps a text-only mode for those who have graphics turned off.

Here is a typical Web page with the Meta operator:

```
<HTML><HEAD>
<META HTTP-EQUIV="Refresh"
      CONTENT="0" URL="http://internet_path/cgi-bin/program">
<TITLE> Company XYZ </TITLE></HEAD>
<BODY>
<!- Place Optional Web page Body Here -->
</BODY> </HTML>
```

This page will come up for a brief second and then immediately go to the cgi-bin program. If the browser does not use the Meta operator, the optional Web page will appear.

Meta Ping Pong

WHILE A cgi-bin program startup is a valuable first use of the Meta operator, it is not the only way this unique capability can be used. The HTML Meta line can be sent from a cgi-bin program just like any other HTML. This means that now you have a rudimentary way of controlling time-out, and it allows the Meta operator also to be used for other special effects. To demonstrate this capability, we begin by creating two Web pages with Meta operators that force them to toggle or Ping Pong back and forth. We call this Meta Ping Pong. We begin by creating a Meta Ping Pong with only HTML. This will then be changed to a cgi-bin program that provides Meta Ping Pong. In the third stage we begin to develop ways to use this intelligently.

A quick look at the Meta Ping Pong operation is provided by the two following HTML pages:

Web Page 1

```
<HTML><HEAD>
<META HTTP-EQUIV="Refresh" CONTENT="2" URL="http://mypath/page2.html">
<TITLE> PAGE 1 </TITLE></HEAD>
<BODY>
<H1> This is page 1 </H1>
</BODY> </HTML>
```

Web Page 2

```
<HTML><HEAD>
<META HTTP-EQUIV="Refresh" CONTENT="2" URL="http://mypath/page1.html">
<TITLE> PAGE 2 </TITLE></HEAD>
<BODY>
<H1> This is page 2 </H1>
</BODY> </HTML>
```

If you start your browser on page 1, it will show "This is page 1" on the screen for two seconds. Then there will be a flash (the next screen loading) followed by "This is page 2" on the screen for two seconds, then back to page 1, back to page 2, and so on, ad infinitum. It is evident why this is called Ping Pong.

The preceding Web pages are not a very exciting display, but they illustrate the use of the Meta Ping Pong operation. The operation could as easily have created a single page:

```
<HTML><HEAD>
<META HTTP-EQUIV="Refresh" CONTENT="2"; URL="http://mypath/page1.html">
<TITLE> PAGE 1 </TITLE></HEAD>
<BODY>
<H1> This is page 1, I refresh every two seconds </H1>
</BODY> </HTML>
```

This page would be reloaded every two seconds. This is still not very exciting, but the possibilities are becoming more apparent. Knowing from the earlier parts of this book about cgi-bin programs, it is clear that this could be changed to a cgi-bin program as follows:

```c
/*
 * Type C main
 * Purpose: demonstrate Meta capability
 */
/* includes here */
void main()
{
    /* Tell the server HTML is arriving */
    printf("Content-type: text/html\n\n");
    printf("%s\n%s\n%s\n%s\n%s\n%s\n",
        "<HTML><HEAD>",
        "<META HTTP-EQUIV=\"Refresh\" CONTENT=\"1\"",
        "URL=\"http://internet_path/cgi-bin/this_program\">",
        "<TITLE> Company XYZ </TITLE></HEAD>",
        "<BODY>",
        "<!- Place Optional Web Page Body Here -->",
        "</BODY> </HTML>"
    );
}
```

Meta Tickle

Now every second (Content="1"), the Meta times out and reactivates our cgi-bin Web page. If we changed this_program to another program, it would be possible to have two cgi-bin programs Ping Pong back and forth into eternity. Of course, since we are working on the Internet, the two URLs for the different cgi-bin programs do not have to be on the same machines or even in the same locations. In fact, they could be in different cities or even on different continents. Additionally, since we are using cgi-bin programs, we could change the HTML content slightly with each Ping Pong. In more complex operations, it would be possible to allow something to be processed that would extend beyond the timers allowed for the Internet by passing information into the HTML and then back to the cgi-bin program. As an example of this last case, consider an advanced chess program in which you want to allow the computer to take up to one half hour to determine its move. On the Internet, the request would time out way before the half hour elapsed. But suppose you could save status, either in a file or in hidden variables every 10 seconds. Now you can use the Meta Ping Pong to keep the Internet connection alive. On each move the state of the board move will be passed back as a hidden variable file along with the elapsed time. The new request will begin from the previous place and continue adding to the elapsed time. This creates a "tickle" to hold up the Internet connection. When the final decision to move is made, the HTML would be sent without the Meta operator. The user would then be allowed to make a new move. Figure 12.1 illustrates the control of timed input using cgi-bin programs with Meta control.

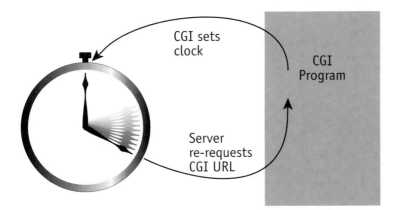

Figure 12.1   Meta: Timed effects produce some of the most dramatic web experiences.

Meta Examples

Let's continue with our simple example of Meta Ping Pong. First the cgi-bin sends out the information to the user, and then the Meta results in information coming back to the server. Before continuing, we should allow for one more possibility, user intervention. Instead of setting the timer at 1 second, suppose it is set at 10 seconds. Furthermore, let's include the initial Web page sent from the cgi-bin program with additional anchors to other URLs. Now if the user clicks on one of the URL anchors before the 10-second time-out, the new request takes precedence over the Meta operator and the user continues merrily on his or her way.

By setting the Meta at a reasonable value, one can allow time for intervention by the user before the Meta time-out. For example, in the chess game developed in Chapter 10, we could add a timer to the game. If a person did not make a move in a given time interval, the Meta would send a message back that the person had lost his or her move. We could even allow the time-out to be set from an initial form.

The use of the Meta operator in conjunction with cgi-bin programs can open up a whole new area of capabilities for the Internet. It can provide potential real-time applications such as monitoring the weather or other monitoring equipment, and providing continuous display changes.

Many institutions are beginning to examine how the Internet can provide internal benefits to make it easier to accomplish their goals. Many of these applications are done at secure sites behind protective firewalls. These sites are prime candidates for experimentation with Meta control in conjunction with cgi-bin programs.

A word of caution: The Internet only operates at the speed of the link and is affected by other people using the service. This means that real-time processing cannot be done with precision intervals. Therefore, it makes more sense to think in terms of monitoring of events that can have errors in the seconds. For example, updates of weather conditions would be unaffected if the update was once every 4 to 10 seconds. In fact, using a 20- or 30-minute interval might be reasonable. On the other hand, a game that fired a rocket and resulted in an explosion four to eight seconds later would prove incredibly uncomfortable.[1]

Anyone who reflects on the early stages of computers will understand these kinds of problems. Immediate response and real-time simulation only became available when methods were developed to speed up response times. The same constraints have shifted to the Internet and will be solved when the speed of response or bandwidth concerns are eliminated. A great deal of work is going on regarding how to accomplish these kinds of goals. But it is premature to think of them as possible at this time. Therefore, you should limit your Meta programs to situations in which moderate and variable response times are acceptable.

The Meta Class

WITH THIS IN MIND, HERE is a simple Meta class to get you started.

```
class _Meta
public:
    _Meta() { ; };
```

---

[1]   This type of application is better accomplished on the server side.

```
        void html(char* url, char* metatime);
};
```

About the _Meta class. . . . .

This class starts with the basic ability of sending out HTML that includes the Meta
operator and a settable URL and time-out.

. . . .

```
/*
 * Type C++ class subroutine
 * Purpose: demonstrate meta operation from a class
 */
// This routine puts a META string onto stdout
void
_Meta::html(char* url, char* metatime)
{
    char out_string[MAXLINE];

    strcpy(out_string, "<META HTTP-EQUIV=\"Refresh\" CONTENT=\"
    strcat(out_string, metatime);
    strcat(out_string,"; URL=\"";
    strcat(out_string, page);
    strcat(out_string,"\">\n");
    cout << out_string;
}
// This could be made more efficient by using a buffered ostream.
/*
 * Type C++ class subroutine
 * Purpose: meta demo
 */
// This routine puts a meta string onto stdout
void
_Meta::html(char* page, char* metatime)
{
    char out_string[MAXLINE];
    ostream dest(MAXLINE, out_string);
    dest << "<META HTTP-EQUIV=\"Refresh\" CONTENT=\" <<
        metatime << "; URL=\"" <<page << "\">\n";
    cout << out_string;
}
```

The program looks similar in C:

```
/* This routine puts a meta string onto stdout */
/*
```

```
 * Type C subroutine
 * Purpose: meta html subroutine
 */
void
meta_html(char* page, char* metatime)
{
        char out_string[100];
    sprintf(out_string,"%s%s%s%s%s",
        "<META HTTP-EQUIV=\"Refresh\" CONTENT=\",
        metatime,
        " URL = \"",
        url,
        "\">\n"
    );
    printf("%s", out_string);
}
```

More Meta Examples

HAVING DEVELOPED THIS KIND OF capability, it makes sense to think of where you might want to use it. Certainly, the final decision will depend on what it is you do, but here are some possibilities that may trigger your imagination.

1. **Games**   The chess game has already been mentioned, but there are numerous other games that could benefit from a timer.
2. **A slide show**   Set up a bunch of GIF files and Meta through the slides. These could be training slides or an actual product presentation.
3. **Timed learning**   The programmed learning environment discussed in Chapter 7 could be timed. By allowing the timer to be settable, the user could set his or her own learning pace.
4. **Stocks and other Finances**   Put up your favorite stocks and then have their status updated every 10 minutes.

In the next two programs, we will expand the Meta operator to include changing something before sending back the new HTML. There are two options that we will look at. In the first example, the request for the change will be handled by command line arguments using argc and argv[]. Since the URL is created by our cgi-bin program, we can use the program to append arguments to the URL. Let's explore this with a simple slide show of four GIF pictures.

```
#define GIF1 "http://internet_path/slide1.gif"
#define GIF2 "http://internet_path/slide2.gif"
#define GIF3 "http://internet_path/slide3.gif"
#define GIF4 "http://internet_path/slide4.gif"
#define DEFAULT_ARGV "slide1"
```

```cpp
class _Meta : public Standard
{
private:
    char local_argv[20];
    char slide[60];// http for slide to show
    void change_argv();
    void send_html(char* url, char* metatime, char* argv_string);
public:
    _Meta() { strcpy (local_argv, DEFAULT_ARGV);
    // overload the html routine
    void html();
    // move the argc and argv handler into the class
    void get_argv (int argc, char* argv[]);
};
/*
 * Type C++ class subroutine
 * Purpose: Meta get the argv[] value to a temp agrv[]
 */
// Set local_argv or leave it at the default value that was put in by the constructor
void _Meta::get_argv(int argc, char* argv[])
{
    if(argc > 1)
    {
        strcpy (local_argv, argv[1]);
    }
}
void _Meta::change_argv()
{
    if(strcmp(local_argv, "slide1") == 0)
    {
        strcpy(local_argv, "slide2")
        strcpy(slide, GIF1);
    } else
    if(strcmp(local_argv, "slide2") == 0)
    {
        strcpy(local_argv, "slide3")
        strcpy(slide, GIF2);
    } else
    {
        // other slides for show
    }
}
/*
 * Type C++ class subroutine
 * Purpose: Meta send out the html
 */
```

```cpp
void _Meta::send_html()
{
    // change the local_argv and the GIF file to show
    change_argv();
    // Tell the server HTML is being sent
    cout << "Content-type: /text/html\n\n";
    // Send some basic HTML here -- title, background ...
    // Send the Meta
    sprintf(out_string,"%s%s%s%s%s%s%s",
        "<META HTTP-EQUIV=\"Refresh\" CONTENT=\",
        metatime,
        " URL = \"",
        url,
        "?",
        local_argv,
        "\">\n"
    );
    cout << out_string;

    // send some more HTML
    // send the image
    sprintf(out_string,"%s%s%s",
        "<IMG SRC= \"",
        slide,
        "\" >\n"
    );
    cout << out_string;
    // send the closing HTML
}
void main(int argc, char* argv[])
{
    Meta mymeta;
    // do the getopt in the META class
    mymeta.get_argc(argc, argv[]);
    send_html();
}
```

In the next example, a random variable is used to change the output

A Flashing Sign

HERE IS ANOTHER SIMPLE PROJECT—namely, creating a flashing sign similar to the type used for stores. Since this project will involve working with the Internet, use the now familiar Hello Internet World for a sign.

To make things interesting, use the built-in function rand() to choose randomly which word or words get displayed.

```
/*
 * Type C++ class subroutine
 * Purpose: Meta create hello world flashing sign
 */
void
_Meta::hello()
{
    int random_value;
    random_value = rand() % 8;        // get a random value between 0 and 8
    start_msg();                      // send the start msg to the server
    switch(random_value)
    {
    case 0:
        /* meta_html is the META function. It will send the Meta HTML using the values of
         * the URL and time sent into the function. */
        meta_html("http://mypath/this_cgi_program", "1");
        cout << "<BR> HELLO Internet World<BR>\n";
        break;
    case 1:
        meta_html("http://mypath/this_cgi_program", "1");
        cout << "<BR> HOLA EL MUNDO DE INTERNET<BR>\n";
        break;

    case 2:
        meta_html("http://mypath/this_cgi_program", "1");
        cout << "<BR> CIAO MONDO INTERNET<BR>\n";
        break;
    case 3:
        meta_html("http://mypath/this_cgi_program", "1");
        cout << "<BR> HELLO INTERNET BUDDIES<BR>\n";
        break;
    case 4:
        meta_html("http://mypath/this_cgi_program", "1");
        cout << "<BR>Hallo, Internet Wereld<BR>\n";
        break;
    case 5:
        meta_html("http://mypath/this_cgi_program", "1");
        cout << "<BR> CHAO QUI VI, THE GIOI INTERNET<BR>\n";
        break;
    case 6:
        meta_html("http://mypath/this_cgi_program", "1");
        cout << "<BR> HELLO DUDES ON THE INTERNET<BR>\n";
        break;
```

```
    default:
    case 7:
        meta_html("http://mypath/this_cgi_program", "1");
        cout << "<BR> BONJOUR MONDE DE INTERNET<BR>\n";
        break;
    }
    end_msg();
}
```

Ping Ping Pong

In the next version the Ping Pong is used with the Internet ping routine. This results in the name Ping Ping Pong. The Internet ping routine is used to verify that an IP address associated with a network facility is active (alive).

```
/*
 * Type C subroutine
 * Purpose: Meta hello to the Internet World
 */
#include <stdio.h>
main()
{
    FILE* stream;
    char tempstring[100];
    char instring[100];
    random_value = rand(getpid()) % 8;
    start_msg();
    meta_html("http://mypath/this_cgi_program", "1");
    switch(random_value)
    case 0:
        strcpy( tempstring, "ping 199.182.120.202" );
        break;
    case 1:
        strcpy( tempstring, "ping 500.100.140.000" );
        break;
    case 2:
        strcpy( tempstring, "ping 500.200.160.001" );
        break;

    /* other case statements */
    ...
    case 7:
        strcpy( tempstring, "ping 500.300.999.002" );
        break;
```

```
        if(( stream = popen(tempstring, "w")) == 0)
        {
            return;
        }
        fgets ( instring, 90, stream );

        printf ("<H1>%s\n%s</H1>\n", tempstring, instring );
        pclose(stream);
        end_msg();
    }
```

About the hello function . . . .

This function can be called from the cgi-bin main. It first sends out the required
start information in HTML. It then uses the rand function to get a random number.
The modulo 8 operation returns a random value between 0 and 7. The switch statement provides the different Hello Internet World strings that are sent to stdout. The
Internet is asked for status using the ping operation and will return "alive or not
alive." The status is then sent to the screen. Finally, an end message is sent.

You will get back a message like this:

```
ping 500.300.999.002
Is Alive
```

To assure randomness, the unique process ID is used to seed the rand function. A
modulo 8 produces the required range for the case statements.

A Cartoon Show

ONE FUN USE FOR THE Meta operator is to create cartoons. The technique shown
here can also be used to create some basic animation. Everyone has probably experienced the animation that results from flipping cards that have figures on them;
the figures move gradually from one position to another. The effect is the percep-
tion of movement. The same thing can be done with Meta control. While this could
be done on standard HTML pages, the advantage of cgi-bin programs is that the program can feed in an extra parameter that will be used to speed up or slow down the
display rate or the rate at which the cartoons flip. For this example, we control the
rate by the content value fed to the Meta string.

First it will be necessary to create the cartoon GIF files. They are called

```
cartoon.1.gif
cartoon.2.gif
...
cartoon.6.gif
...
```

These can be scanned in or created directly in a program that saves files in GIF format or uses other techniques discussed later in this book. For now, just assume that the necessary cartoons in GIF format are available.

Next create the C++ classes. To make things simple, inherit the earlier developed _Html_page class.

```cpp
class _Cartoon : public _Html_page
{
public:
    _Cartoon() { ; };
    void show(int gif_number);
    void meta(int which, int time);
};
/*
 * Type C++ class subroutine
 * Purpose: Meta cartoon show
 */
void
Cartoon::show(int gif_number)
{
    char cartoon_string[80];
    char gif_char[2];
    gif_char[0] = gif_number + '0';
    gif_char[1] = 0;
    strcpy(cartoon_string,"cartoon");
    strcat(cartoon_string, gif_char);
    strcat(cartoon_string, ".gif");
    cout << "<IMG SRC= \"" << cartoon_string << "\ >";
}
```

Or, using ostream,

```cpp
/*
 * Type C++ class subroutine
 * Purpose: Meta another version of cartoon show
 */
void
Cartoon::show(int gif_number)
{
    char cartoon_string[80];
    dest = ostream(80,cartoon_string);
    dest << "cartoon" <<
        (gif_number) <<
        ".gif";
    cout << "<IMG SRC= \"" << cartoon_string << "\ >";
}
```

Or, simpler yet and returning a string,

```
/*
 * Type C++ class subroutine
 * Purpose: Meta and one more version of cartoon show
 */
char*
Cartoon::show(int gif_number)
{
    /* ostream dest in the constructor */
    dest << "<IMG SRC= \"" <<
        "cartoon" <<
        (gif_number) <<
        ".gif" <<
        "\ >";
    return(dest);
}
```

C Version

```
char* cartoon_show(char* buffer, int gif_number)
{
    char cartoon_string[MAXLINE];
    char gif_char[2];
    gif_char[0] = gif_number + '0';
    gif_char[1] = 0;
    strcpy(cartoon_string,"cartoon");
    strcat(cartoon_string, gif_char);
    strcat(cartoon_string, ".gif");
    sprintf( buffer, "%s%s%s", "<IMG SRC= \"", cartoon_string, "\ >");
    return(buffer);
}
/*
 * Type C++ subroutine
 * Purpose: Meta subroutine for cartoon show
 */
void meta(int which, int time)
{
/*
 * Which -> determines which cartoon to put up and which URL to send back with the META.
 * Time -> time period to put in the content.
 */
    char* url;
    char* cartoon_gif;
    char period[5];
    char buffer[MAXLINE];
```

```
    /* Always set the meta for the next cartoon */
    switch(which)
    {
    case 1:
        url="http://html_path/cgi-bin/cartoon?-c2";
        cartoon_gif=show(buffer, 1);
        break;
    case 2:
        url="http://html_path/cgi-bin/cartoon?-c3";
        cartoon_gif=show(buffer, 2);
        break;
    case 3:
        url="http://html_path/cgi-bin/cartoon?-c4";
        cartoon_gif=show(buffer, 3);
        break;
    case 4:
        url="http://html_path/cgi-bin/cartoon?-c1";
        cartoon_gif= show(buffer, 4);
        break;
    default:
        return;
    }
    start_msg();
    html(START)
    cout << "<META HTTP-EQUIV=\"refresh\" URL=\""
        << url <<\" NAME=\"A\"<< "CONTENT="
        << itoa(time) << ">";
    body(START);
    img(cartoon_gif);
    body(END);
    html(END);
}
```

C++ main

```
/*
 * Type C++ main
 * Purpose: Meta cartoon show
 */
void main(argv, *argc[])
{
    Cartoon myCartoon;
    /* getopt see above */
    case c:
        myCartoon.meta(atoi(optarg), 1);
        break;
}
```

That's all there is to it. Some readers are saying, What about the promise of being able to control the time? There are a couple of ways to go on this one. But be smart. Since overloading is available, just overload the argument to main.

First rewrite the Meta function with a minor modification. The incoming time will be merged onto the end of the URL argument following the ?.

```c
/*
 * Type C subroutine
 * Purpose: Meta with timed control
 */
void meta(int which, int time)
{
/*
 * Which -> determines which cartoon to put up and which URL to send back with the META.
 * Time -> time period to put in the content.
 */
    char* url[50];
    char* cartoon_gif;
    char period[5];
    /* Always set the meta for the next cartoon */
    switch(which)
    {
    case 1:
        strcpy(url,"http://internet_path/cgi-bin/cartoon?-c2");
        strcat(url, itoa(time));
        cartoon_gif=show(1);
        break;
    case 2:
        strcpy(url, "http://internet_path/cgi-bin/cartoon?-c3");
        strcat(url, itoa(time));
        cartoon_gif=show(2);
        break;
    case 3:
        strcpy(url, "http://internet_path/cgi-bin/cartoon?-c4");
        strcat(url, itoa(time));
        cartoon_gif=show(3);
        break;
    case 4:
        strcpy(url, "http://internet_path/cgi-bin/cartoon?-c1");
        strcat(url, itoa(time));
        cartoon_gif= show(4);
        break;
    default:
        return;
    }
    start_msg();
```

```
        html(START)
        cout << "<META HTTP-EQUIV=\"" << url << "\" NAME=\"A\"" << "CONTENT="
             << itoa(time) << ">";
        body(START);
        img(cartoon_gif);
        body(END);
        html(END);
}
```

C Version (with some simplifications)

```
/*
 * Type C++ subroutine
 * Purpose: Meta and overloading
 */
```

Next modify to handle the overloading.

```
void meta(int which, int time)
{
/*
 * Which -> determines which cartoon to put up and which URL to send back with the META.
 * Time -> time period to put in the content.
 */
    char* url[50];
    char* cartoon_gif;
    char period[5];
    /* Always set the meta for the next cartoon */
    switch(which)
    {
    case 1:
        strcpy(url,"http://html_path/cgi-bin/cartoon?-c2");
        break;
    case 2:
        strcpy(url, "http://html_path/cgi-bin/cartoon?-c3");
        break;
    case 3:
        strcpy(url, "http://html_path/cgi-bin/cartoon?-c4");
        break;
    case 4:
        strcpy(url, "http://html_path/cgi-bin/cartoon?-c1");
        break;
    default:
        return;
    }
    strcat(url, itoa(time));
```

```
        cartoon_gif= show(which);
        start_msg();
        html(START)
        printf("%s%s%s%s%s%s",
            "<META HTTP-EQUIV=\"refresh\" URL=\"",
            url, "\" NAME=\"A\" CONTENT=",
            itoa(time), ">");
        body(START);
        img(cartoon_gif);
        body(END);
        html(END);
}
/*
 * Type C++ main
 * Purpose: Meta cartoons with overloading
 */
main(argv, *argc[])
{
        CARTOON Cartoon;
        int gif_val;
        int time_val;
        /* getopt see options section on argc and argv[] */
        case c:
            gif_val = *((char *)(optarg)) - '0';
                time_val = atoi(optarg+1);
                cartoon.meta(gif_val, time_val);
            break;
}
/*
 * Type main
 * Purpose: Meta cartoons with overloading
 */
main(argv, *argc[])
{
        /* getopt see option sections on argc and argv[] */
        case c:
            cartoon.meta((*((char *)(optarg)-'0'),
                    atoi(optarg+1));
            break;
}
```

Now start the program with a URL that looks like this:

```
http://html_path/cgi-bin/cartoon?12
```

The 1 in 12 will start with cartoon.1.gif. The 2 will set the timing for two seconds in the Meta operators. One technique that makes for good laughs is to take some pictures of people around the office and graft their heads onto your favorite cartoons. Just be sure you do not offend anyone who is overly sensitive.

The Meta operator provides you with a means to develop timed control. The Ping Pong program can be used to provide continuous input from the Internet on a periodic basis when used in conjunction with cgi-bin programs.

PROGRAM EXERCISES

1. Create a cgi-bin heartbeat. On each beat of the heart, have it provide visible output of status. (**Advanced:** Change the rate based on changing conditions. How might argc and argv[] be used?)
2. Create an index file that starts a cgi-bin program. Demonstrate that this is operational by starting the index file as a URL from the browser and verifying that the cgi-bin program is activated.
3. Create your own cartoon show using your own IMaGes and the Meta operator.

PROBLEMS

1. Describe in detail the operation of the Meta operator. Include as part of your description different ways it can be used with HTML Web pages and cgi-bin programs. Explain the use of the Content field. Explain what it can be used for and what its limitations are. Show examples of the Meta operator in HTML and how it can be produced from C++ and C.
2. Describe some of the issues associated with index files. Do not limit your descriptions to cgi-bin programs. Discuss issues about connecting to search engines, such as Yahoo and Lycos. Describe the alternative to an index page. Examine alternatives to having your cgi-bin program as the initial starting point. What advantages do both alternatives provide? When would either alternative make more sense?
3. In the discussion of the Meta operator, a program was developed to output a cartoon. Since people will be using modems, 56K, and T1 lines to access your Web page, since they will be using different browsers sometimes with load images disabled, and since they will be accessing during times of the day when your system is busy or relatively unused, what kinds of concerns should you examine when developing this kind of capability? How could you optimize your testing of your cartoon?

13

Page Access Counters

Developing Page Counters
Developing the Count Files
Invisible Counters
Visible Counters

Developing Page Counters

PAGE COUNTERS CONTINUE TO BE a valuable asset for Internet page developers. The purpose of a Web page counter is to get an indication of how many times people are accessing your Web page. While page counters may not be 100% accurate, since a page can be reseen through local cache memory, they are good relative indications. Many people, however, find the idea of a page count somewhat offensive. A number glares out at you on virtually every page looked at, telling how often the Web page has been accessed. This problem can be resolved by a hidden page counter, which keeps track of the number of hits but keeps the count off the Web page.

Developing the Count Files

VISIBLE AND INVISIBLE PAGE COUNTING can be done in a number of ways. For any page counter, the essential requirements are

- a place to keep the counts and
- a way to increment the counts.

```
class _Counter
{
Private:
FILE* stream;

Public:
    _Counter() { ; };
    char* increment(); // increment the counter and return value
};
#define COUNT_FILE "unix_path/count_file";
char* _Counter::increment()
{
    char buffer[10];
    int value;
    stream = fopen(COUNT_FILE, "r");
    fgets(buffer, 10, stream);
    fclose();
    value = atoi(buffer);
    value++;
    stream = fopen(COUNT_FILE, "w");
    fprintf(stream, "%s", itoa(value));
    fclose();
    return value;
}
```

About this subroutine . . . .

1. The program reads in the value of the count file.
2. The count is incremented.
3. The new count is put back into the file.
4. The count is returned.

. . . .

Here is a slightly different version in C:

```
/*
 * Type C++ or C subroutine
 * Purpose: Basic counter
 */
int increment(char* filename)
{
    char buffer[2];
    stream = fopen(filename, "r");
    fgets(buffer, 2, stream);
    fclose();
    ++buffer;
```

```
        stream = fopen(filename, "w");
        fprintf(stream, "%d", buffer);
        fclose();
        return atoi(buffer);
    }
```

The count is kept in raw form, and the file is an optional name to allow for multiple counters.

The idea of multiple counts for different pages makes sense, but multiple files seem a bit much. Here is a single file version with multiple counters:

```
/*
 * Type C++ or C subroutine
 * Purpose: Counter with single file
 */
#define COUNT_FILE "unix_path/count_file";
char* _Counter::increment(char* html_name)
{
    char* buffer[MAXLINE];
    FILE* tmp_stream;
    char tmp_buffer[50];
    stream = fopen(COUNT_FILE, "r");
    tmp_stream = fopen("unix_path/tmp_file", "w");
    while(stream != EOF)
    {
        fgets(buffer, 100, stream);
        if(strncmp(html_name, buffer, strlen(html_name) != 0)
        {
            fprintf(tmp_stream, "%s", buffer);
        } else
        {
            /* Increment value */
            value = atoi(buffer
            + strlen(html_name) + 1);
            value++;
            /* Replace old value with new value */
            strcpy(buffer, html_name);
            strcat(buffer, " ");
            strcat(buffer, itoa(value));
            fprintf(tmp_stream, "%s", buffer);
        }
    fclose(tmp_stream);
    fclose(stream);
    /* Now move the tmp file to the real file */

    stream = fopen(COUNT_FILE, "w");
    fprintf(stream, "%c", buffer);
```

```
        fclose();
        fprintf(tmp_buffer, "mv %s %s\n",
            "unix_path/tmp_file", COUNT_FILE);
        system (tmp_buffer);
        /* Don't remove this file since someone else may be recreating it right behind us */
        return value;
    }
```

This version uses a single file and the HTML page name for lookup. The advantage of this is that only one file is used, but a disadvantage is that collisions can occur if the number of Web pages increases. Even the multiple files will have potential collisions if the same Web page is accessed at the exact same time. Most sites only require a rough estimate, so these algorithms should suffice. Figure 13.1 shows the flow from the client side to the cgi-bin program with its hidden counter algorithms.

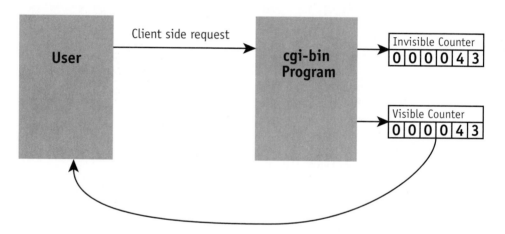

FIGURE 13.1   Counters: The number of accesses of your Web sites can be hidden from your users.

In C++ these versions could be overloaded:

```
class _Counter
{
Private:
    FILE* stream;

Public:
    _Counter() { ; };
    char* increment(); // increment the counter and return value
    char* increment(char* html_file);
    int increment();
    int increment(char* html_file);
};
```

Invisible Counters

THERE ARE A NUMBER OF ways to use the count files. The simplest application is to use the now familiar pass Thru mode.

```
/*
 * Type C++ main
 * Purpose: Invisible counter
 */
#define HTML_FILE "unix_path/file.html"
void main()
{
    FILE* html_stream;
    char buffer[MAXLINE];
    COUNTER Counter;
    cout << "Content-type: text/html\n\n";
    html_stream = fopen(HTML_FILE, "r");
    while ( html_stream != EOF)
    {
        fgets(buffer, MAXLINE, stream);
        puts(buffer);
    }
    (void ) Counter.increment(); /* pick the increment to use */
}
```

The same thing could be done using an image, which is on a Web page, instead of the entire Web page output. This could improve response speed since the image to activate the counter could be very small, even just a little colored dot.

```
/*
 * Type C++ main
 * Purpose: Hidden counter with GIF
 */
#include <stdio.h>
#include <stdlib.h>
#define CNTGIF "/d/markf/redball.gif"
void
main(argc, argv)
int argc;
char* argv[];
{
    FILE* stream;
    char buffer[10];
    int value;
    char c;
    char filename[MAXLINE];
    if(argc > 1)
```

```
{
        strcpy(filename, argv[1]);
        stream = fopen(argv[1], "r");
        fgets(buffer, 10, stream );
        fclose(stream);
        value = atoi(buffer);
        value++;
        stream = fopen(argv[1], "w");
        fprintf(stream, "%d\n", value);
        fclose(stream);
}
/*
 * This code is explained in Chapter 16 on IMaGe control. Send out the GIF file.
 */
fprintf(stdout, "Content-type: image/gif\n\n");
stream = fopen( CNTGIF, "r");
while(fgets(buffer, 2, stream) != 0)
        fprintf(stdout, "%c", buffer[0]);
fflush(stdout);
fclose(stream);
}
```

Now any HTML page that includes

```
<IMG SRC="http://internet_path/gif_counter?unix_path/countfile" >
```

will cause the counter to increment. This type of approach is valuable for sites that use a uniform logo on each page and merely want a general count of access to the site, not to any particular page. The only disadvantage of the GIF approach is for persons who turn off images or use a nongraphical browser: Counts will not increment for these accesses.

Visible Counters

TO MAKE THE COUNT VISIBLE, there are also a number of options. One approach is to have a special comment line in the HTML file. When a match occurs on the comment line, the count is put out in its place.

```
/*
 * Type C++ main
 * Purpose: Visible counter
 */
#define HTML_FILE "unix_path/file.html"
#define COMMENT_STRING "<!- COUNTER -->
void main()
```

```
{
    FILE* html_stream;
    char buffer[MAXLINE];
    COUNTER Counter;
    cout << "Content-type: text/html\n\n";
    html_stream = fopen(HTML_FILE, "r");
    while ( html_stream != EOF)
    {
        fgets(buffer, MAXLINE, stream);
        if(strncmp(buffer, COMMENT_STRING,
            strlen(COMMENT_STRING) ==0)
        {
            puts(Counter.increment());
        `} else
        {
            puts(buffer);
        }
    }
}
```

Now the HTML file looks like this:

```
<HTML> <HEAD> <TITLE> Counter HTML </TITLE> </HEAD>
<BODY>
== Any HTML Here ==
<B> This page has been accessed </B>
<!- COUNTER -->
<B> times since June of 1996 </B>
</BODY> </HTML>
```

When the HTML file is passed through the cgi-bin program, the comment line will be replaced and the final outputted HTML will look like this:

```
<HTML><HEAD> <TITLE> Counter HTML </TITLE></HEAD>
<BODY>
== Any HTML Here ==
<B> This page has been accessed </B>
30
<B> times since June of 1996 </B>
</BODY> </HTML>
```

It is also possible to create counters using images. One approach is to create a software Light Emitting Diode (LED) and use the color mapping algorithms developed in Chapter 17. The segments of the LED can be used to create different numbers.

One other approach that bridges both modes is to send the count inside an
HTML comment sent back from the cgi-bin as part of the program's HTML output.
The advantage of this is that it does not put the count on the page, but the count is
easily viewable by using view the source with any browser.

```
/*
 * Type C++ main
 * Purpose: Counter inside html comment
 */
void main()
{
    FILE* html_stream;
    char buffer[MAXLINE];
    COUNTER Counter;
    cout << "Content-type: text/html\n\n";
    html_stream = fopen(HTML_FILE, "r");
    while ( html_stream != EOF)
    {
        fgets(buffer, MAXLINE, stream);
        if(strncmp(buffer, COMMENT_STRING,
            strlen(COMMENT_STRING) ==0)
        {
            puts("<!-- ");
            puts(Counter.increment());
            puts(" -->\n");
        } else
        {
            puts(buffer);
        }
    }
}
```

Now the final HTML sent to the server will have a hidden count inside a comment
field.

You now have the ability to create either visible or hidden counters. These
counters can be very useful in getting feedback on how often your Web resources
are being used.

PROGRAM EXERCISES

1. Develop a file counter using the Thru mode and the Comment mode. Make the counter
   visible. Redo and make the counter invisible.

2. Using one of the forms developed earlier, develop a counter that only counts the activation of the starting form. (For example, in the chess game the count would only occur when the game was started, not for each move made.)

3. Develop a visible counter that uses GIF files. Verify operation from the browser. Verify operation when you go from 9 to 10. How about 99 to 100? 9999 to 10,000. (**Hint:** One way to deal with this is to have blank place holders instead of leading zeros. What other methods might work?)

PROBLEMS

1. Come up with at least four different ways to provide counters. Separate each of these into visible or invisible. Can you think of a way to create a counter that would use argc and argv[] to determine if it is visible or invisible? Examine the effect of browser caching on your counters. Will you get an additional count if the file is cached? Is there a way to force a count even when caching is being done? How?

2. How could you create a counter that would only count the first time a person accessed your Web page (**Hint:** Use the server environment.)

3. Discuss the advantages and disadvantages of visible versus invisible counters. Examine methods for assuring that counts are accurate. What are some of the factors that will lead to inaccurate counts? Given these factors, what considerations should you make when examining counts? Are there any capabilities in UNIX that could be used to increase your accuracy?

Database and WAIS

Search-and-Retrieve Database Lookup

HAVING BECOME FAMILIAR WITH THE Internet, you have used the search tools that help you navigate around the various Web pages. These search tools are frequently referred to as Wide Area Information Servers System (WAIS), which is the name of one of the early popular versions that provides search-and-retrieve database lookup capability.

Typically, the process consists of four stages, three of which are familiar to you by now:

Stage 1: Presentation of an Input form   The first stage is very straightforward. A form is presented to the user via the client software. Normally, the form will contain text input fields, but this is not the only method. Any of the different techniques for entering form information can and often will be used. These include options, radio buttons, checkboxes, and even password input. The form is then sent in the normal way (submit) to a cgi-bin program.

Stage 2: Program Processing   The program processing stage is somewhat different from earlier versions. In an information retrieval system, there are normally several subsections.

Logical operations are required to deal with empty fields and to parse logic operators. For some database searches, the logic is implied. For example, if there are two fields, one for name and a second for social security number, then it might be implied logic to use both for the search if they are both available, but to use either if only one is available.

The second type of logic is *forced logic.* This is provided by logical operators such as AND, OR, and NOT. These key words will be used to activate the appropriate logic as part of the search. For example, a search for *Solar* OR *Energy* would find any entry in the database that includes either the term *Solar* or the term *Energy*. If the search was repeated using "*Solar* AND *Energy*", only items that contained both the word *Solar* and the word *Energy* would be retrieved. There may also be *implied logic*. For example, what would be searched for if the entry was *Solar Energy*? Most search tools default to the OR logic, but this may be inappropriate.

Logic can be imposed with many mechanisms. For example, the AND logic is often provided with quotation marks (""). This would make a search for

    Solar Energy

search for either word. While a search for

    "Solar Energy"

would search for both words.

There are many aspects to the search logic. For example, would a search for "*Solar* AND *Energy*" return the following item?

    In a recent discussion, scientists talked about the energy impact of solar flares on the sun.

Special Search Factors

MOST SEARCHES AVAILABLE TODAY WOULD return the preceding item. However, there are a number of factors that could be placed in logic operations that might result in this item not being returned:

- **Case Sensitivity:** Both *solar* and *energy* begin with lowercase letters, while the search used uppercase letters.
- **Order Sensitivity:** The word *energy* occurs before the word *solar,* while the search request had them in the opposite order.
- **Juxtaposition Sensitivity:** The two words are separated by the words *impact of,* while the search request had them next to each other.

These and other logics can be built into the logic-parsing routines. Decisions on how to parse your information may be important to the specifics of your operations. Early analysis of the nature of your information database will allow you to make the correct decisions about how best to set up your logic-searching capability. Some of the examples given in this chapter should help with this process. However, they should not be seen as the only possible approaches. Numerous texts are available on database searching. While interfacing to the Internet does offer some unique capabilities, you should still use sound, well-established techniques.

Database search and retrieval, is the next component of the processing, is the actual search of the database for the critical information. This has already made an assumption—specifically, that the database already exists. Later, some simple programs will be developed to create your own word database. While more expensive databases can provide extensive capabilities, a simple word document database is frequently a quick way to make the Internet work for you. At a bare minimum, the database will need to have two fields: the acceptable search words and the place where the actual text associated with the search words can be found.

Most Internet search tools are set up to locate the occurrence of a word or phrase inside a short document (usually an HTML Web page). While this is useful for searching for Web pages, it may be of limited value for your requirements. However, if you have a large amount of information that tends to be compartmentalized into smaller documents, these same tools can be extended. If, on the other hand, you have very large documents or files, other database tools will need to be provided to allow smaller segments to be accessed.

Stage 3: HTML Output to the User   The next stage really consists of two components. Having retrieved the document or documents that contain the key search words along with their logic operations, you must now create HTML that can provide access to any or all of these documents. Normally, this is done using the anchor capability in HTML. The documents themselves may be in HTML, PDF, PostScript, Raw Text, or some other appropriate format. Since there can and often will be more than one document that meets the search criteria, your job is to provide a cgi-bin program that will allow the user to select the specific item he or she wishes to view.

Stage 4: Creation of the Lookup Tables   The final step should be considered as a separate part of the process. The creation of the lookup table will frequently require a separate program that runs independent of the Internet. A simple lookup table will consist of two fields. The first field will be possible search words. The second field will be the filename for the document associated with this search word. The search word will occur for multiple documents, and the same document will be associated with different search words.

The important part of this stage will be to reduce the set of search words to a manageable number. Certain words will need to be eliminated, such as *the, to,* and *but.* Other words will be relevant but will occur multiple times in the same document. If this is the case, only one entry should occur in the word search table for this search word and document. While there are many ways to accomplish these goals, the simplest is to combine a frequency check with a redundancy check. The frequency check will count how many times a search word occurs. Most common words will exceed a base number (three to five is a reasonable number). If they exceed the base, they are eliminated from the search database. The redundancy or duplication check is for recurrences of the same item. If the same item is seen more than once in a single document, the second occurrence is eliminated from the lookup table. A number of occurrence or "hit" counter can be used to show the frequency of occurrence.

Stage 1: Presentation of the Input Form

TYPICAL HTML FOR A database search will consist of a standard form. The following HTML is an example of what this might look like:

```
<HTML><HEAD><TITLE>Database Search</TITLE></HEAD>
<BODY><CENTER><I>WAIS Search Proprietary Restricted</I></CENTER><HR>
<H1>Database Search</H1>
Searches Information Database
<P><FORM ACTION="http://internet_path/cgi-bin/db_program" METHOD="POST">
<B>Enter text:</b> <INPUT TYPE=text NAME="request" SIZE=50 MAXLENGTH=250>
<BR>
<INPUT TYPE="submit" VALUE="Request">
<INPUT TYPE="reset" VALUE="Reset Fields">
        Max_hits:<INPUT TYPE=text name="x" VALUE="40" SIZE=4 MAXLENGTH=4>
</FORM></BODY></HTML>
```

The form consists of input text that is sent to the cgi-bin program called db_program. The user request is sent to stdin as Posted data. The input data can be parsed out in the cgi-bin program using form routines developed in Chapter 4. Because the data are text, they can be multiple words that include logical operators. Recall from the earlier discussions of forms that the spaces between the words will be sent as %20, representing their hexadecimal value.

An additional field called Max_hits is used to determine how many items will be sent back to the screen. In some modifications of database searching, a score value is kept and used as part of the search. The items are shown in the order of the number of score the word has in the document. This will result in documents with higher occurrence of a word appearing first. Other statistics that could be equally valuable for organizing the information include the following:

frequency of access

priority

value or cost.

As always, careful analysis is the critical factor in determining what is essential for your particular site.

Stage 2: Program Processing

To PROVIDE LOGICAL ANALYSIS, develop parsing routines that can provide the required logic.

```
class Logic
{
Private:
        char parse_string[100];
        int logic_state;
        char search_string1[20];
        char search_string2[20];
Public:
        Logic() { ; }; // empty constructor
        inline
        void add_string(char* mystring)
                    { strcpy(parse_string, mystring); };
        short check_logic(int state, char* logic_string); // check for logic state

};
/* Definition of logic state */
enum{
        AND
        OR
        ANDOR
}
/*
  * Type C++ class subroutine
  * Purpose: Database logic
  */
short Logic::check_logic(int logic_state, char* logic_string)
{
        /* The C routine strstr() returns NULL if the search string is not found, otherwise it
          * returns a positive pointer to the location of the search string in the logic string.
          */
        switch(logic_state)
        case AND:
            if(strstr(logic_string, "AND") != NULL)
            {
                    return TRUE;
            } else
```

```
            {
                return FALSE;
            }
        case OR:
            if(strstr(logic_string, "OR") != NULL)
            {
                return TRUE;
            } else
            {
                return FALSE;
            }
        case ANDOR:
            if(strstr(logic_string, "ANDOR") != NULL)
            {
                return TRUE;
            } else
            {
                return FALSE;
            }
        default:
            reuturn FALSE;
    }
}
```

This is a rather trivial logic routine, but it illustrates what can be done to create logic parsing.

Stages 3 and 4: User Output and Table Creation

THE NEXT PART OF THE program will read the indexing file and determine if the words being searched for are referenced. It will then return the URL of the document that contains the search word. A simplified index would look like this:

```
space      "http://internet_path/document1.pdf"
space      "http://internet_path/document2.pdf"
satellite  "http://internet_path/document1.pdf"
satellite  "http://internet_path/document3.pdf"
shuttle    "http://internet_path/document2.pdf"
shuttle    "http://internet_path/document4.pdf"
```

The word *space* appears in document1.pdf and document2.pdf, the word *satellite* appears in document1.pdf and document3.pdf, and the word *shuttle* appears in document2.pdf and document4.pdf. In a larger system, a layered indexing might be needed. It would look something like this:

```
space     doc1; doc2
satellite doc1; doc3
shuttle   doc1; doc4
...
doc1      "http://internet_path/document1.pdf"
doc2      "http://internet_path/document2.pdf"
doc3      "http://internet_path/document3.pdf"
...
```

WAIS

ONE OF THE AVAILABLE INDEXING systems, called WAIS, is available as public domain software. The WAIS[1] indexing system includes programs to create the index and to read the index. The WAIS programs are available through FTP.[2] The WAIS is a set of programs that were developed to help retrieve information over networks. The retrievable information can be text, pictures, voice, or formatted documents. The WAIS programs are very usable with forms since they generate documents that contain requested information based on a server-accepted English language question. This will normally be a text string generated from a client form. The user's request is examined against a lookup table that contains vocabulary (key words) and associated documents. Matches are sent back (e.g., in HTML anchor format) and the user can then select any relevant documents for viewing.

Here is a C++ program to read in a WAIS indexed request:

```
/*
 * Type C++ main
 * Purpose: wais
 */
/* cgi_wais.c */
#include <stdio.h>
#include <stdlib.h>
#include <iostream.h>
#include <strings.h>
#define WAISD "unix_path/index " /* wais index directory */
void main()
{
    char wais_string[500];
```

---

[1]   The information on WAIS is compiled from man (manual) pages.

[2]   See the URLs in the rear of the book.

```
FILE* fp;
char buffer[100];
int i;
int j = 1;
char input[50]; /* string from FORM */
char search[20]; /* string to search for */
char source[20]; /* name of source file created by wais */
/*
waisq -c $waisd -m 3 -f - -S ${src}.src -g search_xyz
 */
    gets(input);
    strcpy(search, variable(input, "search="));
    strcpy(source, variable(input, "source="));
    cout << "Content-type: text/html\n\n"
        << "<HEAD><TITLE>WAIS Catalog</TITLE></HEAD>\n"
        << "<BODY><h1>WAIS Catalog</H1>\n";

    sprintf(wais_string, %s%s%s%s%s%s%s,
        "waisq -c ",
        WAISD,
        "-m 3 -f - -S ",
        source,
        "-g ",
        search,
        " 2> /dev/null | grep headline"
        );
fp= popen(wais_string, "r");
while(fgets(buffer,80,fp) !=0)
{
    for(i=0; i< strlen(buffer); i++)
    {
        if(strncmp(buffer+i, "\"http", 5) == 0)
        {
            break;
        }
            }
        cout <<
                "<A HREF=" <<
                buffer+i <<
                "> Reference " ,,
                j++ <<
                "</A>\n";
    }
    cout << "</BODY></HTML>\n";
}
```

About cgi_wais . . . .

1. The program uses a software pipe to retrieve the information. The program waisq will return strings that include lines that look like this:

```
headline: "http://internet_path/document.pdf"
```

The headline: is stripped off and the URL is added after the HREF as an anchor. When the page appears on the screen, each reference that contained the search word will be part of an HTML anchor on the Web page. The user selects the pages in order, and they come up on an appropriate viewer. In this case, the documents are in PDF format so a reader such as Acroread™ from Adobe™ is needed.

2. The required command for the pipe is set up using the sprintf command. If you get hold of WAIS or another available search program, you can experiment to determine the right command for your requirements and then set up the sprintf to create the command.

The program to create the indexes will need to be developed separately. Programs like WAIS include these as part of the package. If you want to develop your own application, you will need to develop your own programs. Database development is a relatively sophisticated skill, so it will not be covered here.

. . . .

Connecting to an Existing Database

WHEN DEVELOPING DATABASE ACCESS FROM a cgi-bin program, the usual problem will be the server environment, which will not include variables required by the database routines. In this next routine, the required server environment is set up to allow the database routines to be used. Most standard databases provide C++ and/or C interface capability. Figure 14.1 illustrates some of the many kinds of information available from database access.

```
/*
 * Type C++ main
 * Purpose: Existing database connection - using putenv
 */
void main()
{
    /* For variable read */
    char outmsg[100];
    char msg[100];
    char buffer[200];
    /* Database initialization code */
    /*
```

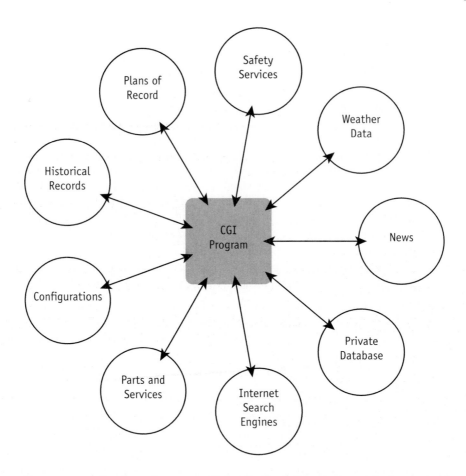

FIGURE 14.1   Database: Access to existing databases becomes straight-forward with existing
programming languages.

```
   * A database application will often require special environmental variables. Normally,
   * you would set these with your .profile. In the case of a cgi-bin program, you have no
   * control over the profile since it is the server that will be running the program.
   * Instead, use putenv to set up the database environment.
   */
putenv("KSHON=y");
putenv("DIR=\/tech\/markf\/d");
putenv("MODE=USER");
putenv("MACH=sun4");
putenv("UNIX=BSD");
/*
   * Using C++ or C routines available to interface to the database, locate the areas where
   * stdin and stdout are being used. Modify stdin to use the input from your FORM.
   * Modify stdout to include the command to the server and the needed HTML.
```

```
    */
    /* stdin from FORM */
    gets(msg);
    /* Clean up the message */
    (void) clear_hex(outmsg,
    variable(outmsg, msg, "search="));
    /* The database routines for access */
    setup_data_base(...);
    data_base_read(...);
    /* stdout - initial Content type and HTML */
    printf(
    "Content-type: text/html\n\n",
        /*
        * The Pragma client request is used to turn off caching to assure that every
        * database request will get new information.
        */

        "Pragma: no-cache\n\n",
    "<HTML>\n",
    "<BODY bgcolor=#f0f0f0 </BODY>\n",
    "<Body> <center> <p>\n",
    "<H2>Response From Database</H2><PRE>\n" );
    fflush(stdout);
    /* The canned database output routine */
    Display_Begin__0_1( );
    /* The terminating HTML */
    printf("%s", "</PRE></BODY></HTML>\n");
    fflush(stdout);
    exit( 0 );
}
```

About this program. . . . .

The main difference between this and other cgi-bin programs is the use of putenv(...) to set up environmental variables needed to access the database. Once these are in place, the normal routines available with many databases are used along with the form routines developed previously. The information retrieved from the database is formatted inside HTML. This is then sent to the browser.

In this chapter you have developed some fundamental skills in doing database searches. In addition, you have learned how to build your own document search tools using publicly available WAIS software. The use of putenv() provides a means to set up the environment needed for standard databases. The logic parsing and various database techniques can be combined to provide powerful access using Internet forms.

PROGRAM EXERCISES

1. Develop a form and related cgi-bin program that takes the input of a string and then parses out the logic operators. Using a simple text file, test your logic operations by retrieving sentences that have the expected words in them.
2. FTP the WAIS software to your site and develop a WAIS interface.
3. Using a database available at your site, develop an application that will access the database on demand.

PROBLEMS

1. Explain the different ways of looking at information logically. What additional alternatives come to mind? Where would they be applicable?
2. Explain the functioning of WAIS. How is a WAIS set up on the Internet? Give a step-by-step analysis of how you would develop your own WAIS application.
3. Explain the requirement to connect to an existing database. Give a detailed explanation for a known database.
4. Using Figure 14.2, explain database retrieval over the Internet.

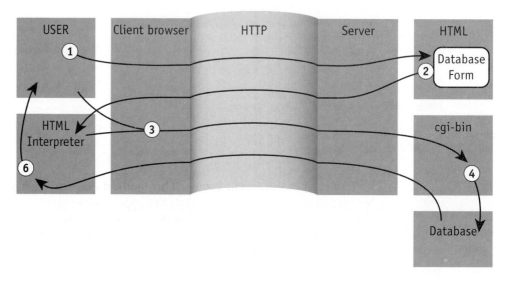

FIGURE 14.2

15

IMaGe Maps

IMaGe Input

The submit form[1] is not the only way that a form can be sent to a cgi-bin program. One of the alternative available input methods is the use of different areas of an image or GIF file to activate different events. This method takes advantage of the IMaGe input, which differs from all other input types. Where other inputs take information into a variable and then send the information to the cgi-bin program when the submit occurs, the IMaGe input is activated by clicking the mouse anywhere inside the specified image. The information sent to the cgi-bin program are the *x*

---

[1] Submit form refers to an HTML form that has its user information sent to a cgi-bin program by clicking the mouse on the submit button. This chapter provides another method to send the user data to the cgi-bin program.

and *y* coordinates of the place where the mouse was clicked. By creating a complex image that contains different sections that can be used to move the user to different capabilities, the IMaGe input provides a special kind of form. While the primary goal of the IMaGe input will normally be to send this coordinate information, as we will see, other variable information can also be sent.

Many users who surf the Internet have experienced interactive maps and other pictures that have clickable regions. While some of these use an older technique called ISMAP, the IMaGe input provides the same type of ability in a much easier manner.[2]

To do IMaGe input, you need the following components:

IMaGe Components

1. An image, either Graphic Interface Format (GIF) or Joint Photographic Expert Group (JPG). Normally, this will be a composite image so that different regions or subsections will be used to follow different pathways or, more specifically, to activate different URLs. You can think of the image as if it were multiple anchors. The different sections of the image will be mapped so that clicking different parts of the image acts the same way as clicking on different anchors. However, since the output is sent to a cgi-bin program, other computer-controlled actions can also take place. In this respect, the IMaGe input is very similar to the form submit.

2. An HTML page with a form area with an IMaGe input type. This will create a Web page with the initial image on it. This image will appear on the Web page like any other image, except that when the mouse is clicked on any area of the image, the cgi-bin program will be activated and the *x* and *y* coordinates where the mouse was clicked will be sent to the cgi-bin program. Any other variables, either hidden or visible, will also be sent at this time.

3. A cgi-bin program that can process the *x* and *y* coordinate information and any other user input. Its job is to provide appropriate responses, which will normally include sending back HTML pages (although it could also include other types of Web pages, such as PDF, audio, video, or other acceptable Web formats).

A typical GIF file is shown next. When doing IMaGe forms, it is common practice to use pictures in which different subsections suggest different types of information. The user then clicks on the appropriate area of the picture to retrieve the desired information.

The HTML for the IMaGe type looks very similar to other forms. Here is an example of a typical section used to create a form with image inputs.

---

[2]   Netscape provides a client-side image map capability. The advantage of server-side image mapping is the ability to provide more computer control. Access to databases or critical sections of the computer requires server-side control.

```
<FORM ACTION="http://internet_path/cgi-bin/cgi_xy" METHOD="post">
<INPUT TYPE="image" SRC="http://internet_path/image.gif" >
</FORM>
```

x and *y* Coordinates

THE FORM STATEMENT IS similar to others we have encountered in other sections. The action tells which cgi-bin program to run when the mouse is clicked on the IMaGe. A method is specified as in other forms and it defaults to the Get method if none is specified. The difference is in the second line. Here an input type image is specified with the name of an SRC for the IMaGe. This GIF or JPG file will be placed on the screen, and clicking on it will cause the action to occur. The input data to the cgi-bin program will include the *x* and *y* coordinates. The coordinate variables are sent as *x* and *y*. So a typical coordinate information string would look like this:

```
x=35&y=28
```

Here is a simple Web page with which to get started testing this capability. You can add your own text around it to create the effects you need.

```
<HTML><TITLE> Image Form </TITLE>
<BODY>
<H1> This is an IMaGe form </H1>
<H2> Click on the Image to Send Out the x and y Coordinates </H2>
<FORM ACTION="http://internet_path/cgi-bin/cgi_xy" METHOD="post">
<INPUT TYPE="image" SRC="http://internet_path/image.gif" >
</FORM>
</BODY></HTML>
```

This will place the GIF file named image.gif, which can be displayed by accessing the

```
URL="http://internet_path/image.gif"
```

on the screen as an IMaGe form type. If the mouse is clicked on the image, the cgi-bin program called cgi_xy will be activated by the server. The *x* and *y* coordinates of the location where the mouse was clicked on the image will be sent to the cgi-bin program. Since the method is Post, the information will be sent in stdin. Had the method been Get, it would have been sent as a command line argument (argc and argv[]).

What is meant by *x* and *y* coordinates? Actually, they are horizontal (*x*) and vertical (*y*) distances along the GIF (or JPG) pictures starting from the origin (left top corner). In other words, the motion is the same way you would read a book (left to right and top to bottom). The upper left corner is designated 0,0, or $x = 0$ and $y = 0$. But how large is each *x* and *y* unit?[3] While there is an exact dimension to this, fortunately you do not need to have it to make images work for you. Instead, there is a simple getting-started program that will send the x and y coordinates back to the screen to help you map out your pictures. Figure 15.1 shows IMaGe areas connected to various resources.

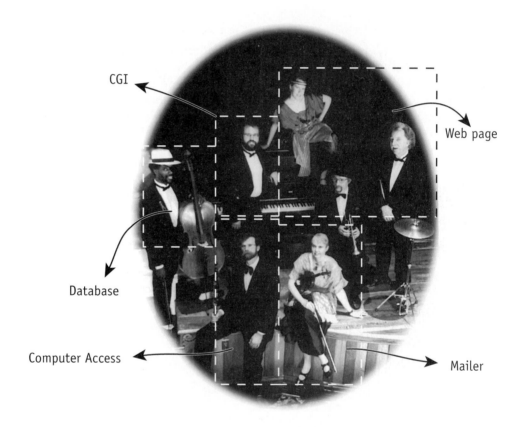

FIGURE 15.1   IMaGe Maps: Subsections of IMaGes are mapped to server-side control points.

The Coord Class

To EXPAND THE x and y coordinated capability, a coordinate class is developed.

```
#include <stdio.h>
#include <stdlib.h>
#include <sys/time.h>
```

---

[3]   This is equated to the GIF dimension. If the GIF image is 24×36, then the x goes from $0 \leq x < 24$ and y goes from $0 \leq y < 36$.

```
#include <unistd.h>
#include <string.h>
class _Coord
{
Private:
    char coord[100];    // holder for the variables input by the FORM
    int x_coord;        // value of the x coordinate
    int y_coord;        // value of the y coordinate
    char return_msg[MAXLINE];
    char* get_variable( char* msg, char* start_msg);
Public:
    _Coord();           // the constructor
    void show();        // send out HTML to the client server
};
```

The coordinate class has a private string to retrieve the string containing the coordinates. It has two integer variables to hold the coordinates, and it has the variable function discussed earlier to separate out the value of the coordinates as a string. Since coordinate information is sent in exactly the same format as other form information, the same form routines can be used. In fact, the form class could be inherited to make things easier.

For the public subroutines there is the constructor and the public function show(), which will be used to send HTML back to the screen that includes the x and y coordinates.[4]

```
/*
 * Type C++ class subroutine
 * Purpose: constructor for image mapping class
 */
/*
 * The constructor does most of the work
 */
_Coord::_Coord()
{
    gets(coord); /* read the data from stdin */
    /* get the x coordiate value */
    x_coord=atoi(get_variable(coord, "x="));
    /* get the y coordinate value */
    y_coord=atoi(get_variable(coord, "y="));
}
```

---

[4]   The coordinates for an image will not change, even if the font or Web page is resized. However, resizing the image will change the coordinates proportionately.

About the constructor ·

The constructor will run the first time the Coordinate class is created. Since our
plan is to have this happen as soon as the cgi-bin program runs, most of the hard
work has been built into it.

1. First the gets() routine is used to read in the posted information from stdin.
   The char string called coord is used as a holding place for the information.

2. Next the integer x_coord is set to the value of the *x* coordinate. This is done by
   getting a pointer to the string that represents the value of the *x* coordinate in
   ASCII. This will follow the variable name, which is always x= for IMaGe forms.
   The routine atoi() turns the ASCII string into an integer.

3. The *y* coordinate is retrieved in a similar value. Its value is in the variable y=. It
   is placed into the integer y_coord. Since the values of x_coord and y_coord are
   available to any subroutine in the class Coord, they will be accessed easily when
   the show() routine is called.

· ·

```
/*
 * Another subroutine for separating a message out of the input data sent from a FORM. You
 * can substitute your favorite choice.
 */
char* _Coord::get_variable(
     char* msg,          /*
                          * Pointer to the user message from the server.
                          */
        char* var_name   /*
                          * Pointer to the name of the variable.
                          */
)
{
     char* msg_ptr;
     char* tmp_ptr;
     int i =0;
     /* The function strstr returns a pointer to the second string which in this case is the
      * start of the variable name. If it returns NULL, the variable was not found in the
      * string.
      */
     if((msg_ptr = strstr(var_name, msg)) == NULL)
     {
          return ("") ;
     }
     /* If there is an ampersand following the variable name, put in up to the ampersand;
      * otherwise the variable value is the rest of the message to the end.
      */
```

```
        if(strstr(msg_ptr, "&") != NULL) /* check for ampersand */
        {
            strncpy(return_msg, msg_ptr,
            /* The difference between the ptr returned by strstr and the pointer msg_ptr is the
             * length of the variable value. This is used as the count value to strncpy.
             */
            (strstr(msg_ptr,"&") - msg_ptr));
        } else
        {
            strcpy(return_msg, msg_ptr);
        }
        return(return_msg);
    }
```

About the get_variable subroutine . . . .

Alternatives to this subroutine are described in Appendix 1. The subroutine is reworked here to make this chapter easy to read as a standalone section. It is another version of the form decision routine.

. . . .

```
    /*
     * Type C++ class subroutine
     * Purpose: Show the x and y coordinates
     */
    void _Coord::show()
    {
        /*
         * Send a message to the server that HTML text is coming. Then send out the HTML
         * with the coordinates.
         */
        cout<< "Content-type: text/html\n\n" <<
                "<HTML><TITLE>x and y Coodinate Demo</TITLE>\n" <<
                "<BODY> <H1> Your x and y coordinates are "<<
                x_coord <<" " << y_coord << " </H1></BODY></HTML>\n";
    }
```

About the show subroutine . . . .

This subroutine sends back some required HTML (see Chapters 1 and 2); then it sends out the *x* and *y* coordinates; then it sends out the ending HTML to complete the HTML.

. . . .

```
    /*
     * Type C++ main
     * Purpose: show the coordinates
```

```
        */

void main()
{
        COORD Coord;                    // The constructor will take place automatically
        Coord.show();                   // Send back the coordinate information
        return;
}
/*
  * C Version - Includes a check for the coordinates and an HTML file sent back through the
  * cgi-bin program based on the coordinates sent.
  */
#include <stdio.h>
#include <stdlib.h>
#include <sys/time.h>
#include <unistd.h>
#include <string.h>
/*
  * Type C subroutine
  * Purpose: sending out with Thru mode based on x and y coordinates
  */
/*
  * This routine is used to send different HTML pages out to the user depending on the
  * section of the image that is activated by the mouse. The information will be x and y
  * coordinates of the position on the image where the mouse was located when it was
  * clicked.
  */
void
file_out(
        char* filename /* The path and filename of the HTML */
)
{
        FILE* fp; /* file point to point to the HTML */
        char buffer[90]; /* buffer to read in the HTML */
        fp=fopen(filename, "r"); /* open the HTML for reading */
        /*
          * Read in the HTML and then send it back to stdout, which is the server
          */
        while(fgets(buffer,80,fp)!= 0)
        {
                printf("%s", buffer);
        }
        fclose(fp); /* close the HTML file */
}
```

Using Coordinates to Control Output

IN THE C VERSION THAT follows, the coordinate information is obtained in a similar manner as in the C++ program. It is then used to send an HTML file out to the screen based on the *x* and *y* coordinates selected. Typically in IMaGe forms, the screen is separated into rectangular areas. If this is done, a test of whether the *x* coordinate falls between two values and the *y* coordinate falls between two values will isolate a particular rectangular area. More complex areas can be mapped by using rectangular slices.

```c
/*
 * Type C main
 * Purpose: Read in coordinates
 */
/*
 * Subroutine that reads the coordinate data out of the input from the server. The x and y
 * coordinates are set using pointers to integer variables.
 */
void
read_coord(int* x_coord, int* y_coord)
{
    char coord[100];
    gets(coord);        /* read the data from stdin */
                        /* get the x coordiate value */
    *x_coord=atoi(get_variable(coord, "x="));
                        /* get the y coordinate value */
    *y_coord=atoi(get_variable(coord, "&y="));
    /* Send a message to the server that HTML text is coming.
     * Why not here instead of later?
     */
    printf("Content-type: text/html\n\n");
}
/*
 * Type C main
 * Purpose: Coordinates with validation
 */
void
main()
{
    int x_coord, y_coord;
    read_coord(&x_coord, &y_coord);
    /* check for coordinate ranges */
    if((x_coord > 0) && (x_coord < 69) &&
    (y_coord > 0) && (y_coord < 66))
    {
        file_out("unix_path/file1.html");
```

```
    } else
    if((x_coord > 0) && (x_coord < 69) &&
    (y_coord > 80) && (y_coord < 120))
    {
        file_out("unix_path/file2.html");
    } else
    if((x_coord > 78) && (x_coord < 142) &&
    (y_coord > 9) && (y_coord < 64))
    {
        file_out("unix_path/file3.html");
    } else
    if((x_coord > 78) && (x_coord < 142) &&
    (y_coord > 80) && (y_coord < 120))
    {
        file_out("unix_path/file4.html");
    } else
    {
        file_out("unix_path/default.html");
    }
}
```

Depending on the coordinates' range, a different file is sent out to the client and then to the user. The Thru mode (see Chapter 7) is used to send the different files out to the client. Each of the files must be in standard HTML. The content type is sent out prior to the HTML in the file_out routine. The path to these files must be accessible by the server software since it is running the cgi-bin program.

x/y Coordinate Range

A WORD ABOUT THE TESTING of the coordinate ranges: These ranges are tested using a rectangular area. The minimum and maximum x values determine the length of the top and bottom of the rectangle, while the minimum and maximum y values determine the range of the two vertical sides of the rectangles.

While the preceding program is a simple way to get these dimensions, there are a number of alternative methods for mapping out the x and y coordinate areas. There are a number of UNIX or windows programs that will give x and y information.

giftrans   Will give the height and width of a GIF file. Once this is known, you can use any measuring ruler to determine various points relative to these points. For example, if the height is 50, then half the height is 25.

xv   Will actually show you the x and y coordinates as you move the positioner across the image with the mouse.

Photoshop   Will give x and y coordinates in pixels suitable for mapping.

Irregular Shapes

WHILE RECTANGLES WILL WORK FOR most images that you want to map, you may
want to map out more irregular images. This can be done by making multiple rectangles and then having the program send the same HTML for different coordinate
ranges that overlap the picture area. By making the rectangle small enough, virtually any level of control can be realized. While it is not recommended practice, you
could map out every *x* and *y* coordinate on an image with response controllable on
a point by point basis. For most applications this would be absurd, and the use of
rectangles makes more sense. Most users will tend to click in the center of the various sections of the image. If moderately large subsections are used in your image
maps, you should not have any complaints. If you are making public accessible
images, it is a good idea to think about your users. Give them images that are not a
test of their coordination. Figure 15.2 shows different ways of breaking up the same
IMaGe.

Location

THE PREVIOUS EXAMPLE USED Thru mode files to send different HTML output depending on the *x* and *y* coordinates. An alternative is to use the server directive Location:.
Location works in a manner similar to Content type: except that it sends back the
requested URL. The advantage of Location is that your IMaGe forms can be used to
send back URLs associated with either local or remote sites.

```
/*
 * Type C main
 * Purpose: Transfer to location based on coordinates
 */
void
main()
{
    int x_coord, y_coord;
    read_coord(&x_coord, &y_coord);
    /* Check for coordinate ranges */
     if((x_coord > 0) && (x_coord < 69) &&
     (y_coord > 0) && (y_coord < 66))
     {
    printf("%s\n\n",
          "Location: http://internet_path/file1.html");
    } else
    if((x_coord > 0) && (x_coord < 69) &&
    (y_coord > 80) && (y_coord < 120))
    {
        printf("%s\n\n",
```

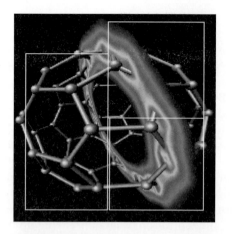 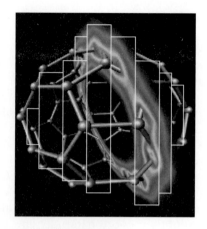

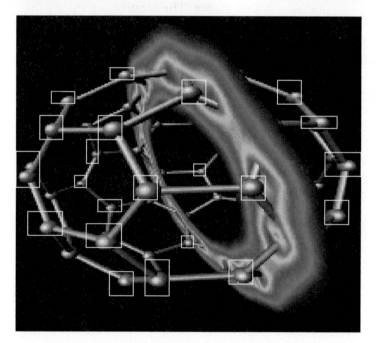

FIGURE 15.2   Mapping of IMaGes: Slicing sections allows the different areas to be mapped
to Internet events.

```
                    "Location: http://internet_path/file2.html");
          } else
          if((x_coord > 78) && (x_coord < 142) &&
          (y_coord > 9) && (y_coord < 64))
          {
              printf("%s\n\n",
```

```
                    "Location: http://internet_path/file3.html");
        } else
        if((x_coord > 78) && (x_coord < 142) &&
        (y_coord > 80) && (y_coord < 120))
        {
            printf("%s\n\n",
                    "Location: http://internet_path/any.html");
        } else
        {
            printf("%s\n\n",
                    "Location: http://internet_path/default.html");
        }
    }
```

A couple of key points about Location. The Location request replaces the Content-type: request. It is not in addition to it. The actual URL is sent without any quotes. Again, remember that the URL need not be a local reference.

IMaGe Input and Other User Information

THE USE OF THE IMaGe input method as a method for sending user information to a cgi-bin program does not mean that only *x* and *y* coordinates can be sent. An IMaGe input type can include other input variables that will be sent along with the *x* and *y* coordinates. Here is an example of a section of HTML code that includes other user information.

```
<HTML><TITLE> Image Form With Other Information </TITLE>
<BODY>
<H1> This Is an IMaGe FORM </H1>
<H2>
Click on the Image to Send Out the x and y Coordinates
<BR>
And the Other Information
</H2>
<FORM ACTION="http://internet_path/cgi-bin/cgi_xy" METHOD="post">
<INPUT TYPE="image" SRC="http://internet_path/image.gif" >
<H2>
Do You Like Entering Information This Way?
</H2>
YES<INPUT TYPE="radio" NAME="info1" VALUE="yes" SELECT>
NO<INPUT TYPE="radio" NAME="info1" VALUE="no" >
</FORM>
</BODY></HTML>
```

Now when you click on the IMaGe, your radio box selection will also be sent in the Posted string.

This capability can be used to design your own custom *select* buttons. Just make a small GIF picture of a button and use it in an IMaGe type form. Then discard or ignore the x and y coordinate information, and you have your own custom buttons.

In this chapter you have learned how to create an IMaGe type input form that sends the x and y locations of the mouse when it is clicked on the image. You have also learned how to map these coordinates and use them to send back different HTML pages using the Thru mode and Location. You have discovered that IMaGe forms do not stop you from sending other user information. In fact, you have seen examples where this can be used to create your own custom buttons. IMaGe input types are very popular on the World Wide Web. While some recent browsers provide HTML support for IMaGe mapping, they can never provide the levels of control available when the capabilities of compiled programs are added through cgi-bin program control.

PROGRAM EXERCISES

1. Create an IMaGe map form. Create a cgi-bin program that will map out the x and y coordinates of the image. Using the mouse, form and program map out different areas of the IMaGe. Using a program such as giftrans, compare your image mapping with the x and y coordinates returned from your program.

2. Create a complex image and map it out using rectangular sections. Create the cgi-bin program to respond to the sectioning. Create a Thru mode response to the area mapping.

3. Create an IMaGe map cgi-bin program using the Location: directive. Verify that using this method you can use coordinate information to go to URLs that are off site. Using hidden variables, send at least one of the locations as a hidden variable. Verify that changing the URL in the hidden variable redirects the response. (**Note:** Watch out for caching.)

PROBLEMS

1. Explain the structure of an IMaGe map form. How does this differ from a submit form? Explain the way the x and y coordinates arrive when the mouse is clicked on the IMaGe. Explain the parsing routines needed to isolate out the x and y coordinates. Explain the use of atoi() in this procedure.

2. Explain the alternative methods for isolating out the IMaGe area in the cgi-bin program. Explain how function pointers might assist in this process. Explain the purpose of Location instead of http. What is the advantage of Location? When would Thru mode have advantages?

3. Explain the distinction between GIF and JPG images. What are the advantages and disadvantages of each? How will they differ in terms of mappings in the IMaGe form? What will be the effect of interleaving the image? How can more than one IMaGe be used with IMaGe forms? How might hidden variables help in this type of project? How might argc and argv[] help in this type of project?

4. What is the effect of including an argv[] as an ?argument in conjunction with the Get method?

16

CGI Image Control

CGI Programs for IMaGes

UP TO THIS POINT, THE discussion of cgi-bin programs has focused on their use as the primary URL or their use in response to a form being submitted. In both cases, the output of the cgi-bin program was HTML text. In this chapter, the discussion turns to the use of a cgi-bin program to provide output directly to an IMaGe. While some of the earlier discussions could have been accomplished with shell programming languages, the control of images can only be accomplished with compiled programs.

Recall for the moment the normal format for a command to display an image in HTML.

```
<IMG SRC="http://internet_path/picture.gif" ALIGN="top">
```

This HTML code says that an image is to be placed on the screen and the *source* (SRC) for the image is the file addressed by

```
URL="http://internet_path/picture.gif"
```

In other words, the image will be in GIF format. The rest of the information is optional information about the image. In this instance it is an alignment instruction, but it could also have included HEIGHT and WIDTH information, for a faster display and other image options.

Even if other optional arguments are provided, the basic format remains the same—that is, the source for the image is the GIF format or JPG formatted image.

For most browsers, the in-line images are displayed in parallel with the rest of the Web page. This results in the experience of seeing the pictures appear on the screen partially while the text comes into view. There are a number of tools that can be used to improve this situation. One is interlacing, which is available on better graphics programs. It makes the GIF picture appear in much the same manner as a TV screen. First some sections throughout the picture from top to bottom and then more sections are added throughout the picture until the entire picture is present. This and other factors allow you, on some browsers (for example, Netscape), to hit the Stop button during partial loading and get the text even though all IMaGes will not be present. The importance of this will become apparent later when we try to take more and more control of the image.

The thing of interest at this point is that the SRC part of the image is really a request to a location known by the browser for image data. It can, in fact, be a URL for a cgi-bin program, provided that the cgi-bin program will send back binary image data. This may seem remarkable at first, but it is really a fact. You can send an image to the screen from a cgi-bin program. Begin the development of this capability with a simple pipe. It will merely substitute the cgi-bin program for the path to picture.gif. This is similar to the original programs in Chapter 1, that substituted HTML passed through a cgi-bin program. It is accomplished with the following HTML line:

```
<IMG SRC="http://html_path/cgi-bin/picture_cgi" >
```

Now the request for the image is going to the cgi-bin rather than directly accessing a GIF or JPG formatted image. To make this work, two things will be necessary. First the cgi-bin program will have to send a command to the server to say that an image is coming, just as before it had to tell the server that HTML text was going to be sent. Then the cgi-bin program will have to send out binary data that look exactly like a GIF or JPG file. (For these illustrations, GIF format will be used.)

To accomplish these two goals, a cgi-bin program will be created to provide the necessary GIF data. The easiest approach is to read in a known good GIF file and then send it back out to stdout. Since stdout is the server when a cgi-bin program is being run, this should work. (Later, methods will be demonstrated for modifying these data to create remarkable results.)

Begin as always with a basic class, as shown in the next section.

Picture Class

```
class Picture
{
private:
    File* stream;        // use data hiding on the file stream
    char buffer[2];      // a buffer to get the characters
public:
    Picture() { ; };     // put in a constructor just for grins
    void show();         // public subroutine to do the whole thing
};
/*
 * Type C++ class subroutine
 * Purpose: Show a GIF picture
 */
void
Picture :: show()
{
    /*
     * This line is needed to tell the server that an image is coming.
     */
    fprintf(stdout,"content-type: image/gif\n\n");
    /*
     * Set up a stream between the buffer and the file.
     */
    stream = fopen("/unix_path/picture.gif", "r");
    /*
     * This instruction appears to read two characters and output one. This is not the case.
     * Only one character is read in and one sent out.
     */
    while(fgets(buffer, 2, stream ) // get the gif data
    {
        fprintf(stdout, "%c", buffer[0]);
        // send the image data back to IMG
```

```
        }
        fclose();
    }
```

Important Note: The line

```
        fprintf(stdout, "%c", buffer[0]);
```

does not use cout. This is not by accident. The routine cout in C++ includes formatting capabilities that will not work with the raw GIF binary data.

Here is the main:

```
    /*
     * Type C++ main
     * Purpose: Show a picture
     */
    void main()
    {
        Picture myPicture;
        myPicture.show();
    }
```

About this program . . . .

1. The initial statement tells the server that a GIF image is coming.

   ```
   fprintf(stdout,"content-type: image/gif\n\n");
   ```

   The equivalent for jpg is

   ```
   fprintf(stdout,"content-type: image/jpg\n\n");
   ```

   This looks almost identical to the earlier way the server was informed about HTML text. You may be wondering about the use of fprintf instead of cout or printf. Both would work for this line, but they will not work for the binary data from the GIF file. Since we are going to need fprintf for the binary IMaGe, use it here for consistency. Notice that the file print is sent to stdout. As always, this is the server.

2. The GIF image is read in as a stream and then sent out to the server one byte at a time. The file is then closed and the program returns. If we wanted to get a little fancier, we could have had the constructor open the file and created a destructor to close the file.

Alternatively, in C,

```
/*
 * Type C subroutine
 * Purpose: show a picture GIF
 */
#define GIF_CONTENT "Content-type: image/gif\n"
#define GIF_LENGTH "Content-length: %d\n\n " /* blank line follows the length */
#define GIF_PICTURE "/unix_path/picture.gif"
void show()
{
    File* stream;
    char buffer[2];
    int gif_length = NUMBER_OF_BYTES_IN_GIF;
    /*
     * This line is needed to tell the server that an image is coming.
     */
    fprintf(stdout, GIF_CONTENT);
    /* The use of GIF_LENGTH is not required. However, it can increase transfer speed and
     * minimize errors. */
    fprintf(stdout, GIF_LENGTH , gif_length);
    /*
     * Set up a stream between the buffer and the file.
     */

    stream = fopen(GIF_PICTURE, "r");
    while(fgets(buffer, 2, stream )!= EOF) {
        fprintf(stdout, "%c", buffer[0]);
    }
    fclose(stream);
}
```

Here is the main:

```
/*
 * Type C main
 * Purpose: GIF output
 */
void main()
{
    show();
}
```

About this program. . . . .

One critical change is the addition of Content-length. This directive to the server provides the number of bytes in the IMaGe file. While this is not needed, its use will speed up download time. There are a number of ways to speed up the time of IMaGe download:

1. Specify the number of bytes through Content-length.
2. Specify the HEIGHT and WIDTH of the IMaGe in the HTML IMaGe request.
3. Minimize the size of the IMaGe by scanning at the resolution required for the goal of the display.
4. If IMaGes are of a high enough quality, it is possible to send out a small version across the client-server network interface and then have the browser use the height and width information for resizing. This can be especially useful for patterned background IMaGes.
5. Finally, there is the technique called interleaving, which allows the IMaGe to be sent in parallel with the information.

· ·

Accessing GIF IMaGes

ONE KEY POINT TO BE sure to notice: The GIF file is accessed by the program as a UNIX file, not using a URL. Be sure to set up your permissions correctly before trying this. Since this is a GIF image, you should be able to access this directly as a URL from your browser, just as you can directly access a GIF file with a browser. Just enter the URL of the cgi-bin program (be sure it was put in the cgi-bin after being compiled) and see if the same picture appears as it would if you viewed the GIF directly with the browser.

The next step is to add the same cgi-bin program to an HTML document. Just build a simple document with an image in it, and then replace the SRC part with the URL of the cgi-bin program. Here is an example:

```
<!- Regular Image HTML -->
<HTML> <TITLE> IMaGe TEST </TITLE>
<BODY>
<H1> SHOW AN IMaGe </H1>
<IMG SRC="http://internet_path/picture.gif" >
</BODY></HTML>
```

Here is the same thing with the cgi-bin program:

```
Now the same thing with the cgi-bin program
<!- Image created by a cgi-bin program -->
<HTML> <TITLE> CGI-BIN IMAGE TEST </TITLE>
<BODY>
<H1> SHOW AN IMAGE FROM A CGI-BIN PROGRAM </H1>
```

```
<IMG SRC="http://internet_path/cgi-bin/cgi_image" >
</BODY></HTML>
```

If everything is set up right, both of these programs should create the same IMaGe.

Web Usage of IMaGes

LET'S CONTINUE OUR EXPLORATION of IMaGes with some simple tricks. Now that the IMaGes can come from a cgi-bin program, numerous possibilities will open up. Since images are one of the most powerful parts of the World Wide Web, this is a very powerful capability.

Before giving some examples of ways to use this capability, it is worth your time to think of all the places that IMaGes can be used on Web pages.

1. **IMaGes Directly Accessed as a URL**   This is the case in which the URL of the IMaGe is sent directly from the browser.

   ```
   http://internet_path/image.gif
   ```

2. **Simple IMaGe**   This is the example of the preceding section in which the IMaGe is just placed onto the page.

   ```
   HTML
   <IMG SRC="http://internet_path/image.gif" >
   ```

   or

   ```
   <IMG SRC="http://internet_path/cgi-bin/cgi_image" >
   ```

3. **IMaGe as a Background**   Instead of using a color for the background, an IMaGe can be repeated over and over again to create the background.

   ```
   HTML
   <BODY BACKGROUND="http://internet_path/image.gif"> Any text </BODY>
   ```

   or

   ```
   <BODY BACKGROUND="http://internet_path/cgi-bin/cgi_image">
       Any text </BODY>
   ```

4. **IMaGes Replacing or Along With Text in an Anchor**   An IMaGe or an IMaGe with words can be used to activate an URL through an HTML anchor.

```
HTML
<A HREF="http://internet_path/page.html"> optional text
    <IMG SRC="http://internet_path/image.gif> optional text </A>
```

or

```
<A HREF="http://internet_path/page.html"> optional text
    <IMG SRC="http://internet_path/cgi-bin/cgi_image> optional text </A>
```

5. **IMaGes or IMaGes and Words in a Table**   An IMaGe can be part of the items in a table.

```
HTML
<TABLE>
<TR><TD> optional words
    <IMG SRC="http://internet_path/image.gif> optional words
<TD> optional words
    <IMG SRC="http://internet_path/image.gif> optional words
</TABLE>
```

or

```
<TABLE>
<TR><TD> optional words
    <IMG SRC="http://internet_path/cgi-bin/cgi_image> optional words
<TD> optional words
    <IMG SRC="http://internet_path/cgi-bin/cgi_image> optional words
</TABLE>
```

6. **IMaGes as Part of an IMaGe Form**   These are IMaGes that are placed into a form, where the type is IMaGe. When this is done, x and y coordinates where the mouse is clicked on the image are sent to the cgi-bin program.

```
HTML
<FORM METHOD=POST ACTION="http://internet_path/cgi-bin/cgi_form">
<INPUT TYPE="image" SRC="http://internet_path/image.gif">
</FORM>
```

or

```
<FORM METHOD=POST ACTION="http://internet_path/cgi-bin/cgi_form">
<INPUT TYPE="image" SRC="http://internet_path/cgi-bin/cgi_image"> </FORM>
```

In the final case, a cgi-bin program is used both as the action for the form and as the input to the *x/y* coordinate figure used to activate the form.

Since any of these are shown replaced by an appropriate cgi-bin program that sends IMaGes, there are lots of new possibilities that are opened up by this capability.

Random IMaGes

HAVING ESTABLISHED OUR BASIC PROGRAM, it is now possible to think about some of the things that might be done with this capability. One easy possibility is to change the IMaGe. This is not a bad idea, especially if you have a Web site that gets visited frequently by the same people. Here is a program that randomly selects the IMaGe from five possible pictures and then puts out the one selected.

```
/*
 * Type C++ class subroutine
 * Purpose: output random images
 */
void
_Picture :: show()
{
    int random_select;
    /*
     * This line is needed to tell the server that an image is coming.
     */
    fprintf(stdout,"content-type: image/gif\n\n");
    /*
     * Get a random number between 0 and 4. The process id is used as a seed to the
     * random number generator. This will change every time the program is run by the
     * server. The modula operator (%5) is used to reset the random number to the desired
     * range.
     */
    random_select = rand(getpid()) % 5;
    /*
     * Use the random number to pick one of the five pictures for viewing.
     */
    switch(random_select)
    {
    case 0:
        stream = fopen("/unix_path/picture0.gif", "r");
        break;
    case 1:
        stream = fopen("/unix_path/picture1.gif", "r");
        break;
    case 2:
```

```
                    stream = fopen("/unix_path/picture2.gif", "r");
                    break;
              case 3:
                    stream = fopen("/unix_path/picture3.gif", "r");
                    break;
              default:
              case 4:
                    stream = fopen("/unix_path/picture4.gif", "r");
                    break;
        }
        /*
          * Send the image to the client-server software.
          */
        while(fgets(buffer, 2, stream )!= EOF  // get the gif data
        {
               fprintf(stdout,"%c", buffer[0]); // send data to IMG
        }
        fclose();
   }
```

C Version

```
    /*
      * Type C subroutine
      * Purpose: output random images
      */
    void show()
    {
        File* stream;
        char buffer[MAXLINE];
        char* show_picture[5];
        fprintf(stdout,"content-type: image/gif\n\n");
        show_picture[0]="/unix_path/picture0.gif";
        show_picture[1]="/unix_path/picture1.gif";
        show_picture[2]="/unix_path/picture2.gif";
        show_picture[3]="/unix_path/picture3.gif";
        show_picture[4]="/unix_path/picture4.gif";
        stream = fopen(show_picture[rand(getpid())%4], "r");
        while(fgets(buffer, 2, stream )
        {
               fprintf(stdout,"%c", buffer[0]);
        }
        fclose(stream);
    }
```

Create a main() and compile:

```
/*
 * Type C main
 * Purpose: main for random images
 */
void main()
{
    show();
}
```

Compile cc -o show_cgi show.c
Place the file in the cgi-bin. Now create the required HTML home page:

```
<HTML>
<HEAD>
<TITLE> Random GIF Show </TITLE>
</HEAD>
<BODY>
<IMG SRC="internet_path/cgi-bin/show_cgi" >
<!-- OTHER HTML HERE -->
</BODY>
</HTML>
```

Now every time users come to this Web page, they will get a randomly selected picture that provides variety.

Scheduled IMaGes

HERE IS A SLIGHTLY MORE useful version. It uses the function time() to get the time of day. Then it figures out which day of the week it is. Once determined, it displays a different picture for each day of the week.

C++ Class and subroutine to get the day of the week

```
#include <sys/time.h>
class Day
{
private:
    struct timeval *tp;
    struct timezone *tzp;
    long day;
public:
    long get_day_of_week();
};
```

```
/*
 * Type C++ class subroutine
 * Purpose: produce scheduled images
 */
long
Day::get_day_of_week()
{
    (void )gettimeofday(tp, tzp);
    /*
     * Modula the number of seconds weekly seconds since Jan 1, 1970. Then find out how
     * many days have passed in the final week.
     */
    day = (tp->tv_sec % (24*60*60*7)) % (24*60*60);
    /* Do a sanity check */
    if((day > 6) || (day <0)) /* days are 0-6 */
        return(0);
    return(day);
}
```

C Version subroutine to get the day of the week

```
/*
 * Type C subroutine
 * Purpose: produce scheduled images
 */
#include <sys/time.h>
long get_day_of_week()
{
    struct timeval *tp;
    struct timezone *tzp;
    long day;
    (void )gettimeofday(tp, tzp);
    /*
     * Modula the number of seconds weekly seconds since Jan 1, 1970.
     */
    day = tp->tv_sec % (24*60*60*7);
    /*
     * Now find out how many days have passed in the final week.
     */
    day = day % (24*60*60);
    if((day > 6) || (day <0)) /* days are 0-6 */
        return(0);
    return(day);
}
```

Add this to the show routine:

```
/*
 * Type C subroutine
 * Purpose: scheduled images
 */
void show()
{
    File* stream;
    char buffer[100];
    char* show_picture[5];
    fprintf(stdout,"content-type: image/gif\n\n");
    show_picture[0]="/unix_path/sunday.gif";
    show_picture[1]="/unix_path/monday.gif";
    show_picture[2]="/unix_path/tuesday.gif";
    show_picture[3]="/unix_path/wednesday.gif";
    show_picture[4]="/unix_path/thursday.gif";
    show_picture[5]="/unix_path/friday.gif";
    show_picture[6]="/unix_path/saturday.gif";
    /*
     * The array value is set based on the day of the week.
     */
    stream = fopen(show_picture[(int )get_day_of_week()], "r");
    fprintf(stdout,"content-type: image/gif\n\n");
    while(fgets(buffer, 2, stream )
    {
        fprintf(stdout,"%c", buffer[0]);
    }
    fclose(stream);
}
```

About This Program.

This program is similar to the random version except that the GIF file selected is based on the day of the week. The day of the week is returned as an integer value that is used as the argument to the array of pointers to GIF files. Each day of the week is represented by a different GIF file. Other routines can easily be added to get the date, hour of the day, or other time-based information.

IMaGes argv[] and Function Pointers

YOU CAN INCREASE YOUR IMAGE capability by adding the argc and argv[] to the cgi-bin program. The IMaGe can even be selected by a form request. In the next example, four pictures in four angles of rotation are created. A form is used to request the specified rotated picture. You may be wondering if the picture could be rotated directly. The answer is yes, but doing so requires advanced algorithms to generate the GIF file on the fly. The techniques developed here may lead some readers to explore creating GIF pictures on the fly. Since doing so requires the study of compression algorithms, some preliminary discussions are included in Chapter 10.

```
typedef void (*F_PTR)();/* pointer to a function */
#include <stdio.h>
#include <stdlib.h>
#include <iostream.h>
#include <strings.h>
/* Needed since routines are below main part of program */
extern void rotate_0();
extern void rotate_90();
extern void rotate_180();
extern void rotate_270();
typedef void (*F_PTR)();
static struct degrees
{
    char* subroutine;   /* name of subroutine */
    F_PTR function;     /* pointer to subroutine */
    char* gif;          /* path to gif for subroutine */
};
static struct degrees Degrees[] =
{
    { "rotate_0", &rotate_0, "/unix_path/picture_0deg.gif"; },
    { "rotate_90", &rotate_90, "/unix_path/picture_90deg.gif"; },
    { "rotate_180", &rotate_180, "/unix_path/picture_180deg.gif"; },
    { "rotate_270", &rotate_270, "/unix_path/picture_270deg.gif"; },
};
extern void gif_out(char* filename);
/*
 * Type C++ or C subroutines
 * Purpose: Degree rotation routines - demonstrate use of function pointers
 */
void rotate_0()
{
    gif_out(Degrees[0].gif);
}
void rotate_90()
{
    gif_out(Degrees[1].gif);
}
void rotate_180()
{
    gif_out(Degrees[2].gif);
}
void rotate_270()
```

```
{
     gif_out(Degrees[3].gif);
}
/*
 * Type C++ or C subroutine
 * Purpose: output rotated GIF file
 */
void gif_out(char* filename)
{
    /*
     * Send the picture.
     */
    stream = fopen(filename "r");
    fprintf(stdout,"content-type: image/gif\n\n");
    while(fgets(buffer, 2, stream )!= EOF )
    {
        fprintf(stdout,"%c", buffer[0]);
    }
}
```

Now the main looks like this:

```
/*
 * Type C++ or C main
 * Purpose: Rotation main
 */
void main(int argc, char* argv[])
{
    int i;
    for(i=0; i<4; i++)
    {
        if(strcmp(argv[1], Degrees[i].subroutine) == 0)
        {
            Degrees[i].function();
            return;
        }
    }
}
```

About this program. . . . .

This program introduces the use of tables with pointers to functions, which is a useful technique for cgi-bin programming.

   1. A typedef is created that defines a pointer to a function.

2. A struct is created that includes the name of the function, the pointer to the function, and the path to the GIF file to be used with the function.

3. The four rotation functions are developed. In this example, they are simple functions that send out the specified GIF file.

4. In the main, the value of argv[1] is the name of the function to call. The table is used to look up this function and then send out the required GIF file.

· ·

Here is the same program with integer drivers:

```
#include <iostream.h>
#include <stdlib.h>
#include <strings.h>
extern void rotate_picture(int rotation);
typedef void (*F_PTR)();
static struct degrees
{
     char* subroutine;   /* name of subroutine */
     F_PTR function;     /* pointer to subroutine */
     char* gif;          /* path to gif for subroutine */
};
static struct degrees Degrees[] =
{
     { "rotate_0", &rotate_0, "/unix_path/picture_0deg.gif"; },
     { "rotate_90", &rotate_90, "/unix_path/picture_90deg.gif"; },
     { "rotate_180", &rotate_180, "/unix_path/picture_180deg.gif"; },
     { "rotate_270", &rotate_270, "/unix_path/picture_270deg.gif"; },
};
extern void gif_out(int rotation);
/*
 * Type C++ or C main
 * Purpose: table rotation routines
 */
void rotate_0()
{
     gif_out(0);
}
void rotate_90()
{
     gif_out(1);
}
void rotate_180()
{
     gif_out(2);
}
```

```
void rotate_270()
{
    gif_out(3);
}
/*
 * Type C++ or C subroutine
 * Purpose: Table-driven GIF output
 */
void gif_out(int rotation)
{
    /*
     * Send the picture.
     */
    stream = fopen(Degrees[rotation].gif, "r");
    fprintf(stdout,"content-type: image/gif\n\n");
    while(fgets(buffer, 2, stream ) != EOF)
    {
        fprintf(stdout,"%c", buffer[0]);
    }
}
```

Now the main looks like this:

```
/*
 * Type C++ or C main
 * Purpose: main for table-driven rotation
 */
void main(int argc, char* argv[])
{
    int i;
    for(i=0; i<4; i++)
    {
        if(strcmp(argv[1], Degrees[i].subroutine) == 0)
        {
            Degrees[i].function();
            return;
        }
    }
}
```

Name the file rotate-cgi.c, compile it, and place it in the cgi-bin.

```
cc -o rotate-cgi rotate-cgi.c
```

Here is the HTML form page:

```
<HTML>
<HEAD>
<TITLE> PICTURE ROTATION </TITLE>
</HEAD>
<BODY>
<H1> PICTURE ROTATION </H1>
<FORM ACTION = "http//internet_path/rotate-cgi"
    METHOD="GET">
<P>
ENTER DESIRED ROTATION IN DEGREES:
[<INPUT TYPE="checkbox" NAME="deg" VALUE="rotate_0" CHECKED> 0 deg]
[<INPUT TYPE="checkbox" NAME="deg" VALUE="rotate_90" CHECKED> 90 deg]
[<INPUT TYPE="checkbox" NAME="deg" VALUE="rotate_180" CHECKED> 180 deg]
[<INPUT TYPE="checkbox" NAME="deg" VALUE="rotate_270" CHECKED> 270 deg]
<p> <INPUT TYPE="submit"> <INPUT TYPE=reset>
</FORM>
</BODY> </HTML>
```

Bring up the HTML page in the normal way from a browser. Select the degrees required and then submit. Since the method is Get, the degree value will be appended to the cgi-bin request as argv[1] in the format rotate-cgi?degXXX (where XXX is the selected number of degrees). (**Note:** Since this method is using argv, it will only work with browsers that support command line arguments. By modifying this to use METHOD="post", a read routine can be used in the program and any browser that allows GIFs should work.)

The new main will look like this:

```
/*
 * Type C++ main
 * Purpose: Image rotation
 */
void main()
{
    char input[MAXLINE];
    /* Create your own rotate class */
    Rotate* myRotate = new(Rotate);
        myRotate->picture( *(cin >> input) != 0 ? input : "0");
}
/* C version main for post option */
void main()
{
    char input[30];
    gets(input);
    picture(strlen(input) > 0 ? input : "0");
}
```

While this program has opened up many possibilities to anyone with a good imagination and some creative programming skills, the real gain is still to come. In the next section the actual makeup of the GIF file will be altered. The ability to alter images will create a whole new world of possibilities that is only limited by a person's creativity, patience, and programming skills. We begin this venture by altering a GIF file's color mapping.

Changing the Color Maps

ONE OF THE MORE INTERESTING techniques with IMaGes that is straightforward to implement involves changing the *color maps*. While it is difficult to create an entire GIF picture on the fly, each GIF picture contains header information that includes the color maps. The color maps are a definition of what colors exist in the picture. These are kept at a specific location in the GIF file and continue until the colors are exhausted or until the maximum colors (256) has been reached. The colors are each represented by three hexadecimal values. These three values combine to create a single color and are each numbered sequentially, with each three-valued color in the color map having a single number attached to it. This number is then used to create the actual picture. Suppose, for example, that there are six colors represented as follows:

```
Color 1 0xFF 0xFF 0xFF
Color 2 0xFD 0xC0 0xB0
Color 3 0xC0 0xD0 0xB0
Color 4 0xAF 0xFF 0xFF
Color 5 0xFB 0xCC 0x0B
Color 6 0xFF 0x00 0x00
```

In the simplest mapping, if the sixth (6) color is red (0xff, 0x00, 0x00); then every time 6 occurs in the data part of the file, it will be replaced by red when recreated on the browser screen. All that would be needed are the horizontal and vertical lengths, which tell when to go back to the left edge of the picture and down one row. The picture could then be created with little squares of the selected colors put side by side in much the same way as a TV picture is created. In actuality, compression algorithms are used, so this is not exactly the case. Since the same color will frequently recur multiple times, it is possible to create smaller files by using intelligent algorithms. Therefore, some study would be needed to understand the method used to create the final picture.[1] Fortunately, the color maps are simple, so it is straightforward to locate them and change them in a cgi-bin program.

---

[1] For detail on the Lempel, Ziv, Welch (LZW) compression algorithms used to create the data part of the GIF file, see the URLs in the rear of the book.

Changing the color maps with a cgi-bin program can create fascinating effects. Since the algorithms are simply replacing the colors at the appropriate locations throughout the picture, the result of changing the color maps will be that the new color is placed at the same location as the original color. Instead of changing the color everywhere in the file, you merely change the three hexadecimal values for color 6. If you change the color from blue to red and then everyplace blue would have appeared, you will get red. One effective trick is to change certain colors to be very close to the background color. For example, if the background is 0x00 0x00 0x00, the new color 0x00 0x00 0x01 will be virtually the same to the human eye. In this manner, sections of the picture can be changed by fading them into the background.

Altering the color mapping is an especially good technique if the display is a geometric figure, with only a few colors, rather than a photographic image, in which colors are blended together as pixels. Real photographs tend to consist of blends of colors in different areas that require more complex algorithms to accomplish color changes. This is not to say that they cannot be done, but only that simpler pictures are a good place to start. Even with just a few colors, changing the color maps is somewhat difficult, so persons using these techniques should proceed with care.

Starting on page 321 additional information is provided on how color and other parts of the GIF image mapping work, which should make it easier to accomplish amazing effects. Care should be taken to use simple colors for the first experiments. This will allow knowledge of this technique to be gained before continuing to more complex projects. Once you accomplish a few working programs, you will find yourself doing amazing things with your images. One area that need not concern you is whether the cgi-bin program will have any adverse effect on your image responses. Because you are using compiled programs, standard GIF files and your altered files will respond with equal speed. In fact, any slowness in response is not due to the cgi-bin program response time but to responses in the client-server software. I mention this because sometimes people experience slowness with their Internet services and may fear that their programs are what is creating the degradation. Rest assured that they are not. More than likely, you are experiencing normal delays from the other people timesharing on your service. If you have any doubts, retry during a time when the system is not busy (for example, late at night).

Steps for Color Mapping

THE COLOR MAPPING TECHNIQUE is a bit more complex since it requires the following steps:

1. Skip over the header and trailer information associated with the GIF picture file.
2. Identify the bytes in the file associated with a particular color. For a GIF file, the colors are kept in a color map area starting at byte 14. There are a number of techniques that can be used to modify the colors. One that works

requires a color mapping program, such as xv on UNIX machines or Photo-shop on a PC. First create the GIF picture. Then rename the picture and change the colors to other values. It is only necessary to change a single color since the maps are maintained sequentially. However, to gain experience initially, it may make sense to change several or all colors to assure an understanding of the color mapping. Later, alternative methods will be developed that will make this process easier. Record the values before and after the changes. Most GIF creation programs provide color mappings as three values, *red, green,* and *blue.* The values range from 0 to 255 (decimal) or 0x00 to 0xFF (hexadecimal) for each of the three colors.

> **Note: It is possible to identify the color maps by understanding the methods used to develop GIF color mapping. In many ways this is easier than the technique discussed here. If you want the quick method, skip to the next section. This discussion is included here because it provides a method to access all kinds of information about image files, and some people will want to do their own experiments in image manipulation.**

The method uses a software tool that will turn the binary image file (in this example a GIF file) into a readable format. This is done by outputting the file with a counter of which byte is being read followed by the decimal value of the byte. This is a useful technique if you are planning to do GIF modifications. Recall that in the program that output the GIF file to the client server, the values were sent as chars, or single bytes of binary data. These would not print out on the screen. Many of them would be strange control characters and even nonprintable characters. By printing them as decimal numbers, the image file can be easily examined.

One easy way to find out where the color mappings are is to make two pictures with just one of the colors changed. If we do this and if the program will give us the three values of the initial and changed colors, then the difference between the two outputs should be the single color being changed in the color maps.[2]

This program is a tool or utility for identifying the color mappings; it is not a cgi-bin program in its present state. The purpose of this program is to print all the values in the GIF file as integers. Since the color values are the only ones that have been changed, the difference between the two files will reflect the location of the color mappings. The file must be changed to integers since the normal values of the GIF file are not in printable format. (For example, the value 0 is a true 0 ASCII

---

[2] One word of warning before you try this: Recall from an earlier discussion that the compression of the final data is a little more than you expect. Because of this, some changes can actually modify the file size and result in several differences between the two files. When you first try this, check the file size.

   ls -l filename1.gif
   ls -l filename2.gif

If the files are not the same size, you may want to try changing the same color again until you get two files the same size.

that will be printed as ^A; this would be extremely difficult to decipher.) The value of the counter i is also printed to show at which byte location the color maps occur. Later, this value will be used to locate the color map and change it to a new color.

Color Map Tool

```
/*
 * Type C++ or C main
 * Purpose: GIF color mapping tool
 */
/* TOOL program to print out the values of the bytes in a file */
void
main()
{
    File* stream;
    char buffer[2];
    int i=1;
    /*
     * Set up a stream between the buffer and the file.
     */
    stream = fopen("/unix_path/picture.gif", "r");
    while(fgets(buffer, 2, stream ) != EOF ) // get the gif data
    {
        /*
         * Send the data back to stdout preceded by the counter.
         *
         */
        fprintf(stdout, "%d %d\n", i++, (int )buffer[0]);

    }
    fclose();
}
```

Rather than hard coding the filename, you can use argc and argv[] for a generic version.

```
/*
 * Type C main
 * Purpose: expanded GIF color mapping tool
 */
```

Here is the same program in C with argc and argv[] options:

```
void main(int argc, char* argv[])
{
    File* stream;
    unsigned char buffer[2];        /* the unsigned char will eliminate the negative numbers
                                     * shown in the example */
    int i=1;
    /*
     * Set up a stream between the buffer and the file.
     */
    if(argc <=1)
    {
        printf("You must give a gif file as an argument\n");
        return;
    }
    stream = fopen(argv[1], "r");
    while(fgets(buffer, 2, stream ) != EOF)
    {
        fprintf(stdout, "%d %d\n", i++, (int )buffer[0]);
    }
    fclose(stream);
}
```

About the program . . . .

1. The program first checks if there is an argument on the command line. If there is not, it prints an error message.
2. If there is, it reads in the file and then sends out the counter i and the decimal value of the byte.
3. It increments the counter and then continues step 2 until all the bytes have been sent out. While this will normally go to stdout, the redirect operator > in UNIX can be used to send it to a file.

. . . .

Now run the program from the command line and redirect the output to a file. In UNIX the command would look like this:

```
myprogram picture1.gif > outputfile.1
```

Repeat the procedure after changing one or more colors in the GIF file to alter color maps in the picture:

```
run the command again:
myprogram picture2.gif > outputfile.2
```

Now compare the two files for differences. In UNIX you can use the command

```
diff outputfile.1 outputfile.2
```

It may make sense to redirect this output if there are lots of colors changed.

```
diff outputfile.1 outputfile.2 > diff.file
```

Here is the diff output from a file with nine colors changed:

```
< 14 -55
< 15 -108
< 16 -2
< 17 1
< 18 1
< 19 75
< 20 92
< 21 -102
< 22 -29
< 23 -82
< 24 -1
< 25 -1
< 26 -4
< 27 111
< 28 93
< 29 -27
< 30 -32
< 31 56
< 32 -74
< 33 72
< 34 -86
< 35 -84
< 36 -101
< 37 0
< 38 0
< 39 -1
< 40 -46
> 14 -56
> etc. Rest of results not shown.
```

The lines beginning with < are the lines found different in file 1, and the ones starting with > are the ones found different in file 2. The numbers 14 to 40 are the values of the integer i in the program. As will be seen shortly, the *14th byte* is always the start of the color maps. This can be used to eliminate the need for the two-file process. By examining the byte values starting from byte 14, it is possible to locate easily the three bytes associated with any color. The numbers represent the three values of a color mapping, with values ranging from 0 to 255. When the numbers are negative, the numbers are subtracted from 256. Therefore, the value −1 is the same as 255 and the value 0 represents the value 0. This is just a product of the way C++ and C output the bytes.[3]

Having recorded each of the color mappings obtained, it is now possible to write a program that will change the color mapping. There are a possible $256 \times 256 \times 256$ which comes out to 16,777,216 possible colors in each location. There are 256 possible different colors in the color map. It is possible to have $16{,}777{,}216 \times 16{,}777{,}216 \times \ldots \times 16{,}777{,}216$, with the multiplication occurring 256 times. When you finish multiplying these numbers by each other, you get a very large number. This is the number of GIF files you can have with one file for every color combination. Using cgi-bin programs, one template can be kept. Then, by replacing the color values, any color map can be put on the screen.

Remapping Colors on the Fly

HERE IS THE PROGRAM FOR changing some of the colors on the fly. In this example, there are nine colors in the color map that will be changed to different colors.

Change the identified bytes to a new color:

```
/*
 * Type C++ class subroutine
 * Purpose: changing color mapping for a GIF file
 */
void
_Picture :: show()
{
     int i=1;   /* Byte counter used to locate the color maps */
               /*
                * Set up a stream between the buffer and the file.
                */
     stream = fopen("/unix_path/picture.gif", "r");
     /*
      * This line is needed to tell the server that an image is coming.
      */
     fprintf(stdout,"content-type: image/gif\n\n");
     while(fgets(buffer, 2, stream )!= EOF) // get the gif data
     {
          /*
           * Start with byte 14 and continue in groups of three until the completion of byte
           * 40. Some arbitrary values are given as the replacement values. In an actual
           * program you want to change the values based on some effect you are trying to
           * create.
           */
          if((i>=14) && (i=<40))
          {
               /*
```

---

[3]   The second example eliminates this problem by using unsigned chars.

```
                    * Change the colors if they are in the start of the color map area beginning
                    * with byte 14.
                    */
                   switch(i)
                   {
                   case 14:
                        buffer[0]=-5;
                        break;
                   case 15:
                        buffer[0]=12;
                        break;
                   case 16:
                        buffer[0]=27;
                        break;
                   /* etc thru byte 40 */
                   }
              }
              fprintf(stdout, "%c", buffer[0]);
              // send same data back to IMG
              i++;
         }
         fclose();
    }
    /*
     * Type C subroutine
     * Purpose: changing color mapping for a GIF file
     */
```

C Version

```
    #define START_CHG 14
    #define END_CHG 40
    void show(char* gif)
    {
         FILE* stream;
         char buffer[2];
         char tmp_buff;
         int i;
         /*
          * Set up a stream between the buffer and the file.
          */
         stream = fopen(gif, "r");
         /*
          * This line is needed to tell the server that an image is coming.
          */
         fprintf(stdout,"content-type: image/gif\n\n");
         while(fgets(buffer, 2, stream )!= EOF)
         {
              if((i >= START_CHG) && (i <= END_CHG))
```

```
{
        /* change the colors */
        if(buffer[0] - (i*2) < 0)
        {
                buffer[0] += (i*2);
        } else
        {
                buffer[0] -= (i*2);
        }
    }
    fprintf(stdout, "%c", buffer[0]);
    i++;
    }
    fclose(stream);
}
```

In a real application, it would make sense to change the colors systematically in a predefined way. This is possible since the values can be determined using GIF viewing programs and then altered according to plan with the cgi-bin program.

Using this technique, it is possible to create elaborate figures and allow the user to change the color mappings interactively. Other knowledge about image files would allow other parameters to be created (for example, morphing, animation, GIF merging, and creating a GIF file on the fly). As mentioned previously, the internals of GIF files are complex, requiring knowledge of compression algorithms, so these more advanced topics are not discussed here. Instead, the next section discusses some related techniques that can be used to create some of these effects.

Chess Game Revisited

RECALL THE EARLIER EXAMPLE of the chess game. How could this new capability be used to reduce the overhead required? Previously, a GIF file was required for each piece on each of the two background colored squares and for each of the two colors of the pieces. With the color mapping techniques, a single GIF can be used for each type of piece. Then the background color of the square and the foreground color of the piece can be altered depending on position on the board and the piece selected. Now all that is required are the following GIF files:

```
pawn -> piece can be black or white, background can be white or gray
rook -> same
bishop -> same
knight -> same
queen -> same
king -> same
```

The six GIF files can create the entire chess board by remapping the colors of the pieces and the colors of the background square. Note that no GIF was provided for the empty gray and empty white squares. These can be created easily from any of the others by changing the piece to a color that is only one digit from the background. The piece will disappear into the background.

Begin by creating the six pieces. Each piece will consist of three colors, the background, the edge of the piece, and the color of the piece. The edge will be needed if you want to allow for white pieces on a white background. You could reduce this to two colors if the foreground and background colors were never the same (for example, using red and blue pieces on gray and white squares). Even if gray is used for the background, the edge will make the pieces stand out. But these are decisions for your artistic and aesthetic skill and need not concern us here.

Having created our pieces, we use our program created previously to locate the three colors for each piece. For simplicity, we will assume that all color maps start at location 14 and go to location 22 (three colors). In other words, there are no other colors on the GIF file, such as borders. Further, we will set up the colors so the first color is the background, the second is the edge, and the third is the color of the piece.

Start with some defines. These will be placed in a header file.

```
chess.h.
/*
 *          chess.h
 */
#define BACKGROUND_1 14/* background bytes 14-16 */
#define BACKGROUND_2 15
#define BACKGROUND_3 16
#define EDGE_1 17/* edge color bytes 17-19 */
#define EDGE_2 18
#define EDGE_3 19
#define PIECE_1 20/* color of piece bytes 20-22 */
#define PIECE_2 21
#define PIECE_3 22
/* Used for edge */
#define RED_1 0
#define RED_2 -1
#define RED_3 0
/* Used for light squares and light pieces */
#define WHITE_1 -1
#define WHITE_2 -1
#define WHITE_3 -1
/* Used for dark pieces */
#define BLACK_1 0
#define BLACK_2 0
#define BLACK_3 0
/* Used for dark squares */
#define GRAY_1 50
```

```
#define GRAY_2 50
#define GRAY_3 50
```

You should be able to see where we are heading. The colors will be changed based on our knowledge of where the piece is and what color the piece is. We learned earlier in the original chess program that a simple test could determine the color of the square.

if the x and y coordinates are both even or both odd, it is a dark square.
else if
the x coordinate is even and the y coordinate odd, or vice versa, then it is a light square.

Since the modula 2 operation x%2 and y%2 will return zero for even numbers and one for odd numbers, it is simple to devise a background color test. The foreground color is based on which piece is being moved to the new location.

Increased GIF IMaGe Control

WHILE THE PRECEDING TECHNIQUES are a simple way to control and change GIF images, you can optimize these effects if you have a real understanding of how the GIF file is actually put together. In this section the GIF image is first divided into its constituent parts. This is followed by some simple subroutines that will allow you to read the different components. While there are many programs available to provide this output (such as giftrans on UNIX), these subroutines should be of value to people who wish to develop cgi-bin programs that systematically manipulate images. Figure 16.1 shows the basic breakdown of a GIF IMaGe.

You can think of a GIF file as consisting of four distinct sections:

```
/*************************************************************
 * HEADER - This provides the information about the file
      TYPE - either GIF87a or GIF89a (Bytes 1-6)
      WIDTH - (Bytes 7-8)
      HEIGHT - (Bytes 9-10)
      BITPIXEL or NUMBER OF COLORS AND COLOR RESOLUTION -> (Byte 11)
      BACKGROUND - (Byte 12)
      ASPECTRATIO - (Byte 13)
      COLOR MAPS - (Byte 14 to Byte 14 + (BITPIXEL * 3))
 * BODY - The actual compressed image information. This is where the major difference
 * between GIF types will exist.
 * CONTINUATION - An optional exclamation mark ('!')
      Transparency Information - only if a continuation
 * TERMINATION - A single byte with a semicolon (';') in it
```

By using this information, it is possible to create more intelligent IMaGe control. For example, you could obtain the aspect ratio and then use it to compute the

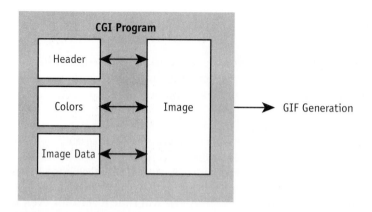

FIGURE 16.1   IMaGe Control: The direct output of an IMaGe from a cgi-bin program creates powerful effects.

number of colors in the color map. This would allow you to write more systematic programs for generically altering the color map. Simple examples include taking any GIF file and searching for the color green anywhere in the color map and then changing it to red. The width and height information might also have value. In a transparent image, by shifting the background value you could change which color was transparent for the image. Finally, you can use the tools developed in the image section and experiment with other special effects on your own. You might even try some experiments on the **BODY** of the image.

The following subroutines are simple algorithms for obtaining the different sections of the GIF image.

```
********************************************************************/
/*
 *---------------------------------------------------------------
 * The following code is modified from the giftoppm program[4]
 *---------------------------------------------------------------
```

---

[4]   Sections of this code are based on the following:
```
/*
 * tkImgFmtGIF.c —
 * A photo image file handler for GIF files. Reads 87a and 89a GIF files. At present there is no write function.
 * Derived from the giftoppm code found in the pbmplus package and tkImgFmtPPM.c in the tk4.0b2 distribution by -
 * Reed Wade (wade@cs.utk.edu), University of Tennessee. Copyright (c) 1995 Sun Microsystems, Inc.
 * See the file "license.terms" for information on usage and redistribution of this file, and for a disclaimer of all warranties.
 * This file also contains code from the giftoppm program, which is copyrighted as follows:
 * | Copyright 1990, David Koblas.||
 * | Permission to use, copy, modify, and distribute this software | and its documentation for any purpose and without fee |
 * | is hereby granted, provided that the above copyright notice appear in all copies and that both that copyright notice |
 * | and this permission notice appear in supporting documentation. This software is provided "as is" without express or |
 * | implied warranty. */
```

```
*/
#include <stdio.h>
#include <stdlib.h>
#include <string.h>
/*
 * A macro for determining if a bit in a byte is set.
 */
#define BitSet(byte, bit)(((byte) & (bit)) == (bit))
/*
 * A macro to left shift a byte eight times and then "OR" it with another byte.
 */
#define LM_to_uint(a,b) (((b)<<8)|(a))
/*
 * A macro to read a byte from file and verify that the read is OK.
 */
#define ReadOK(file,buffer,len)(fread(buffer, len, 1, file) != 0)
/*
 * The defines required for these subroutines.
 */
#define INTERLACE          0x40
#define LOCALCOLORMAP      0x80
#define MAXCOLORMAPSIZE    256
#define COLORMAP_RED       0
#define COLORMAP_GREEN     1
#define COLORMAP_BLUE      2
#define MAX_LWZ_BITS       12
/* Extern all functions to allow them to be shown in correct order */
extern ReadGifHeader(...);
extern ReadColorMap(...);

...
/*
 * This routine gets all the information from the header up to the color maps.
 */
static int
ReadGIFHeader(FILE* f, int* widthPtr, int* heightPtr)
{
    unsigned char buf[7];
    if ((fread(buf, 1, 6, f) != 6)
         || ((strncmp("GIF87a", (char *) buf, 6) != 0)
         && (strncmp("GIF89a", (char *) buf, 6) != 0))) {
        return 0;
    }
    if(strncmp("GIF87a", (char *) buf, 6) == 0)
    {
        printf("GIF87a\n");
    } else
    {
```

```
            printf("GIF89a\n");
        }
        if (fread(buf, 1, 4, f) != 4) {
            return 0;
        }
         *widthPtr = LM_to_uint(buf[0],buf[1]);
         *heightPtr = LM_to_uint(buf[2],buf[3]);
        printf("Width=%d Height=%d\n", *widthPtr, *heightPtr);
        return 1;
}
/*
 * This routine reads the color maps and places them into the two-dimension buffer array.
 */
static int
ReadColorMap(FILE* fd, int number, unsigned char buffer[3][MAXCOLORMAPSIZE])
{
    int i;
    unsigned char rgb[3];
    for (i = 0; i < number; ++i) {
        if (! ReadOK(fd, rgb, sizeof(rgb)))
            return 0;
        buffer[COLORMAP_RED][i] = rgb[0] ;
        buffer[COLORMAP_GREEN][i] = rgb[1] ;
        buffer[COLORMAP_BLUE][i] = rgb[2] ;
        printf("Color %d %d %d %d\n",
            i, rgb[0], rgb[1], rgb[2]);
    }
    return 1;
}
/*
 * This routine is used by the extension section to get additional information from the
 * extension fields.
 */
static int
GetDataBlock(FILE* gif_file, unsigned char* buf)
{
    unsigned char count;
    int i;
    if (! ReadOK(gif_file, &count, 1)) {
        return FAILURE;
    }
    if ((count != 0) && (! ReadOK(fd, buf, count))) {
        return FAILURE;
    }
    return count;
}
/*
```

```
 * This routine reads the extension information.
 */
static int
DoExtension(FILE* gif_file, int label, int* transparent)
{
    static unsigned char buf[256];
    int count = 0;
    switch (label) {
        case 0x01: /* Plain Text Extension */
            printf("Plain Extension\n");
            break;
        case 0xff: /* Application Extension */
            printf("Application Extension\n");
            break;
        case 0xfe: /* Comment Extension */
            printf("Comment Extension\n");
            break;
        case 0xf9: /* Graphic Control Extension */
            printf("Graphic Control Extension\n");
            count = GetDataBlock(gif_file, (unsigned
                char*) buf);
            if (count < 0) {
                return 1;
            }
            if ((buf[0] & 0x1) != 0) {
              *transparent = buf[3];
                printf("Transparent = %d\n",
                  *transparent);
            }
            break;
    }
    do {
     count = GetDataBlock(gif_file, (unsigned char*) buf);
    } while (count > 0);
    return count;
}
/*
 * This is the main subroutine. It reads all the GIF header information and prints it to the
 * screen.
 */
static int
FileReadGIF(
 FILE* gif_file /* The image file, open for reading. */
)
{
    int fileWidth, fileHeight;
    unsigned char buf[100];
```

```
    int bitPixel;
    unsigned int colorResolution;
    unsigned int background;
    unsigned int aspectRatio;
    unsigned char localColorMap[3][MAXCOLORMAPSIZE];
    unsigned char colorMap[3][MAXCOLORMAPSIZE];
    int useGlobalColormap;
    int transparent = -1;
    if (!ReadGIFHeader(gif_file, &fileWidth, &fileHeight)) {
        return FAILURE;
    }
    if ((fileWidth <= 0) || (fileHeight <= 0)) {
        return FAILURE;
    }
}
if (fread(buf, 1, 3, gif_file) != 3) {
    return 0;
}
bitPixel = 2<<(buf[0]&0x07);
colorResolution = (((buf[0]&0x70)>>3)+1);
background = buf[1];
aspectRatio = buf[2];
printf("Number of
Colors=%d\ncolorResolution=%s\nbackground=%d\naspectRatio=%d\n",
        bitPixel, colorResolution>0?"TRUE" : "FALSE",
            background, aspectRatio);
if (BitSet(buf[0], LOCALCOLORMAP)) { /* Global Colormap */
    printf("Global Colormap\n");
    if (!ReadColorMap(gif_file, bitPixel, colorMap)) {
     return FAILURE;
    }
}
while (1) {
    if (fread(buf, 1, 1, gif_file) != 1) {
        /*
         * Premature end of image. We should really notify the user, but for now just show
         * garbage.
         */
        break;
    }
    if (buf[0] == ';') {
        /*
         * GIF terminator.
         */
        break;
    }
    if (buf[0] == '!') {
        /*
```

```
                    * This is a GIF extension.
                    */
            if (fread(buf, 1, 1, gif_file) != 1) {
                    goto error;
            }
            if (DoExtension(gif_file, buf[0], &transparent) < 0) {
                    goto error;
            }
            continue;
        }
        if (buf[0] != ',') {
                /*
                 * Not a valid start character; ignore it.
                 */
                continue;
        }
        if (fread(buf, 1, 9, gif_file) != 9) {
                goto error;
        }
        useGlobalColormap = ! BitSet(buf[8], LOCALCOLORMAP);
        bitPixel = 1<<((buf[8]&0x07)+1);
        if (!useGlobalColormap) {
                if (!ReadColorMap(gif_file, bitPixel, localColorMap)) {
                        goto error;
                }
        }
    }
    return SUCCESS;
error:
        return FAILURE;     /* Define FAILURE = -1 */
}
/*
 * The main program takes as an argument the name of the GIF file with its path, if needed.
 * It then goes through the subroutines to obtain and print out the header information.
 */
main(int argc, char* argv[])
{
    FILE* gif_file;
    printf("%s%s\n", "opening file ", argv[1] );
    gif_file= fopen(argv[1], "r");
    FileReadGIF( gif_file );
    fflush(stdout);
    fclose( gif_file );
}
```

Creating a Software LED

IN THE NEXT PROJECT THE equivalent of a numeric light emitting diode (LED) is created in software. A numeric LED is an electronic device made up of seven segments. The seven segments are arranged in two squares, one on top of the other, with a single common leg horizontally across the center. The numbers 0 through 9 are created by lighting up different sections. To produce the equivalent of the numeric LED in software over the Internet, advantage is taken of the color mapping methods. The seven-segment numeric LED is created using a GIF file template. Each of the segments in the template is done in a different color to allow the segments to be located in the color maps. The segment can be made to disappear into the background by changing the section's color to that of the background. It is made to appear by changing the section's color map to the required foreground color.

```c
#include <stdio.h>
#include <stdlib.h>
#include <iostream.h>
#include <strings.h>
/* Red Green Blue values to turn on a segment */
#define ON1 -1
#define ON2 -1
#define ON3 -1
/* Red Green Blue values to turn off a segment */
#define OFF1 0
#define OFF2 0
#define OFF3 0
/*
 * Type C++ or C subroutine
 * Purpose: turn on a section of the LED
 */
void segment_on()
{
    fprintf(stdout, "%c%c%c", ON1, ON2, ON3);
}
/*
 * Type C++ or C subroutine
 * Purpose: turn off a section of the LED
 */
void segment_off()
{
    fprintf(stdout, "%c%c%c", OFF1, OFF2, OFF3);
}
/*
 * Type C++ or C subroutine
 * Purpose: LED segment handler
 */
```

```
void set_segments(char* sections)
{
    int i;
    for(i=0; i<7; i++)
      *(sections+i) == 0 ? segment_off() : segment_on();
}
int set_seven_segments (int number)
{
    switch(number)
    {
        case 0:
            set_segments("1111110");
        break;
        case 1:
            set_segments("1100000");
        break;
        case 2:
            set_segments("1011011");
        break;
        case 3:
            set_segments("1110011");
        break;
        case 4:
            set_segments("1100101");
        break;
        case 5:
            set_segments("0110110");
        break;
        case 6:
            set_segments("0111101");
        break;
        case 7:
            set_segments("1100010");
        break;
        case 8:
            set_segments("1111111");
        break;
    default:
        case 9:
            set_segments("1100111");
        break;
    }
    return (3*7);        /* 7 colors set with 3 values each */
}
/*
  * Type C++ or C main
```

```
  * Purpose: LED control
  */
void main(int argc, char* argv[])
{
     FILE* stream;
     char buffer[2];
     int number;
     int i=1;
     number = atoi(argv[1]);
     stream = fopen("led_template.gif", "r");
     fprintf (stdout, "Content-type: image/gif\n\n");
     while (fgets (buffer, 2, stream) != 0)
     {
          /* check if in the color mapping area */
          if( (i < 14) || (i > (14 + (3*7)))))
          {
               /* no just send the byte */
               fprintf(stdout, "%c", buffer[0]);
          } else
          {
               /* remap the colors to light the segments */
               i += set_seven_segments (number);
          }
     }

}
```

About the program . . . .

1. The program locates the IMaGe map section by watching for byte 14 (the start of the IMaGe maps).

2. The routine set_segments() turns on or off the color segment based on whether a 0 (off) or a 1 (on) is active for the segment. If the segment is turned on, the color mapping is set to the on color. If it is off, the reverse or off color is set. Since the off color is the background color, only the on segments will be seen. The use of on and off could be expanded so each of the numbers 0 to 9 represented different colors. Use of the alphabet could expand this even further.

. . . .

Selecting Colors on the Fly

THE NEXT PROJECT TAKES advantage of the ability to gain information from the GIF header. Instead of having a predefined image map, as in the previous examples, this program will determine how many IMaGe maps are present from the header. It will then examine each IMaGe map on the fly to determine if the color falls inside a predefined color window. (For example, is the color one of a range of reds?) When it falls inside the color window, the color is changed to a different color. In the example shown, a totally new color is chosen, but the color could as easily have been saturated. Such techniques can be used for a variety of purposes. The color blindness and color weakness tests use disguised letters to test a person's red-green or total lack of color pigmentations. By varying these colors with color mapping techniques, more sensitive tests could be developed. Satellite images frequently require color enhancement to show certain patterns. Again, the color mapping techniques could provide important methods for obtaining this information.

```c
#include <stdio.h>
#include <stdlib.h>
#include <iostream.h>
#include <strings.h>
/*
 * Class to read in the header information from a GIF file.
 */
class _GIFheader
{
private:
    char type[7];
    char width[2];
    char height[2];
    char bitpixel;
    char background;
    char aspect_ratio;
public:
    _GIFheader() { ; } ;
    inline int get_type()
        { return( strncmp("GIF87a", type, 6)==0 ? 0 : 1 ); } ;
    inline int get_width()
        { return( (width[1] << 8) | width[2] ); } ;
    inline int get_height()
        { return( (height[1] << 8) | height[2] ); } ;
    inline int get_color_total()
        { return( 2 << (bitpixel & 0x70) ); } ;
    inline int get_color_resolution()
        { return(((bitpixel & 0x70) >> 3) +1); } ;
    inline int get_aspect_ratio()
        { return( aspect_ratio); } ;
void get_header(FILE* stream);
};
/*
```

```
 * Read in all the header bytes and then place them in the appropriate places. Then send the
 * header information out to stdout (the server).
 */
void _GIFheader::get_header(FILE* stream)
{
    char buffer[14];
    fread( buffer, 1, 13, stream );
    strncpy(type, buffer, 6);
    width[0] = *(buffer+7);
    width[1] = *(buffer+8);
    height[0] = *(buffer+9);
    height[1] = *(buffer+10);
    bitpixel = *(buffer+11);
    background = *(buffer+12);
    aspect_ratio = *(buffer+13);
    /* send the header back out to stdout */
    for(int i=0; i<13; i++)
        fprintf(stdout, "%c", *(buffer+i));

}
#define START_COLOR_MAPS 14 /* start of the color maps */
/*
 * Struct is used to define the range for RGB that will be used to remap a color. Each color in
 * the GIF color map table will be checked to see if the RGB values fall between the minus
 * and plus values. If all three are between the two values, the color is remapped to the
 * three new values for red, green, and blue.
 */
struct _Range
{
    unsigned char red_minus;
    unsigned char red_plus;
    unsigned char red_new;
    unsigned char green_minus;
    unsigned char green_plus;
    unsigned char green_new;
    unsigned char blue_minus;
    unsigned char blue_plus;
    unsigned char blue_new;
};
typedef struct _Range RANGE;
/*
 * Three RGB bytes to check for remapping.
 */
struct _Color_bytes
{
    unsigned char red;
```

```
        unsigned char green;
        unsigned char blue;
};
typedef struct _Color_bytes COLOR_BYTES;
class _Remapper : public _GIFheader
{
private:
        RANGE range;
        COLOR_BYTES rgb;
        int byte_counter;
        int end_of_colors;

public:
        _Remapper(); // constructor
        void remap(char* buffer);
        int colormap_check(); // check if in the GIF color map area
        int remap_check(); // check if color is in the remap range
        void set_end_of_colors() {
            end_of_colors = START_COLOR_MAPS +
                (get_color_total() * 3); } ;
        void set_byte_counter(int increment) { byte_counter += increment; } ;
        void set_color(char* buffer){
            rgb.red = *buffer;
            rgb.green= *(++buffer);
            rgb.blue = *(++buffer); };
};


/*
 * Defines for the remapping. These will be set to values based on the specifics of what is
 * being remapped.
 */
#define RED_MINUS 240
#define RED_PLUS 255
#define RED_NEW 25
#define GREEN_MINUS 240
#define GREEN_PLUS 255
#define GREEN_NEW 25
#define BLUE_MINUS 240
#define BLUE_PLUS 255
#define BLUE_NEW 25
_Remapper::_Remapper()
{
    /*
     * Set the high, low, and new value for the three color components (RGB). If all three
     * values for the color in the GIF color map table fall inside the minus-plus range, the
     * color values will be remapped to the new values.
```

```
        */
    range.red_minus = RED_MINUS ;
    range.red_plus = RED_PLUS ;
    range.red_new = RED_NEW ;
    range.green_minus = GREEN_MINUS ;
    range.green_plus = GREEN_PLUS ;
    range.green_new = GREEN_NEW ;
    range.blue_minus = BLUE_MINUS ;
    range.blue_plus = BLUE_PLUS ;
    range.blue_new = BLUE_NEW ;
    byte_counter = 0;
}
#define FALSE 0
#define TRUE 1
void _Remapper::remap(char* color_buffer)
{
    set_color(color_buffer);
    if( remap_check() == TRUE)
    {
        fprintf(stdout, "%c", range.red_new);
        fprintf(stdout, "%c", range.green_new);
        fprintf(stdout, "%c", range.blue_new);
    } else
    {
        fprintf(stdout, "%c", rgb.red);
        fprintf(stdout, "%c", rgb.green);
        fprintf(stdout, "%c", rgb.blue);
    }
    set_byte_counter( 3 );
}


/*
 * Return TRUE if in the GIF color map area.
 */
int _Remapper::colormap_check()
{
    if( byte_counter < 14)
        return FALSE;
    if( byte_counter > end_of_colors)
        return FALSE;
    return TRUE;
}
int _Remapper::remap_check()
{
    if( (range.red_minus < rgb.red && range.red_plus < rgb.red) &&
        (range.green_minus < rgb.green && range.green_plus < rgb.green) &&
```

```
                (range.blue_minus < rgb.blue && range.blue_plus < rgb.blue) )
            {
                return FALSE;
            } else
            {
                return TRUE;
            }
        }
        class _Gif : public _Remapper
        {
        private:
            FILE* stream;
        public:
            _Gif(char* gif_file);
            ~_Gif() { fclose ( stream ); } ;
            void set_colors();
            void send_gif_data();
        };

        _Gif::_Gif(char* gif_file)
        {
            stream = fopen( gif_file, "r");
            get_header(stream);
            set_byte_counter( 13 );
            set_end_of_colors();
            set_colors();
            send_gif_data();

        }
        void _Gif::send_gif_data()
        {
            char buffer[2];
            while(fgets(buffer, 2, stream) != 0)
                fprintf(stdout, "%c", buffer[0]);
        }
        void _Gif::set_colors()
        {
            char color_buffer[3];
            while( colormap_check() )
            {
                fread( color_buffer, 1, 3, stream );
                remap(color_buffer);
            }
        }
        void do_error_routine() { ; }
        void main(int argc, char* argv[])
```

```
    {
        GIF* mygif;
        if(argc < 2)
        {
            do_error_routine();
            return;
        }
#ifndef DEBUG
        fprintf(stdout,"%s",
            "Content-type: image/gif\n\n");
#endif

        mygif = new GIF(argv[1]);
    }
```

About the program . . . .

This program illustrates how information about the GIF file can be obtained from
the header and then used as part of the decision process for color remapping.
Other information, such as the aspect ratio or the type of GIF file, could have also
been used.

. . . .

Recursive IMaGes and HTML in the Same Program

THE NEXT PROGRAM ILLUSTRATES the use of one program for handling HTML and
images.[5] The division is made using getopt() and argv[]. If the program is called with

       ?-ifilename.gif

the image GIF file is sent out to stdout with the content type of image/gif. If the same
program is called with

       ?-hfilename.html

the HTML file is sent through using Thru mode. The HTML file can include an image
request for the same program with the -i option set. When this is done, the program is run iteratively (that is, the output of the first call results in the second call
to the same program). Since process identifiers will separate the two calls, this is
totally acceptable.

---

[5]   The use of the term *recursive* to describe this process may not be an exact meaning of the word. Typi-
      cally, *recursive* and *iterative* describe a situation in which a function calls itself. In the description here,
      the recall is done by the HTML sent out by the program, through the HTML interpreter, not directly
      by the program. Nevertheless, the term is descriptive of what occurs.

```
* multiarg.c */
/*
 * Type C++ or C main
 * Purpose: handle images and html in same program
 */
#include <stdio.h>
#include <stdlib.h>
#include <sys/time.h>
#include <unistd.h>
#include <string.h>
extern char *optarg;
extern int opterr;
extern int getopt();
void
main(int argc, char *argv[])
{
    int optchar;        /* arg for getopt */
    opterr = 1;         /* disable printing an error msg*/
    /***********************************************************
     *          OPTIONS
     ***********************************************************/
    while ((optchar = getopt(argc, argv, "I:H:")) != EOF)
    {
        switch(optchar)
        {
         case 'I': /* image routines */
             image_routine(optarg);
             return;
         case 'H': /* send out the HTML */
             thru_mode(optarg);
             return;
         default:
             /* send error message */
             break;
        }
        error_routine();
    }
}
```

About the program . . . .

1. The program puts out an GIF image if called with the -I option and HTML if
   called with the -H option.
2. If the -H option includes an HTML line that uses the same program in the
   IMaGe mode with the -I option, the program will run recursively. When this
   occurs, different versions of the same program can be running simulta-

neously to produce the HTML and IMaGe shown to the browser. The process ID will distinguish the two versions from each other.

. . . .

Case Study 3: Quilt Program

THIS CASE STUDY WAS DEVELOPED as part of a project to support the showing of Native American crafts. The goal for the project was to support a group who make hand-crafted quilts. The actual result of this project can be viewed at http:// www.dash.com/netro/tribal/Quilt.html or http://www.alphacdc.com/prentice/cgi-book.html. A complete C listing of this project is available in Appendix 4 of this book.

This project illustrates a number of the principles outlined in this book. This program and the chess program are two large programs that are included in this book. Both illustrate some fascinating capabilities, so they have been included in their entirety in Appendix 3 and 4. Every attempt has been made to divide these up in a way that will make it easy to read and to gain insights into cgi-bin programming.

The objective of the Quilt program was to create an interactive Web page that would allow people to design their own quilts. The Star Quilt[6] was selected because of its unique geometry.

The Star Quilt cgi-bin program is made up of several different components:

1. **An IMaGe creator**   This section sends GIF images from the cgi-bin program with the color maps set to the selected values. The values are passed into the program as a string of nine numbers in argv[1]. Each number represents a color for one of the circular sections of the Star Quilt.

2. **An HTML generator**   This section sends out HTML to the client-server software. Part of the HTML sent is an IMaGE request. This IMaGe request is for the cgi-bin image in component 1. Included in the IMaGe request is the string of nine digits representing the user's color mapping request. Note that the user is being allowed to select the color mappings through an interactive form.

3. **A form processing section**   This section processes the information Posted by users when they submit their requests for new colors. In addition, users can use a checkbox to request cost information and a mail option to request a mailer to make a purchase.

4. **An HTML mail form**   This section sends out an email form if the user has selected the mail option.

5. **A mail form processor**   This section processes the mail request and sends the user's information to the purchasing agent. The colors selected by the user for the quilt are carried to the mailer as a hidden variable along with the user's entered information.

---

[6]   The Star Quilt is shown on the book cover.

6. **A cost provider**   This section brings up cost information only on request
   from the user.

As is readily apparent, the Star Quilt cannot be created with rectangular
geometry. Each star layer consists of a circle of diamonds that can be one of nine
unique colors. The techniques developed in the chess game required rectangular
construction. Since GIF files are rectangular, there is no way to cut up the screen
and piece together the Star Quilt picture. By designing a nine-layer quilt, each star
layer can be one of nine colors. Furthermore, the colors are interchangeable, and
different layers can have the same color. The result is nine to the ninth power possible star quilts, or 387,420,489 possible combinations. It would take a lot of disk
memory to create all the GIF files to provide this number of different combinations.
Doing so would probably require all the disk memory on your system if you were to
use different GIF files, not to mention the time and energy required to produce all
these different combinations. I shudder just thinking about what it would take to
keep track of all the combinations.

By using color mapping, only one GIF template file is required and one cgi-bin
program. Of course, this program does a lot of different things, but that is the
power of cgi-bin programming. Here's how it works from the user's point of view.
The program starts with the Star Quilt on the screen with default color mappings.
The user then selects desired colors through interactive form control located
under the picture. For the actual program, the HTML option was used, but this program could have used radio buttons with the nine possible choices. The option
capability was easy to implement since it used repeated code. It also gives an easy-to-
use pull-down list of the colors. The user selects a color for each of the nine color
circles. Fascinating effects can be produced by using the same color in several
places.

The request for the new colors is then submitted. The request for new colors
is processed by a cgi-bin program, which then sends HTML back to the client-server
software. Included in this HTML is a request for an IMaGE from the cgi-bin program.
Included in this IMaGE request is the string representing the user's requested colors:
an argv[1] string appended to the cgi-bin program line. It looks something like this:

```
<IMG SRC="http://internet_path/cgi-bin/cgi_program?-i122448891" >
```

When the browser attempts to process this line, it will first determine that it is
expecting an image. Next it will determine that the source is the given

```
url="http://internet_path/cgi-bin/cgi_program?-i122448891"
```

When it requests the image from the server, the server will run the cgi-bin program.
The ? will be replaced with a space and the -i122448891 will be placed in argv[1]. It
does not matter if the earlier cgi-bin request has completed or not. Multiple copies
of the same program can be run without conflict. In fact, if there are different users
requesting the same URL, this will definitely be the case. The UNIX system keeps
these separate with different processes.

When the argv[1] is received by the program, it first goes through the routine getopt(), which isolates out the -i option for image. The rest of the string, 122448891, which represents the colors for each of the nine circles of the quilt, is sent to the image-processing software. The image-processing software reads in the GIF template file, which is the Star Quilt GIF with any nine colors. Using the string representing the colors, it changes the colors in the color map to the user's request, and then sends it along with the other GIF binary data back to the client-server software. The user now sees the new IMaGe on the screen with the changed colors.

In addition, there are a couple of special options. One allows the user to see the cost information. This is a nice twist since it does not require the person to see purchasing information unless he or she wants to see it. A person could just play with the colors on the Star Quilt.

If users do request the prices, an additional option appears that allows them to activate a mailer. If they activate the mailer, the mailer is sent back in HTML format. The colors they have selected are passed along at each stage, so when they complete the mailing, the colors they have selected are included as part of the mailing.

The Star Quilt is an interesting project because it combines a number of different aspects on a single site. First, it is entertaining. A person can play with the HTML/cgi-bin page without ever purchasing a quilt. Changing the colors provides unique new and interesting designs. To assure that this is the case, the user is given a checkbox for cost information. Only if the box is checked will options appear that relate to buying a Star Quilt. Without this box checked, the page becomes an interactive entertainment site.

The foremost challenge for the Star Quilt project was to come up with a way to change the color mappings. The previous sections (on color mapping) explain the method used. A GIF file of the Star Quilt was created using a drawing and coloring program. In the actual project, the drawing was done on UNIX using xcip and the coloring done with xv. While there are probably better choices, such as Photoshop for Windows, this was what was available and it worked well even if it did take a little extra time.

Once the GIF was created, the color mapping techniques were used to determine the nine colors. It is important to note that the actual colors on the template GIF were not critical. All that is necessary is that they be unique colors since the program will later remap these to other colors. In the actual development, an attempt was made to use colors close to the expected colors even though it was not necessary.

The next step was to locate the color maps. This was done in conjunction with the development of the program since the program is required (at least in part) to determine the mappings. A built-in option allowed the same program to be used in the tool mode suggested previously.

To make it easier to connect the program to external search facilities, a method was provided to start the program from an HTML page. This page is the same as the HTML that will be sent back by the cgi-bin when a new Star Quilt is requested. It includes an IMaGe request for the cgi-bin part of the program that sends back the Star Quilt with the color string set to 123456789, the default color selection.

The program uses HTML and cgi-bin programs. The cgi-bin program puts out both HTML text and GIF images. It uses both the Get and Post methods and uses command line arguments (argv[]) to separate the different states. To accomplish all this functionality in a single program, the program must perform the following functions:

1. Begin from HTML input. This was done for a number of reasons. First, if the starting point is HTML, the initial request will appear familiar to users. It will also be easier to get this added to public search engines, such as Lycos. Finally, the HTML will be easy to provide with minor modifications, such as changes in the title. The initial page can also provide branches. In the case of the Star Quilt, an option was allowed for a smaller picture that would download more quickly on modems.

2. The cgi-bin program is departmentalized into its different sections. For the Star Quilt, these consist of the following:

   a. The GIF output section, including the color mapping changes.

   b. The Star Quilt HTML page, which is the most complex part of the program. This includes constant parts of the Web page (Title, Heading, etc.) and the variable sections of the Web page (the in-line arguments that will be sent out as the image request and the cost information). This is the real heart of the program, since the HTML text sent from the program includes a call to the same cgi-bin program for the GIF. This recursive technique is totally legal in C++ or C since multiple versions of the program can be run with different arguments and consequently with different outputs. In this case advantage is taken of the fact that the same program can send HTML text and GIF images based on the arguments given.

   c. The mailer form provides a standard input screen to allow the user to input his or her purchase information.

   d. Subroutines are performed to send the mail to the required agent.

   e. The option handlers determine whether to send HTML data or GIF data from the cgi-bin program.

The actual program, which uses many expansions of techniques discussed in this book, is shown in Appendix 4.

Quilt Program

```
/****************************************************************
 *       Quilt.C
 ****************************************************************/
/* This program is owned by Mark Felton and Chris Cota. Any sections may be
 * reused, but reproduction of the Star Quilt program is prohibited.
 */
/*
 * These are built-in libraries.
```

```
     */
#include <stdio.h>
#include <stdlib.h>
#include <sys/time.h>
#include <unistd.h>
#include <string.h>
#include "Quilt_defines.h"
// Name of GIF file used for image template
#define GIF_FILE "unix_path/star_quilt.gif"
// Name of HTML file used to start the program
#define HTML_FILE "unix_path/star_quilt.html"


IMaGe ROUTINES FOR QUILT
/***********************************************************
 *          IMaGe routines
 ***********************************************************/
```

The major new class that is needed for the Star Quilt is the Color_IMaGe class. This class will provide the ability to pass a GIF file out through the server to the client. The color map of the GIF image is altered based on the new colors requested. An array of possible color values is set up initially. These can be indexed from a list of color defines. To change a color, the location of the original color in the color map and a new colors index are required.

To allow multiple color changes, a type is created that consists of both the color map location and the new color. These can then be passed in as a vararg list of any length into the Color_IMaGe class.

```
/*
 * A pallet contains the three values required to produce a color. These are the red, green,
 * and blue components ranging from 0 to 255 decimal or 0 to 0xFF hexadecimal.
 */
static struct Pallet
{
    char select[3];
} PALLET[9] = {
        222, 90, 57,/* A nice red */
        255, 250, 255,/* Off white */
        // rest of colors

    };
class _Color_IMaGe {
private:
    PALLET Color_pallet[TOTAL_COLOR_CHOICES];
    int Color_map[TOTAL_COLOR_MAPS]
    create_pallet();
    create_default_map();
```

```
    public:
        _Color_IMaGe(); // constructor
        void show_star(char* gif, COLOR_MAP* color_change, ...);
    };
    /* This is the Quilt IMaGe Constructor */
    _Color_IMaGe::_IMaGe()
    {
        // Create a pallete of colors for remapping
        create_pallet();
        // Map the template GIF to an internal map
        create_default_map();
        // Turn off showing purchase information as the default
        purchase_info=OFF;
    }
    void
    _Color_IMaGe::show_star (char* color_select)
    {
        int byte_count;      // counter of bytes
        /* read the colors */

        for(color_select=0; color_select < MAX_SELECT; color_select++)
        {
            // The colors are in the string that came from argv[1]
                set_color (color_select);
        }
        // read in the template star
        // Tell the server an IMaGe is coming
         fprintf(stdout,"Content-type: image/gif\n\n");
         // Read in the IMaGe file, altering as required
        stream = fopen(GIF_FILE, "r");
        while(fgets(buff,2,stream) != 0)
        {
            // Check if we are in the color map area
            if( (byte_count >= GIF_COLORMAP_START) &&
                (byte_count <= ( TOTAL_COLORS * 3) )
            {
                // If yes remap the color
                remap_color ( byte_count );
            }

            // Send the IMaGe byte to stdout
            fprintf(stdout, "%c", buff[0]);
            // Use this line instead for decimal output
            //   fprintf(stdout, "%d %d\n", i, buff[0]);
            byte_count++;
        }
```

```
        fclose(stream);
    }
```

This completes the routines required to create an IMaGe of the Star Quilt with remapped colors based on a string.

The next section is the Quilt class, which is the main class for the Star Quilt project. It basically acts like a traffic cop, first reading in the Posted information and then sorting it and deciding which subobjects are needed to create the client output.

HTML Quilt Routines

```
/*****************************************************************
 *                          Quilt HTML routines
 *****************************************************************/
```

Creating a quilt for the user requires the IMaGe and a form to read in the user's color selection as variable input.

```
class _Quilt : public _Color_IMaGe, _Form {
private:
    char show_string[10];
    // other stuff
public:
    _Quilt();  // constructor does nothing
    void html();
    void default();
};
/*
 * This is the main part of the program. It sends the Quilt HTML to the client along with an
 * IMaGe string. The IMaGe string will cause the cgi-bin program to be called from the HTML
 * with options that will send the GIF image back to the client.
 */
_Quilt::html(char* input_string)
{
    gets(input);
    /*
     * The colors have been submitted as a FORM input, with values ranging from "1" to
     * "9". Get the values of the user's requested colors and put them in the appropriate
     * arrays for processing. These will later be sent as argv when the same cgi-bin program
     * is called to request the GIF IMaGe output.
     */

    get_color_choice("color1=");
    get_color_choice("color2=");
    // continue for all colors
```

```
    get_color_choice("color9=");
    /*
     * If you are using the optional mailer, check if an email request has been sent.
         if(check_mail()) { return; }
     */

    /*
     * If you are showing the optional purchase information, check if the user wishes to
     * see the purchase information.
     */
        purchase_information = check_purchase();

// Send the HTML for the IMaGE
        send_image_html();
    /*
     * Change from ascii to ints for the Options in the
     *    FORMS
     */
        get_variables();

    /*
     * Send the fixed part of the star quilt HTML to stdout
     */
    printf("Content-type: text/html\n\n");
    printf( "<HTML>\n");
    printf("<BODY bgcolor=#f0f0f0 </BODY>\n");
    printf("<BODY>\n");
    /*
     * Now deal with the variable sections of the HTML
     */

    /*
     * A check on whether to use the modem mode. If the modem is used, a smaller IMaGe
     * is sent and the cgi-bin option for requesting the image is changed from
     * -I -> large image to
     * -i -> small image
     */
    if(option_small!=1)
    {
        printf(%s%s%s%s%s,
            "<FORM ACTION=",
            "\"http://info.dr.att.com/cgi-bin/dev/markf/cgi-bin/Qmain?-h\"",
            "METHOD=POST>\n",
            "<IMG HEIGHT=184 WIDTH=186 SCR= ",
            "\"http://info.dr.att.com/cgi-bin/dev/markf/cgi-bin/Qmain?-i\"");
    } else
```

```
{
      printf(%s%s%s%s%s,
            "<FORM ACTION= ",
            "\"http://internet_path/cgi-bin/Qmain?-H\"",
            "METHOD=POST>\n",
            "<IMG HEIGHT=369 WIDTH=373 SRC= ",
            "\"http://internet_path/cgi-bin/Qmain?-I\"");
}
/*
  * Since the user will be able to change the colors again, an option FORM is sent to the
  * screen as HTML. However, since the C++ or C program has knowledge of which colors
  * are already selected, some intelligence is added to make these the selected colors in
  * the option fields.
  */
printf("%s\">", show_string);
printf("<H2> Select Color For Each Star Element </H2>\n");
printf("<BR>");
for(i=0; i<9; i++)
{
      printf("%s%d%s", "_", i, "_\n");
      printf("%s%d%s", "<SELECT NAME = \"color",
            i+1, "\">Element Color\n");
      for(j=1; j<=9 ; j++)
      {
            option_html ( colorname, i, j );
      }
      printf("</SELECT>\n");
      if((i==2) || (i==5))
      {
            printf("<BR><BR>\n");
      }
}
/*
  * Next show a checkbox that allows the user to request
  * cost information
  */
printf("<BR><BR>\n<BR><BR>\n");
printf("%s%s\n",
      "[<INPUT TYPE=\"checkbox\" NAME=\"purchase_info\"",
      "VALUE=\"on\"> Show Purchase Infomation]");

if(purchase_information == ON)
{
      // send HTML with price information
      show_cost_information();
}
```

```
        printf("%s%s%s",
            "<P>Submit Color Selection <INPUT TYPE=\"submit\"","VALUE=\"Select Colors\"",
            "> <INPUT TYPE = \"reset\">\n");
        /*
         * Complete the HTML output
         */
        printf("</FORM></BODY></HTML>\n");
}
/*
 * Use the HTML Thru mode to send the default
 * HTML to the client
 */
void _Quilt::default()
{
    char* buffer;
    buffer = new(char * 80); // allocate an 80 character buffer
    printf("Content-type: text/html\n\n");
    stream = fopen(HTML_FILE, "r");
    while(fgets(buffer, 80, stream) != EOF)
    {
        puts (buffer);
    }
    free (buffer);
}
```

Quilt Main

```
/***************************************************************
 *         main
 ***************************************************************/
/* This program is owned by Mark Felton and Chris Cota.
 * Any unauthorized use is prohibited
 */
extern char *optarg;
extern int opterr;
extern int getopt();
void
main(int argc, char *argv[])
{
    /* Allow a choice of a small or large picture on the screen */
    int option_small = OFF;
    /*
     * Since the same program will
     * create the HTML
     * put out the GIF IMaGe
     * send the mail
```

```
       * depending on what options it is called with, it makes sense to use pointers. That
       * way, you can only instantiate the required classes.
       */
      QUILT* Quilt;
      COLOR_IMAGE* IMaGe;
      MAIL* Mail;
```

Quilt Options

```
      /**********************************************************
               OPTIONS
      **********************************************************/
      while ((optchar = getopt(argc, argv, "i:I:hHm")) != EOF)
      {
          switch(optchar)
          {
          /* IMaGe Options */
          case 'i':              // small image
              option_small=ON;
              return;
          case 'I':              // large image
              IMaGe = new(COLOR_IMAGE);
              IMaGe->show_star(gifsm, optarg);
              return;
          /* star quilt HTML option */
          case 'h':              // HTML for small image
              option_small=ON;
          case 'H':              // HTML for large image
              Quilt = new(QUILT);
              Quilt->html();
              return;
      /* Mail Option */
          case 'm':
              Mail = new(MAIL);
              Mail->submittal();
              return;
          default:
              break;
          }
      }
      /*
       * If there are no options, the program will put out the starting HTML program.
       * This is a protection against someone entering the cgi-bin program as a URL request.
       */
              Quilt = new(QUILT);
              Quilt->default();
  }
```

The flow of the program requires some careful examination. The user enters the program with the HTML file Quilt.html shown next. While it would be possible to use a default in the cgi-bin to produce this same HTML, the advantage of an HTML file is that it can be customized easily and will have a normal URL for search engines.

```
<!-- Quilt.html -->
<HTML>
<HEAD>
<TITLE>Star Burst Quilts</TITLE>
</HEAD>
<BODY bgcolor=#f0f0f0 >
<IMG SRC="http://internet_path/cgi-bin/Qmain?-i123456789">
<FORM ACTION="http://internet_path/cgi-bin/Qmain?-H">
<H2> Select Color for Each Star Element </H2>
    _1_
    <SELECT NAME = "elem1">
    <OPTION SELECTED> RED
    <OPTION> WHITE
    <OPTION> BLACK
    <OPTION> YELLOW
    <OPTION> BLUE
    <OPTION> GREEN
    <OPTION> ORANGE
    <OPTION> CYAN
    <OPTION> FUSHA
    </SELECT>
  _2_
    <SELECT NAME = "elem2">
    <OPTION> RED
    <OPTION> WHITE
    <OPTION> BLACK
    <OPTION> YELLOW
    <OPTION> BLUE
    <OPTION SELECTED> GREEN
    <OPTION> ORANGE
    <OPTION> CYAN
    <OPTION> FUSHA
    </SELECT>
  _3_
    <SELECT NAME = "elem3">
    <OPTION> RED
    <OPTION> WHITE
    <OPTION> BLACK
```

```
    <OPTION> YELLOW
    <OPTION> BLUE
    <OPTION> GREEN
    <OPTION SELECTED> ORANGE
    <OPTION> CYAN
    <OPTION> FUSHA
    </SELECT>
    <BR>
    <BR>
_4_
    <SELECT NAME = "elem4">
    <OPTION> RED
    <OPTION> WHITE
    <OPTION> BLACK
    <OPTION> YELLOW
    <OPTION SELECTED> BLUE
    <OPTION> GREEN
    <OPTION> ORANGE
    <OPTION> CYAN
    <OPTION> FUSHA
    </SELECT>
_5_
    <SELECT NAME = "elem5">
    <OPTION> RED
    <OPTION> WHITE
    <OPTION> BLACK
    <OPTION> YELLOW
    <OPTION> BLUE
    <OPTION> GREEN
    <OPTION> ORANGE
    <OPTION> CYAN
    <OPTION SELECTED> FUSHA
    </SELECT>
_6_
    <SELECT NAME = "elem6">
    <OPTION> RED
    <OPTION> WHITE
    <OPTION> BLACK
    <OPTION> YELLOW
    <OPTION> BLUE
    <OPTION> GREEN
    <OPTION> ORANGE
```

```
        <OPTION SELECTED> CYAN
        <OPTION> FUSHA
        </SELECT>
<BR>
        <BR>
        _7_
        <SELECT NAME = "elem7">
        <OPTION> RED
        <OPTION> WHITE
        <OPTION> BLACK
        <OPTION SELECTED> YELLOW
        <OPTION> BLUE
        <OPTION> GREEN
        <OPTION> ORANGE
        <OPTION> CYAN
        <OPTION> FUSHA
        </SELECT>
_8_
        <SELECT NAME = "elem8">
        <OPTION> RED
        <OPTION SELECTED> WHITE
        <OPTION> BLACK
        <OPTION> YELLOW
        <OPTION> BLUE
        <OPTION> GREEN
        <OPTION> ORANGE
        <OPTION> CYAN
        <OPTION> FUSHA
        </SELECT>
_9_
        <SELECT NAME = "elem9">
        <OPTION> RED
        <OPTION> WHITE
        <OPTION SELECTED> BLACK
        <OPTION> YELLOW
        <OPTION> BLUE
        <OPTION> GREEN
        <OPTION> ORANGE
        <OPTION> CYAN
        <OPTION SELECTED> FUSHA
        </SELECT>
<BR>
```

```
[<INPUT TYPE="checkbox" NAME="purchase_info" VALUE="on">
     Show Purchase Info]
     <BR>
<P>Submit Color Selection <INPUT TYPE = "submit">
     <INPUT TYPE = "reset">
</FORM>
</BODY>
</HTML>
```

The initial HTML program uses a cgi-bin for input for the image. It also uses the same cgi-bin program for the action when the form is submitted.

When the HTML is invoked by a browser, the client sends the server a request for an IMaGe file from the cgi-bin program. The URL for this IMaGe is

```
URL = "http://internet_path/cgi-bin/Quilt?-i123456789"
```

If you have not found this in the HTML, you should do so now, since it is essential for understanding how this project works.

The IMaGe part is called the cgi-bin program as

```
Quilt -I123456789
```

The cgi-bin Quilt program reads in the string in argv[1] as

```
"-I123456789"
```

The -I option is a request for an IMaGe to be sent, and the numbers

```
"123456789"
```

are the pallet values for the colors to be used in the nine areas of the star. In this case color 1 goes to area 1, color 2 to area 2, etc. But this will not have to be the case. Users can now use the options to select a rearrangement of the colors in any order they wish. The options provide the variable input for the users' selections. Users can make two or more colors the same if they want. There is also a checkbox on the form to show the purchase information. In the actual implementation, this is a two-stage process. The first request shows a phone number and provides a second check-box for sending email. If this is checked, an email input form is sent to the user. If the user sends out the email, his or her choices of colors are also sent at the same time. Maintained hidden variables are used to provide the person's color choices.

If the email request is not activated, the person's color choices are sent to the cgi-bin script as a Post. In this case there is nothing on the command line except the ?-H. This is found in the action part of the HTML.

```
ACTION="http://internet_path/cgi-bin/Quilt?-H"
```

This is the previously discussed use of a Post and an agrv[1] at the same time. Since the method is Post, the user information will arrive as stdin. At the same time, the ?-H will be in argv[1] as a -H.

The program processes the -H option and sends the program off to produce new HTML output. The cgi-bin program reads in the user's input, translates to a GIF string, and then sends HTML back to the client.

Now comes the important part. The HTML includes in it a request for an IMaGe to be put on the screen. This is a URL. The URL is a call to the same cgi-bin program with the -I option as argv[1]. In addition, the -I has appended to it a new string representing the new way to map the colors. When the client reaches the <IMG> part of the HTML, it sends a new request to the server for the image. The cgi-bin program is invoked with the image (-I) option, followed by the string of colors (1 to 9) to use in each Quilt section. It then sends the IMaGe with the color mappings changed back into the HTML that was just sent.

The other options are relatively straightforward. The -i and -h do the same thing as -I and -H, except that they use a scaled down image for people using modems. The -m option occurs when the mail form is submitted. It sends out mail and then sends back the default Star Quilt page.

> **Note: A special trick was used in the real program. If a color is repeated, an offset is used and incremented to assure that no two colors in the color map are exactly the same. The offset is so small (one unit) that the user will not see any significant change in the colors on the screen.**

Low-Level Routines for Image Mapping

```
void _Color_IMaGe::create_default_map()
{
    // set all colors to defaults
    //
    for(i=0; i < TOTAL_COLOR_MAPS; i++)
    {
        Color_map[i] = DEFAULT_MAP;
    }
}
/*
```

Each color map item is set to the value sent to the form in the argv[1] string called the color string. Because it is ASCII, the value of 0 must be subtracted. For example, if the color_string that came from argv[1] is 331772135, and if the value of color_select is 3 for the fourth color in the color map, the value of Color_map[4] will be 1, which is the third number in the string. This 1 will later be used to select the first color in the pallet when the fourth color in the GIF file is remapped to a new color.

```
*/
int _Color_IMaGe::set_color(int color_select)
{
    Color_map[color_select] =
        *((char *) (color_string + color_select) - '0' ;
    // do some error checking here
}
void _Color_IMaGe::create_pallet()
{
    /* initiate color values for template */
    PALLET pallet[] = {
        222, 90, 57,/* A nice red */
        255, 250, 255,/* Off white */
        // rest of colors
    };
}
// Use the byte count to determine which pallet and which value in the specific pallet
void remap_color( int byte_count )
{
    byte_count = byte_count - 13; // set to zero offset
    new_color = Color_map[byte_count % 3];
    // If new color is -1 leave the color alone
    if(new_color != -1)
    {
        buff[0]=
            pallet[new_color].value[byte_count % 3];
    }
}
```

Low-Level Routines for HTML Output

```
/*
This subroutine is used to map the user's input to the color variables to an integer value. It
uses table lookup to determine the value.   */
static struct color_table
{
    char* color_name;
    char color_value;
} COLOR_TABLE = {
    "RED", '1',
    "WHITE", '2',
    // other choices here
    "END", 'Z'
};
```

```
// Return a color value located in the table above
```

```
char _Color_table::return_color_val(char* var_str)
{
    int i = 0;
    while (color_table[i++].color_value != 'Z')
    {
        if(strcmp(color_table[i].color_name, var_str) == 0)
        {
            return (color_table[i].color_value);
        }
    }
}
void _Quilt::get_color_choice(int item, char* variable)
{
    var_str=variable(variable);
  *(show_string + item) = color_val(var_str);
}
#define MAX_ITEMS 9         /* nine color circles */
void _Quilt::get_variables()
{
    char color_variable[15];
    strcpy(color_variable, "colorX=")
    for(item=0; item < MAX_ITEMS; item++)
    {
        // replace X with a number from 1 to 9
        *(color_variable + 5 ) = item = '0';
        get_color_choice ( item, color_variable );
    }
}
#define OFF 0
#define ON ~OFF
int check_purchase_information()
{
    var_str=variable("purchase_info=");
    return ( strcmp(var_str, "on") == 0 ) ? ON : OFF;
}
void Quilt::show_cost_information()
{
        printf("<H4>Quilt Prices</H4>\n");
        printf("<UL>\n");
        printf(" <LI>Queen Size $250\n");
        printf("<LI>Full Size $225\n");
        printf("<LI>Twin Size $175\n");
        printf("<LI>Baby Crib $95\n");
        printf("<LI>Baby Small $75\n");
        printf("</UL>\n");
        printf("<BR>To order by Phone Call 303-xxx-xxxx\n");
```

```
            printf("<BR>To order by Email Turn On The EMAIL OPTION");
            printf(" Below And Submit the Form\n");
            printf("<SELECT NAME = \"email\">Email Purchase<BR>");
            printf("<OPTION SELECTED> OFF\n");
            printf("<OPTION> ON\n");
            printf("</SELECT>\n");
    }
```

Optional Additions

An optional mailer can also be added. This mailer is interesting because it sends the hidden variable containing the user's color choices as part of the mailing.

```
    class Mail
    {
    private:
    public:
        void request(char* quilt_hidden);
        void submittal();
    };
    void Quilt::option_html( int i, int j )
    {
        printf("<OPTION ");
        printf("%s", (show_string[i] == j ? "SELECTED>" : ">"));
        printf("%s\n",_color_table[j].color_name);
    }
    int check_mail()
    {
        var_str=variable("email=");
        if(strcmp(var_str, "ON") == 0)
            return YES;
        else
            return NO;
    }
    start_mail()
    {
        MAIL* Mail;
        Mail = new(MAIL);
        Mail->request(show_string);
        return;
    }
    /*
     * This routine creates the mail FORM that is sent as HTML to the client screen
     */
    void
    Mail::request(char* quilt_hidden)
    {
```

```
    printf("%s%s%s%s%s%s%s%s%s%s%s%s%s%s%s%s%s%s%s%s%s%s%s%s%s%s%s%s%s%s",
        "Content-type: text/html\n\n",
        "<HTML><HEAD><TITLE>Quilt Mail Form</TITLE></HEAD>\n",
        "<BODY bgcolor=#ffffff </BODY>\n",
        "<H1> STAR QUILT ORDER FORM </H1>\n",
        "<BR>\n",
        "If you are submitting this form, you are requesting purchase of the",
        "Quilt you have designed. Because of differences in computer screens,",
        "the colors may not be an exact match to those shown on your screen.",
        "Every attempt has been made to get these as correct as possible.",
        "Your colors have been automatically recorded. Please verify them below.",
        "\n<BR>\n",
        "<FORM ACTION=\"http://internet_path/cgi-bin/Qmain?-m\" METHOD=POST>\n",
        "<P>\n",
        "<B>Send To </B>: <INPUT VALUE=\"cota@dash.com\" SIZE=40 NAME=\"to\"><BR>\n",
        "<B>Your Name </B>: <INPUT VALUE=\"\" SIZE=40 NAME=\"name\"><BR>\n",
        "<B >Your Email</B>: <INPUT VALUE=\"\" SIZE=40 NAME=\"from\"><BR>\n",
        "<B> Including Area Code </B> <BR>\n",
        "<B> Phone </B>: <INPUT VALUE=\"\" SIZE=40 NAME=\"phone\"><BR>\n",
        "<B>Size</B>: <INPUT VALUE=\"\" SIZE=40 NAME=\"size\"><BR>\n",
        "<P><INPUT TYPE=\"HIDDEN\" NAME=\"quilt\" VALUE=\"",
        quilt_hidden,
        "\"></P>",
        "<B> Any Special Comments </B>\n",
        "<P><TEXTAREA ROWS=10 COLS=60 NAME=\"body\"></TEXTAREA></P>\n",
        "<P><INPUT TYPE=\"submit\" VALUE=\"Send the mail\">\n",
        "<INPUT TYPE=\"reset\" VALUE=\"Start over\"></P>\n",
        "</FORM>\n",
        "<HR>\n",
        "</BODY></HTML>\n");
}
/*
 * This routine is used to process the input from the mail FORM and send the mail out to the
 * designated person.
 */
void Mail::submittal()
{
    FILE* fp;
    char mail_str[1000];
    gets(mail_str);
    strcpy(mail_str, clear_all(mail_str));
    fp= popen("mail myname@myloc", "w");
    fprintf(fp,"%s\n", mail_str);
    pclose(fp);
}
```

List of Quilt Routines

The files and subroutines for the Quilt program are as follows:

File: Quilt.h

This file contains the main classes used for this program.
public:

Quilt()   The constructor sets all values to default.

Quilt()   In this implementation the destructor has no function, it is a null destructor.

void show_sample(char* gif, int mode)   This routine is included for possible expansion of the program to include a demonstration of sample quilts. It is not called in the program shown.

void form_out(char* form_string)   This is the main form subroutine. It takes as an argument the string containing the user's color requests and requests for cost and email information. It generates an output that is the same form again with the IMG section changed to request the user's colors. If an email request is sent, it will put up the email form instead.

void show_star(char* gif, int mode, char* g_colors)   This routine is the image routine. It takes as arguments the GIF file to use for the image (this is done to allow alternative images) and a mode variable, which is used to find the color mapping during initial development, but will be set to show the image during normal usage and the list of colors in order as a string variable.

// mode=0 normal image, mode=1 diff data

void send_mail(char* mail_str)   This routine sends the mail to the person in charge of purchasing. The argument mail_str is a string containing the colors selected by the user in order, from the inner star to the outer star.

void mail_form(char* quilt_hidden)   This routine sends out the mail form as HTML. The argument quilt_hidden is the string list of the colors presently selected by the user. If the user submits the form, the hidden variable is sent to send_mail and then sent out with the mail.

File: Bus.h   This file contains the inherited class Formin. This class is used to process the information that comes from the form in a primitive format. The functions are Formin()-Null constructor

The rest of the functions separate submitted data that arrive in the format&variable_name_1=value1&variable_name2=value2, etc., into a variable separated format. By using these routines in the correct order, the actual submitted value of the variable can be obtained. The proper use of these subroutines is shown in the C++ code. Each function returns a character string that consists of the submitted message in its newly formatted state. With each progression it gets closer to the real value. On the final stage, the actual value of a single variable is returned.

char* variable(char* msg, char* start, char* end)

char* variable_clr(char* msg, char* start, char* end);

char* clear(char *);

char* clear_cr(char *);

char* clear_sp(char *);

The ability to control images can be extended in many ways. A C project called GD (see the discussion of URL listing) allows users to create their own GIF geometries. This and other types of capabilities can be connected to cgi-bin image control to create graphs, maps, geometries, and other exciting image capabilities. The potential to produce real-time images exists by combining image creation programs with cgi-bin image control.

In this chapter you learned how to use IMaGe files in forms and how to produce images from cgi-bin programs. The ability to manipulate and control graphics on the screen is one of the most underrated capabilities of the Internet. The primary focus to this point has been on what IMaGes should be placed on Web pages, not on how to connect graphics and programming skills to produce interactive graphic effects. Most programmers have incorrectly assumed that graphics programming is only relevant on local computers with loads of memory and direct control. The demonstration programs included here reveal that this is not the case. The Internet provides a new dimension for graphics control programs. The fact that these will reach significant audiences should influence programmers to explore how to activate these fascinating capabilities.

PROGRAM EXERCISES

1. Create a tool that will isolate out the header and image mapping information from a GIF file. Create a simple GIF file. Using GIF tools, verify the values of the colors in the color mapping area. Using the tool you developed, verify that you can read the same information with your tool.

2. Using the IMaGe created in program exercise 1, send the image through a cgi-bin program. Verify that you can send the image back to the screen as a URL. Change one of the colors using the color mapping techniques. Verify that the color changes on the screen.

3. Create a program that systematically changes the color maps to create the letters A through E by color mapping a template. (**Hint:** See the software LED in Chapter 16.)

PROBLEMS

1. Explain the different sections of a GIF file. Explain the role of each section. Examine ways that this information could be used to alter and control images systematically. Examine the various situations in which images are used and tell how you might use

color mapping techniques to create special effects. (**Advanced:** How could these techniques be used along with the animation discussed in Chapter 18?).

2. Explain the critical line that differentiates IMaGes from HTML when sending to the server. How would this line need to be changed if a JPG image was used instead of a GIF?

3. List some applications that relate to your field of expertise and might benefit from IMaGe mapping techniques. Explain in detail what would be required to produce the expected goals. Detail a step-by-step procedure to work through to completion. Include points at which debugging and validation can be done as part of the process. Rework your plan until each stage is a manageable size. Rework the plan until each stage appears to be implemented easily. Rework the plan until one of the stages is an obvious starting point. Rework the plan until the starting point would require less than one day. Rework the starting point until the starting point would require less than one hour.

4. Animated GIF IMaGes are available at many locations on the Web. One of the problems with them is that there is no way to stop them. Is there any way to use the GIF cgi techniques from this chapter to eliminate this problem? How would you go about breaking down and then reconstructing one of these images using the IMaGe tool?

17

Debugging

Debugging cgi-bin Programs

WHILE IT IS NOT DIFFICULT to debug a cgi-bin program, doing so requires special techniques. Remember that the final cgi-bin program will be run by the server. Because problems can arise at any point in a program, normal tools can frequently be used to solve basic problems. These include debugging tools that allow a programmer to step through a program from start to finish and change variables in order to cause the code to follow various paths. However, these are not the only tools available to the cgi-bin programmer.

Using stdout

BECAUSE THE OUTPUT OF a cgi-bin program will go to stdout, this can be used to great advantage to determine how a program will operate. Recall that normally (without the client-server software) standard output is the screen of your computer. Only when the cgi-bin program is being run through a browser will the output first pass through the server and then through the browser, including the browser's HTML interpreter. If we examine step by step how this occurs, it is possible to gain real insights into debugging.

Step 1: The user enters a URL as a form action, as an anchor, or directly on the URL command line from the browser. The URL is a request for the cgi-bin program.

Step 2: The browser sends the request type (for example, HTML text request or image request) to the server along with the URL. In addition, if the request is a form request, the data in the form are sent to the server as part of the data transmission. Certain servers also separate any lines following a ? into an argument sent to the program as a command line argument (in C jargon, argv[1-n]).

Step 3: The server interprets the URL. Using the URL, it locates the cgi-bin program and executes it. It also sends any Post method form information into stdin and any ? or Get Method form information as argv[].

Step 4: The cgi-bin performs its operations and then sends output to stdout. However, stdout is not the screen, it is the server.

Step 5: The server receives the output of the cgi-bin program. It checks the initial line to verify that the type of information being sent matches the type that has been requested (e.g., HTML text or an image). If there is a match, it sends the rest of the data to the browser. If there is not a match, it sends nothing to the browser, eventually resulting in a time-out.

Step 6: The browser interprets the data as standard HTML text or as standard image information and places the data on the screen accordingly.

Anyone planning to debug cgi-bin programs would do well to spend some time studying this sequence of events. As complicated as it may appear at first, a great deal of time can be saved by understanding this process.

Executing the Program

How DOES ONE BEGIN TO debug a cgi-bin script? The first step should always be to execute the program before putting it in the cgi-bin. This is an important first step since you will probably never be invited back again if you place a program in the cgi-bin that results in major problems.

First and foremost, execute the program from the command line as if it were going to be used like a normal program. If your program is called cgi_main after you have compiled it, simply type cgi_main from the UNIX prompt. This will find simple errors, such as core dumps.

Debugging with argc and argv[]

IF YOU HAVE OPTIONS IN your program, again execute with the options. For example, if you expect to see cgi_main?-i as a request from a form, simply type

```
cgi_main -i
```

and see what happens.

This is the same method you will use to test a form with Get as the method. Recall that the Get method will send all requested variables as a single string in argv[]. These will normally be in argv[1], but + can be used to forces them into successive argv[].

The next step is to capture the output and examine it. In UNIX this is done by redirecting the output to a file. The new commands would be

```
cgi_main > file1
cgi_main -i > file2
```

The output files called file1 and file2 can now be examined. If the expectation is HTML, the output will be an actual HTML page with the exception that the first lines are the request to the server. Just delete these lines and look at the HTML with a standard browser. The browser will allow a look at a file if the argument file:// is used instead of http://, or you can place the file in a legitimate HTML area on the server and view in the standard manner.

Debugging Graphics GIF Files

IF THE OUTPUT OF YOUR cgi-bin program is GIF formatted data, audio, or some other special formatted data, the debugging is slightly more complex. It is suggested that you temporarily comment out the command line to the server and then execute the cgi-bin program and redirect it to a file. You can now view the GIF file or listen to the audio using your browser and see if the changes you expected have taken place. Another option is to create a debugging option to your program. This will set a flag that can block the server command. The code would look something like this:

```
void main(int argc, char* argv[])
{
    int option_debug=OFF;
    /* getoption see above */
    case 'd': /* debug option */
        option_debug=ON;
        break;
    if(option_debug==OFF)
    {
```

```
        cout << "Content-type: image/gif";
    }
    /* rest of GIF, AUDIO or other FORMAT here */
}
```

To disable the server command, execute with the -d option.

```
cgi_main -d [other options] > filename.gif
```

Testing Forms: stdin Post Method

TESTING FORMS IS SLIGHTLY MORE difficult but merely requires some additional ingenuity. The input to a Post form is stdin. Suppose our form is expecting to see a string that looks like the following:

```
msg1=xxx&msg2=xxx&msg3=xxx ...
```

Here is a UNIX command to send the string into our cgi_main program and output the result to a file:

```
echo "msg1=xxx&msg2=xxx&msg3=xxx ..." | cgi_main > output_file
```

There is only one problem with this approach. The last character in a Post is a 0D hex or carriage return. There are a number of ways to get around this for testing purposes. One is to use a test for variables that will accept either an end of string or a carriage return.

```
if((*char == "\n") || (*char == 0))
{
    break;
}
```

This will work for both testing and the real form. Since a null (0) will never occur on the real output from the form, it should cause no problem if this is left in the final code. The second alternative is to use the debug option mentioned previously. In C the debug option could be made global so it could be used in different sub-routines. In C++ it might be part of an inherited Debug class. The third option is to execute the program and then manually type in the variable string. This must be the entire string that would be sent by the server. When you type it in directly, you will get the required \n at the end by pressing the return key.

One thing that is essential to note is the use of quotation marks around the echoed string. This is required because of the & characters that are used in form strings. In UNIX the & is used to put a process into the background. An alternative would be to use the \ in front of each ampersand.

```
echo msg1=xxx\&msg2=xxx\&msg3=xxx ... | cgi_main > output_file
```

The \ removes the special meaning of the ampersand. The quotation marks do the same thing.

Another consideration is punctuation and control characters. Since these will be sent in the %XX format, you will need to echo them or enter them into your debug string in this format:

```
echo "myvariable=Hello%20Internet%20World" | myprogram > output_file
```

The pipe | is used to send the echo into the program as stdin. If the string is short enough, you could also type it in from the command line after executing the program.

What can be done if it is discovered that there is still a problem? One approach is to have the program send something right onto the Web page, or alternatively, log to a debug file. If a very complex cgi-bin program is being developed, a log routine may be needed.

Testing Forms: argc and argv[]

IF THE Get method is used or command line arguments are sent using ?, the debugging is straightforward. Merely send the argument string as a command line argument. Here is the earlier Post replaced by Get.

```
cgi_main msg1=xxx\&msg2=xxx\&msg3=xxx ... > output_file
```

Logging Errors

ANOTHER EFFECTIVE DEBUGGING PROCEDURE is to log errors to a log file. You can place log outputs in any of your error subroutines. You can also log status information on normal paths. Here is a simple error-logging routine. You can modify this to a subroutine and hard code the name of your error file instead of using argv[].

```
#include <stdio.h>
#include <stdlib.h>
#include <iostream.h>
void log(char* logfile, char* logmsg)
{
    FILE* fp;
    fp=fopen(logfile, "a");
    fprintf(fp, "%s\n", logmsg);
    fclose(fp);
}
```

```
void main(int argc, char* argv[])
{
    log(argv[1], argv[2]);
}
```

Things to Watch For

1. Paths that look different to the server than to the user. Using complete paths can eliminate this problem.
2. Permissions set wrong for the server but not for the user. Verify all permissions on directories and files, especially UNIX paths and UNIX accessed files.
3. Placing writable files in the cgi-bin area. This is a very dangerous practice and should always be avoided.
4. Confusing UNIX paths and URLs. The more you learn to determine which type to use where, the less useless time you will spend debugging your code.

This chapter explained methods for debugging your cgi-bin programs. Techniques were developed for Get and Post methods, for agrv[] and stdin, for stdout, and for HTML and IMaGes. Debugging techniques are essential if you are to create interesting cgi-bin programs.

PROGRAM EXERCISES

1. Using an available program, send the output to stdout and capture it in a file using redirection. Remove the Content... line with a standard editor. Using a browser, display the file using the file://unix_path for the URL. Place the file in an appropriate area and redisplay using the http://internet_path for the URL. Validate that both displays are correct.
2. Test a Post method form using an echo of the expected variables and piping them into stdin. Verify the output by capturing stdout and examining it. (Use either an editor or the method in program exercise 1.) Repeat the experiment by executing the program and typing in the variables as keyboard input. Verify the output. (**Note:** To capture the output, you may need to use "tee".)
3. Repeat program exercise 2, but change it to a Get method. Send the variables into the program as argc and argv[1]. Verify the output as in program exercise 2.
4. Create a cgi-bin program that will change the IMaGe maps. Comment out the Content... line or disable it with a debug option. Send the output to a file using redirection. Place it in an appropriate area and view it as a GIF file with the browser. (**Note:** Be sure the file is named somename.gif). Verify that if you do not remove the Content... line, the file will not be viewable. Why not?

PROBLEMS

1. Explain the different methods for debugging cgi-bin programs. What are some of the techniques that are unique to cgi-bin programs? Explain the different error subroutines that may need to be tested.

2. Create a hidden variable file program that uses a count to establish the sizing for new or malloc. What will happen if a malicious person changes the value of count in his or her saved copy of your Web page? How about if the person eliminates it? What types of defensive programming can you do to avoid these and other problems? How could you use the environment IP address to catch malicious offenders? How could you then disable their access to your system?

3. Explain what is meant by the statement, "The best debugging method is careful programming, good code reading, and adequate testing."

18

Animation and Mixed Modes

Animation and Other Special Effects

WHILE GIF CONTROL REPRESENTS an especially interesting way to produce unique GIF output, it is not the only way available. There are several special Content-types (MIME-types) that can be used to produce other special effects. The multipart/x-mixed-replace allows the creation of animation or overlay capability. It can use as its output GIF, JPG, or any other standard type. The format for multipart/x-mixed-replace is

```
Content-Type: multipart/x-mixed-replace; boundary="any_boundary_string"
```

This Content-type includes two arguments. The first tells that the type is multipart/x-mixed-replace. The second argument, which follows the semicolon, is the *boundary string* that tells that the next image or file is about to start.

Boundary Conditions

AFTER EACH IMAGE IS completed, the boundary condition string is sent, preceded by two dashes (--). The boundary condition must start a new line (preceded by a carriage return) and end with a carriage return. The boundary condition can be placed in quotation marks, which will allow punctuation to be included. Without the quotation marks, certain punctuation will not work. The boundary condition can be any unique string that does not occur in the actual files being sent. The maximum length for the boundary condition string is 70 characters.

A second Content-type must also be sent before each file to identify the type of file being sent. The multipart/x-mixed-replace is stopped when the boundary condition string is followed by two additional dashes. The multipart/x-mixed-replace Content-type can be placed in an endless loop to produce continuous animation or can be sent through a single time to produce a single animation.

Animation[1] should be used sparingly over the Internet. There are a number of reasons for this. First, it can be distracting. The screen motion tends to draw your eye away from other things of interest on the screen. While it can be stopped, using the stop button, it is a good idea to limit its use. One way to do this is with a *loop counter* that exits after a finite count. It is often a good idea to include your own stop button if you are using continuous animation. The second concern is bandwidth utilization. The Internet was set up to have a file downloaded and then surrender any network facilities. When animation is used, the network is continually accessed (although caching will minimize some of this if images are repeated).[2]

A Simple Animation Program

WITH THESE WARNINGS IN place, here is a simple animation program.

```
/*
 * Type C++ or C subroutine
 * Purpose: animation demo
 */
/*
 * These are built-in libraries
 */
#include <stdio.h>
```

---

[1] There are other methods for providing animation, such as the GIF89A animated GIF image. This is a client-side continuation animation. The main disadvantage of this approach is that it cannot be stopped. Since animation tends to be distracting, this will be inappropriate for certain applications. The server-side cgi-bin animation can be created for a finite interval. The other approach, Java animation, will require more messages: First the HTML is sent, then the requested Applet, and then the animation files. It can produce similar effects.

[2] Quick animations tend to optimize when produced from the server side. Longer animations may be better implemented from the client side.

```
#include <stdlib.h>
#include <sys/time.h>
#include <unistd.h>
#include <string.h>
/*
 * Defines for the GIF files that make up the animation
 */
static char* GIF1 = "unix_path/animate1.gif"
static char* GIF2 = "unix_path/animate2.gif"
static char* GIF3 = "unix_path/animate3.gif"
static char* GIF4 = "unix_path/animate4.gif"
static char* GIF5 = "unix_path/animate5.gif"
#define GIF6 "unix_path/animate6.gif"
void
animate ( int delay )
{
    FILE* stream;
    char buff[2];        /* Character buffer for the GIF file */
    char* gif ;          /* The path to the GIF file */
    int tmp_delay;       /* Allows delay to be added to the output */
    int j=0;
    int i=0;
    int flag=0;
    /* set the delay */
    tmp_delay = delay;
    /* Initial request for multi-part content type */
    fprintf( stdout,
        "Content-type: multipart/x-mixed; boundary=\"xyzcom\"\n" );
    for(;;)                 /* loop forever to animate continuously */
    {
    /*
     * Use the modulo operator to sequence through the GIF files
     */
        switch(j%6)
        {
        case 0:
            gif = GIF1 ;
        break;
        case 1:
            gif = GIF2 ;
        break;
        case 2:
            gif = GIF3 ;
        break;
        case 3:
            gif = GIF4 ;
```

```
            break;
        case 4:
            gif = GIF5 ;
          break;
        default:
        case 5:
            gif = GIF6 ;
        break;
    }
    /* Delay is produced by repeating GIFs multiple times */
    if(tmp_delay <= 0)
    {
        tmp_delay = delay+1;
        j++;            /* Setup for next GIF file */
    }
    --tmp_delay;
    /* Send out the boundary message */
    fprintf( stdout, "%s", "\n--xyzcom\n" );
    /* Send out the Content-type for the file */
    fprintf( stdout, "%s", "Content-type: image/gif\n\n" );
    /* Send out the GIF binary data */
    stream = fopen( gif, "r" );
    while( fgets( buff,2,stream ) != 0 )
    {
            fprintf(stdout, "%c", buff[0]);
    }
    fclose( stream );
    /* comment out this line to loop forever - not recommended */
    if(j > MAXSENDS) break; /* exit forever loop */

    }
    /* Send out a final boundary message */
    fprintf(stdout, "%s", "\n--xyzcom--\n");
}
/*
 * Type C++ or C main
 * Purpose: animation main
 */
/*
 * The main retrieves any delay from argv[] and then calls the
 * animate routine
 */
void main(int argc, char* argv[])
{
    int delay = 1;
    if(argc>1)
```

```
        {
             delay = atoi( argv[1] );
        }
        animate( delay );
    }
```

About the program . . . .

1. The multipart message is sent to the server. It includes the boundary condition.

2. An infinite loop is established. On each loop the value of j is incremented. It is then used in a switch statement with a modulo for the number of GIF files. The case statements are offset by –1, so they go from zero (0) to the number of GIF files minus one.

3. Once the GIF path and name are copied into the string, the program sends out the actual Content-type of the file. In this example, GIF files are used for the animation.

4. This is followed by the actual GIF binary data, which are read through in the same manner as was done with earlier image techniques.

5. When the GIF is finished, the boundary string is sent, preceded by two dashes.

6. The program then loops back and sends out the next Content-type message and the next GIF file.

. . . .

Techniques Animation

ANIMATION TENDS TO WORK BEST if the GIF images are all set to the same size. GIF transparencies can produce fascinating effects, creating the illusion of motion across the Web page. Animation is not an easy technique to use. Be prepared to spend some time working on your images to get them to produce the desired effect. You may also want to create timing loops at various spots in the program to create delays needed for your particular effect.[3] Figure 18.1 shows a basic view of cgi-bin generated animation.

In the next example, a slightly more generic version is created. It includes the following features:

1. Reads the GIF files from a flat file

---

[3] There are a number of ways to create delays. One is to repeat the images over several times; a second is to use the sleep command or other software delay loops. On some systems, the second method will not work very well since the images will not start to display until a certain amount of information has been sent to the client. It may be necessary to experiment to determine the best method for your system.

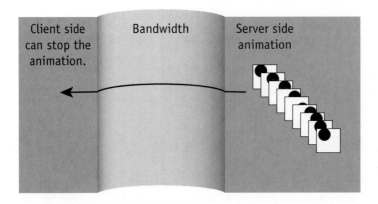

Figure 18.1   Server-controlled animation.

2. Breaks out after a defined number of loops

```
struct _Gif_file
{
    char* name;
    struct _Gif_file* next;
};
class _Animate
{
Private:
    /* Used to read and send binary GIF data */
    FILE* stream;
    char buff[2];              // Character buffer for the GIF file
    /* the present GIF file being sent out */
    char gif_buffer[80];       // The path to the GIF file
    char filename[100];
    /* used in the animation routine */
    int delay;
    int break_value;
    int number_of_gifs;        // counter of the number of GIF files
    _Gif_file gif_file;        // list of gif_files
    int tmp_delay;             // Allows delay to be added to the output
    void send_multi-mix();     // could be added to the html base class
    void send_gif( char* gif );
    void send_end_boundary();
Public:
                               // The constructor will need to do some work
    _Animate( int argc, char* argv[] );
    void show();       // The actual animation
};
```

```
/*
 * Type C++ class constructor
 * Purpose: animation constructor
 */
// constructor
_Animate::_Animate(int argc, char* argv[])
{
    char* tmp_gif_file;
    char* previous_gif_file;
    // set up the defaults
    break_value = delay = gif_file.next =
        gif_file.name = gif_file.next = number_of_gifs = 0;
    // getoption moved to constructor (see earlier getopt program)
    while ( ...see getoptions... )
    switch( ...see getoptions... )
    {
    case d: // delay
        delay = atoi( optarg );
        break;
    case f: // filename
        strcpy( filename, optarg );
        break;
    case b: // value to break out of loop on
        break_value = atoi( optarg );
        break;
    default:
        break;
    }
    // read the file with the paths and names of the GIFs
    if(stream = fopen(filename, "r") == NULL)
    {
        // do error leg
        exit -1;
    }
    // get the GIF file names from the input file and build a link list
    while(fgets( gif_buffer, MAXLINE, stream) != EOF)
    {
        tmp_gif_file = new gif_file; /* create next gif_file struct */

        tmp_gif_file->name = new char[strlen(gif_buffer)];
        strcpy(tmp_gif_file->name , gif_buffer);
        if(number_of_gifs)
        {
            previous_gif_file->next =
                tmp_gif_file;
            previous_gif_file = tmp_gif_file;
```

```
            }
            number_of_gifs++;
        }
    }
    /*
     * Type C++ class subroutine
     * Purpose: animation multimix message
     */
    void Animate::send_multimix()
    {
        /* Initial request for multipart Content type */
        fprintf( stdout,
            "Content-type: multipart/x-mixed; boundary=\"xyz.com\"\n" );
    }
    /*
     * Type C++ class subroutine
     * Purpose: animation boundary message
     */
    void _Animate::send_end_boundary()
    {
        /* Send out the boundary message */
        fprintf( stdout, "%s", "\n--xyz.com\n" );
    }
    /*
     * Type C++ class subroutine
     * Purpose: animation GIF and Content-type messages
     */
    void _Animate::send_gif(char* gif)
    {
        /* Send out the boundary message */
        fprintf( stdout, "%s", "\n--xyz.com\n" );
        /* Send out the Content-type for the file */
        fprintf( stdout, "%s", "Content-type: image/gif\n\n" );
        /* Send out the GIF binary data */
        stream = fopen( gif, "r" );
        while( fgets( buff,2,stream ) != 0 )
        {
                fprintf(stdout, "%c", buff[0]);
        }
        fclose( stream );
    }
    /*
     * Type C++ class subroutine
     * Purpose: animation
     */
    void _Animation::show()
```

```
{
    int gif_counter = 0;
    int break_counter = 0;
    send_multimix();
    tmp_gif_file = gif_file; /* start with 1st file */
    for(;;) // go forever
    {
        send_gif(tmp_gif_file -> name);
        // inc & reset of loop counter
        if(++gif_counter >= number_of_gifs)
        {
            gif_counter = 0;
            tmp_gif_file = gif_file;
            continue;
        }
        // check for break;
        if(break_counter++ == break_cnt)
        {
            break;
        }
        // delay code here
        // get the next file
        tmp_gif_file = tmp_gif_file->next;
    }
    send_end_boundary();
}
```

Here is a typical file for use with the animation class. (As an example, name this "animation.file.")

```
/unix_path/gif_file1
/unix_path/gif_file2
/unix_path/gif_file3
...
/unix_path/gif_filen
```

The main is straightforward:

```
/*
 * Type C++ main
 * Purpose: animation
 */
void main()
{
    Animation MyAnimation;
    MyAnimation.show();
```

```
     }
     CC -o animate animate.C
```

To run the animation, use the following:

```
http://internet_path/cgi-bin/animate?-f/unix_path/animate.file
```

Continuous Animation

IF YOU ARE RUNNING A continuous animation loop, add signal catching to your main to catch the stop button, back button, or request for a URL. This will cause your cgi-bin animation program to exit after these events. Without signal catching, the cgi-bin program will continue to run indefinitely.

```
/*
 * Type: C++ or C exit function
 */
void func_exit()
{
    fprintf(stdout, "%s", "\n--brought to you by xyzcom--\n");
    exit(-1);
}
/*
 * Type: C++ or C main
 * Usage: Demonstrate signal catching for a continuous animation.
 */
#include <signal.h>
void main()
{
    void (*func)();
    func= &func_exit;
    /*
     SIGHUP 1 hangup
     SIGINT 2 interrupt
     SIGQUIT 3* quit
     SIGILL 4* illegal instruction
     SIGTRAP 5* trace trap
     SIGABRT 6* abort (generated by abort(3) routine)
     SIGEMT 7* emulator trap
     SIGFPE 8* arithmetic exception
     SIGKILL 9 kill (cannot be caught, blocked, or ignored)
     SIGBUS 10* bus error
     SIGSEGV 11* segmentation violation
     SIGSYS 12* bad argument to system call
```

```
    SIGPIPE 13 write a pipe or other socket with no one to read it
    SIGALRM 14 alarm clock
    SIGTERM 15 software termination signal
    SIGURG 16@ urgent condition present on socket
    SIGSTOP 17+ stop (cannot be caught, blocked, or ignored)
    SIGTSTP 18+ stop signal generated from keyboard
    SIGCONT 19@ continue after stop
    SIGCHLD 20@ child status has changed
    */
    signal(SIGPIPE, func);
    signal(SIGHUP, func);
    signal(SIGINT, func);
    signal(SIGQUIT, func);
    signal(SIGTRAP, func);
    signal(SIGABRT, func);
    signal(SIGTERM, func);
    signal(SIGURG, func);
    signal(SIGSTOP, func);
    signal(SIGTSTP, func);
    /* rest of program here */
}
```

Other Special Content-Types

THERE ARE TWO OTHER Content-types that can provide special effects.

Multipart/Parallel

The multipart/parallel capability allows mixed media to be run in parallel. For example, audio files and GIF files can be provided in parallel. The parallel subtype works in the same manner as the multipart/x-mixed discussed previously. The primary distinction is that the order of the files is unimportant as long as they are in different media. When this is the case, the browser will attempt to run both at the same time.

```
/*
 * Type C++ or C subroutine
 * Purpose: binary image output
 */
void send_binary( char* filename)
{
    FILE *stream;
    char buff[2];
    /* Send out the the binary data */
    stream = fopen(filename, "r" );
```

```
      while( fgets( buff,2,stream ) != 0 )
      {
              fprintf(stdout, "%c", buff[0]);
      }
      fclose( stream );
}
/*
 * Type C++ or C subroutine
 * Purpose: mixed parallel
 */
void
mixed_parallel (char* gif_file, char* audio_file)
{
    /* Initial request for multipart Content-type */
    fprintf( stdout,
        "Content-type: multipart/parallel; boundary=\"xyzcom\"\n" );
    /* Send out the boundary message */
    fprintf( stdout, "%s", "\n--xyzcom\n" );
    /* Send out the Content-type for the file */
    fprintf( stdout, "%s", "Content-type: image/gif\n\n");
    /* Send out the binary data */
    send_binary(gif_file);
    /* Send out the boundary message */
    fprintf( stdout, "%s", "\n--xyz.com\n" );
    /* Send out the Content-type for the file */
    fprintf( stdout, "%s", "Content-type: image/audio\n\n" );
    /* Send out the binary data */
    send_binary(audio_file);
    /* Send out a final boundary message */
    fprintf(stdout, "%s", "\n--xyzcom--\n");
}
/*
 * Type C++ or C main
 * Purpose: mixed parallel
 */
void main()
{
    if(argc == 3)
    {
        mixed_parallel(argv[1], argv[2]);
    } else
    {
        /* send an error message */
    }

}
```

Multipart/Alternative

The multipart/alternative is presently implemented as a client-side feature in Netscape as the LOWSRC option for images. This capability provides a low-resolution and a high-resolution version of the same file. The low-resolution version will be displayed prior to the high-resolution version. If the browser cannot display the high-resolution version either due to bandwidth limitations or other factors, then the low-resolution version will perseverate. The multipart/alternative is used in the exact same way as the multipart/parallel, except that order is critical. The low-resolution version should occur prior to the high-resolution file.

```
/*
 * Type C++ or C subroutine
 * Purpose: mixed alternative
 */
void
mixed_alternative (char* gif_low_file, char* gif_high_file)
{
    int i = 0;
    /* Initial request for multipart Content-type */
    fprintf( stdout,
        "Content-type: multipart/alternative; boundary=\"xyzcom\"\n" );
    while(i < 2)
    {
        /* Send out the boundary message */
        fprintf( stdout, "%s", "\n--xyz.com\n" );
        /* Send out the Content-type for the file */
        fprintf( stdout, "%s", "Content-type: image/gif\n\n" );
        /* Send out the binary data */
        send_binary(i==0 ? gif_low_file : gif_high_file);
        i++;
    }
    /* Send out a final boundary message */
    fprintf(stdout, "%s", "\n--xyzcom--\n");
}
```

In this chapter you learned how to create special effects that include overlays and animation using special MIME-types. As part of this, you learned about boundary strings and special Content-types. The HTML standard will continue to expand to meet user requests. As part of this process, MIME-types and their associated Content-types will be expanded. Many of the browsers will incorporate the basic capabilities, allowing them to be accessed directly from HTML. However, the direct use of cgi-bin programs will continue to provide the maximum flexibility and control over these special capabilities.

PROGRAM EXERCISES

1. Create an animation program that loops three times through the image set. Add the animation as an image on an HTML Web page. Verify the animation using a browser.
2. Rework program exercise 1 so the animations can be selected from a text file. Place the names of the GIFs in the file and activate the animation. Change the GIF names and do the animation again.
3. Create a program that combines sound and pictures using the correct multipart. Verify with a browser.
4. Using either program from exercise 1 or 2, try different methods for creating image delay. Vary the delay and validate the changes. Using argc and argv[], come up with a way to input the delay value as arguments to the program.

PROBLEMS

1. Explain boundary condition and what role it plays in the various multimodes. Show an example of a boundary condition. Explain the restrictions on boundary conditions. Why are quotes normally used around the boundary string?
2. Explain the steps required to develop an animation. What are some considerations that you might use for selecting images? What are the disadvantages of continuous animation?
3. Explain the different Content... required for mixed mode operations. Explain the ending boundary condition.

Analysis

Analysis

WHEN DEVELOPING A cgi-bin program, several stages can be identified that will increase your productivity:

- Identifying the goal
- Dividing into components
- Separating HTML components from other parts
- Identifying special applications

- Providing for debugging

- Writing the public interfaces

- Writing the private layers

- Testing the code

- Telling the Internet world

Stage 1: Identifying the Goal

THIS IS THE MOST DIFFICULT PART of the project. It is where the end product of the Internet project is identified, and it is the creative part of the process. A person who starts an Internet Web page already knows where he or she is going. The goal may be a game, such as the chess game, or the presentation of some important information. The person may have some idea about the end goal and even have some presentation material that is already available from other sources.

But the identification must go further than this basic level. In the case of the chess game, it was determined that the goal was to allow people to play chess, not just to give information about how to play chess. This is an important distinction since it determines both the kinds of Internet resources that will be needed and the level of commitment to the project that will be required.

In many ways, the goals should be based on external factors. How skilled is the developer in cgi-bin programming and in HTML? How much time is available for the project? What are the potential benefits from the project? What are the costs involved and what are the potential gains? What is the available budget? What are the estimated costs? Is this a must-complete project for school or perhaps for a paying customer? Or is it a side hobby that will be completed in the margins? Is there a modular approach that might allow different completion points to be reached? For example, the initial chess program can be used in its present state, but it might not be considered complete if the goal is to add computer algorithms so the users can play against the computer across the World Wide Web. In any event, the goal should be as clearly defined as possible. This will not mean that information obtained during development cannot be used to modify and or enhance the goal; it merely sets some direction that will be used to drive the project forward.

As you develop your goals, you should try to use words that will move you forward. Object analysis is an almost perfect fit for Web pages. If you describe your Web page as a table that displays database information, you will have an easy time picking up the table class. The other important thing is the database, so you will need to provide a database object. The word *display* suggests either the Thru mode or one of the standard HTML classes. If properly described, the Web page and the cgi-bin program will almost build themselves.

Stage 2: Dividing into Components

AN INTERNET PROJECT, PARTICULARLY THOSE involving cgi-bin programs, may require multiple components. The components can be divided into the following:

- HTML versus C++
- HTML versus cgi-bin
- Form versus output screen
- Normal output versus error legs
- CGI images versus cgi HTML
- Reusable code versus new algorithms

The better these initial breakdowns are done, the more object based and efficient the design will be. This will result in less rework and will provide valuable tools for future projects, which increases productivity.

In developing our various cgi-bin programs, every attempt has been made to follow this process. The more complex the program under development, the more detailed the level of component division. The object-oriented approach was used because it is such a powerful methodology for working these kinds of problems. But in addition, different alternatives, such as the Thru mode, were presented because a programming unit may provide unique advantages for a particular application. The standard classes also provide a foundation for persons who expect to be doing a great deal of cgi-bin work. If you are planning to do multiple applications, the more modular your software tools are, the more time you can spend doing the important task of analysis. By building good modularity, you will also be able to make better time estimates on how quickly you can deliver a grouping of Web capabilities.

Stage 3: Separating HTML Components from Other Parts

BECAUSE HTML IS A SPECIAL part of the process, it is often a good idea to create clear divisions between the HTML and the rest of the project. This will include HTML files and HTML generated from the cgi-bin program or using the Thru mode. By separating these components, clear options will emerge between the different methods discussed in this book. The Internet page developer will have organized the project in a manner that will suggest whether to use the HTML class or the Thru mode or merely to generate the HTML directly using either cout or printf to send the output to stdout. The variable sections of the HTML output can be clearly delineated and effective interfaces provided at these points.

The identification of variable parts of the HTML output is a critical part of this stage. Decisions will need to be made about whether to use hidden variables or comment messaging. The type of information that will be varied will also need to be examined. Is it a form, a table or an anchor that is going to be altered in the HTML?

During this stage you will also identify the cgi-bin components that will be used in the HTML. Will argv[] change or will all information arrive through a Post? Will there be hidden variable or nonhidden components of the HTML that will change as the result of user input or state changes? Will transition states need to be maintained in the HTML output?

Stage 4: Identifying Special Applications

IMaGe control and other special cgi-bin applications should be examined separately. These may require special testing or the development of special algorithms. Because they represent an unique cgi-bin capability, they should be treated as a separate part of the analysis. Changes in color mapping may require special GIF tools and may even need outside assistance from graphics experts. Because these types of projects are complex, a decision may be made to break them into totally separate projects. If this is the case, methods for connecting the independently developed subsections should be put in place. These need not be formal if the project is of reasonable size.

Stage 5: Providing for Debugging

EXAMINE YOUR PROJECT AND DETERMINE if any special debugging capabilities are needed. If the project is complex, logs may make sense. If the project is unique, it may make sense to talk to others in your organization about what they can provide. Some facilities may include C++ or C language debugging tools. Early discussions can save lots of future headaches.

Equally important to this process are discussions with your systems people about the use of cgi-bin space. Some facilities may only want testing during off hours. Others may have special machines that can be used to test your programs. Concerns about programs that may core dump or other problems should be discussed. Security concerns should be examined early in the cycle. Will there be requirements for inspections of code by the system administrators or by an official group?

Stage 6: Writing the Public Interfaces

THE OBJECT-ORIENTED APPROACH HAS been developed to provide a systematic way to write code. Begin by developing the classes along with the public interfaces. Examine the advantages of inheritance, overloading, and other object tools. If C is being used, develop libraries and modules that provide easy reuse. Separate into header files and source files. If large projects are being undertaken (particularly ones that are being paid for), use source control tools such as the Source Code Control System (SCCS).

Stage 7: Writing the Private Interfaces

TRADITIONALLY, IN OBJECT CODING, the private layers are the last ones written. These are the coded modules (algorithms) that do the dirty work, and they should be coded as efficiently as possible. The biggest problem on the Internet continues to be response time. Despite the enormous growth rate, service providers are unable to create bandwidth as quickly as demand requires. The result is frequent periods in which numerous systems provide slow responses. The worst thing possible would be if your cgi-bin program contributed to this problem. The use of C++ and C should virtually eliminate any performance issues. Only badly designed code could create the same effect. Good coding standards are essential in development of Internet cgi-bin pages.

Stage 8: Testing the Code

THE FIRST LEVEL OF TESTING should always be to execute the code to stdout rather than through the server. This will allow many simple problems to be eliminated early. *Dangling pointers* or other problems can be isolated early and will not be blamed on the server. The debugging techniques discussed in Chapter 17 are extremely valuable for testing code. Only after the code has been completely tested should it be placed in the cgi-bin for testing. Testing from the cgi-bin should be extensive. Again, follow the procedures discussed in Chapter 17.

Stage 9: Telling the Internet World

ONCE THE WEB PAGE IS working, announce it to the world. If it is a publicly accessible page, it can be registered with the various search engines, such as Lycos and Netscape. If it is behind a firewall and is to be used privately, use the methods available to inform the users. For some applications, it may make sense to have a small group test the Web pages prior to making them more widely available.

In this chapter you learned the nine-stage process for developing high-quality Web pages. By developing excellent methodologies, you will optimize your productivity. Figure 19.1 shows the analysis steps.

1 **Identifying the goal**
"What am I trying to accomplish?"

2 **Dividing into components**
"I want one section for new information and another for showing pictures."

3 **Separating HTML Components from Other Parts**
"Which parts are HTML? Where am I sending HTML from CGI? Am I generating images?"

4 **Identifying Special Applications**
"What am I trying to do that hasn't been done before?"

5 **Providing for Debugging**
"How will I fix any problems? How will I check out my work?"

6 **Writing the Public Interfaces**
"This does this with this."

7 **Writing the Private Interfaces**
"They don't need to know how this part works."

8 **Testing the Code**
"My web pages looks okay, but did I really test all of the error legs?"

9 **Telling the Internet World**
"I know people are going to like this page if they can find it... Let's see, there are those search engines, maybe I should see how to register."

FIGURE 19.1   Analysis: Object-oriented analysis allows systematic development of Web pages.

PROBLEMS

1. Why is analysis a critical component in the development of complex cgi-bin capabilities? Explain the various stages in analysis. What other steps do you believe will be of use in your own development of projects? Which of the analysis steps do you tend to minimize or neglect? How might you increase your use of effective analysis?

2. Explain what telling the Internet world means in the context of your projects. Who are you reaching and who are you failing to reach with your information? What can be done to improve this situation? What are some of the methods that you have seen others use to reach their audiences? What kinds of cost, time, and resource constraints are there on some of these?

3. Select an individual or group project and go through the steps of analysis. What additions did you find necessary? Where did you experience the most difficulty? What kind of additional tools might help you move through the cycle more effectively?

20

Advanced Capabilities

Complex Operations

HAVING DEVELOPED ALL THESE VARIOUS capabilities, it makes sense to look for methods to get more information from the computer over to the Internet. In this chapter methods are developed to place the input from external devices onto your Web page. Since this may be why you started looking into cgi-bin programming, you may be thinking, "It's about time." However, a word of caution should precede your reading this chapter. In Chapter 1 you were cautioned about cgi-bin programs being run by the server and therefore presenting security issues. As you begin to access the computer internals, this caution should be restated. Many of the devices discussed in this chapter could result in real problems for you if accessed incorrectly by the wrong people. While every attempt has been made to provide methods that protect against abuse, many of these techniques should only be tried by experienced people with full knowledge of the equipment being accessed.

With this caution in mind, let's examine the creation of a Complex class. The name of this class (Complex) is deliberate. It is called Complex not because it is difficult, but because it can allow you to access all the complexities of the computer world.

```
// Here is an initial COMPLEX class
class _Complex
{
private:
// physical devices
    virtual void read_rs232c(); /* read a device on the
                      s232c connector */
    virtual void read_A_to_D();
    virtual void read_mem();
// software devices
    virtual void read_file();
    virtual void lock_file();
    virtual void lock_audit();
    virtual void log();
// virtual devices
    virtual void read_cgi_in();
    virtual void analysis();
public:
    _Complex();
    virtual void interface();
};
```

About the Complex class . . . .

1. The interface subroutine is the only real public interface. This is an
   important part of the Complex class. As we will see shortly, an indirect
   interface will provide more flexibility. The interface and other routines are
   developed as virtual functions, which in C++ allows other classes that inherit
   this class to create overlay functions with additional capabilities. There is no
   equivalent to virtual functions in C. About the closest you can get is to think
   about an array of *function pointers*. Each pointer will designate one of a
   grouping of functions that all have the same basic goal (for example, access
   from the serial port). With each successive function, the serial I/O
   capabilities become increasingly sophisticated. In many ways this is the same
   as virtual functions, except that the newer functions literally overlay the
   earlier ones while sharing the same name. At the lowest level, you might
   create a serial I/O function that just retrieves a byte of data from the serial
   port. At the highest level, error checking using a cyclic redundancy check
   along with other protocol enhancements might be part of the overlayed
   function. The goal here will not be to get too specific about the nature of
   these virtuals. Instead, the focus will be on the interface between the hidden
   virtuals and the Internet.

2. The programs that interface to the computer are the private virtuals. Each of
   these functions represents a way of obtaining or sending computer-based
   information. As virtuals, they represent a generic capability that can be
   expanded later. They are created in the private area; these functions must be

protected from the Internet users. This is consistent with the strategy we will develop of isolating the computer interfaces from the general public while allowing your cgi-bin programs to use these I/O devices. A distinction has been made in the private area between physical, software, and virtual devices. This is not an essential distinction, but it will remind us about what types of devices we are using. For example, physical devices may require a lot more development time as well as the use of special library functions. Software devices may require subroutines associated with files, pipes, shared memory, etc. Finally, virtual devices may have to be developed as a standalone entity (class) along with the cgi-bin program. Some of the examples may cross over between different types. For example, an RS232C might also use a virtual device.

3. The concept of virtual devices may be new to some readers. An example might be a software light-emitting diode display. (Chapter 16, on IMaGe control, discusses examples of the use of these types of devices on the Internet.) In the example of the virtual LED, the activities of a hardware LED are created in software. This leads to the term *virtual* as opposed to *real* (as in virtual reality). This should not be confused with the use of virtual in C++. While the meaning is similar, the C++ definition is a function place holder that can provide basic functionality. The C++ virtual function can be used, or it can be replaced usually by a more complex function. This is done through inheritance. If you are new to C++, you are encouraged to read up on C++ in one of the many excellent books dedicated to this topic.

· ·

Complex Devices

THE NEXT SECTION PROVIDES AN overview of the private virtuals. These are not the only possibilities.

- read_rs232c() Suggests an input routine that will obtain information from the serial RS232C port. It is virtual to allow different devices to be put on this port and still inherit the same routine. Our virtual function will merely read the byte available on the standard RS232C port. Other routines may be created to do something with the data, use a secondary RS232C, change the baud rate or character mode, etc.

- read_A_to_D() This assumes a computer with an analog-to-digital (A-to-D) board on it. These kinds of boards are available for many computers and could be added to a server. The input to the A-to-D would contain scientific or other information that could be used for output to the Web page. The basic function is a straight read of the device; more advanced versions use the information intelligently.

- read_mem() Some systems allow shared memory resources. This could be EEPROM or other shared memory resources. Once again, our goal is to provide a basic routine and then allow inheriting classes to provide the more complex functionality.

- read_file() This virtual reads in an ASCII file. Again, the basic program will just read in the file and do nothing with it. The classes that inherit this may want to do more complex things, such as in our chess program, where the input file was formatted for chess configurations.

- lock_file() This is another important place holder, since some kind of provision will need to be made for multiple requests for these devices. For example, two people cannot read the RS232C device at the same time.

- lock_audit() Another locking requirement is for a lock when an audit occurs. An audit is a routine that occurs periodically. The advantage of using audits is that a single access device, such as the RS232C, can be read and then written to a file that is accessible to numerous people. The lock is needed to stop people from accessing the file during the short interval when it is being updated. This will assure that they do not get back half of the old data and half of the new data.

- log() Since the goal here is to create unusual conditions, creating a log makes sense. At the very least it can be used to tell how frequently the project is used. It could also be used to determine which capabilities are accessed if the program becomes complex. Finally, logs are useful for error legs. A log would tell if some resource was blocked. A common cause of blockage is the read-write capability for files and directories. If the file access is being used, the permissions have to allow the server to access the file. If this is accidentally changed, the log will tell that this has occurred. In a security application, the logs could keep records of IP addresses to assure that security breaches have not taken place.

- analysis() This is really just a place holder function. It may make more sense to make it a pure virtual, although there are some disadvantages to this approach. (For example, the new operator cannot be used to instantiate classes with pure virtuals.)

Every attempt has been made thus far to assure that the actual examples in this book do not require many extremely complex mechanisms. Because this chapter covers advanced topics, it may occasionally be necessary to venture into some advanced computer capabilities. Readers may wish to skip over these advanced discussions until basic applications have been developed. They are included in this discussion for those readers who may decide to provide highly complex applications. The tools in this book can and should lead some in this direction. These discussions have been added to assure that those people move ahead with the proper cautions. It should always be remembered that a Web page can and often will be accessed simultaneously by multiple people without sophisticated knowledge about your area of expertise.

As more complex Web capabilities are developed, it is essential to develop Internet techniques that are consistent with the object approach. The idea of data hiding so valued in C++ should be extended to the Internet. As a rule, you should make every effort to minimize the number of files that are kept in the cgi-bin area. For example, if you are using the Thru mode, it is better to place the file that will be read into the cgi-bin program in a secondary directory. While this will require additional path information in your program, it will minimize the files in the cgi-bin area. Imagine a file left in the cgi-bin with permissions for the server to write to it. What is going to stop someone from replacing it with a binary or script file that can then be run from the client side? You should minimize this concern by placing the file outside the cgi-bin area. Then changes in the file cannot be passed to the client-server software, except as Thru mode data.

Interface

As a part of this same isolation process, our first goal in providing complex capabilities will be to develop the interface() subroutine, which provides the public interface. To understand what it is that we are undertaking here, let's examine how this situation differs from our previous examples.

1. The private devices and their associated subroutines will be receiving changing information on a regular basis. This is independent of usage, access, or any other occurrences on the Internet. In our previous examples, the changes occurred because of the user submitting a form or just as the result of access to our Web page. The number of submits will change in frequency depending on the amount of Internet usage of our Web page. In complex cases, the external events are totally independent. If we are going to read weather conditions from an analog-to-digital device, the weather will change no matter what happens on our Web pages. If we are reading a monitoring device, such as a heart monitor, through a local area network (LAN) or serial device, the person's heart condition will change independent of the person reading the Web page. If we are accessing camera images from a remote camera, the IMaGes will change independent of Web activity.

2. Something in the computer will have to read the devices. You may be wondering if this was true in some of our past examples, where we read files. The answer is yes, it was true, but no, it is not the same. The difference is that the files were available to multiple people running our cgi-bin program, while devices such as an RS232C port are serial and can therefore only allow a single read at a time. If you allowed direct access to the serial device and the message *Hello Internet World* was waiting in the Univeral Asynchronous Receiver and Transmitter (UART), one person might read the *H* in hello and a second read the *e*. No one would get the entire message when more than one person was accessing at the same time. Furthermore, the hardware devices may have slow response times and issues about how they are accessed. While it would be possible to provide direct access, there are many complex issues outside the

scope of this book that would need to be considered. Figure 20.1 shows satellite data as input to a cgi-bin program. The preference here will be to isolate
the reading of devices from the Web access. As we will see, by doing this we
minimize contention issues and other issues concerning overextending the
resources of the computer.

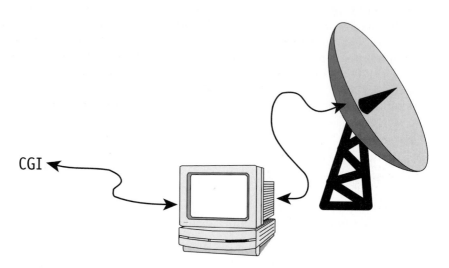

FIGURE 20.1   Advanced Capabilities: Global information sources connect to the Web
to provide widespread availability of important information.

3. If we are going to move changing information across boundaries (as yet
   unspecified), then we will need to assure that there are no periods when
   potential inconsistencies are created. For example, suppose we decided to
   change the contents of a GIF image file by changing its contents. Here we are
   referring to the situation in which the change is done from outside the cgi-
   program. This could be as simple as a manual copy of a different file into the
   same filename. Or something could be done automatically. Suppose that during the period when the changes are occurring, someone is in the process of
   reading in that file and changing its color map. If the file is changed before
   the read has been completed (remember, servers are multitasking), then the
   person could receive uninterpretable data. To assure that this is not the case,
   every effort should be taken to minimize this effect. For example, in the preceding example, it is better to change a list of GIF files in a text file than to
   change the actual GIF file. This approach will minimize the likelihood of a
   bad event. None of these factors are of any consequence if the external
   devices are never changing. It is only when change is occurring that care must
   be taken to deliver the state of the change accurately and completely.

CGI Program and Device Isolation

WITH THESE THREE FACTORS IN mind, the approach we will develop here will be to move information from devices independent of the cgi-bin program. This will be done using separate control programs. The information will be placed into *isolation files*. The cgi-bin program using the interface subroutine will access the device information by reading the created file rather than the device. In more simple terms, the cgi-bin program will read isolation files that have been prepared by other programs (for example, using cronjob). Since we have seen that files are easily managed by cgi-programs, this approach sounds promising. Most important, this approach will mean that the device is only accessed by the external programs that can be run on a predefined schedule. Our concerns about multiple people trying to access a serial device disappear if a single program reads the device and then puts it into an isolation file. The file can then be read by multiple people simultaneously. By doing this, the changes are taken in by a single program that operates without concern for events occurring on the Internet. In the example of the weather information, the analog-to-digital devices are read and their values are placed into a weather file, even when no one is accessing the associated Web page.

The goal is to move information from devices into a single file and then to move information from the file to client-server software in parallel. For the serial port, you would provide a program that reads the serial device and then writes the information in the serial device into a serial device isolation file. When someone accesses the associated Web page, the cgi-bin program reads the serial device isolation file, not the serial device. As long as the file is stable, multiple versions of the cgi-bin program can read the file and send the information to the Internet users.

While this is a major improvement over directly reading the devices, there are still potential problems. For example, we want to make sure the users do not get erroneous information during periods when the file is being updated. However, this is a manageable situation.

Putting Information into Isolation Files

THERE ARE A NUMBER OF different approaches to obtaining information from a device and putting it into a file:

1. **Use a separate program** A program can be written that will access your device and then write the data to a file. By adding an infinite loop, the program can be made to read and write the information on a regular interval. Do not get this confused with the earlier examples of cgi-bin programs. This program can run anywhere on the system and, in fact, should never be placed in the cgi-bin area.

```
#define TIME_TO_SLEEP 3600 /* 3600 second or 1 hour sleep time */
// separate program
void main()
{
    while(TRUE) // do forever
    {
        // read device
        // write file
        sleep (TIME_TO_SLEEP);
    }
}
```

After compiling, run the program in the background and with the nohup option (no hang-up will cause the program to continue even after you log off). This will assure that the program will continue even after you log off the system.

```
nohup my_device_program1 &
```

2. **In UNIX use crontab**   This is a built-in scheduler that will run a program at predefined times. The previous program is now rewritten without the sleep line and without the infinite loop. The crontab is used to provide the scheduling.

```
/* main.c - new program */
void main()
{
        // read device
        // write file
}
```

Compile this as my_program.

```
cc -o my_device_program2 main.c
    // crontab here
01 * * * 1,2,3,4,5,6,7 /unix_path/my_device_program > /dev/null
```

3. **Run the program from a looping Shell script**   This is similar to the first example except that a Shell script is used to schedule the program. This method is especially good during initial development. Later, when you have all the bugs out of your project, you can switch to the crontab option.

```
# Shell script
# Runs my_program every hour
while :
```

```
do
my_device_program2
sleep 3600
done
```

Of the three aforementioned options, the crontab option will continue even after the computer is rebooted, so it is the best option for most situations.

Transitioning the Isolation File

WHILE THESE EXAMPLES WILL WORK, there is still a period in which the information can be only partly there and the user could get bad information: the period when the file is being updated. You can improve on this situation by copying the data into a temporary file and then moving the temporary file to the real isolation file. For almost any situation, this will virtually eliminate the possibility of getting part of one file and part of the other file. This file buffer technique is extremely effective and requires little overhead.

```
/* main.c -> new program */
void main()
{
    // read device
    // write temporary file
    // move temp file to real file
}
```

In some extremely complex projects, the use of lockfiles may be required. Lockfiles are separate files that are created when the data are being changed. Any program trying to read the file will first check to see if the lockfile is present. If it is, the program delays and then checks again. This assures that during the period when material is transitioning, the cgi-bin program will not read the file. If the delay is short enough, the Internet users will not even realize when the delay occasionally occurs.

This technique would be very useful if a device was only read occasionally but the read took a relatively long time. An alternative message could be sent to people accessing the Web page during this period explaining that an update is occurring and that they should check back after an appropriate period of time.

PROBLEMS

1. What options are available to connect a Web page up to a remote camera? Remote sensors? Meters? An audio detection system?

2. What types of complex functions exist in your situation that might provide valuable information if made available through the Internet? If they should only be available for a restricted population, how would you provide security? What is a reasonable interval for accessing data? What are some of the problems that will need to be dealt with to accomplish your goal? What kind of special debugging will be needed?

3. Explain the use of virtuals in developing the complex class.

21

Porting Script and Code

Script Versus Compiled Languages

A GREAT DEAL HAS BEEN said over the years about using PERL and other script languages to develop cgi-bin capabilities. The most compelling argument for this approach has been that script languages are not compiled and therefore can be inspected. While it is true that these languages are open to inspection, the fact is that inspection methodologies are much more rigorous where compiled languages are used because compiled languages are the choice among anyone who is developing serious coding projects, while script languages are normally seen as a interim step for a project. This means that compiled languages will tend to be more transparent when it comes to error legs and potential collisions. In addition, compiled code has the obvious advantage of speed of execution. Most of the examples in this book could not be accomplished in script languages. The chess game and the IMaGe remapping require algorithms that, if implemented in script languages, would time out long before the code completed. Attempts to bring multiple images onto the screen or to access databases or other file I/O will be unlikely to succeed when multiple users begin accessing your Web sites. Swap space and other critical computer resources will be devoured when scripts are used.

All of this is not meant to say, "Do not use script languages." For many projects script languages have the advantage that they can be put in place quickly and debugged easily. This is extremely valuable when you want to get something operational quickly. You may often wish to migrate a project from HTML to script language cgi-bin and then finally to cgi-bin compiled languages. For some of your projects, you may wish to start with existing scripts that can be obtained at FTP sites or other public computer sites. Many of these will allow you to put a mailer or a WAIS in place easily.

However, once you have accomplished your initial goals, you may quickly discover that a compiled version will be more efficient. If this is the case, you need to think about the process of moving script programs to compiled programs. This is a relatively simple procedure that can be organized into a sequence of clearly defined steps.

Breaking Down the Script

1. Get an understanding of the script language and the compiled language. This will usually involve a reference text on both languages or training in both languages.
2. Identify the various modules. Some script languages, such as PERL, include subroutines. These can be identified and used as the initial structure for your compiled program. The movement from a script language to a compiled language begins with a top-down analysis. The same analysis of subparts that was necessary in the creation of a cgi-bin program should be identifiable in the analysis of a script cgi-bin program. The next section discusses some possible ways to identify components in the scripts.

Identifying Components

1. Look for the message going to the server. Since the server will not receive HTML without it, there will have to be a line that includes

   Content type: text/html

2. Look for the HTML output sections. Along with the message to the server, there will be sections that send HTML back to the browser. If you have a working script, you can run some tests from your browser, including viewing the source, to determine more about these messages.
3. Look for the input sections. These will include reads of stdin or command line arguments. There may also be environmental testing for Get versus Post.
4. Locate the interpretation sections. These will include the parsing of variables out from the user data and changing of user input to usable formats. Many script languages are very powerful in these areas (for example, PERL allows

the use of arrays with names for the array identifiers). PERL also contains some very powerful string manipulation routines.

5. Locate the conditionals and other logical operations. This is the final section of the script language. In most cases it will be easy to determine how this operates.

Having broken down the script program into its various components, you will now need to change these to your compiled language. If you can, it is always a good idea to do an object analysis before proceeding. In many instances this may be difficult at this point. The alternative is first to get a coded version operating and later rewrite an object-oriented version. Script languages are normally not object oriented. You want to avoid doing just the first part. While this will have immediate short-term gains, in time you may wish you had created more maintainable code.

Script Conversion Tricks

HERE ARE SOME TRICKS that may help with this process:

1. Script languages use a lot of environmental variables that are created inside the programs. In many cases these can be mapped into #defines in the compiled programs. The use of putenv() can also produce environmental variables.

2. Script languages do not use much variable passing between subroutines. You can create a parallel structure with lots of global variables and then push these variables down to their proper level on a second iteration of the program.

3. String routines in script languages will need to be developed in your compiled programs. Save these routines since they may be of value in future script conversions.

4. The routines system(script arguments) and popen() can be used to get around some problems that script programs will create. For example, a PERL script can call an awk script or a shell script. This means that two layers of script language will need to be handled. By using popen(), you may be able to use the secondary script during initial development.

Connecting to Existing Code

ON THE OPPOSITE END OF the spectrum is the use of existing C++ or C code. Several examples (e.g., WAIS and database connections) have already shown some of the methods used to make these connections. In actuality, the techniques are very similar to those used with scripts.

Locating stdout

Most existing C++ and C routines use stdout as the method for sending output to the user. Places where this occurs will need to be modified to include the Content... message and HTML formatting. In many instances, the best technique is to create your own routines and then substitute them for the routines throughout the program. Both output to stdout and stderr will need to be handled. One approach is to create a generic routine for handling stderr. Here is an example that will work:

```
void
stderr_message( char* output_message)
{
    cout << "Content-type: text/html\n\n";
    cout << "<HTML> <BODY>\n" <<
        "<H2>" << output_message <<
        "</H2></BODY></HTML>\n"
    exit(ERROR);
}
```

If you call the routine with a fault message, it will send the fault back to the user via the browser. Here are some examples:

```
stderr_message("Could Not Find Item in Database");
stderr_message("Could Not Complete Request");
stderr_message("Resource Unavailable at This Time");
```

Locating stdin and argv[]

These will be the inputs from your form or alternative input methods. Frequently, input options should be disabled. The Internet does not lend itself to the typical options provided by programmers. It will often make sense to use the default and disable other options. There may be exceptions, but my tendency is to look for alternative approaches. For example, in the chess program located in Appendix 2, the common mode of starting a game in a partial state is available by modifying the game start state found in one of the hidden variables. This is a much better way of providing this capability than the separate code paths provided in the original algorithms.

The stdin will also need to be examined. Since this is frequently the user's input (for example, in the chess game it is the user's move), it will need to be an input to the program. However, since forms provide the unique input strings (see Chapter 4) that require special parsing routines, you will have to modify the inputs to include clearing and decision capabilities.

Locating File Interfaces

This may prove the most difficult part of your task. Many programs use resources that are located in files, databases, etc. The best techniques for dealing with these will depend on your specific situation. There are a number of alternatives. Frequently the most simple, but potentially most risky, is to use the program files as they would normally be used. The problem with this approach will be the sharing of these files by multiple users over the Internet. A great deal of existing code is set up for the PC environment that will assume a single user. If the files are only being read, this will work (you may need to use putenv() to set up a usable environment for the server). However, if the files are being written, you will need to come up with alternative approaches. The best, but most difficult to implement, is the hidden variable file. An alternative is to use real files. This would require the use of the PID to assure unique names for multiple users. The problem with this approach is possible file cleanup problems (i.e., files may be left even after the user disconnects). Eventually, this could fill up your entire disk space.

These are only some of the many difficulties in adapting existing code to the Internet. Displays may need to be modified; timing issues may affect performance and accuracy; and so on. This should not discourage you from attempting these kinds of projects. The rewards of success in such an endeavor far outweigh the obstacles.

Conclusion

THE cgi-bin AREA HAS BEEN SHOWN to be a powerful tool for developing Internet capabilities. It is certainly not the only way to develop exciting capabilities. HTML, client capabilities, Java, and changes to the server are some of the many other ways to provide Internet enhancements. However, each of these has certain unique qualities that work best for specific applications. The cgi-bin area is clearly the best alternative for forms capabilities and for the extension of forms to other interactive capabilities. Many capabilities developed in cgi-bin initially will eventually migrate into the client-server capabilities. Examples are LOWSRC and IMaGe mapping. This is usually due to the increased popularity of these capabilities, which leads to their migration to the readily available HTML. However, as with all HTML capabilities, when this is done, numerous restrictions must be put in place to assure that there will be no danger from providing the numerous HTML users with these capabilities. This means that the user of cgi-bin control will still have access to many areas of control that are not available under HTML. In many ways, this is very similar to the distinction between script languages and compiled languages. While they often give the same types of appearances, the performance and control capabilities are much greater in the compiled languages.

When cgi-bin programs are used, the compiled programs will give significantly better performance. During development and early testing, this may appear to be unnecessary. However, when multiple people are using your cgi-bin resources at the same time, the computer can run out of resources, such as swap space. Script programs will require significantly more of these resources than compiled programs. The result will be images that only partly appear on the screen or time-outs. By using compiled programs, these problems can be virtually eliminated. This, along with the ability to connect up to the vast amount of C and C++ code already available, makes a powerful argument to provide compiled cgi-bin Internet services.

PROBLEMS

1. Explain the importance of stdin, stdout, and argv[] in changing script programs to C++ or C.

2. What are the important reasons for using compiled languages over script languages?

3. Explain the process of connecting existing C++ or C programs up to the Internet. What is the importance of stdin, stdout, and argv[] in this process? What special routines might be required to accomplish the interface (e.g., putenv())? What approach might be needed to deal with files? Error paths? Options?

4. Locate an existing script cgi-bin program and alter it to C++ or C. Once it is operational, rework the program into a more object-oriented design. (**Note**: Scripts typically are not object oriented.)

5. Locate an existing C++ or C program. Analyze the program interfaces. Separate out the parts that will need to be changed to create an Internet interface. Change as required and test with a browser.

CHAPTER 22

CGI and Java Applets

cgi-bin *or Java*

cgi-bin *and Java*

cgi-bin *Sending Java*

cgi-bin *from Java*

An Interactive Learning Environment

Sockets, Forks, and Threads

cgi-bin or Java

THROUGHOUT THIS BOOK, THERE HAVE been a number of discussions about the new Java language and its implications for cgi-bin programming. In this chapter a number of important issues relating to this topic are discussed:

1. What are the important distinctions between cgi-bin programs and Java programs?
2. In what ways can cgi-bin programs and Java programs interact?
3. What cautions are needed in developing interactive capabilities?

The primary distinction between cgi-bin and Java programs has been stated several times. The cgi-bin is a server-side capability, while the Java language is a client-side capability. To provide client-side memory for the cgi-bin, the hidden variable and hidden file methods have been provided. To provide server-side capabilities from Java, *sockets, forks,* and *threads,* which will be explained shortly, have been developed. The cgi-bin control provides no protections. A programmer can provide complete access to resources within the computer. The Java language, on the other hand, is a protected language that isolates the client from the server to protect against malicious actions.

Before continuing, it is important to make a mild digression and discuss the Java and C sockets, forks, and threads mechanism. A *socket* is a software connection between the client and server that remains present while the client is accessing the Applet associated with the server. Sockets are the backbone for all Internet client-server communications. However, in the case of an Applet, the socket connection can be maintained for as long as the Applet is active. A *fork* and a *thread* are methods for creating duplicate versions of all or some part of a program. When used with Applets, a duplicate fork or thread is created each time a new user makes a request for the same Applet. Since the forks or threads are bonded to a common program, they can provide the same information to multiple users accessing the same Applet. While this may seem to be the same as HTML and cgi-bin programs, the primary difference is that the information can be sent in *real time* since the socket connection remains in place continuously. This includes providing information from the server side. In the case of HTML, the request must be initialized from the client side. The cgi-bin can provide a similar type of server side activation (e.g., the earlier example of continuous animation). When this is done, the distinction between Java and cgi-bin is somewhat fuzzy. The main difference will be in the selection of the connection stream. A cgi-bin program allows the server to select the stream, while a Java program can request a particular socket. In the example developed later in this chapter, a teacher sends information to students as part of a continuous lesson. The use of a selected stream parallels the classroom which is a known location for the teacher.

This combination of continuous socket connections with forks and threads has both advantages and disadvantages when compared to the cgi-bin method. The advantage is that the client can be continually polled from the client or server side.[1] This means that information can be updated if changes occur on the server side. The disadvantage is that the socket is kept active as long as the client is connected to the service. If the person connects to a socket from the client side and then leaves on vacation for a week, the socket will remain active on the server. The cgi-bin program, on the other hand, is server based. This means that information sent to the client must be re-requested. Once the request has completed, the client and server will normally return to a quiescent state.[2]

The other critical factor, mentioned previously, is the level of control available through cgi-bin programs versus Java. The Java language has been deliberately made to protect against invasion of the computer resources. The cgi-bin programming relies on the programmer to create this protection. This allows greater flexibility for the cgi-bin approach when Intranet[3] capabilities are being provided and program security is less of an issue because use is already restricted. Where security is more critical, the Java approach may be preferred.

---

[1] In fact, polling can occur from either side since there is a continuous connection with programs running on both ends of the connection.

[2] The use of cgi-bin continuous animation is a violation of this principle. Because of this, it was not recommended in the chapter on animation.

[3] The term Intranet refers to private Internet facilities protected by firewalls or other forms of security. Some Java programs will not work when accessed through a firewall proxy server.

In addition, there are a number of other important distinctions. Java is its own language. While it bears resemblance to C++ and C, it is neither. It requires special compilers (javac) and has unique coding rules. This means that there are major limitations on creating interfaces to existing code. The cgi-bin programs are written in standard coding languages and can easily be interfaced to existing databases and other code. In addition, cgi-bin programs can be easily integrated with HTML, while Java tends to be a standalone entity with only limited connectivity to HTML. For example, a Java image cannot act as an HTML anchor, while a cgi-bin image can.

Perhaps the biggest advantage for Java is the machine independence of Applets. The compiled Java script is turned into a byte code that can be transferred to any server and viewed by any computer that supports Applets. This is because Java uses an interpreter rather than direct execution, as is done with compiled languages. While interpreters are significantly slower than executables, they have the advantage of portability. The cgi-bin programs must be re-compiled for each server. Since cgi-bin programs send out HTML or standard IMaGes, they are client independent; however, they must be recompiled if moved to a different server. This advantage may be overstated, since most advanced programs will end up on a single machine anyway.

Table 22.1 provides some of the critical distinctions between cgi-bin and Java. Which of the two options should be chosen? This depends on your objectives.[4]

■ Is your project more client or server focused?

■ Are you on the Intranet or Internet?

■ Do you have concerns about your programmer's ability to protect critical resources?

■ Do you have existing code that needs to be connected to your system?

■ Do you need to provide extensive HTML capabilities?

■ Do you feel more comfortable using C++ or C versus a Java compiler?

■ Do you need continual client-server updates?

■ Do you have access to C compilers and/or Java compilers?

Finally, there is the combined question of convenience and reliability. While work on Java will certainly remove some of the lack of reliability, the more thoroughly tested C++ and C compilers and debugging tools may remain the choice for many well into the future. Smaller systems will include C compilers as part of the operating system. Supporting Java compilers may require space and resources not readily available to these operators. Larger companies that can support Java may

---

[4] While this book has been written in support of cgi-bin programming, it is not meant to be a condemnation of Java. One of the major emphasis in this book is using programming skills to enhance and support nonprogramming groups who may feel very comfortable with HTML. In this respect, Java and cgi-bin programming should avoid becoming isolationist. In the early history of the Internet, access was almost solely for computer wizards. The World Wide Web supports different kinds of multimedia skills. It is critical to maintain this in the future.

TABLE 22.1: *CGI versus Java*

Capability	CGI	Java
Server control	Yes	Some through sockets
Client control	Some through hidden variables	Yes
HTML interface	Yes	Restricted—provides parallel capabilities
Computer access	Complete	Provided through sockets
User restrictions	Must be provided through programming	Yes
Programming	Standard languages— C++, C, etc.	Special language and compiler
Cross-machine compatibility	No, requires recompiling for each platform	Yes, Applets become a machine-independent byte code
Connection to existing code	Yes	Some capability through extensibility
Client save of status	Yes—save source	Not presently available
Extensive client-side programming	Limited	Yes
Connection to URLs and HTML	Direct—can be called as a URL and connected into existing HTML	Indirect—must be activated from HTML and requires special Applet HTML
Mail interface	Yes	Indirect
Restrictions	None	Access to single server only[a]
Implementation	Compiled[b]	Interpreted

[a] There are ways in Java to get around these restrictions. The lack of restrictions is often seen as a disadvantage for CGI programs in which security is an issue.

[b] Compiled code will result in a 3× faster response time. The disadvantage is machine portability. Projects for handling distributed objects, such as CORBA, could eventually combine speed with portability.

still take a wait-and-see position. This type of cautious approach is to expected where significant costs can result from implementing products in Java before thorough testing has taken place. For many on-line businesses, the forms option for taking orders will be more straightforward. Techniques, such as the Thru_mode, will provide a simple interface to HTML and IMaGes. The present thinking among some purists that Java will replace cgi-bin is highly unlikely. The more likely future is combinations of both capabilities.[5]

---

[5] One other disadvantage of Java is a complex network. While cgi-bin programs can be used across network file system (NFS) mounted systems, Java programs must be placed on the server to provide server-side capabilities through threads and sockets. This can actually mean less security for Java applications as compared to cgi-bin programs.

cgi-bin and Java

BECAUSE cgi-bin AND JAVA PROGRAMMING are distinct, there are a number of places where use of both capabilities may make sense. There are several basic ways that these languages can interface:

- cgi-bin programs that send Java Applets out as part of the HTML sent from the server to the client. In this instance, the cgi-bin program can be used to change Applet parameters or even the requested Applet.
- cgi-bin programs sent from a Java Applet. Since Java includes the capability to send out URLs for either HTML or IMaGes, it is possible to have a Java script send out a cgi-bin URL.

These basic building blocks could also be combined to allow both capabilities to be used simultaneously and interactively. The learning environment case study at the end of the chapter takes advantage of this. It combines the threads and sockets used to establish a client-server communications path between a Java application on the client side and a C application on the server side, with an isolation file for communication between the same C program on the server side and a cgi-bin program on the server side. This is a very complex example, but is worth study time since it illustrates a number of important capabilities in a single example.

cgi-bin Sending Java

FROM THE POINT OF VIEW OF HTML, a Java Applet has the following structure:[6]

```
<APPLET CODEBASE="http://internet_path/"
CODE="myApplet.class" WIDTH=20 HEIGHT=20>
<ALT="http://internet_path/no_applet.html">
<NAME="myApplet" >
<ALIGN="top">
<VSPACE=10>
<HSPACE=5>
<PARAM VALUE="anywords" >
<PARAM VALUE="image/someimage.gif">
</APPLET>
```

```
/*
 * Type C code function
 *
 * Use: Send the HTML to activate an Applet
```

---

[6] This was also included in the Chapter 11.

```c
    */
char* applet(
    char* codebase,     /* Optional field specifying the base URL of the APPLET. If not
                         * specified, current documents URL is used.
                         */
    char* code,     /* Required applet class name, it must be relative to the codebase */
    char* width,    /* Required width of applet frame on screen */
    char* height,   /* Required height of applet frame on screen */
    char* alt,      /* Optional alternative text if APPLETS are not supported */
    char* name,     /* Name fields allows APPLET to communicate to another APPLET */
    char* align,    /* Alignment on the page—same as IMG align */
    char* vspace,   /* Margin above—same as IMG vspace */
    char* hspace,   /* Margin to side—same as IMG hspace */
    int count,      /* Number of parameters */
    char* param,    /* Multiple parameters and */
    char* value,     * Multiple value fields for the parameter. These can be used to allow
                     * APPLETS to communicate to each other or to provide input
                     * information to the APPLET */

    ...
        )
{
char msg_buffer[MAXLINE];

    sprintf( msg_buffer,
        "<APPLET ", "CODEBASE=\"", codebase,"\" ",
        "CODE=\"", code, "\"",
        (width==NULL ? " " : "WIDTH=\""), width, "\"",
        (height=NULL ? " " : "HEIGHT=\""), height, "\"",
        " [ALT=" << alt << "] ",
        " [NAME=" << name << "] ",
        " [ALIGN=" << align <<"] ",
        " [VSPACE=" << vspace <<"] ",
        " [HSPACE=" << hspace <<"] ",
        ">";
    while(count-- > 0)
    {
        sprintf(msg_buffer,
            "<PARAM name=\",
            /* varargs routine here */
            "value=\"",
            /* varargs routine here */
    }
    sprintf(msg_buffer, "</APPLET>\n");
    printf(msg_buffer);
}
```

```
/*
 * Type: C Code Main
 *
 * Use: Create an HTML Web Page with an Applet
 */
void main()
{
    printf(
        "Content-type: html/text\n\n",
        "<HTML><TITLE> Test Applet </TITLE>\n"
        "<BODY>\n",
        "<H1>This HTML will call up an Applet</H1>";
    applet(
        "http://internet_path/",
        "myApplet.class",
        "20",
        "20",
        "myApplet",
        "",   /* no optional align, vspace or hspace */
        "",
        "",
        "myParam"
    );
    printf(
        "</BODY></HTML>\n"
    );
}
```

Since this routine can be sent as the output from a cgi-bin program, it is possible to select different Applets or provide different parameters. These choices can be provided from a form using either the Get or Post methods or as argc and argv[] using the ?args along with the cgi-bin call.

In the next example, five different Applets have been set up as part of a learning environment. The user selects which Applet will be viewed from a form. The output of the form is sent to a cgi-bin program, which then sends back the required Applet. (See Figure 22.1.)

1. The client browser sends a request to the sever for a URL with Content-type of HTML.

2. The HTML is retrieved and sent from the server to the client.

3. The client recognizes the type as HTML and sends it to the interpreter. It is then placed on the user's screen.

4. In this instance, the HTML is a form. The user is given a choice of five different Java Applets. The user makes a selection and submits the form.

5. The form request is sent to the server using either Post or Get. The server uses the action field to activate the cgi-bin program.

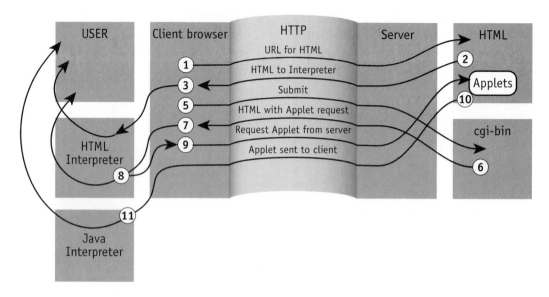

FIGURE 22.1   cgi Sending Java: The cgi-bin program sends out Java Applet requests allowing control over the Applet's parameters.

6. The cgi-bin program uses the user request to send back the HTML to the client. The HTML associated with the requested Applet is included.

7. The client receives the HTML and sends it to the HTML interpreter. The HTML interpreter sends the text back to the screen. It also recognizes the request for the Applet.

8. This Java Applet request is sent to the client, which then sends a request to the server for the Applet. If the Applet is already present, the request will not be sent.

9. The Applet is sent from the server to the client.

10. The client passes the Applet to the Java Applet interpreter.

11. The Applet is placed on the user's screen or provided to the user as multimedia, depending on the Applet.

```
HTML APPLET REQUEST FORM
<HTML><HEAD><TITLE><Applet Request Form</TITLE></HEAD>
<BASE HREF="http://internet_path/" ><BODY>
<H1> Select the Applet to run </H1>
<FORM ACTION="cgi_applet" METHOD="post" >
<INPUT TYPE="radio" NAME="applet" VALUE="1" > Basic Geometry Applet
<BR>
<INPUT TYPE="radio" NAME="applet" VALUE="2"> Mid-Level Geometry Applet
<BR>
```

```
<INPUT TYPE="radio" NAME="applet" VALUE="3"> Advanced Geometry Applet
<BR>
<INPUT TYPE="radio" NAME="applet" VALUE="4"> Calculus and Geometry Applet
<BR>
<INPUT TYPE="radio" NAME="applet" VALUE="5">Tensor Geometry Applet
<INPUT TYPE="submit"> <INPUT TYPE="reset">
</FORM>
<BR>
</BODY></HTML>
```

```c
/*
 * Type: cgi-bin program
 *
 * Use; respond to form request; send back HTML for Applet request
 */
void main()
{
    char buffer[MAXLINE];
    char choice[MAXLINE];
    int userchoice = 0;/* set to default */
    /* Send out the starting HTML */
    printf("Content-type: html/text\n\n ");
    /* retrieve form request */
    gets(buffer);
    /* which choice */
    choice=getvariable(choice, buffer, "VALUE=");
    /* Check which choice */
    /* Alternatively, userchoice = *choice-'0' */
    if ( check_msg( choice, "1")
        userchoice=1;
    else
    if ( check_msg( choice, "2")
        userchoice=2;
    else
    if ( check_msg( choice, "3")
        userchoice=3;
    else
    if ( check_msg( choice, "4")
        userchoice=4;
    else
    if ( check_msg( choice, "5")
        userchoice=5;
    /* send out the HTML */
    printf(
        "<HTML><HEAD><TITLE>");
    switch (userchoice)
```

```
{
    case 1:
        printf("Basic Geometry");
        break;
    case 2:
        printf("Mid-Level Geometry");
        break;
    case 3:
        ...
    default:
        printf("Bad Request");
}
printf("</TITLE></HEAD><BODY>\n");
printf("<H1>");
switch(userchoice)
{
    case 1:
        printf("Basic Geometry");
        break;
    case 2:
        ...
    case 3:
        ...
    default:
        printf("Bad Request");
}

printf("/H1>\n");
switch(userchoice)
{
    case 1:
        applet(
            "http://internet_path/",
            "myApplet1.class",
            "20", "20", 0, "", "", "", "",...);
        break;
    case 2:
        applet(
            "http://internet_path/",
            "myApplet2.class",
            "20", "20", 0, "", "", "", "",...);
        break;
    case 3:
        ...

    default:
        printf("No available Applet\n");
```

```
                break;
        /* send completion of HTML */
        printf("</BODY></HTML>\n");
    }
```

The specifics of the Applet are left to Java programmers.

cgi-bin from Java

IN THE NEXT EXAMPLE, THE Java Applet sends out an URL request for an IMaGe. In this instance, the URL request is for a cgi-bin program to send out the IMaGe. (See Figure 22.2.)

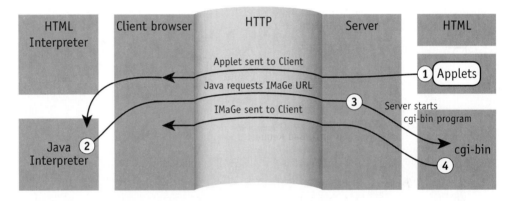

FIGURE 22.2   Java Requests cgi IMaGe: The Java program requests a cgi-bin IMaGe which is then altered under program control.

1. The Java Applet is sent out from the server side. This could involve the earlier sending of Applets from HTML as part of the process.
2. The Applet interpreter sees a request for an IMaGe URL. The request is sent back to the server.
3. The server interprets the request as an IMaGe to come from a cgi-bin program. It starts up the cgi-bin program.
4. The cgi-bin program does database lookups, etc., and determines what IMaGe it is supposed to send back. The IMaGe is sent back to the client, where it is displayed on the screen.[7]

---

[7]   The example uses an IMaGe request, but it could have used other media.

This sample Applet provides the fundamentals of how to provide this capability. The interested reader should consult additional material on Java programming before continuing with this example.

```
// Java Applet CGI_image.Java
import java.awt.*;
import java.awt.image.*;
import java.net.*;
public class CGI_image extends Applet{
    Image img;              // image data type
    String url = "http://internet_path/cgi-bin/image_prog";
    public void init() {
        try { img=getImage(new URL(url));
        } catch (MalformedURLException e) {
        }
    }
    public void paint(Graphics g) {
        showStatus("drawImage: "+url);
        g.drawImage(img,0,0,this);
    }
}
```

Compile javac CGI_image.java[8]

Here is the HTML to call this Applet:

```
<HTML><HEAD><TITLE>CGI & Applet</TITLE>
</HEAD><BODY>
<!- Applet Here -->
<APPLET
 code="CGI_image.class" width=278 height=96 >
 </APPLET>
CGI Image From an Applet
</BODY></HEAD>
```

The HTML is started by requesting the URL for the Web page. When the HTML is sent from the server to the client, the browser HTML interpreter puts out an HTTP request to the server for the CGI_image Applet. The Applet is sent to the client. The Applet interpreter recognizes the request for a URL IMaGe. It sends a request back to the server. The server identifies the IMaGe URL as a program in the cgi-bin. It runs the program and sends the IMaGe output back to the client browser. It is then displayed in the Applet window. The cgi-bin program is not shown. (Examples of IMaGe output control from cgi-bin programs can be found in Chapter 16.)

---

[8]   Java files must have the same name as the primary class with a .java extension (in this case, DoImage.java. The Java compiler (javac) is required to compile the Applet into the class DoImage.class.

Case Study: Learning Environment

In the next example, HTML, cgi-bin, and Java are combined to create a total learning environment. To provide a traditional learning environment, a teacher with multiple students in an electronic classroom is provided. The lessons are passed from the teacher to the learning pool using cgi-bin forms. A continually connected threaded socket is set up to each of the students so that the information from the teacher can be passed out through an Applet interconnection. The subsections are as follows:

HTML Frames

The HTML Frames capability provides separate areas (similar to Windows) inside your browser environment. Each Frame can be used separately to access different Internet resources. These can be URLs associated with HTML Web pages, cgi-bin programs, and Java Applets. For the learning environment, the following Frames are created:

1. **Frame 1** The basic output Frame is used to send information to be learned to the users. The information is sent from a server-side C program that connects through threads to a client-side Java Applet. This is the only section shown in this example; the other frames are left as exercises at the end of the chapter.

   - **Java Applet1** This Applet is connected via a socket to the server-side C program. It provides the user with lessons. On the server side, a C++ or C program acts as the server side of the socket. This is allowed since sockets can be implemented on the server side in any legitimate language. Because a C program is used, an isolation file can also be created that will allow the instructor to modify the Applet's behavior through a form interface to a cgi-bin program.

   - **C socket and fork (or thread) program** This program runs on the server side. It sends information to the Java Applet1 running in the first HTML frame window.

2. **Frame 2** The question Frame provides access to a form from which questions can be entered by the students. It uses a standard cgi-bin form interface to send the questions. The questions are viewed by the teacher through a separate cgi-bin program.

3. **Frame 3** The third Frame shows the users' questions queued up in the order they were asked. The program for this is left to the readers.

4. **Frame 4** The answer Frame allows the teacher to answer questions in the order asked. A reference number is connected to each answer to show which question is being answered. This is also to be implemented by the readers.

5. **cgi-bin Program1** This program is an interface for the instructor. It accepts requests from the teacher and then modifies the Applet's behavior using the

isolation file to send information through the server side of the socket and thread program. The instructor places information into the isolation file using a teacher cgi-bin program. The isolation file is then read by the C program that interfaces to the Java Applets being run by the students. If the information in the isolation file has changed, the thread and socket program sends the new information out to the students.

6. Other interfaces include a way to send the users' questions out to the students along with the teacher's answers. This is left for a project to be done by the readers.

As is evident, this is a very complex project that has been provided to show the levels available when different capabilities are combined into a single project. To understand how a project such as this would be implemented requires an understanding of how cgi-bin programs and socketed Java Applets can communicate. While only the programs required for the main Frame (i.e., the socketed communication between the server-side C code and the client-side Applet) are shown, this constitutes the major part of the project.

Sockets, Forks, and Threads

A socket is a stream network connection. Sockets are the method used for communications on the Internet. When URLs are used, a socket provides a short-term or connectionless communication interface between the client and server. This results in the memoryless protocol associated with HTML and cgi-bin programs. However, there is a second kind of socket interface that stays active for the life of the client-server interconnect. This connection-based socket is what Java can provide. In essence, a private client-server interface is set up. There are presently two types of connection sockets provided by Java.

- Datagram connections are easily established, but provide no validation that the data have reached the other end of the connection. Datagrams are also called UDP (unreliable datagram protocol).
- Stream connections are more complex, but guarantee end-to-end integrity of the data being sent.

Because the Applet may be run by multiple users simultaneously, the server side of the program must provide multiple connections of the same type. This is done using the C language fork. The fork call creates a new version of the program each time a connection is established. Since a single socket can support more than one user, this is perfectly acceptable.

In addition, Java provides threaded processes. A threaded program allows a part of the program to run by itself. This can be used to provide animation or other activities that must run over and over again. A thread differs from a fork in that the initial program continues to function in parallel with the thread. In the case of a fork, the original program is reproduced; in the case of a thread, only a part of the program is reproduced. The fork is needed on the server side, so a new version of the server-side socket program will be available in the event that another user requested the Applet. Recall that the initial version creates the fork when the connection is established to a new Applet request from the client. A thread can serve the same function as a fork, but includes other capabilities (e.g., the ability to recreate only a part of the code). While threads are increasingly replacing forks, the use of forks in the present example provides valuable C++ or C interfaces on the server side. Since compiled code runs faster than interpreted code, there are definite advantages to using C++ or C on the server side. Many systems do not support threads for C++ and C.

In the case of Applets, a request occurs each time a new user starts up the specific Applet.[9] The use of connection sockets with forks or threads allows intercommunications to take place between a single server and multiple clients. This provides a capability similar to traditional media, such as TV and radio. This differs from the normal client-server interface provided by HTML, since the socket and thread remains active as long as the client-side browser is on the Web page that activated the Applet associated with the socket. Only by leaving the Web page and/or stopping the Applet will the socket be broken. Since sockets are created with program threads, all connections to the Applet will exist simultaneously. This means that the server can send messages out to the various clients. In many ways, this contradicts the earlier statement that Applets are totally client based. This is the single exception to that rule. When a socket is activated, the server and client have a communication path available. However, the Applet is running and being interpreted on the client side.

Figure 22.3 shows the communications paths.

1. A socket fork or thread is created between each of the students and the server socket.

2. The students' Applets provide a continuous stream of information on the subject. This can be client-side polled or server-side generated.

3. If the teacher wishes to change the material content, a CGI form request is sent to the cgi-bin program. An isolation file creates a bridge between the output of the cgi-bin form and the input to the C socket program. Information from the teacher is placed into the isolation file by the cgi-bin program, and then the same information is retrieved from the isolation file by the server socket program. A protocol (not shown in the example) is needed to establish when new information has been added to the isolation file. Since the fork created clones of the original server C program, the isolation file information will be sent to each of the users.

---

[9] The code provided here includes a limit on the number of threads allowed. In real applications, several methods are used to limit the number of threads. One method is first come, first served up to the limit allowed. Once the limit is reached, no one else is allowed access. An alternative method is to bump the first person when the limit is exceeded by one, the second person when the limit is exceeded by two, etc. This method stops people from staying on the service too long.

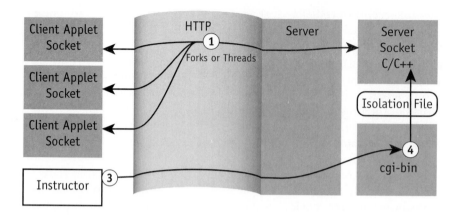

FIGURE 22.3   Sockets: The use of sockets provides a continuously updating multi-user connection.

4. Not shown in Figure 22.3 is the student's ability to ask questions using a separate form that appears in one of the other FRAME windows. Also missing from the figure is a form that allows the students to see answers to questions sent by the instructor. To avoid too much resource demand, each of these is done on demand using forms. This allows the socketed Applet to function only as the education channel.

```
/*
 * Server-Side Socket and Fork Program
 * The HTML, C Code, and Applets in this section are modifications of code provided by
 * Robert Klein.
 * Type: C Program
 * The server side program runs in a continuous loop. It does the following: If a client-side
 * Applet is started from the browser, a new thread is created that provides communications
 * on the socket to the Applet. The thread includes code to check the isolation file, which
 * can be changed through the cgi-bin program. If a change is made, the thread transmits
 * the change out to all users through the enabled threads on the socket.
 */

#include <sys/types.h>
#include <sys/socket.h>
#include <netinet/in.h>
#include <netdb.h>
#include <stdio.h>
#include <signal.h>
#include <sys/errno.h>
#include <dirent.h>
#include <stdio.h>
```

```
extern int errno;
extern char *tzname[];
extern char *getcwd(char*,int);
/*
 * This number must match the number used in the Applet. Certain sockets may be reserved
 * on a particular system. In general, lower numbers are available for general usage.
 */
#define ISSD_SOCKET 2658
/* The maximum number of users for this service */
#define MAX_ISSD_CONNECTIONS 10
/* The names of services that will be part of the connection */
static char hostname[64];
static char domain_name[256];
static char rhostname[64];
static char ihostaddr[64];
/* The number of active connections */
static int nbr_connections = 0;
/* These will get set when the connection is established */
static int server_socket = -1;
static int connection_sock = -1;
/* buffers, pointers, and counters for sending messages back and forth */
static char input_buffer[10*1024];
static char output_buffer[10*1024];
static char *resp_ptr;
static char *arg_ptr;
static int resp_length;
/* available for debug or general logging of events
void
log_msg(char* mystring)
{
    FILE *fileptr;
    fileptr = fopen("unix_path/logfile", "a");
    fprintf(fileptr, "%s", mystring;
    fclose(fileptr);
}
int
readsocket ( int infile, char *buf_ptr, int maxchars )
{
    char nbytes[10];
    int nbr_bytes;
    char c;
    char *cptr;
    nbr_bytes = 0;
    cptr = nbytes;
    while (read(infile,(char *)&c,1) > 0) {
        *cptr++ = c;
```

```
            if (c == '\n') {
                int i;
                sscanf(nbytes,"%d\n",&nbr_bytes);
                if (nbr_bytes > maxchars)
                    nbr_bytes = maxchars;
                cptr = buf_ptr;
                for (i=0; i<nbr_bytes; i++) {
                    read(infile,(char *)&c,1);
                    *cptr++ = c;
                };
                return(nbr_bytes);
            };
        };
        return(-1);
}


/* Termination routine if a signal is caught */
static void terminate ( int sig )
{
        if (server_socket >= 0)
            close(server_socket);
        exit(sig);
}

static void reapchild ( int sig )
{
        int status;
        while ((wait(&status) > 0) && (nbr_connections > 0))
            nbr_connections--;
        signal(SIGCHLD,reapchild);
}


/*
 * This routine sends a buffer out to the Applet(s). The buffer is built using general buffer
 * building routines.
 */
static void put_response ( )
{
        char size[12];
        output_buffer[resp_length++] = '\n';        /* terminate the buffer */
        sprintf(size, "%10d", resp_length);

        if (write(connection_sock, size, 10) < 0)
            terminate(0);
        if (write(connection_sock, output_buffer, resp_length) < 0)
            terminate(0);
```

```
}
/*
 * General purpose routines for putting different kinds of information into the
 * buffer before sending it to the Applet.
 */
void
put_response_int ( int value )
{
    int len;
    sprintf(resp_ptr,"%d",value);
    len = strlen(resp_ptr);
    resp_ptr += len;
    *resp_ptr = '\0';
    resp_ptr++;
    resp_length += len + 1;
}
void
put_response_buffer ( char *buf, int nbytes )
{
    memcpy(resp_ptr,buf,nbytes);
    resp_ptr += nbytes;
    *resp_ptr++ = '\0';
    resp_length += nbytes + 1;
}
void
put_response_string ( char *value )
{
    int len;
    sprintf(resp_ptr,"%s",value);
    len = strlen(resp_ptr);
    resp_ptr += len;
    *resp_ptr = '\0';
    resp_ptr++;
    resp_length += len + 1;
}
/*
 * The main routine for servicing a connection to an Applet. This routine will be recreated as
 * a new thread for each new Applet request up to the maximum allowed.
 */
static void service_connection ( )
{
    int optval;
    char *cp, *s;
    int len;
    /* Used by isolation file */
    FILE *fileptr;
```

```
char data_buffer[MAXLENGTH];
/*
 * Set up the keep alive signal to the Applet. This will maintain connectivity for the life
 * of the Applet.
 */
optval = 1;
setsockopt(connection_sock,
      SOL_SOCKET,
      SO_KEEPALIVE,
      (char *)&optval,
      sizeof(optval));

/*
 * Signals that will terminate the thread when the Applet is no longer in use.
 */
signal(SIGQUIT,SIG_IGN);
signal(SIGTERM,SIG_IGN);
signal(SIGPIPE,terminate);
/*
 * Set up the receive and transmit streams to the Applet. These allow communications
 * to take place to and from the Applet.
 */
optval = sizeof(input_buffer);
setsockopt(connection_sock,
      SOL_SOCKET,
      SO_RCVBUF,
      (char *)&optval,
      sizeof(optval));
optval = sizeof(output_buffer);
setsockopt(connection_sock,
      SOL_SOCKET,
      SO_SNDBUF,
      (char *)&optval,
      sizeof(optval));
/*
 * Look for a request to be intialized from the Applet side. Coding can be done to
 * communicate initially from the server side, if necessary. Just comment out this
 * section and start by generating a server-side message.
 */
/* Begin wait for client side message */
while ((len=readsocket(connection_sock,
      input_buffer,
      sizeof(input_buffer))) > 0) {
           int response_type;
           int request_id;
           if (input_buffer[len-1] == '\n') {
```

```
                        input_buffer[len-1] = '\0';
                        len--;
            };
            resp_ptr = output_buffer;
            resp_length = 0;
            arg_ptr = input_buffer;
            response_type = -1;
            request_id = -1;
            if (sscanf(arg_ptr,"%d",&response_type) <= 0)
                continue; /* invalid request, ignore!! */
            arg_ptr += strlen(arg_ptr) + 1;
            if (sscanf(arg_ptr,"%d",&request_id) <= 0)
                continue; /* invalid request, ignore!! */
            switch (response_type) {
            /* Place the responses to the Applet here */
                case 0:
                break;
                case 1:
                /**************************************************
                 *          ISOLATION FILE CODE
                 */
                /* READ AND SEND THE ISOLATION FILE */
                fileptr=fopen("unix_path/isolation_file",
                    "r");
                fgets(fileptr, data_buffer, MAXLENGTH);
                fclose(fileptr);
                /* put the response into the buffer */
                put_response_string(data_buffer);
                /* send the buffer to the Applet */
                put_response();
                /**************************************************
                 *          END ISOLATION FILE CODE
                 */
            break;
            default:
                /* put some response into the buffer */
                put_response_string("shallom internet world");
                /* send the buffer to the Applet */
                put_response();
            break;
            };
        };
        /* End wait for server-side connection */
        close(connection_sock);
        return;
    }
```

```
/*
 * In the C main routine, allowance is made for optional arguments even though
 * code is not included here for using them. The use of getoptions for handling
 * command line arguments is included in other sections of the text and in
 * most standard books on C++ and C programming.
 */
main ( int argc, char *argv[] )
{
    /* Required data types to create the connection to the Applet */
    struct sockaddr_in server;
    struct sockaddr_in client;
    int rval;
    int optval;
    int i;
    /* parse input arguments—not shown here */
    /* available to handle command line arguments */
    if (argc != 1) {
        exit(1);
    };
    /* enable this is you want only root to run this program */
    /*
    if (geteuid() != 0) {
        exit(1);
    };
    */
    umask(0022); /* only daemon can read/write data files */
    gethostname(hostname,sizeof(hostname));
    /* set up input/output connection socket */
    /*
     * socket creates an end point for communications
     * and returns a descriptor
     */
    server_socket = socket(AF_INET, SOCK_STREAM, 0);
    if (server_socket < 0) exit(1);
    /* name socket */
    server.sin_family = AF_INET;
    server.sin_addr.s_addr = INADDR_ANY;
    /* SMTP input connnections on port ISSD_SOCKET */
    server.sin_port = htons(ISSD_SOCKET);
    optval = 1;
    /* set the socket options */
    setsockopt(server_socket,
        SOL_SOCKET,
        SO_REUSEADDR,
        (char *)&optval,
        sizeof(optval));
```

```
/* bind the socket to the address */
if (bind(server_socket,
 (struct sockaddr *)&server,
 sizeof(server)) < 0) exit(1);

/*
 * listen defines the maximum number of connections that can be established.
 */
listen(server_socket,MAX_ISSD_CONNECTIONS);
/* Catch any critical signals that arrive */
signal(SIGTERM,terminate);
signal(SIGQUIT,SIG_IGN);
signal(SIGHUP,SIG_IGN);
/* run in the background as a daemon */
/*
 * set process group for the main process to a background process.
 */
setpgrp(0,0);
close(0);
close(1);
close(2);
/*
 * The fork creates a child process that is an exact copy of the original process.
 */
if (fork()) exit(0);
signal(SIGCHLD, reapchild);

/* loop forever until we get a termination signal */
while (1) {
    optval = sizeof(client);
    /* wait for a connection from an Applet */
    /*
     * accept takes the first connection waiting on the queue and creates a new
     * socket with the same properties as the original.
     */
    connection_sock = accept(server_socket,
        (struct sockaddr *)&client,&optval);
    if (connection_sock >= 0) { /* got a valid connection */
        int chpid;
        if ((chpid = fork()) == 0) {
            unsigned char *cptr;
            struct hostent *hp;

            /* child process handling
             connection */
            close(server_socket);
```

```
server_socket = -1;
setpgrp(0,0);
/* set remote host name on other
 end of the connection */
cptr =
     (unsigned char *)&client.sin_addr;
sprintf(ihostaddr,"[%d.%d.%d.%d]",
     *cptr,
     *(cptr+1),
     *(cptr+2),
     *(cptr+3));
/*
 * gethostbyaddr returns a
 * pointer to the binary
 * address of the host computer.
 */
hp = gethostbyaddr(
     (char *)&client.sin_addr,
     sizeof(struct in_addr),
     client.sin_family);
if (hp == NULL)
/* used dotted notation */
     strncpy(rhostname,
      ihostaddr,
      sizeof(rhostname));
else
     strncpy(rhostname,
          hp->h_name,
          sizeof(rhostname));
     service_connection();
     exit(0);
};
/*
 * maintain a counter of the number of connections established.
 */
if (chpid > 0)
     nbr_connections++;
else {

     ;
};
/* daemon parent goes to accept next connection */
close(connection_sock);
connection_sock = -1;
}
else { /* connection socket error! */
     if (errno != EINTR) {
```

```
                        /* reset server socket */
                        close(server_socket);
                        server_socket = -1;
                        /* reset input/output connection socket */
                        server_socket = socket(AF_INET, SOCK_STREAM, 0);
                        if (server_socket < 0) exit(1);
                        /* name socket */
                        server.sin_family = AF_INET;
                        server.sin_addr.s_addr = INADDR_ANY;
                        server.sin_port = htons(ISSD_SOCKET);
                        /* SMTP input connnections on port ISSD_SOCKET */
                        optval = 1;
                        setsockopt(server_socket,
                             SOL_SOCKET,
                             SO_REUSEADDR,
                             (char *)&optval,
                             sizeof(optval));
                        if (bind(server_socket,
                             (struct sockaddr *)&server,
                             sizeof(server)) < 0) exit(1);
                        listen(server_socket,MAX_ISSD_CONNECTIONS);
                        };
                };
            };
        }
```

The Applet is set up to provide the other side of the connection. Because forks or
threads are being used, multiple users can be communicating and receiving information from the same Applet. The Applet consists of two parts. The communications and creation of general purpose routines is done in the package mysocket. An
Applet package is similar to a C++ or C library; it contains general-purpose classes
that can be made available to the Applet. The second section of the Java code is the
actual Applet. It is accessed through the HTML and uses the classes and public class
subroutines found in the mysocket package.

```
    /* Applet Code
     * Type Package
     */
    package mysocket;
    // These are usable built in resources
    import java.lang.*;
    import java.net.*;
    import java.io.*;
    import java.applet.*;
    /* This is the public class. This file must have the name mysocket.java. It must compile into
     * the file mysocket.class. It must be placed in a directory named mysocket. The Java Applet
```

```
   * will then be able to use this compiled file.
   */
public class mysocket{
     /*
      * Public Declarations
      * These are used in the main applet. The use of the word "main" is not strictly correct
      * since there is no main() in the Applet code.
      */
     public static String data = "";
     public static booleanConnected = false;
     /*
      * Private Declarations used inside the mysocket package
      */
     // This number must match the port in the server C code
     private static final int port = 2658;
     // created to provide connection to the server
     private static Socket socket;
     private static String server_host;
     private static DataInputStream in = null;
     private static DataOutputStream out = null;
     // general-purpose variables for communications
     private static final String separator = "\0";
     private static int next_arg_start;
     private static int next_arg_end;
     /*
      * This public constructor allows the Java Applet code to use this package. When the
      * class is created by each activation of the Applet from HTML, the constructor
      * establishes a connection to the server. As a result, the server generates a new fork or
      * thread back to the Applet.
      */
     public mysocket(Applet parent) {
          // should only run to create a connection
          if (Connected == true)
               return;
          /*
           * Get the name of the host computer. The server and the Applet must reside on
           * the same host to establish a socket connection. This is part of the Java security.
           */
          server_host = parent.getCodeBase().getHost();
          try {
               // establish the socket connection
               socket = new Socket(server_host, port);
               }
          // Java provides extensive exception handling
          catch (IOException e) {
               shutdown();
```

```
                return;
            };
        try {
            // establish the send and receive streams
            in = new
                DataInputStream(socket.getInputStream());
            out = new
                DataOutputStream(socket.getOutputStream());
            }
        catch (IOException e) {
            shutdown();
            return;
        };
        Connected = true;
    };
    /*
     * A public routine available to shut down the connection. It will only discontinue the
     * single connection between the user and the server. It does not shut down the server
     * side.
     */
    public void shutdown() {
        if (Connected == true) {
            try {
                in.close();
                out.close();
            }
            catch (IOException e) {
            };
            Connected = false;
            if (socket != null) {
                try {
                    socket.close();
                }
                catch (Exception e) {
                };
            };
        };
        in = null;
        out = null;
        socket = null;
    };
    // Send a string to the server side
    private void send_data(String str) throws IOException,
        SecurityException {
        int i;
        int len = str.length();
        String str_len;
```

```
        int llen;
        str_len = Integer.toString(len);
        llen = str_len.length();
        for (i=0; i<llen; i++) {
            byte b = (byte)str_len.charAt(i);
            out.writeByte(b);
        };
        out.writeByte((byte)'\n');
        for (i=0; i<len; i++) {
            byte b = (byte)str.charAt(i);
            out.writeByte(b);
        };
    };
    /* receive data from the server side */
    private String recv_data() throws IOException, SecurityException
    {
        int msgLength = 0;
        int i = 0;
        StringBuffer str = new StringBuffer();
        StringBuffer size = new StringBuffer();
        for (i=0; i<10; i++) {
            char c = (char)in.readByte();
            if (i <= 9 && Character.isDigit(c))
                size.append(c);
        };
        msgLength = Integer.parseInt(size.toString());
        for (i=0; i<msgLength; i++) {
            char c = (char)in.readByte();
            if (i < msgLength-1) str.append(c);
        };
        return str.toString();
    };
    /* server service request interface methods */
    public void put_buffer ( byte buf[], int nbytes ) {
        int i;
        StringBuffer arg = new StringBuffer();
        for (i=0; i<nbytes; i++)
            arg.append((char)buf[i]);
        data = data + arg.toString();
        data = data + separator;
    };
    public void get_buffer ( byte buf[], int nbytes ) {
        String arg;
        int i;
        arg =
        data.substring(next_arg_start,
            next_arg_start+nbytes);
```

```java
            next_arg_start = next_arg_start + nbytes;
            next_arg_end = data.indexOf(separator,next_arg_start);
            for (i=0; i<nbytes; i++)
                    buf[i] = (byte)arg.charAt(i);
            };
    public void initialize_request ( int service_id, int request_id ) {
            data = Integer.toString(service_id) +
                    separator +
                    Integer.toString(request_id) +
                    separator;
    };
    /* Place a string in the data buffer */
    public void put_arg ( String arg_value ) {
            data = data + arg_value;
            data = data + separator;
    };
    /* Send the data to the server side */
    public boolean put_request () {
            try {
                    data = data + "\n";
                    send_data(data);
            }
            catch (Exception e) {
                    return(false);
                    /* request transmit failed! */
            };
            return(true); /* request was sent okay! */
    };
    /* Get data from the server side */
    public boolean get_response ( ) {
            try {
                    data = recv_data();
            }
            catch (Exception e) {
                    return(false);
                    /* response receipt failed! */
            };
            next_arg_start = 0;
            next_arg_end = data.indexOf(separator,next_arg_start);
            return(true);
    };
    public String get_string_arg ( ) {
        String arg;
        String arg_value;
        arg = data.substring(next_arg_start,next_arg_end);
        if (arg.equals("\n") == true) {
        /* no more args looking for more! */
```

```
                    arg_value = "";
                    System.out.println(
                        "server.get_arg: Internal error!");
                    return arg_value;
                };
                arg_value = arg;
                next_arg_start = next_arg_end + 1;
                next_arg_end = data.indexOf(separator,next_arg_start);
                return arg_value;
            };
            /* Applet debugging, goes to the java viewer */
            public void put_screen()
            {
                System.out.println(data);
            };
        }
```

Place this Java package in the directory:

```
        ../mysocket
```

Name the file

```
        mysocket.java
```

Compile

```
        java mysocket.java
```

to create

```
        mysocket.class
```

The Java Applet is now created using the package.

```
    import java.applet.*;
    import java.awt.*;
    import java.io.*;
    import java.net.*;
    import java.util.*;
    import mysocket.*;
    // create a class called AClient that is usable as an Applet
    public class AClient extends Applet {
    // create the local data type for class in the package
    public mysocket Asocket;
    // create an Applet data type
```

```
        Applet applet;
    /* Everything is only done once in init. This is executed in a manner similar to a constructor
     * in a C++ program. Since Java is an interpreted language, not a compiled language, the
     * main is really resident in the interpreter. Since the primary function of the interpreter is
     * to load classes and interpret init code, the init constructor is very similar to a C program
     * main().
     */
    public void init() {
        applet = this;        // set the variable applet to this Applet
        /*
         * Create the socket and connect to the server. The name of this Applet is passed to the
         * mysocket constructor, which uses it to establish the name of the server and other
         * related information. This is required as part of the Java security.
         */
        Asocket = new mysocket(applet);

        // The connection is now established
        // send a request out to the server
        Asocket.initialize_request(1, 1);
        Asocket.put_request();
        // get back the response and put it on the java screen
        Asocket.get_response();
        Asocket.put_screen();
        /*
         * Put the response on the browser screen. Java treats all output like graphics, so the
         * received text is painted onto the screen as if it were a graphic.
         */
        public void paint(Graphics g)
        {
            g.drawString("Hello Students of the Internet World",
                25, 10);
            // paint the public data from the server side
            g.drawString(Asocket.data, 25, 30);
        }
        // other Applet code to continuely receive messages
        /* Note: This code can be vastly improved by creating polling loops from either the
         * client or server side. These exercises are left to the readers.
         */
    }
```

Name this file

AClient.java

It must be located in the same directory that contains the directory mysocket. Now compile this file:

```
javac AClient.java
```

This will create the file

```
AClient.class
```

Here is the HTML:

```
<HTML><HEAD><TITLE>applet socket</TITLE><BODY>
<H1> Stream Socket Applet </H1>
<APPLET code=ClientApplet HEIGHT=300 WIDTH=300>
</APPLET>
</BODY></HTML>
```

To have this run on your server, the following must be present:

1. AClient.class in the public HTML area.
2. myserver.class in a subdirectory of the public HTML area named myserver.
3. The HTML file in the public HTML area.
4. The C server code, which must be running on the server. It can be located in any area.
5. File and directory permissions, which must be set up to allow all isolation files to be accessed and modified by the server. The log files will be created and changed by whoever starts the C code up. Care should be taken if this is done by root. If it is done by you as a user, be sure to place the logfile in one of your directories or in a directory that you are permitted to read and write.

The complete process of setting up the socket is shown in Figure 22.4. The C socket is run on the server side. It is in a continuous loop waiting for a request from the client side. The program can be started by route or by a normal user.

1. The client-side browser requests the initial URL. This is the URL containing the Applet HTML code.
2. The HTML is sent from the server over to the client and then to the HTML interpreter. Part of the HTML results in output to the browser screen.
3. In addition, there is a request for an Applet. This results in a message being sent to the server side requesting the Applet. If the Applet is already present, it will be retrieved locally.
4. The Applet classes are retrieved from the server and sent over to the client. They are passed to the Java interpreter. The code is interpreted. Since the code is in universal byte code, the interpreter is needed rather than direct execution.
5. The Applet code runs, using the Java interpreter on the client side. The Java code establishes a socket connection over to the server. The socket is a bidirectional connection allowing communications in both directions between the client and the server. Since it is an independent socket, the HTTP protocol does not have to be used for communications between the client and server.

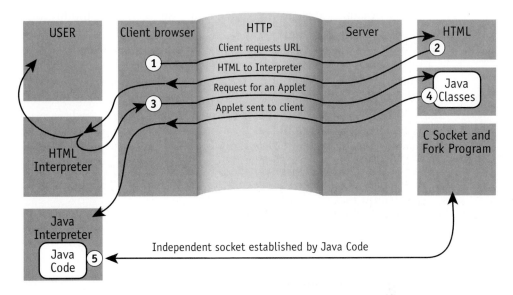

FIGURE 22.4   Socket Activator: Critical runtime steps take place during the activation of a socket.

6. Additional connections, not shown in Figure 22.4 are the server connection to the isolation file, etc.

While the server-side program was shown in C, it could have been written in C++ or even in Java.[10] The use of sockets can include establishing the initial connection on one socket and then moving the connection to another socket. By adding this kind of complexity, it is possible to provide different services. If the initial Applet is sent from a cgi-bin program, it could include IP address security, encryption, etc.

To complete the socket environment, it is necessary to add a continuous update of the information in the isolation file. This can be done in either of two ways:

1. **Client-Side Polling** A request for information is sent out from the client side on an interval schedule. The server receives the request, checks the isolation file for information, then sends the information back to the client. The client retrieves the newly sent information. It then clears the section of the browser screen used to display information and places the new information on the screen.

2. **Server-Side Polling** The server contains a loop and wait. On each loop it retrieves the information from the isolation file and sends it out to the client(s). The client sits in a loop checking for new information to arrive. When

---

[10] Java is a complete language that allows standalone code as well as Applet code. Since sockets and threads are allowed, server software can be written in Java code.

the information arrives, the Applet clears the section of the browser screen used to display information and places the new information on the screen. (Alternatively, the information could be made to scroll, allowing the new information to be added to the end of the text.)

3. **Client or Server Messaging** A third option uses either of the two aforementioned options but sends messages rather than the real data. The message is used to retrieve the information from another source, such as a prepared URL. The client-server information acts like a next button on a viewgraph machine. It selects the slide (URL) to show.

Here is AClient.java extended to include client-side polling of the server:

```java
import java.applet.*;
import java.awt.*;
import java.io.*;
import java.net.*;
import java.util.*;
import mysocket.*;
// create a class called AClient that is usable as an Applet
public class AClient extends Applet implements Runnable{
    // create the local data type for class in the package
    public mysocket Asocket;
    // create an Applet data type
    Applet applet;
    /* Everything is only done once in init. This is executed in a manner similar to a
     * constructor in a C++ program. Since Java is an interpreted language, not a compiled
     * language, the main is really resident in the interpreter. Since the primary function of
     * the interpreter is to load classes and interpret init code, the init constructor is very
     * similar to a C program
     * main().
     */
    public void init() {
        applet = this; // set the variable applet to this Applet

        // The connection is now established creating polling loops from either the client
         * or server side. These exercises are left to the readers.
         */
        // This is the thread that polls the server
        private Thread poll_thread = null;
    }

        public void start() {
        if (poll_thread == null) {
        poll_thread = new Thread(this);
        poll_thread.start();
        }

    }
```

```
        public void stop() {
            if ((poll_thread != null) && (poll_thread.isAlive()))
                poll_thread.stop();
            poll_thread = null;
        }
        // This is the body of the thread, it polls the server
        public void run(){
        /*
         * Create the socket and connect to the server. The name of this Applet is passed to the
         * mysocket constructor, which uses it to establish the name of the server and other
related
         * information. This is required as part of the Java security.
         */
        Asocket = new mysocket(applet);
        for(;;)
            {
                // client side request starts the poll
                Asocket.initialize_request(1, 1);
                Asocket.put_request();
                // server side response is received
                Asocket.get_response();
                Asocket.put_screen();
                // wait 200 ms then try again
                try {Thread.sleep(200); } catch (InterruptedException e);
            }
        }
    }
```

This new Applet includes several important changes. First the Applet is declared as runnable. This is required when using threads. For Java, a thread is needed if a continuous loop is to be created. This allows the main program, which run from the Java interpreter, to return control to the client browser. The next critical parts are the start, stop, and run routines. These create the thread, start the thread, provide a way to stop the thread, and create the thread code segment. The code segment is set to poll the server side every 200 ms. If the responses are server-side generated, the client side request code can be eliminated.

When examining Java Applet programs, it is critical to have an understanding of events. Java Applets are provided with a number of predefined events, including the following:

1. init()   Runs once when the Applet starts up.
2. paint(Graphics g)   Places text on the screen during startup and when the Applet is refreshed in any way (e.g., resizing the screen).
3. mouseUp(), mouseDown()...   Activated by motion of the mouse.
4. start(), stop(), and run()   Events that are associated with threads.

This is only a partial list to give a flavor for the language. (See Figure 22.5.) Events look similar to subroutines, but they will only be activated if the stimulus event that activates them occurs. Some events, such as init() occur only once, while others, such as mouse_down() can occur multiple times. The programmer can define an event or allow the default event (normally a null event) to occur. Events can call other subroutines created by the Java programmer. The other critical component that is not seen in other languages is the exception handling. These are part of the protection built into Java. Exceptions guarantee that certain events are protected against. For example, a request for a URL is protected by an exception. If the URL is not available for some reason, the exception handling will provide an error message on the browser. Java is a developing language, which means that new events and exceptions will develop as the language expands.

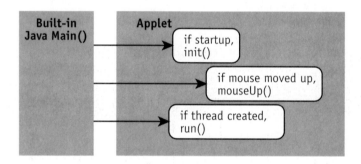

FIGURE 22.5   Applets: Understanding Applets provides new opportunities for cgi-bin programmers.

To complete the learning environment, the cgi interface must be set up to the instructor. This is a standard form that takes input from the instructor, sends it to the cgi-bin program, and then places it in the isolation file. The isolation file is then read by the Java socket and any information is sent back to the students (users who activated the Applets). Because sockets can be spawned to multiple users, the learning environment provides the traditional single-teacher, multiple-student interface. The teacher can monitor progress by setting up a separate window on his or her browser that acts like another student. With this type of setup, additional capabilities can be added easily that will tell how many students are active at any time, when students connect up, etc.

Finally the HTML is provided to create the frames. Recall that frames create different areas (frame windows) for the various URLs to run in. The HTML frame provides different areas with associated URLs for each area. The scrolling mode allows part of the URL to be shown in the frame. If the entire URL is not visible, arrows will be shown along the edge of the frame to allow other parts of the URL to be seen.

```
<HTML><TITLE>Education Frame</TITLE><BODY>
<!-- Divide the browser screen into sections (frame windows) -->
```

```
<FRAMESET ROWS="50,*,50">
<!-- The Applet Socket URL appears in this frame window -->
<FRAME NAME=applet_socket
SRC="http://internet_path/applet.html" noresize
FRAMEBORDER=0
SCROLLING=no>
<!-- The cgi program that allows questions from the students is in this frame window -->
<FRAME NAME=yourquestions
SRC="http://internet_path/cgi-bin/question_input"
SCROLLING=auto>
<FRAMESET COLS="70%,*">
<!-- Answers to student questions -->
<FRAME FRAMEBORDER=0
SRC="http://internet_path/answers.html"
SCROLLING=auto>
<!-- Teacher input only on teacher window -->
<FRAME FRAMEBORDER=0
SRC="http://internet_path/cgi-bin/teacher_input"
SCROLLING=auto>
</FRAMESET>
</FRAMESET>
</BODY></HTML>
```

In this section you learned some fundamentals about how to interconnect cgi-bin programs and Java capabilities. You learned how cgi-bin programs can generate HTML for Java Applets; how Java scripts can activate URLs, including cgi-bin programs; and how sockets and cgi-bin can be interconnected to provide highly complex client-server capabilities.

Javascript and CGI

WHILE JAVA IS A PROGRAMMING language similar to C++ and C, Javascript is a script language similar to shell and PERL. Javascript, unlike Java, cannot be used except with a Web browser. It provides programmable enhancements to HTML. The primary resemblance to Java is the use of a similar object-coding method. However, unlike Java, Javascript is not checked and is subject to bad coding and errors. For UNIX programmers, this is analogous to shell, which uses many of the constructs from C but is not validated by a compiler. In addition, Javascript has none of the security mechanisms found in Java. For example, it is possible to capture someone's Javascript program, alter it, and then reaccess the same Web page. Because of this, Javascript should be used with caution, especially if security is an issue.

Despite these limitations, Javascript does provide some interesting and valuable capabilities for persons developing Web pages. Where security is less of an issue (e.g., Intranet facilities that use firewalls[11] to restrict access), Javascript can provide valuable gains to cgi programs.

One of the most important gains for cgi-bin programmers is the ability to preprocess the user's input on the client side before sending it to the server side cgi-bin program. The use of client-side preprocessing can allow such functions as

1. Range Checking
2. Data Validation
3. Data Compression

to take place before the data are sent to the server cgi-bin program. Because error messages can be generated on the client side, the user is given a quicker response to both a valid and an invalid entry. Corrections take place more quickly if data are entered incorrectly.

The following example HTML Web page with embedded Javascript shows how this works. The goal is to validate whether a user-provided mailing address has a valid format. If it doesn't, the user is prompted for a new address.

```
<HTML>
<HEAD>
<TITLE>Verifying Mail Address Form Input with Javascript</TITLE>
<SCRIPT LANGUAGE="Javascript">
<!--
function runmailTest(form, button) {
  Ret = false;
  if (button.name == "1") Ret = sendmail(form);
  if (button.name == "2") Ret = content(form);
  if (Ret)
    alert ("Mail Sent Successfully!");
}
function sendmail(form) {
  Ctrl = form.inputbox1;
  if (Ctrl.value == "" || Ctrl.value.indexOf ('@', 0) == -1) {
    validatePrompt (Ctrl, "Enter a valid email address")
    return (false);
  } else
    return (true);
```

---

[11] A firewall is a method for limiting access to an Intranet facility. Usually a firewall will restrict access to persons at a particular location or to a specific corporate entity or to a particular institution. Firewalls can be combined with proxy servers to allow external access to the Internet while restricting access to internal Web pages.

```
}
function content(form) {
    Ctrl = form.sendmail;
    if (Ctrl.value == "") {
        validatePrompt (Ctrl, "Please provide a value for this box")
        return (false);
    } else
        return (true);
}
function runSubmit (form, button) {
    if (!sendmail(form)) return;
    if (!content(form)) return;
    alert ("All entries verified OK!");
    document.test.submit();
    return;
}
function validatePrompt (Ctrl, PromptStr) {
    alert (PromptStr)
    Ctrl.focus();
    return;
}
//-->
</SCRIPT>
</HEAD>
<BODY BACKGROUND="#c0c0c0" >
<CENTER>
<H2>Verifying Form Input with Javascript</H2>
</CENTER>
<FORM NAME="test" ACTION="http://internet_path/cgi-bin/mailer" METHOD=POST>
Enter an e-mail address (e.g., markf@alphacdc.com): <BR>
<INPUT TYPE="text" NAME="sendmail">
<INPUT TYPE="button" NAME="1" VALUE="Mailto Input"
onClick="runmailTest(this.form, this)"><P>
Enter mail input (don't leave blank): <BR>
<INPUT TYPE="textarea" NAME="content">
<INPUT TYPE="button" NAME="2" VALUE="Content Input"
onClick="runmailTest(this.form, this)"><P>
<P>
<INPUT TYPE="button" NAME="Submit" VALUE="Submit"
onClick="runSubmit(this.form, this)"><P>
</FORM></BODY></HTML>
```

About the program ·

1. Javascript begins with an HTML request for <SCRIPT language=javascript>. This is provided to tell the browser that a script language is going to be used and to allow for the invention of other script languages in the future.

2. To provide compatibility with older browsers, Javascript can be embedded in an HTML comment. If the browser does not accept Javascript, the section will be ignored rather than causing a browser error.

3. The initial Javascript calls are found at the top of the program in the <HEAD> section. While this is not required, this is the recommended procedure.

4. The two main Javascript functions are the following:

   - **sendmail()**   This function checks that the mail address contains content and that the @ character is present. These are a required part of an email address. If either is not present, the error message is sent back to the user, and the cgi-bin program is never activated.

   - **content()**   This function checks the mail information to verify that some content is present. If there is no information at all, the mail is not sent and an error message is activated.

5. The other functions are as follows:

   - **runSubmit()**   This function is activated when the submit button is clicked on with the mouse. The onClick in the input from the Submit button results in the Javascript function runSubmit() being run. Two arguments are sent to the function: the present form and the contents of the submit button. The contents of the form are then sent into the sendmail() and content() Javascript routines. If both of these are true the successful mail message is sent out as an alert().

   - **runmailTest()**   This function is a common input point for each of the form inputs. It checks which part of the form is being examined and then sends the form information to the correct checking function.

   - **validatePrompt()**   This function is used to send a message box to the user if the test of the user's entry fails.

By using Javascript, the coding on the server side is minimized. If the Javascript is written correctly, error legs may be unnecessary or minimal on the server-side cgi-bin program. As with most script languages, this approach may be especially appealing where quick development is needed. Because the Javascript can be quickly changed without recompiling, type checking can be tested and modified quickly. If you are expecting to see regular modifications in your ranges, this is a very appealing approach. If the project will go through several iterations, Javascript can allow you to get something in place quickly. This can be migrated to the server side once the project is stabilized.

TABLE 22.2   *Javascript Explained*

Type	Description	Example

Values	Numbers, logical, strings, null	Local Variables
		  var myvariable = 10
		  var stringvariable
		  stringvariable="Bonjour"
		Global Variables
		  global_val = 2;

eval	Convert string to number.	
parseInt	Convert string to int.	
parseFloat	Convert string to float.	
Operators	Standard operators as found in Java. These are similar to C operators: +, -, *, /, !, |, &, ^, –, ++, +=, -=, *=, /=, ?:, %, >>, <<, <<<, >>>, &&, ||, ~ (>>> and <<< are zero fill left and right shift found in Java and Javascript but not in C or C++)	a = b * c
Compare	==, <=, >=, !=, <, >	if (a > b)
String Join	String concatenation can be done with the + operator.	mystring = "hello " + "internet " mystring += "world"
Objects	Objects can be accessed using the standard dot notation or using an array access. When arrays are used, the items in the array are the associated string.	toon.zero="show0.gif" toon.one="show1.gif" toon["two"]="show2.gif" *Declaration function* function Quilt(color1, color2, color3, color4) { this.color1=color1; this.color2=color2; this.color3=color3; this.color4=color4 } myQuilt = new Quilt("red", "blue", "green", "yellow")
myobj.arguments.length myobj.arguments[i]	The number of arguments The ith argument	
Functions	Functions are an integral part of Javascript. They are declared with the function key word. This is followed by functions in standard format. Since there is no main in Javascript, functions are declared in a standalone fashion, then called from the HTML code.	function myfunction (args) { function body; } function showstring (string) { documentwrite ("this is my string..." + string) }
Method	A method is a predefined function that is associated with an object.	myobject.mymethod = myfunction;

TABLE 22.2   *Javascript Explained (Continued)*

Type	Description	Example
this	As in C++ and Java, "this" refers to the current object	myfunction(this) With HTML <INPUT TYPE="text" NAME="mailer" SIZE=20 onChange="validate(this, 20, 100)" >
Built-in Objects Math	Trigonometry functions, e.g., Math.sin(myvalue). The argument must be in radians. Use the with(Math) {...} for multiple mathematical computations. Math.asin(...) Math.acos(...) Math.atan(...) Math.sin(...) Math.tan(...) Math.ln2(...) Math.ln10(...) Math.log2E(...) Math.log10E(...) Math.exp(...) Math.pow(base, exponent) Math.PI Math.E Math.sqrt1_2 1/square_root of 2 Math.sqrt2 square root of 2	Y = Math.cos(epsilon); with(Math){ Y= cos(delta); X=sin(delta); }
Date	Create a date string with the format: Month day year hour minute seconds	today = new date() birthday = new("February 11, 1962") aday = new(10, 12, 1970, 11, 0, 0) month=birthday.getMonth somedate=new Date(); somedate=setTime (Date.parse ("Nov 4, 1942");
Statements Conditionals Loops	if...else for, while, break, continue are used in the same way as in C++, C, and Java	
Object Manipulation	for...in new this with(...)	for(variable in object) {...}
Comments	// my comment /* my comment */	/* this is a javascript comment */ <-- this is an HTML comment -!>

TABLE 22.2   *Javascript Explained (Continued)*

Type	Description	Example
History	history.back() history.forward() history.go()	history.go(-2)
Document	document.write("text") document.background—image document.bgColor document.fgColor—foreground document.linkColor—unfollowed link document.alinkColor -activated link document.vlinkColor—followed link document.clear document.referrer—caller's URL	document.bgColor = "#0c0c0c" document.alinkColor = red
events	onClick—mouse is clicked onMouseOver—mouse moves over onBlur—user leaves a required field onFocus—user enters a required field onSelect—same as onBlur and field change onSubmit—form submit function call onLoad—window or frame done loading onUnload—document exited	
Window Self	window.status—change status line window.alert—string in alert window window.open—open a window window.close—close a window self—current window self.close—same as window.close self.status—change the status bar message	
Actions	alert("text message") confirm("text message") prompt("text message", [inputDefault])	
States	checked—true or false state of a check box defaultChecked defaultSelected defaultStatus—default message in status bar defaultValue	
Escape	escape("?")—return the hex value of the quoted characters in %XX format unescape("%0D")	

TABLE 22.2 *Javascript Explained (Continued)*

Type	Description	Example
Forms	value—the value associated with an input name—the name associated with an input target—where to go if form is submitted	
Navigator	navigator.appCodeName - browser codename navigator.appName—browser name navigator.appVersion—browser version navigator.userAgent	if (navigator.appName != "Netscape") { window.alert("You may not have Javascript capability"); }

Length	This is a generic variable that occurs with a number of types:
	formName.length
	frameReference.length
	history.length
	radioName.length
	selectName.length
	stringName.length
	windowReference.length
	
	ARRAYS
	anchors.length
	elements.length
	forms.length
	frameReferences.length
	windowReferences.length
	links.length
	selectName.options.length
	
	Note: The length argument can be used to pass a variable number of arguments to a function. This is similar to va_args().
		if (mystring.length > 5)
		{
		alert("string too long");
		return FALSE;
		}

Parent	The parent is a synonym for a window or frame. There are a number of parent subtypes: parent.propertyName parent.methodName—method associated with window parent.frameName parent.frames[index value]	parent.myframe.location.href = "http://internet_path/cgi-bin/prog"

TABLE 22.2   *Javascript Explained (Continued)*

Type	Description	Example
Top	The topmost navigator window: top.propertyName top.methodName top.frameName top.frames[index value] top.length—number of frames	top.someframe.document.vlinkColor = "green"
Strings	mystring.toUpperCase mystring.toLowerCase mystring.substring(index1, index2)— returns substring from character at index1 to character before index2	str = "ABCD" tmp=str.toLowerCase();
Links Location	link.port—communications port used links[index].port location.port Using search information can be passed totally at the client layer. This requires all data be placed in the HTML and Javascript code! links[index].search—query information location.search links[index].pathname—The URL path links[index].href—The entire URL links[index]..target—The target URL	window.location.href = "http:// internet_path/myname.html"
selectName formName	selectName is the value of the name in the select object in the input to a form formName is the name of a form object or an element in the form array.	mylist.options[2].value

PROBLEMS

1. Explain the distinctions between cgi-bin programs and Java Applets. What are the advantages and disadvantages of each? What additional examples of advantages and disadvantages can you add? Explain in detail.

2. Explain the HTML part of an Applet and how it can be generated from a cgi-bin program. What advantages can you see to this type of approach as compared to standard HTML? How could parameters be used to advantage to create interesting Web pages?

3. Explain the different methods of providing client-server control. How do hidden files and other `cgi-bin` capabilities differ from sockets and other Java capabilities? What are the advantages and disadvantages of each?

4. Discuss the possible areas in which Java security versus `cgi-bin` might result in one method being chosen over the other.

5. How would you go about setting up a mailer in Java? How does this differ from a `cgi-bin` mailer?

6. Explain the different approaches to sockets. How does HTML and `cgi-bin` use of sockets differ from connection datagrams and stream sockets? What is the difference between a fork, thread, and multiple processes?

7. Is it possible to provide IP security with Java? Explain how.

8. In the example chess game, it is possible to start in the middle of a game, delay a game until another day, or back up and redo a move. Why is this extremely difficult to implement in Java?

9. The chess game had to use hidden variable files to create memory across successive moves. How could stream connections provide the same kind of capability? Would this be easier or more difficult to implement?

10. Explain how Javascript might be used in the Quilt program to do preprocessing on the client side.

1 C++ or C Version of Forms Routines

These are general-purpose routines for handling user input from forms.

```c
/* Type: C++ or C subroutine
 * Purpose: Convert a 2-byte ASCII representation of a hex number
 *    to its decimal equivalent (0-255 decimal or 0 to FF hex)
 * Input:
 *    char* msg - pointer to the ASCII string
 * Output:
 *    char - decimal conversion 0-255
 */
char
ahextoi ( char* value )
{
    int ascii_char;
    char return_value=0;
    while ( *value != EOM )
    {
        ascii_char = isupper ( *value++ );
        if (isdigit(ascii_char))
        {
            /* calculate mod 16 */
            return_value = ( ascii_char - '0' ) +
                (return_value * 16 ) ;
        } else
        if (isalpha(ascii_char))
        {
            /* calculate mod 16 */
            return_value = ( ascii_char - 'A' +10 ) +
                ( return_value * 16 ) ;
        } else /* error */
        {
            return 0;
        }
        ++value;
    }
/*
 * Since return_value is on the stack it must be copied into another variable immediately.
 */
```

```
            return ( return_value );
      }
      /*
       * Type: C++ or C subroutine
       * Purpose: Clean up a message for mailing or other use.
       * Input:
       *    char* output_msg - pointer to the return string variable
       *    char* input_msg - pointer to the message before cleanup
       * Output:
       *    char*- pointer to the cleaned-up message
       */
      #define MAX_SIZE 200
      char* clear_msg(
            char* output_msg,
            char* input_msg
      ) {
            char tmp_msg[ MAX_SIZE ]; /* temporary message holder */
            char* tmp_msg_ptr = &tmp_msg[0];
            while ( *msg != EOM )
            {
                  switch( *msg )
                  {
                        case '+':
                              *tmp_msg_ptr = ' ';
                              break;
                        case '&':
                              *tmp_msg_ptr = '\n';
                              break;
                        case ' ':
                              if( *(msg-1) == ' ' )
                                    break;
                              *tmp_msg_ptr = ' ';
                              break;
                        case '%':
                              *tmp_msg_ptr = ahextoi(msg+1 );
                              msg += 2;
                              break;
                        default:
                              *tmp_msg_ptr = *msg;
                              break;
                  }
                  ++msg; ++tmp_msg_ptr;
            }
            tmp_msg_ptr = NULL; /* Null termination for string */
            strcpy( output_msg, tmp_msg_ptr );
            return ( output_msg );
```

```
}
/*
 * Type: C++ or C subroutine
 * Purpose: Isolate the string value of a variable from a FORM
 * Input:
 *   char* output_msg - ptr to the output message to be sent back
 *   char* input_msg - ptr to the user input string including variable
 *   char* start_msg - pointer variable= that precedes value
 * Output:
 *   char* - pointer to the requested variables value as a string
 */
char*
get_variable ( char* output_msg, char* input_msg, char* variable_name )
{
    int length;
    while ( *input_msg != NULL )
    {
        if( strcmpr( /* check for variable name match */
            input_msg,
            variable_name,
            strlen(variable_name) != NULL )
        {
            ++input_msg;
        }
    }
    if( *input_msg == NULL ) /* no match */
        return( "" );
    /* now determine the length of the variable string */
    while( (*(input_msg + length ) != NULL) &&
     (*(input_msg + length ) != '\n') &&
     (*(input_msg + length ) != '&'))
    {
        ++length;
    }
    strncpy ( output_msg, input_msg, length );
    return ( clear_msg (output_msg) );
}
/*
 * Type: C++ or C subroutine
 * Purpose: Validate if a user's variable from a form is equal to an expected value
 * Input:
 *   char* input_value - pointer to user's variable string
 *   char* expected_value - pointer to expected string
 * Output:
 *   int return -
 *       TRUE if Match
```

```
 *          FALSE if Not Match
 */
int
validate( char* input_value, char* expected_value )
{
    if( strncpm ( input_value,
         expected_value,
         stnlen( expected_value) ) == NULL )
         return (TRUE);
    return (FALSE);
}
```

```
C++ Chess Program
#include <stdio.h>
#include <stdlib.h>
#include <iostream.h>
#include <string.h>
extern char* variable(char* msg, char* start_msg);
/*
 * Defines for the HTML IMaGes used to create the chess board on the screen.
 */
#define B_RK_G "http://mypath/rk.gif?-i11\" ALT=\"B_RK\""
#define B_KT_G "http://mypath/kt.gif?-i11\" ALT=\"B_KT\""
#define B_BI_G "http://mypath/bi.gif?-i11\" ALT=\"B_BI\""
#define B_QU_G "http://mypath/qu.gif?-i11\" ALT=\"B_QU\""
#define B_KI_G "http://mypath/ki.gif?-i11\" ALT=\"B_KG\""
#define B_RK_W "http://mypath/rk.gif?-i12\" ALT=\"B_RK\""
#define B_KT_W "http://mypath/kt.gif?-i12\" ALT=\"B_KT\""
#define B_BI_W "http://mypath/bi.gif?-i12\" ALT=\"B_BI\""
#define B_QU_W "http://mypath/qu.gif?-i12\" ALT=\"B_QU\""
#define B_KI_W "http://mypath/ki.gif?-i12\" ALT=\"B_KG\""
#define W_RK_W "http://mypath/rk.gif?-i21\" ALT=\"W_RK\""
#define W_KT_W "http://mypath/kt.gif?-i21\" ALT=\"W_KT\""
#define W_BI_W "http://mypath/bi.gif?-i21\" ALT=\"W_BI\""
#define W_QU_W "http://mypath/qu.gif?-i21\" ALT=\"W_QU\""
#define W_KI_W "http://mypath/ki.gif?-i21\" ALT=\"W_KG\""
#define W_RK_G "http://mypath/rk.gif?-i22\" ALT=\"W_RK\""
#define W_KT_G "http://mypath/kt.gif?-i22\" ALT=\"W_KT\""
#define W_BI_G "http://mypath/bi.gif?-i22\" ALT=\"W_BI\""
#define W_QU_G "http://mypath/qu.gif?-i22\" ALT=\"W_QU\""
#define W_KI_G "http://mypath/ki.gif?-i22\" ALT=\"W_KG\""
#define W_PN_G "http://mypath/pn.gif?-i11\" ALT=\"W_PN\""
#define W_PN_W "http://mypath/pn.gif?-i12\" ALT=\"W_PN\""
#define B_PN_G "http://mypath/pn.gif?-i21\" ALT=\"B_PN\""
#define B_PN_W "http://mypath/pn.gif?-i22\" ALT=\"B_PN\""
#define BLNK_W "http://mypath/bl.gif?-i31\" ALT=\"----\""
#define BLNK_G "http://mypath/bl.gif?-i32\" ALT=\"----\""
/*
 * Continuity is provided by passing the chess board as eight strings, each one representing
 * a row of the chess board. The nomenclature used is
```

```
 *      b | w => black or white
 *      1-6 represent pieces and blank (see defines for pieces)
 * default board strings
 */
#define H1 "\"b0b1b2b3b4b2b1b0\""
#define H2 "\"b5b5b5b5b5b5b5b5\""
#define H3 "\"w6w6w6w6w6w6w6w6\""
#define H4 "\"w6w6w6w6w6w6w6w6\""
#define H5 "\"w6w6w6w6w6w6w6w6\""
#define H6 "\"w6w6w6w6w6w6w6w6\""
#define H7 "\"w5w5w5w5w5w5w5w5\""
#define H8 "\"w0w1w2w3w4w2w1w0\""
#define WHO "\"B\""
/*
 * Each piece on the chess board is represented by a define. The black and white pieces are
 * offset by +6, allowing only the black pieces to be sent in the strings along with the color.
 * The blank is always sent as white.
 */
#define B_ROOK 0
#define B_KNGT 1
#define B_BISH 2
#define B_QUEN 3
#define B_KING 4
#define B_PAWN 5
#define W_ROOK 6
#define W_KNGT 7
#define W_BISH 8
#define W_QUEN 9
#define W_KING 10
#define W_PAWN 11
#define BLANK 12
/*
 * The defines for the background square color.
 */
#define GRAY 0
#define WHITE 1
/*
 * The chess subroutine includes the option of a file. The file can be used to send a
 * predefined default screen to the program. Since the file is sent as argv[1], it can be the
 * name of a file that has been sent via FTP to the site.
 */
void
chess(char* filename)
{
int i, j, k; /* generic counting variables */
/*
```

```
 * To make the board easy to define, array manipulation is used. The arrays are
 *   xpos => pointers to the IMG strings
 *   pos => pointers to the 8x8 squares on the chess board
 */
char* xpos[13][2];
char* pos[9][9];
char order[300]; /* char string used to get the post information */
char color = WHITE; /* The color of the square the piece is on */
int xstart, ystart, xend, yend; /* Piece moved x y start and end position */
char hidden[9][20]; /* strings sent in HTML hidden variables */
/*
 * Determination of POST of GET tells if it is the start of a game or a move taking place.
 */
char* env;
int post_true = 0;
char offset = 0;
int filemode = 0;
FILE* fp;
char buffer[20];
int debug = 0;
/*
 * Allow a file to be input. This is used to simulate end games or preset configurations such
 * as those done in the newspaper.
 */
    if(strlen(filename) > 0)
    {
        filemode=1;
    }
/*
 * Set up a multidimensional array to point at all the possible HTML anchors. These will then
 * be sent back from the cgi-bin program to the client. To make it easier to make changes
 * later, the defines are used for the strings rather than the actual strings.
 */
    xpos[B_ROOK][RED]=B_RK_G;
    xpos[B_KNGT][RED]=B_KT_G;
    xpos[B_BISH][RED]=B_BI_G;
    xpos[B_QUEN][RED]=B_QU_G;
    xpos[B_KING][RED]=B_KI_G;
    xpos[B_ROOK][WHITE]=B_RK_W;
    xpos[B_KNGT][WHITE]=B_KT_W;
    xpos[B_BISH][WHITE]=B_BI_W;
    xpos[B_QUEN][WHITE]=B_QU_W;
    xpos[B_KING][WHITE]=B_KI_W;
    xpos[W_PAWN][RED]=W_PN_G;
    xpos[W_PAWN][WHITE]=W_PN_W;
    xpos[B_PAWN][RED]=B_PN_G;
```

```
    xpos[B_PAWN][WHITE]=B_PN_W;
    xpos[W_ROOK][RED]=W_RK_G;
    xpos[W_KNGT][RED]=W_KT_G;
    xpos[W_BISH][RED]=W_BI_G;
    xpos[W_QUEN][RED]=W_QU_G;
    xpos[W_KING][RED]=W_KI_G;
    xpos[W_ROOK][WHITE]=W_RK_W;
    xpos[W_KNGT][WHITE]=W_KT_W;
    xpos[W_BISH][WHITE]=W_BI_W;
    xpos[W_QUEN][WHITE]=W_QU_W;
    xpos[W_KING][WHITE]=W_KI_W;
    xpos[BLANK][RED]=BLNK_G;
    xpos[BLANK][WHITE]=BLNK_W;
/*
 * Since the server is running the program, it is possible to retrieve information about the
 * request method. In this case the GET method will occur when the program is first invoked
 * and will be used to send back the default screen. After that, the user's request will be
 * added to the screen using the POST method.
 */
    env=getenv("REQUEST_METHOD");
    if(env != 0)
    {
        if(strcmp(getenv("REQUEST_METHOD"),"POST")==0)
        {
            post_true=1;
        }
    }
    /* xtemp -> this is present for debugging */
    // post_true=1;
    if(post_true == 1)
    {
        /*
         * Retrieve the user's request. The eight chess rows are placed in the hidden
         * variables r1 to r8. These are given in the format
         * Color ->     b= black w=white
         * Piece ->     0 = Rook
         *              1 = Knight
         *              2 = Bishop
         *              3 = Queen
         *              4 = King
         *              5 = Pawn
         * The variable who tells whose turn it is.
         */
        gets(order);
        strcpy(hidden[0], variable(order, "r1="));
        strcpy(hidden[1], variable(order, "r2="));
```

```
strcpy(hidden[2], variable(order, "r3="));
strcpy(hidden[3], variable(order, "r4="));
strcpy(hidden[4], variable(order, "r5="));
strcpy(hidden[5], variable(order, "r6="));
strcpy(hidden[6], variable(order, "r7="));
strcpy(hidden[7], variable(order, "r8="));
strcpy(hidden[8], variable(order, "who="));
/*
 * Switch whose move from black to white or vice versa.
 */
strcpy(hidden[8], (hidden[8][0]=='W') ? "B" : "W");
/*
 * Now read the piece to move. The user has created a start position and an end
 * position given by x and y coordinates at the start and at the end. To make the
 * move, the piece at the start must be determined and replaced by a blank. Then
 * the piece must be moved to the end position. Since it may be on the opposite
 * color square at the final destination, this will also need to be determined. For
 * now, though, merely get the start and end x, y positions.
 */
xstart=atoi(variable(order, "x_start="))-1;
ystart=atoi(variable(order, "y_start="))-1;
xend=atoi(variable(order, "x_end="))-1;
yend=atoi(variable(order, "y_end="))-1;
/*
 * This section here is key to the use of the hidden variables. The position of the
 * board has been passed to the C++ or C cgi-bin program in the eight hidden
 * variables representing the rows. The configuration is now used to set the
 * internal mapping to the present passed variables. In this manner, the cgi-bin
 * program has a representation of the state of the chess board. It is now starting
 * from the last state. What is important here is that multiple users playing the
 * chess game at the same time will get different hidden variables based on their
 * moves. This means that different chess games can be played at the same time.
 */
i=0; k=0;
    while(k <= 7)
    {
    while ( i <= 7)
    {
        switch(hidden[k][i*2])
        {
            case 'w':
                offset = B_PAWN + 1;
            break;
            default:
                offset = 0;
            break;
```

```
            }

            color= i%2 == k%2 ? RED : WHITE;
            pos[k][i] = xpos[hidden[k][(2*i)+1]-'0'+offset][color];
            i++; offset=0;


        }
        i=0; k++;
        }
        /* 1st the hidden */
        hidden[yend][xend*2]=hidden[ystart][xstart*2];
        hidden[yend][xend*2+1]=hidden[ystart][xstart*2+1];
        hidden[ystart][xstart*2]='w';
        hidden[ystart][xstart*2+1]='6';
        /* Now move the piece */
        pos[yend][xend]=xpos[hidden[yend][xend*2+1]-'0'+
            (hidden[yend][xend*2]=='b' ? 0 : 6)][(xstart%2 == ystart%2) ? RED : WHITE] ;
        pos[ystart][xstart]=xpos[BLANK][(xstart%2 == ystart%2) ? RED : WHITE];
} else
/*
 * The file mode provides a method for the user to read in a partially played chess game
 * and start from that point. This allows chess setups such as those found in the
 * newspaper to be played and could also allow games to be continued by saving their
 * state at an FTP site.
 */
if(filemode==1)
{
    fp= fopen(filename, "r");
    i=0;
    while(i <=7)
    {
        fgets(buffer,20,fp);
        *(buffer+16) = 0;
        strcpy(hidden[i], buffer);
        i++;
    }
    fclose(fp);
    strcpy(hidden[8], (hidden[8][0]=='W') ? "B" : "W");
    i=0; k=0;
    while(k <= 7)
    {
        while ( i <= 7)
        {
            switch(hidden[k][i*2])
            {
                case 'w':
```

```
                                        offset = B_PAWN + 1;
                            break;
                            default:
                                    offset = 0;
                            break;
                    }

                    color= i%2 == k%2 ? GRAY : WHITE;
                    pos[k][i] = xpos[hidden[k][(2*i)+1]-'0'+offset][color];
                    i++; offset=0;

            }
            i=0; k++;
        }
    } else
    {
/*
 * This code sets up the default board in the normal way a chess game begins.
 */
        strcpy(hidden[0], H1);
        strcpy(hidden[1], H2);
        strcpy(hidden[2], H3);
        strcpy(hidden[3], H4);
        strcpy(hidden[4], H5);
        strcpy(hidden[5], H6);
        strcpy(hidden[6], H7);
        strcpy(hidden[7], H8);
        strcpy(hidden[8], "W");
        pos[0][0]=xpos[B_ROOK][GRAY];
        pos[0][1]=xpos[B_KNGT][WHITE];
        pos[0][2]=xpos[B_BISH][GRAY];
        pos[0][3]=xpos[B_QUEN][WHITE];
        pos[0][4]=xpos[B_KING][GRAY];
        pos[0][5]=xpos[B_BISH][WHITE];
        pos[0][6]=xpos[B_KNGT][GRAY];
        pos[0][7]=xpos[B_ROOK][WHITE];
        pos[7][0]=xpos[W_ROOK][WHITE];
        pos[7][1]=xpos[W_KNGT][GRAY];
        pos[7][2]=xpos[W_BISH][WHITE];
        pos[7][3]=xpos[W_QUEN][GRAY];
        pos[7][4]=xpos[W_KING][WHITE];
        pos[7][5]=xpos[W_BISH][GRAY];
        pos[7][6]=xpos[W_KNGT][WHITE];
        pos[7][7]=xpos[W_ROOK][GRAY];
        for(j=0; j<=7; j++)
        {
```

```
        pos[1][j]= (j%2 != 0) ? xpos[B_PAWN][GRAY] : xpos[B_PAWN][WHITE];
        pos[6][j]= (j%2 == 0) ? xpos[W_PAWN][GRAY] : xpos[W_PAWN][WHITE];
    }
    for(i=2; i<=5; i++)
    {
        for(j=0; j<=7; j++)
        {
            pos[i][j]=(i%2 == j%2) ? xpos[BLANK][GRAY] : xpos[BLANK][WHITE];
        }
    }
}

/*
 * The board is now reconfigured to the new state. This is sent out as HTML code to the
 * client.
 */
    cout << "Content-type: text/html\n\n";
    cout << "<HTML> <HEAD> <Title>CHESS GAME</Title>\n" <<
            "<BODY bgcolor=#f0f0f0 </BODY>" <<
            "</HEAD> <BODY>\n";
    cout << (hidden[8][0]=='W' ? "WHITES" : "BLACKS") << " MOVE<BR>\n";
    cout <<"x -> 1-8<BR>\n";
    cout <<"y<BR>\n";
    cout <<"| 1-8<BR>\n";
    cout <<"v<BR>\n";
    /*
     * The pointers to the IMaGes are used to create the HTML version of the chess board.
     */
    for(i=0; i<=7; i++)
    {
        for(j=0; j<=7; j++)
        {
            cout << "<IMG SRC=" <<
            pos[i][j] <<
            " >\n";
            cout << flush;
        }
        cout<<"<BR>\n";
    }
    /*
     * The HTML form is sent to allow the user to make the next move.
     */
    cout <<
        "<FORM ACTION=\"http://com/cgi-bin/dacs/proj/chess\" METHOD=POST>\n";
    cout << "<BR><I>START</I>\n";
    cout << "<B> X POS</B>\n";
```

```
cout << "<SELECT NAME= \"x_start\">\n";
cout << "<OPTION SELECTED> 1\n";
cout << "<OPTION> 2\n";
cout << "<OPTION> 3\n";
cout << "<OPTION> 4\n";
cout << "<OPTION> 5\n";
cout << "<OPTION> 6\n";
cout << "<OPTION> 7\n";
cout << "<OPTION> 8\n";
cout << "</SELECT>\n";
cout << "<B> Y POS</B>\n";
cout << "<SELECT NAME= \"y_start\">\n";
cout << "<OPTION SELECTED> 1\n";
cout << "<OPTION> 2\n";
cout << "<OPTION> 3\n";
cout << "<OPTION> 4\n";
cout << "<OPTION> 5\n";
cout << "<OPTION> 6\n";
cout << "<OPTION> 7\n";
cout << "<OPTION> 8\n";
cout << "</SELECT>\n";
cout << "<BR><I>FINAL</I>\n";
cout << "<B> X POS</B>\n";
cout << "<SELECT NAME= \"x_end\">\n";
cout << "<OPTION SELECTED> 1\n";
cout << "<OPTION> 2\n";
cout << "<OPTION> 3\n";
cout << "<OPTION> 4\n";
cout << "<OPTION> 5\n";
cout << "<OPTION> 6\n";
cout << "<OPTION> 7\n";
cout << "<OPTION> 8\n";
cout << "</SELECT>\n";
cout << "<B> Y POS</B>\n";
cout << "<SELECT NAME= \"y_end\">\n";
cout << "<OPTION SELECTED> 1\n";
cout << "<OPTION> 2\n";
cout << "<OPTION> 3\n";
cout << "<OPTION> 4\n";
cout << "<OPTION> 5\n";
cout << "<OPTION> 6\n";
cout << "<OPTION> 7\n";
cout << "<OPTION> 8\n";
cout << "</SELECT>\n";
/*
 * The HIDDEN values are sent to pass along the present state of the board.
```

```
        */
    cout << "<BR>\n";
    cout << "<INPUT TYPE=\"HIDDEN\" NAME=\"r1\" VALUE=" << hidden[0] << ">\n";
    cout << "<INPUT TYPE=\"HIDDEN\" NAME=\"r2\" VALUE=" << hidden[1] << ">\n";
    cout << "<INPUT TYPE=\"HIDDEN\" NAME=\"r3\" VALUE=" << hidden[2] << ">\n";
    cout << "<INPUT TYPE=\"HIDDEN\" NAME=\"r4\" VALUE=" << hidden[3] << ">\n";
    cout << "<INPUT TYPE=\"HIDDEN\" NAME=\"r5\" VALUE=" << hidden[4] << ">\n";
    cout << "<INPUT TYPE=\"HIDDEN\" NAME=\"r6\" VALUE=" << hidden[5] << ">\n";
    cout << "<INPUT TYPE=\"HIDDEN\" NAME=\"r7\" VALUE=" << hidden[6] << ">\n";
    cout << "<INPUT TYPE=\"HIDDEN\" NAME=\"r8\" VALUE=" << hidden[7] << ">\n";
    cout << "<INPUT TYPE=\"HIDDEN\" NAME=\"who\" VALUE=" << hidden[8] << ">\n";
    cout << "<INPUT TYPE=\"submit\"> <INPUT TYPE=reset>\n";
    cout << "</FORM>\n";
    cout << "</BODY></HTML>\n";
}
void main(int argc, char* argv[])
{
    if(argc > 1)
    {
        chess(argv[1]); /* file mode */
        return;
    }
        chess(""); /* normal input */
}
```

3 Chess Modifications for ZZZZZZ

```
/*
 * The connections of zzzzzz to the Internet are the property of Native Communications,
 * Chris Cota and Mark Felton. The direct use of this code is prohibited without express
 * permission. Contact cota@dash.com.
 */
/*
 * This code can be connected to the zzzzzz chess algorithms provided in zzzzzz-3.4.tar.
 * G. Wiesenekker. ZZZZZZ a chess program.
 * Copyright (C) 1993-1994 G. Wiesenekker
 * E-mail: wiesenekker@sara.nl
 * This code was compiled for a SUN machine. It may need to be altered
 * to work on other machines.
 *
 */
/* Note:
 * Sections in BOLD should be generic to any chess algorithms
 */
/* In util.c change game time to read */
util.c:#define GAME_TIME1 (1 * 60)
util.c:#define GAME_TIME2 (1 * 60)
/* In util.c change my_printf to be an empty routine */
void my_printf(char *format, ...)
{
    return;
}
/* Add to bottom of util.c */
/* New code */
enum {PAWN = 0, KNIGHT, BISHOP, ROOK, QUEEN, KING};
char in_msg[1000];
char out_msg[1000];
static char* xpos[13][2];
void set_xpos()
{
    xpos[ROOK+OFFSET][GRAY]=B_RK_G;
    xpos[KNIGHT+OFFSET][GRAY]=B_KT_G;
    xpos[BISHOP+OFFSET][GRAY]=B_BI_G;
    xpos[QUEEN+OFFSET][GRAY]=B_QU_G;
    xpos[KING+OFFSET][GRAY]=B_KI_G;
```

```
        xpos[PAWN+OFFSET][GRAY]=B_PN_G;
        xpos[ROOK+OFFSET][WHITE]=B_RK_W;
        xpos[KNIGHT+OFFSET][WHITE]=B_KT_W;
        xpos[BISHOP+OFFSET][WHITE]=B_BI_W;
        xpos[QUEEN+OFFSET][WHITE]=B_QU_W;
        xpos[KING+OFFSET][WHITE]=B_KI_W;
        xpos[PAWN+OFFSET][WHITE]=B_PN_W;
        xpos[ROOK][GRAY]=W_RK_G;
        xpos[KNIGHT][GRAY]=W_KT_G;
        xpos[BISHOP][GRAY]=W_BI_G;
        xpos[QUEEN][GRAY]=W_QU_G;
        xpos[KING][GRAY]=W_KI_G;
        xpos[PAWN][GRAY]=W_PN_G;
        xpos[ROOK][WHITE]=W_RK_W;
        xpos[KNIGHT][WHITE]=W_KT_W;
        xpos[BISHOP][WHITE]=W_BI_W;
        xpos[QUEEN][WHITE]=W_QU_W;
        xpos[KING][WHITE]=W_KI_W;
        xpos[PAWN][WHITE]=W_PN_W;
        xpos[BLANK][GRAY]=BLNK_G;
        xpos[BLANK][WHITE]=BLNK_W;
}
extern int get_board(int k);
/*
 * Send the HTML containing the chess board, hidden variables, and move request to the
 * server.
 *
 * Arguments:
 *    moves - the move history include the present moves
 *    board - the initial board state
 *    init - 0 is a new move, 1 is a start of the game
 */
void display_html_board(char* moves, char* board, char* init)
{
    int i, j;
    int   k = 0;
    int kk;
    int bcnt =0;
    char tmp_board[81];
/*
 * The board is now reconfigured to the new state. This is sent out as HTML code to the
 * client.
 */
    set_xpos();
    printf("Content-type: text/html\n\n");
    printf("<HTML> <HEAD> <Title>CHESS GAME</Title>\n");
```

```
printf("<BODY bgcolor=#f0f0f0 </BODY>");
printf("</HEAD> <BODY><CENTER>\n");
/*
 * The pointers to the IMaGes are used to create the HTML version of the chess board.
 */
for(i=0; i < 8; i++)
{
    for(j=0; j < 8; j++)
    {
        printf("%s%s >\n",
            "<IMG HEIGHT=51 WIDTH=51 SRC=",
            xpos[get_board(k)][background(i,j)]
        );
        k++;
    }
    printf("<BR>\n");
}
printf("You are %s Computer's move was %s\n",
    colour_as_string[my_colour],
    moves);
/*
 * The HTML FORM is sent to allow the user to make the next move.
 */
printf("%s METHOD=POST >\n",
    "<FORM ACTION=
    \"http://info.com/cgi-bin/dacs/chess/chessw?x\" " );

/* Set up the hidden and visible variables */
printf("%s%d%s\n",
    "<INPUT TYPE=\"hidden\" NAME=\"bcnt\" VALUE=\"",
    (strlen(board)/80) + (( strlen(board) % 80 ) > 0
        ? 1 : 0),
    "\" SIZE=\"4\" >");
printf("%s%s%s",
    "<INPUT TYPE=\"hidden\" NAME=\"init\" VALUE=\"",
    init,
    "\" >\n");
printf("%s\n%s%s\n",
    "<INPUT TYPE=\"text\" NAME=\"move\" VALUE=\"\" SIZE=6><BR>",
    "<BR><A HREF=
    \"http://info.com/~markf/chess.help.html\">",
    " Example Input: a2a4</A>"
);
kk =0;          /* safety for too many moves */
for(;;)
{
```

```
                    tmp_board[kk] = *board;
                    if(kk==79 || *board == 0)
                    {
                            printf("%s%d%s%s%s%d%s\n",
                                "<INPUT TYPE=\"hidden\" NAME=\"board",
                                    bcnt,
                                    "\" VALUE=\"",
                                    tmp_board,
                                    "\" SIZE=",
                                    strlen(tmp_board)+2,
                                    ">");
                            bcnt++;
                            kk=-1;
                    }
                    if(*board==0 ) { break; }
                    tmp_board[kk+1] = 0;
                    kk++; board++;
            }
            printf("%s\n%s\n",
                "<INPUT TYPE=\"submit\" VALUE=\"send\"> <INPUT TYPE=reset>",
                "</FORM>");
            printf("</CENTER></BODY></HTML>\n");
            fflush(stdout);
            exit(0);
}
/*
 * Parsing routine to get the value of a variable.
 */
char* variable(char* msg, char* start_msg)
{
        int start_flag=0;
        int length;
        int start_length;
        int j;
        int i = 0;
        strcpy(in_msg, msg);
        length = strlen(in_msg);
        start_length = strlen(start_msg);
        out_msg[0]=0;
        while(i <= length)
        {
            if(strncmp(in_msg+i, start_msg, start_length-1) !=0)
            {
                    i++;
            } else
            {
```

```
                    start_flag=i+start_length;
                    break;
                }
        }
        i+=start_length;
        j=0;
        while(i <= length)
        {
            if((*(char *)(in_msg+i) == '&') || /* 38 */
                (*(char *)(in_msg+i) == ' ') ||
                (*(char *)(in_msg+i) == 13) ||
                (*(char *)(in_msg+i) == 0))
            {
                break;
            }
            out_msg[j++]=*(in_msg+i);
            i++;
        }
        out_msg[j]=0;
        return(&(out_msg[0]));
}
/*
 * read_game reads the moves played so far and returns the number of moves done by white
 * and by black.
 */

int new_read_game(char *moves)
{
        char line[LINE_MAX];
        char move[LINE_MAX];
        int iroot;
        int nwhite, nblack;
        int i=0;
        int j=0;
        char c = 0;
        nwhite = nblack = 0;
        while(*(moves+i) != 0)
        {
        /* This is an HTML hidden file routine.
         * The letters 'z' and 'Z' separate the white and black moves. Letters are used to
         * minimize the length of HTML form strings.
         */
            j =0;
            for(;;)
            {
                c = *(moves+i++);
```

```
        if((c == 'z') || (c == 'Z') || (c==0))
        {
            move[j]=0;
            break;
        }
            move[j++]=c;
    }

/*
 * These are the algorithms used by zzzzzz; for other chess programs these will need to be
 * changed.
 */
    gen_root();
    BUG((iroot = search_root
        (move, MOVE_STRING_ANY, FALSE, TRUE)) == INVALID)
    do_move(root[iroot].root_move);
    if (your_colour == WHITE_COLOUR)
        nwhite++;
    else
        nblack++;
    }
    compact_lists();
    if (my_colour == WHITE_COLOUR)
        return(nwhite);
    else
        return(nblack);
}
/*
 * Change FORM %XX to ASCII equivalent.
 */
char ahextoi(char* val_msg)
{
    char i = 0;
    char j = 0;
    char temp = 0;
    while(*val_msg !=0)
    {
        if((*val_msg >= 'a') && (*val_msg <= 'f'))
        {
            temp = *val_msg - 'a' + 10;
        } else
        if((*val_msg >= 'A') && (*val_msg <= 'F'))
        {
            temp = *val_msg - 'A' + 10;
        } else
        {
```

```
                temp = *val_msg - '0';
            }
            i = temp + (i * (j==0 ? 1 : 16));
            val_msg++; j++;
        }
        return i;
    }
/*
 * Take a FORM string and alter any %XX to ASCII equivalent.
 */
char* clear_hex(char* message)
{
char tmp_hex[3];
int i = 0;
char* xmessage;
    strcpy(in_msg, message);
        xmessage = in_msg;
    while(*xmessage != 0)
    {
        if(*xmessage == '+')
        {
            out_msg[i] = ' ';
        } else
        if(*xmessage != '%')
        {
            out_msg[i] = *xmessage;
        } else
        {
            xmessage++;
            tmp_hex[0] = *xmessage;
            xmessage++;
            tmp_hex[1] = *xmessage;
            tmp_hex[2] = 0;
            out_msg[i] = ahextoi( &tmp_hex[0] );
        }
            xmessage++; i++;
        out_msg[i] = 0;
        if(i >= 100) break;
    }
    return(&out_msg[0]);

}
/*
 * Plus (+) and Number (#) are used for check and mate displays. For economy these
 * are removed since the rebuild will occur without them.
 */
```

```c
char* clear_string(char* instring)
{
char tmp_string[8];
char* tmp_ptr;
int i = 0;
    tmp_ptr = instring;
    for(;;)
    {
        if(*tmp_ptr== '+')
        {
            tmp_string[i++] = ' ';
        } else
        if(*tmp_ptr== '#')
        {

            ;
        } else
        {
            tmp_string[i++] = *tmp_ptr;
        }
            tmp_ptr++;
            if(*tmp_ptr == 0) { break; }
    }
    tmp_string[i] = 0;
    strcpy(instring, tmp_string);
    return(instring);
}
/*
  * An HTML routine that sends a message to the user rather than the Chess board. Used
  * for a variety of situations, such as invalid moves, check mate, stale mate, error, ...
  */
void
display_state(char* message)
{
    printf("Content-type: text/html\n\n");
    printf("%s%s%s%s\n",
        "<HTML><HEAD><TITLE>Chess</TITLE></HEAD><BODY>\n",
        "<H1>",
        message,
        "</H1></BODY></HTML>\n");
    fflush(stdout);
    exit (0);
}
/*
  * play_game plays a game under simulated tournament conditions.
  */
void new_play_game(int xxxxxx, int yyyyyy, int state)
```

```
{
    int ngame_moves;
    time_t wall1, wall2;
    int wall;
    int iroot;
    char string[LINE_MAX];
    char name[50];
    char zzz_move[20];
    char remove_string[100];
    char move[LINE_MAX];
    char mystart[LINE_MAX];
    char board_string[11];
    char bline[10];
    int bcnt;
    int i;
    char* mymoves;
    char* line;
    int your_move=0;
    /*
      * The bcnt tells how many board move lines are present in hidden variables. The safety
      * is 1000 lines max. This should never occur.
      */
    i=0;
    while( i<10 )
    {
        bline[i] = (char )getc(stdin);
        if(bline[i] == '&') break;
        ++i;
    }
    bline[i] = 0;
    bcnt = atoi(variable(bline, "bcnt="));
    if((bcnt <= 0) || (bcnt >1000)) display_state("Too many moves");
    mymoves = malloc (sizeof(char) * bcnt * 80 + 300);
    line = malloc (sizeof(char) * bcnt * 80 + 300);
    /*
      * Retrieve the output from the server as a FORM.
      */
    if (gets(line) == NULL) display_state("Error: No input strings");
    /* Clean up the sets of moves and build them into a string */
    strcpy(mymoves, clear_hex(variable(line, "board0=")));
    i=1;
    while(i< bcnt )
    {
        sprintf(board_string, "board%d=", i);
        strcat(mymoves, clear_hex(variable(line,
        board_string)));
```

```
            i++;
    }
        /*
         * Get the state of the board at the start of the game. If it isn't there, assume the
         * default board.
         */
        strcpy(mystart, clear_hex(variable(line, "init=")));
        if(strlen(mystart) < 2)
        {
            strcpy(string, MYSTART);
            strcpy(mystart, MYSTART);
        } else
        {
                strcpy(string, mystart);
        }

        while(TRUE)
        {

            /* set up the initial state of the board */
            fen_to_board(string, TRUE);

            /* make the moves from the move history */
            ngame_moves = new_read_game(mymoves);
            /* a little trick to get the board displayed at the right time */
        if(your_move == 1)
        {
            your_move++;
        } else
        if(your_move == 2)
        {
                display_html_board(zzz_move, mymoves, mystart);
        }
        /*
         * Check if this is an initialization. If it is, show the board without making any moves.
         */
        if(state == 1)
        {
            display_html_board("", "", mystart);
        }

        /*
         * A check for game draw based on previous moves.
         */
        if (draw_by_repetition(TRUE))
        {
```

```
        display_state("Draw By Repetition");
}

/*
 * Some more state checks.
 */
gen_root();
if (nroot == 0)
{
    if (i_am_check(my_colour, your_colour))
        display_state("Check Mate");
    else
        display_state("Stale Mate");
    }
    else
    {
        /*
         * The computer moves followed by checks.
         */
        if (xxxxxx == my_colour)
        {
            if (nroot == 1)
            {
                display_state("Forced");
                jroot = 0;
                root[jroot].root_score = 0;
            }
            else
            {
            /* calculate time limit */
            if (ngame_moves
                < NGAME_MOVES1)
            {
                TimeLimit =
                (GAME_TIME1 - GAME_MARGIN -
                GameTimeUsed) /
                (NGAME_MOVES1 - ngame_moves);
            }
            else if (ngame_moves <
            (NGAME_MOVES1 + NGAME_MOVES2))
            {
                TimeLimit =
                    (GAME_TIME1 + GAME_TIME2 -
                    GAME_MARGIN - GameTimeUsed) /
                    (NGAME_MOVES1 + NGAME_MOVES2 -
                    ngame_moves);
```

```
        }
        else
        {
            TimeLimit = 90;
        }
        if (TimeLimit < 0)
        {
            TimeLimit = 1;
        }
        wall1 = time(NULL);
        do_root();
        wall2 = time(NULL);
        wall = (int) difftime(wall2,
            wall1) + 1;
        GameTimeUsed += wall;
        }
    move_to_san_string(
    root[jroot].root_move, TRUE);
    /* move the computer's move onto the move string */
     strcpy(zzz_move, move_string);
     strcat(mymoves,
         clear_string(move_string));
     strcat(mymoves, "Z");
}
else
{
    /*Just for information.
     get_book_move(); */
    while(TRUE)
    {
        /* That trick to time the display */
        your_move = 1;
        /* Get the move sent in the FORM
            and clean it up */
        strcpy(line, variable(line, "move="));
        (void )clear_hex(line);
        if (sscanf(line, "%s", move) != 1)
            continue;
        iroot = search_root(move, MOVE_STRING_ANY,
            FALSE, FALSE);
        /* A validity check */
        if (iroot == INVALID)
        {
         display_state("Invalid");
        }
    /*
```

```
                              * Add the move to the history string with a 'z' termination for the user's
                              * moves.
                              */
                             strcat(mymoves, clear_string(move_string));
                                     strcat(mymoves, "z");
                             /* check for mate here */
                             if(*(move_string + strlen(move_string) - 1) == '#')
                             {
                                     display_state("You Have Check Mate");
                             }
                             break;
                             }
                     }
                 }
             }
    }
    /* Set up some configuration parameters */
    void new_read_config()
    {
         DepthMax = 32;
         TimeLimit = 3;
         options.random_opening = 1;
         options.print_dbase = 1;
         options.print_distrib = 1;
    }
    /*
     * This routine is used if the program is called with no arguments. It sends back a startup
     * chess board to the user in HTML.
     */
    void display_html_default()
    {
         int i, j;
         int  k = 0;
         char* pos[8][8];
         set_xpos();
         pos[0][0]=xpos[ROOK+OFFSET][WHITE];
         pos[0][1]=xpos[KNIGHT+OFFSET][GRAY];
         pos[0][2]=xpos[BISHOP+OFFSET][WHITE];
         pos[0][3]=xpos[QUEEN+OFFSET][GRAY];
         pos[0][4]=xpos[KING+OFFSET][WHITE];
         pos[0][5]=xpos[BISHOP+OFFSET][GRAY];
         pos[0][6]=xpos[KNIGHT+OFFSET][WHITE];
         pos[0][7]=xpos[ROOK+OFFSET][GRAY];
         pos[7][0]=xpos[ROOK][GRAY];
         pos[7][1]=xpos[KNIGHT][WHITE];
         pos[7][2]=xpos[BISHOP][GRAY];
```

```
        pos[7][3]=xpos[QUEEN][WHITE];
        pos[7][4]=xpos[KING][GRAY];
        pos[7][5]=xpos[BISHOP][WHITE];
        pos[7][6]=xpos[KNIGHT][GRAY];
        pos[7][7]=xpos[ROOK][WHITE];
        for(j=0; j<=7; j++)
        {
            pos[1][j]= (j%2 != 0) ?
            xpos[PAWN+OFFSET][WHITE] : xpos[PAWN+OFFSET][GRAY];
            pos[6][j]= (j%2 == 0) ?
            xpos[PAWN][WHITE] : xpos[PAWN][GRAY];
        }
        for(i=2; i<=5; i++)
        {
            for(j=0; j<=7; j++)
            {
                pos[i][j]=(i%2 == j%2) ?
                xpos[BLANK][WHITE] : xpos[BLANK][GRAY];
            }
        }
    /*
     * The board is now reconfigured to the new state. This is sent out as HTML code to the
     * client.
     */
        printf("Content-type: text/html\n\n");
        printf("<HTML> <HEAD> <Title>CHESS GAME</Title>\n");
        printf("<BODY bgcolor=#f0f0f0 </BODY>");
        printf("</HEAD> <BODY><CENTER>\n");
        /*
         * The pointers to the IMaGes are used to create the HTML version of the chess
         * board.
         */
        for(i=0; i < 8; i++)
        {
            for(j=0; j < 8; j++)
            {
                printf("%s%s >\n",
                 "<IMG HEIGHT=51 WIDTH=51 SRC=",
                        pos[i][j]
                );
              k++;
            }
            printf("<BR>\n");
        }
        printf("%s\n", colour_as_string[my_colour]);
        /*
```

```
         * The HTML FORM is sent to allow the user to make the next move.
         */
      printf("%s% METHOD=POST >\n",
           "<FORM ACTION=
           \"http://info.com/cgi-bin/dacs/chess/chessw?x\" ");
      printf("%s%s\n%s\n%s\n%s\n%s\n%s\n",
           "<BR><BR><A HREF=
               \"http://info.com/~markf/chess.help.html\">",
               "Example Input: a2a4 </A>",
           "<INPUT TYPE=\"hidden\" NAME=\"bcnt\" VALUE=\"1\" SIZE=\"4\" >",
           "<INPUT TYPE=\"hidden\" NAME=\"init\" VALUE=\"\" >",
           "<INPUT TYPE=\"text\" NAME=\"move\" VALUE=\"\" SIZE=6 >",
           "<INPUT TYPE=\"hidden\" NAME=\"board0\" VALUE=\"\" SIZE=5 >",
           "<INPUT TYPE=\"submit\" VALUE=\"send\"> <INPUT TYPE=reset>",
           "</FORM>"
           );
      printf("</CENTER></BODY></HTML>\n");
      fflush(stdout);
      exit (0);
}
/*
 * The substitute main. You can either replace main with this or call it from main.
 */
int new_main(int argc, char **argv)
{
/*    char *p; */
      set_options();
      if(argc == 1)
      {
               display_html_default();
      }

      /* Parse command line options */

      new_read_config();
      GameTimeUsed *= 60;
      initialize();
      /*
           new_play_game(WHITE_COLOUR, BLACK_COLOUR, 0);
       */
      if(*(argv[1]) == 's')
      {
           new_play_game(BLACK_COLOUR, WHITE_COLOUR, 1);
      } else
      {
           new_play_game(BLACK_COLOUR, WHITE_COLOUR, 0);
```

```
        }
        return(EXIT_SUCCESS);
}
int main(int argc, char **argv);
int main(int argc, char **argv)
{
        new_main(argc, argv);
}
/* Add to the bottom of zzzzzz.c */
/* New code */
/*
 * This routine takes the state of the board as known by the chess algorithms and turns it
 * into a state usable by the HTML display code. The routine will need to be customized for
 * other chess algorithms.
 */
int get_board(int k)
{
int offset;
    offset = (nota_colour[board[map[k]]->board_colour] == 'w')
        ? 0 : OFFSET;
    if (board[map[k]] == &empty)
    {
            /* empty square background */
                return BLANK;
    }
    switch(nota_kind[board[map[k]]->board_kind])
    {
        case 'P':
            return PAWN+offset;
        case 'N':
            return KNIGHT+offset;
        case 'B':
            return BISHOP+offset;
        case 'R':
            return ROOK+offset;
        case 'Q':
            return QUEEN+offset;
        case 'K':
            return KING+offset;
        default:
            return BLANK;
    }
}
/* Include along with zzzzzz.h */
#ifndef _new_h
#define _new_h
```

```c
/* This was needed to find some missing defines */
#include <unistd.h>
/* Definition of the default state for the chess board. Continuity is provided by passing the
 * chess board start state as a string and the history of moves as a sequence of strings.
 */
#define MYSTART "rnbqkbnr/pppppppp/8/8/8/8/PPPPPPPP/RNBQKBNR w KQkq - 0 1"
#ifndef FILENAME_MAX
#define FILENAME_MAX 40
#endif
#define BLANK 6 /* A blank square on the board */
/*
 * Defines for the HTML IMaGes used to create the chess board on the screen. These
 * will need to be customized for your site.
 */
#define MYPATH www.xxx.com
#define B_RK_G "\"http://MYPATH/rook_b.g.gif\" ALT=\"B_RK\""
#define B_KT_G "\"http://MYPATH/knight_b.g.gif\" ALT=\"B_KT\""
#define B_BI_G "\"http://MYPATH/bishop_b.g.gif\" ALT=\"B_BI\""
#define B_QU_G "\"http://MYPATH/queen_b.g.gif\" ALT=\"B_QU\""
#define B_KI_G "\"http://MYPATH/king_b.g.gif\" ALT=\"B_KG\""
#define B_RK_W "\"http://MYPATH/rook_b.gif\" ALT=\"B_RK\""
#define B_KT_W "\"http://MYPATH/knight_b.gif\" ALT=\"B_KT\""
#define B_BI_W "\"http://MYPATH/bishop_b.gif\" ALT=\"B_BI\""
#define B_QU_W "\"http://MYPATH/queen_b.gif\" ALT=\"B_QU\""
#define B_KI_W "\"http://MYPATH/king_b.gif\" ALT=\"B_KG\""
#define W_RK_W "\"http://MYPATH/rook.gif\" ALT=\"W_RK\""
#define W_KT_W "\"http://MYPATH/knight.gif\" ALT=\"W_KT\""
#define W_BI_W "\"http://MYPATH/bishop.gif\" ALT=\"W_BI\""
#define W_QU_W "\"http://MYPATH/queen.gif\" ALT=\"W_QU\""
#define W_KI_W "\"http://MYPATH/king.gif\" ALT=\"W_KG\""
#define W_RK_G "\"http://MYPATH/rook.g.gif\" ALT=\"W_RK\""
#define W_KT_G "\"http://MYPATH/knight.g.gif\" ALT=\"W_KT\""
#define W_BI_G "\"http://MYPATH/bishop.g.gif\" ALT=\"W_BI\""
#define W_QU_G "\"http://MYPATH/queen.g.gif\" ALT=\"W_QU\""
#define W_KI_G "\"http://MYPATH/king.g.gif\" ALT=\"W_KG\""
#define W_PN_G "\"http://MYPATH/pawn.g.gif\" ALT=\"W_PN\""
#define W_PN_W "\"http://MYPATH/pawn.gif\" ALT=\"W_PN\""
#define B_PN_G "\"http://MYPATH/pawn_b.g.gif\" ALT=\"B_PN\""
#define B_PN_W "\"http://MYPATH/pawn_b.gif\" ALT=\"B_PN\""
#define BLNK_W "\"http://MYPATH/blank.gif\" ALT=\"----\""
#define BLNK_G "\"http://MYPATH/blank.g.gif\" ALT=\"----\""
/*
 * The defines for the background square colors and piece colors.
 */
#define WHITE 0 /* piece and background */
#define GRAY 1 /* background */
```

```
#define BLACK 1 /* piece */
#define OFFSET 7 /* offset from white to black pieces in array */
/*
  * This macro is used to determine the background color based on the x and y
  * coordinates.
  */
#define background(a, b) ( ((a) % 2) == ((b) % 2) ? WHITE : GRAY )
#endif
```

Star Quilt Program

```
/***************************************************************
 *      Quilt.C
 ***************************************************************/
/* This program is owned by Mark Felton and Chris Cota. Any unauthorized use is prohibited.
 */
/*

 * These are built in libraries.
 */
#include <stdio.h>
#include <stdlib.h>
#include <sys/time.h>
#include <unistd.h>
#include <string.h>
#include "Quilt_defines.h"
extern void Quilt();
extern char* xitoa(int);
extern char* clear_cr(char* );
extern char* clear_sp(char* );
extern char* clear_amp(char* );
/***************************************************************
 *      IMaGe routines
 ***************************************************************/
struct _Color_values
{
    char select[3];
};
typedef struct _Color_values COLOR_VALUES;

int element[9];
int offset[9];
int purchase_info;
int option_small;
class _Image {
private:
    COLOR_VALUES Color_values[10];
    FILE* stream;
    char buff[2];
```

```cpp
public:
    _Image(); // constructor
    void show_star(char* gif, char* g_colors, int mode);
};
typedef class _Image IMAGE;
/* This is the Quilt IMaGe Constructor */
_Image::_Image()
{
int i;
    for(i=0; i<9; i++)
    {
        element[i]=i;
        offset[i]=0;
    }
    /* initiate color values for template */
    Color_values[0].select[0] = 222; /* RED */
    Color_values[0].select[1] = 90;
    Color_values[0].select[2] = 57;

    Color_values[1].select[0] = 255; /* WHITE */
    Color_values[1].select[1] = 250;
    Color_values[1].select[2] = 255;

    Color_values[2].select[0] = 66; /* GREEN */
    Color_values[2].select[1] = 132;
    Color_values[2].select[2] = 156;

    Color_values[3].select[0] = 247; /* YELLOW */
    Color_values[3].select[1] = 247;
    Color_values[3].select[2] = 74;

    Color_values[4].select[0] = 247; /* Orange */
    Color_values[4].select[1] = 165;
    Color_values[4].select[2] = 66;

    Color_values[5].select[0] = 74; /* Blue */
    Color_values[5].select[1] = 99;
    Color_values[5].select[2] = 132;

    Color_values[6].select[0] = 57; /* Purple */
    Color_values[6].select[1] = 41;
    Color_values[6].select[2] = 41;

    Color_values[7].select[0] = 214; /* Dk Red */
    Color_values[7].select[1] = 57;
    Color_values[7].select[2] = 49;
```

```
            Color_values[8].select[0] = 66; /* Drk Green */
            Color_values[8].select[1] = 132;
            Color_values[8].select[2] = 156;
            Color_values[9].select[0] = 255;
            Color_values[9].select[1] = 255;
            Color_values[9].select[2] = 255;
                  purchase_info=OFF;
}
void
_Image::show_star (char* gif, char* g_colors, int mode=0)
{
int j;
int i=0;
int flag=0;
      /* Read the colors */

      for(j=0; j<9; j++)
      {
            element[j] = *((char *)(g_colors + j))-'0' -1;
            if((element[j]<0) || (element[j]>8))
                  { element[j]=0; }
      }
      /* Read in the template star */
      fprintf(stdout,"Content-type: image/gif\n\n");
stream = fopen(gif, "r");
while(fgets(buff,2,stream) != 0)
{
            if((flag==0) && (mode==0))
            switch(i)
            {
            case 16:
            case 17:
            case 18:
                  buff[0]= Color_values[element[0]].select[i-16]
                        + (i==17 ? offset[0]++ : 0);
                  break;
            case 19:
            case 20:
            case 21:
                  buff[0]= Color_values[element[7]].select[i-19]
                        + (i==20 ? offset[1]++ : 0);
                  break;
            case 22:
            case 23:
            case 24:
                  buff[0]= Color_values[element[2]].select[i-22]
```

```
                            + (i==23 ? offset[2]++ : 0);
                    break;
            case 25:
            case 26:
            case 27:
                    buff[0]= Color_values[element[1]].select[i-25]
                            + (i==26 ? offset[3]++ : 0);
                    break;
            case 28:
            case 29:
            case 30:
                    buff[0]= Color_values[element[3]].select[i-28]
                            + (i==29 ? offset[4]++ : 0);
                    break;
            case 31:
            case 32:
            case 33:
                    buff[0]= Color_values[element[4]].select[i-31]
                            + (i==32 ? offset[5]++ : 0);
                    break;
            case 34:
            case 35:
            case 36:
                    buff[0]= Color_values[element[5]].select[i-34]
                            + (i==35 ? offset[6]++ : 0);
                    break;
            case 37:
            case 38:
            case 39:
                    buff[0]= Color_values[element[6]].select[i-37]
                            + (i==38 ? offset[7]++ : 0);
                    break;
            case 40:
            case 41:
                    buff[0]= Color_values[element[8]].select[i-40]
                            + (i==41 ? offset[8]++ : 0);
                    break;
            /*
             * On the final byte of the color map, the flag is set up to speed up the rest of the
             * output.
             */
            case 42:
                    buff[0]= Color_values[element[8]].select[i-40]
                            + (i==41 ? offset[8]++ : 0);
                    flag=1;
                    break;
```

```
                default:
                    break;
                }
                if(mode==0)
                {
                    fprintf(stdout, "%c", buff[0]);
                } else
                {
                    fprintf(stdout, "%d %d\n", i, buff[0]);
                }
                i++;
        }
        fclose(stream);
            for(i=0; i<9; i++)
            {
                offset[i]=0;
            }
}

char
color_val(char* var_str)
{
        if(strcmp(var_str, "RED") == 0)
        {
            return(0 + '1');
        } else
        if(strcmp(var_str, "WHITE") == 0)
        {
            return(1 + '1');
        } else
        if(strcmp(var_str, "GREEN") == 0)
        {
            return(2 + '1');
        } else
        if(strcmp(var_str, "YELLOW") == 0)
        {
            return(3 + '1');
        } else
        if(strcmp(var_str, "ORANGE") == 0)
        {
            return(4 + '1');
        } else
        if(strcmp(var_str, "BLUE") == 0)
        {
            return(5 + '1');
        } else
```

```c
        if(strcmp(var_str, "PURPLE") == 0)
        {
                return(6 + '1');
        } else
        if(strcmp(var_str, "CYAN") == 0)
        {
                return(7 + '1');
        } else
        if(strcmp(var_str, "FUCHSIA") == 0)
        {
                return(8 + '1');
        } else
        {
                return(0 + '1');
        }

}
/********************************************************************
 *              Quilt HTML routines
 ********************************************************************/
class _Quilt {
private:
        char show_string[10];
        int send_mail;
        FILE* stream;
public:
        _Quilt();
        void html();
        void default();
};
typedef class _Quilt QUILT;

_Quilt::_Quilt()
{
int i;
        /* Set the colors to the defaults */
        show_string[9]=0;
        for(i=0; i<9; i++)
        {
                show_string[i] = '1' + i;
        }
        send_mail = -1;
}

/*
 * Use the HTML file input output mode to send the default HTML to the client.
```

```
  */
#define HTML_FILE "unix_path/star_quilt.html"
void _Quilt::default()
{
char* buffer;
     buffer = new(char * 80); // allocate an 80 character buffer
     printf("Content-type: text/html\n\n");
     stream = fopen(HTML_FILE, "r");
     while(fgets(buffer, 80, stream) != EOF)
     {
          puts(buffer);
     }
}
/*
 * This is the main part of the program. It sends the Quilt HTML to the client along with an
 * IMaGe string. The IMaGe string will cause the cgi-bin program to be called from the HTML
 * with options that will send the GIF image back to the client.
 */
_Quilt::html(char* input_string)
{
     int i, j;
     char get_val[50];
     char* var_str;
     char temp_str[10];
     MAIL* Mail;
     j=0;
     gets(get_val);
     /*
      * The colors have been submitted as a FORM input with values ranging from 0 to 9.
      * Get the values of the user's requested colors and put them in the appropriate arrays
      * for processing. These will later be sent as argv when the same cgi-bin program is
      * called to request the GIF IMaGe output.
      */
     var_str=variable(input_string,"elem1=", "&elem2=");
     *(show_string + 0) = color_val(var_str);
     var_str=variable(input_string,"&elem2=", "&elem3=");
     *(show_string + 1) = color_val(var_str);
     var_str=variable(input_string,"&elem3=", "&elem4=");
     *(show_string + 2) = color_val(var_str);
     var_str=variable(input_string,"&elem4=", "&elem5=");
     *(show_string + 3) = color_val(var_str);
     var_str=variable(input_string,"&elem5=", "&elem6=");
     *(show_string + 4) = color_val(var_str);
     var_str=variable(input_string,"&elem6=", "&elem7=");
     *(show_string + 5) = color_val(var_str);
     var_str=variable(input_string,"&elem7=", "&elem8=");
```

```
*(show_string + 6) = color_val(var_str);
var_str=variable(input_string,"&elem8=", "");
*(show_string + 7) = color_val(var_str);
var_str=variable(input_string,"&elem9=", "");
*(show_string + 8) = color_val(var_str);
strcpy(temp_str,var_str);
/*
 * Check if an email request has been sent.
 */
var_str=variable(input_string,"&email=", " ");
if(strcmp(var_str, "ON") == 0)
{
    Mail = new(MAIL);
    Mail->request(show_string);
    return;
}
/*
 * Check if the user wishes to see the purchase information.
 */
var_str=variable(input_string,"&purchase_info=", "");
purchase_info = strcmp(var_str, "on") == 0 ? ON : OFF;
/*
 * Change from ASCII to ints for the Options in the FORMs.
 */
for(i=0; i<9; i++)
{
    element[i]= *(show_string+i) - '0';
}

/*
 * Send the fixed part of the star quilt HTML to stdout.
 */
printf("Content-type: text/html\n\n");
printf( "<HTML>\n");
printf("<BODY bgcolor=#f0f0f0 </BODY>\n");
printf("<BODY>\n");
/*
 * Now deal with the variable sections of the HTML.
 */

/*
 * A check on whether to use the modem mode. If the modem is used, a smaller
 * IMaGe is sent and the cgi-bin option for requesting the image is changed from
 * -i -> large image to -I -> small image.
 */
if(option_small==1)
```

```
{
    printf("<FORM ACTION=\"http://info.com/cgi-bin/dev/markf/cgi-bin/Qmain?-
            J\" METHOD=POST>\n");
    printf("<IMG HEIGHT=184 WIDTH=186 SRC=\"http://info.com/cgi-bin/dev/
            markf/cgi-bin/Qmain?-I");
} else
{
printf("<FORM ACTION=\"http://info.com/cgi-bin/dev/markf/cgi-bin/Qmain?-j\"
        METHOD=POST>\n");
printf("<IMG HEIGHT=369 WIDTH=373 SRC=\"http://info.com/cgi-bin/dev/
        markf/cgi-bin/Qmain?-i");
}
/*
 * Since the user will be able to change the colors again, an option FORM is sent to the
 * screen as HTML. However, since the C++ or C program has knowledge of which colors
 * are already selected, some intelligence is added to make these the selected colors in
 * the option fields.
 */
printf("%s\">", show_string);
printf("<H2> Select Color For Each Star Element </H2>\n");
printf("<BR>");
for(i=0; i<9; i++)
{
    printf("%s%d%s", "_", i, "_\n");
    printf("%s%d%s", "<SELECT NAME = \"elem",
     i+1, "\">Element Color\n");
    for(j=1; j<=9 ; j++)
    {
        printf("<OPTION ");
        printf("%s", (element[i] == j ? "SELECTED>" : ">"));
        switch(j)
        {
        default:
        case 1:
            printf(" RED\n");
        break;
        case 2:
            printf(" WHITE\n");
        break;
        case 3:
            printf(" GREEN\n");
        break;
        case 4:
            printf(" YELLOW\n");
        break;
        case 5:
```

```c
                    printf(" ORANGE\n");
            break;
            case 6:
                printf(" BLUE\n");
            break;
            case 7:
                printf(" PURPLE\n");
            break;
            case 8:
                printf(" CYAN\n");
            break;
            case 9:
                printf(" FUCHSIA\n");
            break;
            }
        }
        printf("</SELECT>\n");
        if((i==2) || (i==5))
        {
            printf("<BR><BR>\n");
        }
    }

    /*
     * Next show a checkbox that allows the user to request cost information.
     */
    printf("<BR><BR>\n");
    printf("<BR><BR>\n");
    printf("[<INPUT TYPE=\"checkbox\" NAME=\"purchase_info\" VALUE=\"on\"> Show
            Purchase Infomation]\n");
    if(purchase_info == OFF)
    {
        ; /* Show no cost information */
    } else
    {
        /*
         * Show cost information
         */
        printf("<H4>Quilt Prices</H4>\n");
        printf("<UL>\n");
        printf(" <LI>Queen Size $250\n");
        printf("<LI>Full Size $225\n");
        printf("<LI>Twin Size $175\n");
        printf("<LI>Baby Crib $95\n");
        printf("<LI>Baby Small $75\n");
        printf("</UL>\n");
```

```
                    printf("<BR>To Order by Phone, Call 303-674-9228\n");
                    printf("<BR>To Order by Email, Turn on the Email Option");
                    printf(" Below and Submit the Form\n");
                    printf("<SELECT NAME = \"email\">Email Purchase<BR>");
                    printf("<OPTION SELECTED> OFF\n");
                    printf("<OPTION> ON\n");
                    printf("</SELECT>\n");
        }
        printf("<P>Submit Color Selection",
            "<INPUT TYPE = \"submit\" VALUE=\"Select Colors\"");
        printf("> <INPUT TYPE = \"reset\">\n");
        /*
         * Complete the HTML output
         */
        printf("%s%s%s", "</FORM>", "</BODY>", "</HTML>\n");
}


class _Mail
{
private:
public:
        void request(char* quilt_hidden);
        void submittal();
};
class _Mail MAIL;


/*
 * This routine creates the mail FORM that is sent as HTML to the client screen.
 */
void
_Mail::request(char* quilt_hidden)
{
printf("%s%s%s%s%s%s%s%s%s%s%s%s%s%s%s%s%s%s%s%s%s%s%s%s%s%s%s%s%s%s%s%s",
    "Content-type: text/html\n\n",
    "<HTML><HEAD><TITLE>Quilt Mail Form</TITLE></HEAD>\n",
    "<BODY bgcolor=#ffffff </BODY>\n",
    "<H1> STAR QUILT ORDER FORM </H1>\n",
    "<BR>\n",
    "If you are submitting this form, you are requesting purchase of the",
    "Quilt you have designed. Because of differences in computer screens,",
    "the colors may not be an exact match to those shown on your screen.",
    "Every attempt has been made to get these as correct as possible.",
    "Your colors have been automatically recorded. Please verify them below.",
    "\n<BR>\n",
    "<FORM ACTION=\"http://info.com/cgi-bin/dev/markf/cgi-bin/Qmain?-m\"
METHOD=POST>\n",
```

```
    "<P>\n",
    "<B> Send To </B>: <INPUT VALUE=\"cota@dash.com\" SIZE=40
NAME=\"to\"><BR>\n",
    "<B> Your Name </B>: <INPUT VALUE=\"\" SIZE=40 NAME=\"name\"><BR>\n",
    "<B> Your Email </B>: <INPUT VALUE=\"\" SIZE=40 NAME=\"from\"><BR>\n",
    "<B> Including Area Code </B> <BR>\n",
    "<B> Phone </B>: <INPUT VALUE=\"\" SIZE=40 NAME=\"phone\"><BR>\n",
    "<B> Size </B>: <INPUT VALUE=\"\" SIZE=40 NAME=\"size\"><BR>\n",
    "<P><INPUT TYPE=\"HIDDEN\" NAME=\"quilt\" VALUE=\"",
    quilt_hidden,
    "\"></P>",
    "<B> Any Special Comments </B>\n",
    "<P><TEXTAREA ROWS=10 COLS=60 NAME=\"body\"></TEXTAREA></P>\n",
    "<P><INPUT TYPE=\"submit\" VALUE=\"Send the mail\">\n",
    "<INPUT TYPE=\"reset\" VALUE=\"Start over\"></P>\n",
    "</FORM>\n",
    "<HR>\n",
    "</BODY></HTML>\n");
}
/*
 * This routine is used to process the input from the mail FORM and send the mail to the
 * designated person.
 */
void
_Mail::submittal()
{
FILE* fp;
pid_t pid;
char filestring[150];
char send_string[200];
char mail_xtr[1000];
char* mail_str;
    gets(mail_xtr);
    mail_str=clear_cr(mail_xtr);
    mail_str=clear_sp(mail_str);
    mail_str=clear_amp(mail_str);
    strcpy(filestring,"/tmp/mif.tmp");
    pid = getpid();
    strcat(filestring, (xitoa((int )pid)+1));
    if((fp= fopen(filestring, "w")) == 0)
    {
        return;
    }
    fprintf(fp,"%s\n", mail_str);
    fclose(fp);
    strcpy(send_string, "mail markf@drmail < ");
```

```
        strcat(send_string, filestring);
        system(send_string);
        strcpy(send_string, "rm ");
        strcat(send_string, filestring);
        system("sleep 1");
        system(send_string);
}

/*
 * These are the FORM parsing subroutines.
 */

char* clear_cr(char* msg)
{
}

char* clear_amp(char* msg)
{
}

char* clear_sp(char* msg)
{
}

char* variable(char* msg, char* start_msg, char* unused)
{
}
/* Subroutine to turn integer to ASCII */
char* xitoa(int n)
{
}
/************************************************************
 *    main
 ************************************************************/
/* This program is owned by Mark Felton and Chris Cota. Any unauthorized use is prohibited.
 */
extern char *optarg;
extern int opterr;
extern int getopt();

void
main(int argc, char *argv[])
{

    int optchar; /* arg for getopt */
    char* gif="/home/markf/cgi-bin/star.gif";
```

```
char* gifsm="/home/markf/cgi-bin/star.sm.gif";
QUILT* Quilt;
IMAGE* Image;
MAIL* Mail;
option_small=0;
opterr = 1; /* disable printing an error msg*/
/**********************************************************
 *              OPTIONS
 **********************************************************/
while ((optchar = getopt(argc, argv, "i:I:mjJs")) != EOF)
{
switch(optchar)
{
    /* IMaGe Options */
     case 'i':
         Image = new(IMAGE);
         Image->show_star(gif, optarg);
         return;
     case 'I':
         Image = new(IMAGE);
         Image->show_star(gifsm, optarg);
         return;
    /* Star quilt HTML option */
     case 'J':
         option_small=1;
     case 'j':
         Quilt = new(QUILT);
         Quilt->html();
         return;
    /* Mail Option */
     case 'm':
         Mail = new(MAIL);
         Mail->submittal();
         return;
     default:
         break;
    }
}
    /*
     * If there are no options, the program will put out the starting HTML program. This is
     * a protection against someone entering the cgi-bin program as a URL request.
     */
        Quilt = new(QUILT);
        Quilt->default();
}
#ifndef _Quilt_h
```

```
#define _Quilt_h
/*****************************************************************
 *              Quilt.h
 *****************************************************************/
/* These are libraries */
#include <stdlib.h>
#include <string.h>
#include <iostream.h>
#include "Bus.h"
#include "Bexterns.h"

struct _Color_values
{
    char select[3];
};
typedef struct _Color_values COLOR_VALUES;

/* The main object that controls how the quilt appears on the computer screen */
class _Quilt : public _Formin
{

    send_gif(int type, int color); // create the quilt gif
    int element[9]; // The nine quilt star areas
    int offset[9];
    int purchase_info; // flag to show purchase info
    COLOR_VALUES Color_values[10]; // included none
public:
    _Quilt(); // constructor
    ~_Quilt() { ; }; // null destructor
    void show_quilt();
    void show_sample(char* gif, int mode);
    void build_quilt();
    void get_user_input();
    void form_out();
    void show_star(char* gif, int mode);
            // mode=0 normal, mode=1 diff data
    void get_form();
    void get_formx();// test mode
};
typedef class _Quilt QUILT;
#endif
```

Further Reading

Derek Coleman et al. *Object-oriented Development: The Fusion Method,* Prentice Hall, 1994

Franklin Davis et al. *WAIS Interface Protocol Prototype Functional Specification, Thinking Machines.* Available from Franklin Davis (fad@think.com) or Brewster Kahle (brewster@think.com).

Margaret A. Ellis and Bjarne Stroustrup. *The Annotated C++ Reference Manual,* Addison-Wesley, 1990.

Delores M. Etter. *Introduction to ANSI C for Engineers and Scientists,* Prentice Hall, 1996.

David Flanagan. *Java in a Nutshell,* O'Reilly & Associates Inc., 1996.

Ian S. Graham. *HTML Sourcebook,* John Wiley & Sons, Inc., 1995.

Kris Jamsa. *The C Library,* McGraw-Hill, 1985.

Brian W. Kernighan and Rob Pike. *The UNIX Programming Environment,* Prentice Hall, 1984.

Brian W. Kernighan and Dennis M. Ritchie. *The C Programming Language, 2nd edition,* Prentice Hall, 1988.

Ed Krol. *The Whole Internet User's Guide & Catalog,* O'Reilly & Associates, Inc., 1994.

Marc J. Rochkind. *Advanced UNIX Programming,* Prentice Hall, 1985.

Mary Shaw and David Garland. *Software Architecture,* Prentice Hall, 1996.

Bjarne Stroustrup. *The C++ Programming Language, 2nd edition.* Addison-Wesley, 1991.

Larry Wall and Randal L. Schwartz. *Programming PERL,* O'Reilly & Associates, Inc., 1992.

Keith Weiskamp and Bryan Flamig. *The Complete C++ Primer,* Academic Press, Inc., 1990.

Mark Williams Company. *ANSI C: A Lexical Guide,* Prentice Hall, 1988

URLs and FTPs

GIF compression: Yi-Jou-Chen: LZW Compression and Decompression, http://www.tc.cornell.edu/Visualization/contrib/cs490-94to95/yijou/myproj.html

Chess: ftp://caissa.onenet.net/pub/chess/Unix

HTML: http://www.sandia.gov/sci_compute/elements.html

PERL: http://jau.ece.utexas.edu/perl/perl.html

PERL: http://www.ijs.si/perl/

UNIX Man Pages: http://www.nova.edu/Inter-Links/search/man.html

Star Quilt: http://www.dash.com/netro/tribal/Quilt.html

URL: http://www.sandia.gov/sci_compute/html_ref#URL
http://www.w3.org/hypertext/www/Addressing/URL/5_BNF.html

CGI Internet Programming <C++ & C> Code Listings: ftp://alphacdc.com/pub/cgi
http://www.alphacdc.com/prentice/cgi-book.html

Playable Chess Game: http://www.alphacdc.com/chess/

Create GIFs C Code: http://www.boutell.com/gd/

Terminology

cgi-bin A special area on the same computer and accessed by the server software that can be used to respond to form requests or can provide other computer controlled output to the client by passing it through the server.

class A C++ type that includes both data types, similar to a struct and subroutines. A C++ class is self-enclosed module. Only the public segments can be accessed from outside the class. The private components are only available to the other parts of the class. While it is not a requirement, standard C++ practice is to place all data types in the private area and then to provide public class functions if it is necessary to change the data from outside of the class.

client The user's side of the software used on the Internet. Popular server softwares are Netscape, Internet Explorer, Mosaic, and lynx.

client-server software Refers to the complete process of moving data through client software located at the same site as the cgi-bin program and HTML files and then out to the server software, which resides on the user's computer.

color map A special section in a GIF file that maps colors to a single number. Colors in the color map are represent by three numbers that range from 0 to 255. The numbers represent the amount of the three pigments red, green, and blue.

cout A C++ command that acts similar to printf in C. It sends its output to stdout.

form An HTML element that allows user selectable or hidden data to be sent from a Web page to a cgi-bin program.

Get method A form method that sends the user's request into the program as command line arguments (equivalent to argc and argv[] in C++ and C).

hidden variable A value that will not be shown on the user screen but will be sent along with other user input when a form is sent to a cgi-bin program.

HTML HyperText Markup Language. The script language used to send formatting, identification, and control information between the client and server. The formatting capability allows you to set up tables, change font size, center, etc. The control information provides hyperlinks to other documents, and identifies animations, images, sound, Applets, or other media. HTML is what gives Web pages interesting layouts, including multimedia.

HTTP HyperText Transfer Protocol. The protocol used for sending and receiving HTML, cgi-bin, and other client-server information.

IMaGe (IMG) A picture that can be sent across the Internet as part of a Web page. Standard IMaGe formats are GIF and JPG, but special browsers can support other formats. Images that can be used on the Web can be obtained from scanners, digital cameras, or special graphics programs.

Image Input Form A form that is sent when the user clicks on an IMaGe. The IMaGe input form will send the x and y coordinates of the location where the mouse is clicked on the IMaGe along with any other user input.

inheritance In C++ it is possible to define a base class, which can then become a part of another class. When this is done, the base class is said to be inherited.

object An object comes into existence in C++ (object-oriented programming) when an instance of a class type is created. For example if the class type is a form, then the declaration of form myform instantiates the object myform of type form.

overloading In C++ it is possible to have the same symbol serve multiple purposes provided that there is a way for the compiler to identify which version is being used. Overloading can be done with function names, operators, or data types.

parse Any processing done by a program that separates out components of a string is said to parse the string. In cgi-bin programming, parsing will be needed to separate out the components of a form string. The use of parsing can be extended to logic in databases and other applications.

Post method A form method that sends the user's request to a cgi-bin program as stdin. The user's request can be retrieved by the cgi-bin program using any stdin routine (e.g., gets()).

server The HTML Web page and cgi-bin program side of the Internet. Server software will send out requested HTML or cgi-bin Web pages along with IMaGes and other multimedia.

stdin Standard input. The keyboard and mouse are the major ways for providing stdin from the computer. The primary distinction for the Internet is that stdin will come into forms in a specially formatted string that includes alphanumeric characters in their normal manner, while punctuation and control characters are sent in a special hexadecimal mode.

stdout Standard output. Normally the computer screen, but when sent from a cgi-bin script, stdout passes through the client software which interprets the HTML requests before putting things onto the screen.

Thru mode A method of sending an HTML file through a cgi-bin program and out to the client-server software.

URL Universal resource locator. A mnemonic address that will be mapped into an IP address. The URL can be used to access multimedia resouces that include HTML Web pages, cgi-bin programs, GIF and JPG image files, audio files, video files, PDF, etc. The URL consists of four basic parts and one subpart (not identified in the standard).

aaaa://bbb.bbb.bbb/ccc/ccc/ccc/ccc?ddd+eee

aaaa   access method

http   HyperText Transfer Protocol

https   HyperTest Transfer Protocol Secure

file   internal file accessible by the browser. Uses unix_path to determine the location

mailto   email form

news   netnews

nntp   local news

wais   wide area information server

gopher

telnet   followed by user ID to telnet session

cid   content identifier for MIME body type

mid   message identifier for elecronic mail

afs   AFS file access

prospero   PROSPERO link

x-exec   executable program

bbb.bbb.bbb   The Internet node (default is PORT 80)

ccc/ccc/ccc   The Internet Path

?ddd   options

+eee   part of options will separate as argv[1-n] for cgi-bin programs

WAIS   Wide Area Information Server. A publicly available database search program. WAIS includes programs that create a word seach index from a group of files in specified directories. A second program is also provided that can be used to search through the created indexes and send back URLs for the documents that contain the searched word. WAIS includes logical AND, OR, and NOT. The WAIS indexing tool removes common words, such as *the* and *a* from the index automatically.

Web page   Any HTML page that can be sent out to the server software and then to the user. A Web page may be produced using HTML, cgi-bin programs and multi-media. The home page is a special Web page that is the normal starting point for one or more Web pages. A group of Web pages need not all be at the same site since they can be interconnected or anchored through their URLs.

Index

Index of Terms

ASCII to HTML Forms

ASCII	HTML Form	Hex	Dec	Nomenclature
^A or ^a	%01	01	1	control A SOH
^B or ^b	%02	02	2	control B STX
^C or ^c	%03	03	3	control C ETX
^D or ^d	%04	04	4	control D EOT
^E or ^e	%05	05	5	control E ENQ
^F or ^f	%06	06	6	control F ACK
^G or ^g	%07	07	7	control G BEL
^H or ^h	%08	08	8	control H BS
^I or ^i	%09	09	9	control I HT
^J or ^j	%0A	0A	10	control J NL
^K or ^k	%0B	0B	11	control K VT
^L or ^l	%0C	0C	12	control L NP
^M or ^m	%0D	0D	13	control M CR
^N or ^n	%0E	0E	14	control N SO
^O or ^o	%0F	0F	15	control O SI
^P or ^p	%10	10	16	control P DLE
^Q or ^q	%11	11	17	control Q DCL
^R or ^r	%12	12	18	control R DC2
^S or ^s	%13	13	19	control S DC3
^T or ^t	%14	14	20	control T DC4
^U or ^u	%15	15	21	control U NAK
^V or ^v	%16	16	22	control V SYN
^W or ^w	%17	17	23	control W ETB
^X or ^x	%18	18	24	control X CAN
^Y or ^y	%19	19	25	control Y EM
^Z or ^z	%1A	1A	26	control Z SUB
	%1B	1B	27	ESC
	%1C	1C	28	FS
	%1D	1D	29	GS
	%1E	1E	30	RS
	%1F	1F	31	US
SPACE	%20	20	32	SP
!	%21	21	33	EXCLAMATION
"	%22	22	34	QUOTE
#	%23	23	35	NUMBER
$	%24	24	36	DOLLAR

ASCII to HTML Forms *(Continued)*

ASCII	HTML Form	Hex	Dec	Nomenclature
%	%25	25	37	PERCENT
&	%26	26	38	AMPERSAND
'	%27	27	39	TICK
(	%28	28	40	LEFT PAREN
)	%29	29	41	RIGHT PAREN
*	%2A	2A	42	ASTERISK
+	%2B	2B	43	PLUS
,	%2C	2C	44	COMMA
_	%2D	2D	45	
.	%2E	2E	46	PERIOD
/	%2F	2F	47	FORWARD SLASH
0–9	0–9	30–39	48–57	
:	%3A	3A	58	COLON
;	%3B	3B	59	SEMI-COLON
<	%3C	3C	60	LEFT ARROW LESS THAN
=	%3D	3D	61	EQUAL
>	%3E	3E	62	RIGHT ARROW GREATER THAN
?	%3F	3F	63	QUESTION MARK
@	%40	40	64	AT
A–Z	A–Z	41–5A	65–90	
[	%5B	5B	91	LEFT BRACKET
			5C	92	
]	%5D	5D	93	RIGHT BRACKET
^	%5E	5E	94	UP ARROW
_	%5F	5F	95	
`	%60	60	96	BACK TICK
a–z	a–z	61–7A	97–122	
{	%7B	7B	123	RIGHT CURLY BRACKET
|	%7C	7C	124	PIPE
}	%7D	7D	125	LEFT CURLY BRACKET
~	%7E	7E	126	TILDA
DEL	%7F	7F	127	DELETE